Buying National Security

The tools of American statecraft—defense, diplomacy, foreign and security assistance, homeland security and intelligence—are rarely examined together. Adams and Williams fill this gap by examining how these tools work, how they are planned for, and how they are budgeted. Seeing policy through the lens of the budget can help decision-makers and ordinary citizens discern the genuine priorities of national leaders from the oftentimes illusory ones portrayed in rhetoric. Simply put, policies and strategies cannot be carried out without a corresponding allocation of resources.

Buying National Security weaves a tapestry around the institutions, organizations, tools, and processes that support planning and resource allocation across the breadth of the American national security enterprise. The authors analyze the planning and resource integration activities across agencies of the executive branch as well as examine the structure and processes Congress uses to carry out its national security oversight and budgetary responsibilities. Finally, they review the adequacy of the current structures and process and explore proposals for ways both might be reformed to fit the demands of the 21st century security environment.

Gordon Adams is a professor of international affairs at the School of International Service at American University and a Distinguished Fellow at the Stimson Center. He is the author of *The Iron Triangle: The Politics of Defense Contracting* and co-author of *Transforming European Militaries: Coalition Operations and the Technology Gap*.

Cindy Williams is a principal research scientist in the Security Studies Program of the Massachusetts Institute of Technology. She is the editor of *Holding the Line: U.S. Defense Alternatives for the Early 21st Century* and *Filling the Ranks: Transforming the U.S. Military Personnel S*

D1041424

Buying National Security

How America Plans and Pays for Its Global Role and Safety at Home

Gordon Adams and Cindy Williams

Routledge
Taylor & Francis Group

NEW YORK AND LONDON

First published 2010
by Routledge
270 Madison Ave, New York, NY 10016

Simultaneously published in the UK
by Routledge
2 Park Square, Milton Park, Abingdon, Oxon OX14 4RN

Routledge is an imprint of the Taylor & Francis Group, an informa business

© 2010 Gordon Adams and Cindy Williams

Typeset in Minion by Wearset Ltd, Boldon, Tyne and Wear
Printed and bound in the United States of America on
acid-free paper by Edwards Brothers, Inc.

Library of Congress Cataloging in Publication Data
Adams, Gordon, 1941–
Buying national security: how America plans and pays for its
global role and safety at home/Gordon Adams and Cindy
Williams.
p. cm.
1. National security–Economic aspects–United States.
2. United States–Defenses–Economic aspects. 3. United
States–Foreign relations administration–Economic aspects.
4. Budget–United States. 5. National security–United States–
Planning. 6. United States–Defenses–Planning. 7. United
States–Economic policy–2001– 8. United States. Dept. of
Defense–Planning. 9. United States. Executive Office of the
President–Planning. 10. United States. Congress–Planning.
I. Williams, Cindy, 1947– II. Title.
HC110.D4A59 2009
355′.033573–dc22

2009028241

ISBN10: 0-415-95439-8 (hbk)
ISBN10: 0-415-95440-1 (pbk)
ISBN10: 0-203-86150-7 (ebk)

ISBN13: 978-0-415-95439-6 (hbk)
ISBN13: 978-0-415-95440-2 (pbk)
ISBN13: 978-0-203-86150-9 (ebk)

To Phyllis Goodnow and Barry Posen for their unstinting encouragement and support throughout this project.

Contents

Illustrations

Figures

Tables

Acknowledgments

This book was made possible through the generous support of the John D. and Catherine T. MacArthur Foundation, the Carnegie Corporation of New York, the Ploughshares Fund, and the Frankel Foundation. We also wish to acknowledge the contribution of the Woodrow Wilson International Center for Scholars and the Stimson Center, which provided valuable support for the work.

The authors gratefully acknowledge the ideas, presentations, comments, and encouragement provided through much of the writing of this book by the members of the Working Group on National Security Resource Allocation: Rodney Bent, Hugh Brady, Steve Daggett, Bruce A. Dauer, Arnold Donahue, the late Philip DuSault, James Dyer, Mike Gilmore, Thomas C. Hone, Steven Kosiak, Bruce Lawlor, Alice Maroni, David Morrison, Richard Nygard, Ann Reese, Anne C. Richard, Courtney Richardson, Kim Savit, and Sharon Weiner. Special thanks, as well, to Rodney Bent, Lincoln Bloomfield, Jr., Richard Nygard, Jon Rosenwasser, Sharon Weiner, and others who must remain unnamed for their constructive reviews of various drafts of the manuscript.

Between 2005 and 2009, we interviewed more than 150 scholars, practitioners, and officials to gain insight into the organizations, processes, and tools of planning and resource allocation in use in the national security community. Many thanks to every one of those experts and practitioners.

We are also very grateful to Amy Belasco, William Bonvillian, Matthew Bunn, Richard Burke, Larry Byrne, Michèle Flournoy, John Gannon, Theresa Gerton, Edward Gnehm, Robert Goldberg, Vance Gordon, Kathleen Hicks, G. William Hoagland, Patrick Kennedy, Gregory Koblentz, Eric Lief, James Locher, David McIntyre, Clark Murdock, Kathy Peroff, Alice Rivlin, Richard Sokolsky, John Whitley, and Dov Zakheim for their valuable assistance.

The book would never have been completed without the exceptional contributions of our research assistants, Joshua Itzkowitz-Shifrinson, Miranda Priebe, David Glaudemans, Daniel Melleby, Tim Cooke, Brian Harding, Rebecca Williams, Ngalula-Kapinga Kabundi, and Jen-Ella Mann. We are also deeply appreciative of the help and expertise of Harlene Miller and Caitlin Adams in preparing the manuscript.

The challenge in preparing a list of acknowledgments for a project to which so many people have contributed is that inevitably someone will be left out. We apologize for any inadvertent oversights.

Acronyms

A	State, Bureau of Administration
ACDA	Arms Control and Disarmament Agency
ACOTA	African Contingency Operations Training and Assistance program
ACP	Andean Counterdrug Program
ADF	African Development Fund
AEC	Atomic Energy Commission
AECA	Arms Export Control Act
AF	State, Bureau of African Affairs
AfDB	African Development Bank
AIA	US Air Force, Air Intelligence Agency
AsDB	Asian Development Bank
ASPR	HHS, Assistant Secretary for Preparedness and Response
ATA	State, Antiterrorism Assistance program
AU	African Union
BA	Budget Authority
BBG	Broadcasting Board of Governors
BEA	Budget Enforcement Act of 1990
BES	Budget Estimate Submission
BMDO	Ballistic Missile Defense Organization
BPP	State, Bureau Program Plan
CA	State, Bureau of Consular Affairs
CAIG	DOD, Cost Analysis Improvement Group
CBO	Congressional Budget Office
CBP	DHS, Customs and Border Protection
CCC	Commodity Credit Corporation
CCP	Consolidated Cryptologic Program
CDC	Centers for Disease Control and Prevention
CERP	Commander's Emergency Response Program
CFO	Chief Financial Officer
CGI	Coast Guard Intelligence
CIA	Central Intelligence Agency

CIAP	Central Intelligence Agency Program
CIO	State, Contributions to International Organizations account
CIPA	State, Contributions to International Peacekeeping Activities account
CIS	DHS, Citizenship and Immigration Services
CMA	Community Management Account
CMS	Community Management Staff
COCOMs	Combatant Commanders
COM	State, Chief of Mission
COMINT	Communications Intelligence
COP	State, Country Operational Plan
CPA	Chairman's Program Assessment
CPA	Coalition Provisional Authority
CPMs	DOD, Capability Portfolio Managers
CPR	DOD, Chairman's Program Recommendation
CRS	Congressional Research Service
CSCS	State, Capital Security Cost-Sharing
CSF	Coalition Support Funds
CSH	USAID, Child Survival and Health account
CSI	DHS, Container Security Initiative
CTFP	Combating Terrorism Fellowship Program
CTR	DOD, Cooperative Threat Reduction
D&CP	State, Diplomatic and Consular Programs
DA	USAID, Development Assistance account
DAD	OMB, Deputy Associate Director
DAS	Deputy Assistant Secretary
DAWG	DOD, Deputy's Advisory Working Group
DCHA	USAID, Bureau of Democracy, Conflict, and Humanitarian Assistance
DCI	Director of Central Intelligence
DDNI/M	Deputy Director of National Intelligence, Management
DEA	Drug Enforcement Administration
DHS	Department of Homeland Security
DIA	Defense Intelligence Agency
DIRINT	US Marine Corps, Directorate of Intelligence
DNI	Director of National Intelligence
DOD	Department of Defense
DOE	Department of Energy
DOJ	Department of Justice
DOL	Department of Labor
DRL	State, Bureau of Democracy, Human Rights, and Labor
DS	State, Bureau of Diplomatic Security
DSCA	Defense Security Cooperation Agency

E	State, Under Secretary for Economic, Business and Agricultural Affairs
E&E	USAID, Bureau for Europe and Eurasia
EAP	State, Bureau of East Asian and Pacific Affairs
EBRD	European Bank for Reconstruction and Development
ECOWAS	Economic Community of West African States
EDA	Excess Defense Articles
EGAT	USAID, Bureau of Economic Growth, Agriculture, and Trade
ELINT	Electronics Intelligence
EOP	Executive Office of the President
EPA	Environmental Protection Agency
ERMA	State, Emergency Refugee and Migration Assistance account
ESF	Economic Support Funds
EUR	State, Bureau of European and Eurasian Affairs
EX–IM	Export–Import Bank
EXBS	Export Control and Related Border Security
F	State, Office of the Director of Foreign Assistance
FAA	Foreign Assistance Act
FAO	Food and Agricultural Organization
FAR	Federal Acquisition Regulations
FARC	Federal Acquisition Regulatory Council
FAS	Dept. of Agriculture, Foreign Agricultural Service
FBI	Federal Bureau of Investigation
FCIP	Foreign Counterintelligence Program
FDA	Food and Drug Administration
FEMA	Federal Emergency Management Agency
FFP	USAID, Food for Peace program
FLETC	Federal Law Enforcement Training Center
FMF	Foreign Military Financing
FMS	Foreign Military Sales
FSA	Freedom Support Act
FSN	State, Foreign Service National
FSO	Foreign Service Officer
FY	fiscal year
FYDP	Future-Years Defense Program
FYHSP	Future-Years Homeland Security Program
G	State, Under Secretary for Democracy and Global Affairs
GAO	Government Accountability Office
GDIP	General Defense Intelligence Program
GEF	Global Environment Facility
GEOINT	Geospatial Intelligence
GH	USAID, Bureau of Global Health
GHCS	State, Global Health and Child Survival account
GPOI	State, Global Peace Operations Initiative

GPRA	Government Performance and Results Act
GTR	Global Threat Reduction
HHS	Department of Health and Human Services
HIPC	Heavily Indebted Poor Countries
HPSI	House Permanent Select Committee on Intelligence
HR	State, Bureau of Human Resources
HRDF	State, Human Rights and Democracy Fund
HSC	Homeland Security Council
HUMINT	Human Intelligence
IA	Information Assurance
IADB	Inter-American Development Bank
IAEA	International Atomic Energy Agency
IAF	Inter-American Foundation
IBRD	International Bank for Reconstruction and Development
IC	Intelligence Community
ICASS	State, International Cooperative Administrative Support Services
ICE	DHS, Immigration and Customs Enforcement
IDA	International Development Association
IDFA	USAID, International Disaster and Famine Assistance account
IFAD	International Fund for Agricultural Development
IFC	International Finance Corporation
ILEAs	International Law Enforcement Academies
ILO	International Labor Organization
IMET	State, International Military Education and Training account
IMF	International Monetary Fund
IMINT	Imagery Intelligence
INATR	DHS, Office of International Affairs and Trade Relations
INL	State, Bureau of International Narcotics and Law Enforcement
INLE	State, International Narcotics and Law Enforcement account
INR	State, Bureau of Intelligence and Research
INSCOM	US Army Intelligence and Security Command
IO	State, Bureau of International Organizations
IO&P	State, International Organizations and Programs account
IRM	Information Resource Management
IRTPA	Intelligence Reform and Terrorism Prevention Act of 2004
ISN	State, Bureau of International Security and Nonproliferation
ISR	Intelligence, Surveillance, and Reconnaissance
ITA	International Trade Administration
JCS	Joint Chiefs of Staff
JIOCs	Joint Intelligence Operations Centers
JPG	Joint Programming Guidance

LAC	USAID, Bureau of Latin America and the Caribbean
LRD	OMB, Legislative Reference Division
M	State, Under Secretary for Management
MAP	Department of Agriculture, Market Access Program
MAP	State, Military Assistance Program
MASINT	Measurements Intelligence
MCC	Millennium Challenge Corporation
MCIA	Marine Corps Intelligence Activity
MDA	Missile Defense Agency
MDBs	multilateral development banks
ME	USAID, Bureau for the Middle East
MEBN	BBG, Middle East Broadcasting Network
MEPI	State, Middle East Partnership Initiative
MFPs	Major Force Programs
MIP	Military Intelligence Program
MOP	State, Mission Operational Plan
MPP	State, Mission Program Plan
MRA	State, Migration and Refugee Assistance account
NADB	North American Development Bank
NADR	State, Nonproliferation, Antiterrorism, Demining, and Related Programs account
NAFTA	North American Free Trade Agreement
NATO	North Atlantic Treaty Organization
NCPC	National Counterproliferation Center
NCTC	National Counterterrorism Center
NDAA	National Defense Authorization Act
NDF	Nonproliferation and Disarmament Fund
NEA	State, Bureau of Near Eastern Affairs
NED	National Endowment for Democracy
NFIP	National Foreign Intelligence Program
NGA	National Geospatial-Intelligence Agency
NGIC	US Army, National Ground Intelligence Center
NGO	Nongovernmental organization
NGP	National Geospatial-Intelligence Program
NIAID	National Institute of Allergies and Infectious Diseases
NIH	National Institutes of Health
NIMA	National Imagery and Mapping Agency
NIMC	US Navy, National Intelligence Maritime Center
NIP	National Intelligence Program
NNSA	National Nuclear Security Agency
NPR	National Performance Review
NRO	National Reconnaissance Office
NRP	National Reconnaissance Program
NSA	National Security Agency

NSC	National Security Council
NSDD	National Security Decision Directive
NSPD	National Security Presidential Directive
OAS	Organization of American States
OBO	Overseas Building Operations
OCDETF	Organized Crime and Drug Enforcement Task Force
ODNI	Office of the Director of National Intelligence
ODNN	Department of Energy, Office of Defense Nuclear Nonproliferation
OE	USAID, Operating Expenses account
OECD	Organization for Economic Cooperation and Development
OFDA	USAID, Office of Foreign Disaster Assistance
OFFM	OMB, Office of Federal Financial Management
OFFP	USAID, Office of Food for Peace
OFPP	OMB, Office of Federal Procurement Policy
OGAC	State, Office of the Global AIDS Coordinator
OIA	DHS, Office of Intelligence and Analysis
OIC	DOE, Office of Intelligence and Counterintelligence
OIRA	OMB, Office of Information and Regulatory Affairs
OMB	Office of Management and Budget
ONDCP	Office of National Drug Control Policy
ONI	Office of Naval Intelligence
ONSI	DEA, Office of National Security Intelligence
OPIC	Overseas Private Investment Corporation
OSD	Office of the Secretary of Defense
OSD SO/LIC	OSD, Special Operations/Low-Intensity Conflict
OSTP	Office of Science and Technology Policy
OTA	Treasury, Office of Technical Assistance
OTFI	Treasury, Office of Terrorism and Financial Intelligence
OTI	USAID, Office of Transition Initiatives
OVP	Office of the Vice President
P	State, Under Secretary for Political Affairs
PA&E	DOD and DHS, Office of Program Analysis and Evaluation
PAD	OMB, Program Associate Director
PAHPA	Pandemic and All-Hazards Preparedness Act
PAO	State, Public Affairs Officer
PART	Program Assessment Rating Tool
PBDs	Program Budget Decisions
PCC	NSC, Policy Coordination Committee
PDM	Program Decision Memorandum
PEPFAR	State, President's Emergency Plan for AIDS Relief
PKO	State, Peacekeeping Operations account
PM	State, Bureau of Political-Military Affairs
PMA	President's Management Agenda

PNAC	Project for the New American Century
POM	Program Objective Memorandum
PPBE	Planning, Programming, Budgeting, and Execution
PPBS	Planning, Programming, and Budgeting System
PPC	USAID, Bureau for Policy and Program Coordination
PRM	State, Bureau of Population, Refugees and Migration
PRTs	Provincial Reconstruction Teams
PSC	Personal Services Contractor
QDR	Quadrennial Defense Review
QHSR	Quadrennial Homeland Security Review
R	State, Under Secretary for Public Diplomacy and Public Affairs
RFE	Radio Free Europe
RL	Radio Liberty
RMOs	OMB, Resource Management Offices
S	Secretary of State
S/CRS	State, Coordinator for Reconstruction and Stabilization
S/CT	State, Office of the Coordinator for Counterterrorism
S/H	State, Legislative Affairs
S/L	State, Office of the Legal Advisor
S/P	State, Policy Planning Staff
S/RM	State, Bureau of Resource Management
S&R	Stabilization and Reconstruction
SAO	State, Security Assistance Organization
SAPs	OMB, Statements of Administration Policy
SCA	State, Bureau of South and Central Asian Affairs
SDIO	Strategic Defense Initiative Organization
SDRs	Special Drawing Rights
SEED	Support for Eastern European Democracy Act
SIGINT	Signals Intelligence
SLRG	DOD, Senior Leadership Review Group
SPG	Strategic Planning Guidance
SSCI	Senate Select Committee on Intelligence
T	State, Under Secretary for Arms Control and International Security Affairs
TCP	MCC, Threshold Country Plan
TDA	Trade and Development Agency
TFCA	Tropical Forest Conservation Act
TIARA	Tactical Intelligence and Related Activities
TIATA	Treasury International Affairs Technical Assistance office
TOA	Total Obligational Authority
UN	United Nations
UNDP	United Nations Development Program
UNICEF	United Nations Children's Fund

USAEDS	US Atomic Energy Detection System
USAID	United States Agency for International Development
USD(AT&L)	Under Secretary of Defense for Acquisition, Technology and Logistics
USD(I)	Under Secretary of Defense for Intelligence
USD(P)	Under Secretary of Defense for Policy
USD(P&R)	Under Secretary of Defense for Personnel and Readiness
USD(C)	Under Secretary of Defense, Comptroller
USDA	United States Department of Agriculture
USFCS	United States Foreign Commercial Service
USG	United States Government
USIA	United States Information Agency
USTR	United States Trade Representative
USUN	United States Mission to the United Nations
VCI	State, Bureau of Verification, Compliance, and Implementation
VOA	Voice of America
WFP	World Food Program
WGMA	Working Group on Multilateral Assistance
WHA	State, Bureau of Western Hemisphere Affairs
WHO	World Health Organization

Chapter 1

Money is Policy

Planning and Budgeting for Security and Foreign Affairs

US policymakers on both sides of the political aisle emphasize the importance of employing a wide range of domestic and international tools—including defense, diplomacy and public diplomacy, foreign assistance, intelligence, and homeland security—to make the country secure and advance its international interests and policies. During the current decade, the United States has increased funding in all of those areas. Including the cost of operations in Iraq and Afghanistan, combined spending for national security, including national defense, international affairs, and homeland security, was more than three-quarters of a trillion dollars in fiscal year (FY) 2009, about 80 percent more in real terms than in FY 2001.

Spending for national security constitutes nearly 20 percent of total federal outlays and more than 5 percent of US gross domestic product. The Department of Defense (DOD), Department of State, Department of Homeland Security (DHS), and the US Agency for International Development (USAID) account for most of the total. Homeland security activities are widely dispersed across the federal government, however, so nearly every department and independent agency has some share of the national security total.

Money is Policy

National security budgets are the most dependable reflection of US security policy. Seeing things through the lens of the budget can help decision-makers and ordinary citizens discern the genuine priorities of national leaders from the oftentimes illusory ones portrayed in rhetoric. For example, in speeches and strategy documents, Republican and Democratic leaders often say that the proliferation of nuclear, biological, and chemical weapons and the prospect of such weapons falling into the hands of terrorists are among the greatest threats facing the United States. Yet only two-tenths of 1 percent of national security spending goes toward helping other governments prevent the dispersal or theft of nuclear materials or weapons, and an even smaller share goes toward inspecting US-bound shipping containers for nuclear materials. The Department of Energy spends nearly twice as much annually on new earth penetrating and low-yield nuclear weapons as on securing Russian fissile material.

In another example, policymakers sometimes argue that the United States is committed to development assistance that funds development for its own sake, not because such assistance is connected to vital national interests. At the same time, the budget reveals that the fastest growing bilateral assistance program is one that links assistance to the success of combat missions executed by forward-deployed US troops. The disjunction between rhetoric and budgets often reflects an underlying contradiction between the talk and the real priorities.

As with any area of the federal budget, decisions about how much money to spend on security and foreign affairs as a whole or on any single activity of national security result from a complex mix of public and elite perceptions of security interests, domestic politics, and institutional forces. The choices of priorities to emphasize, programs to pursue, and levels of spending can depend strongly on the preferences and abilities of individual leaders in federal departments and agencies, in the White House, and Congress. They also depend on the machinery each of those institutions has created to bring information to those leaders and help them make choices about which programs and activities to pursue and how to divide resources among them. This book focuses on that machinery.

That machinery is in flux. Arrangements for strategic planning, resource allocation, and budgeting within federal departments, in the White House, and in Congress have undergone substantial changes during the past decade. Scholars, think tanks, and multiple committees and commissions have tabled numerous proposals for additional reforms. In this book, we concentrate on how things stand today and offer only a glimpse into how things may change in the coming years.

This book focuses on the breadth of the US government's structures and processes for national security planning and resource allocation. While there are some excellent studies of the topic for national defense, there are none for international affairs or homeland security. Nor is there a literature on the treatment of budgets in the interagency process, or one that links the executive branch to the Congress across the range of national security resource planning. This study is rooted in the proposition that all the tools of national security policymaking ought to be considered together, if policymakers are right that we need to use them in synergy.

The remainder of this chapter provides a brief overview of the volume.

Planning and Budgeting for International Affairs

Chapters 2 through 7 deal with planning and resource-allocation arrangements in the federal departments and agencies of the executive branch that have major roles in national security. Chapters 2, 3, and 4 discuss the complex machinery and processes that deal with budget Function 150, the international affairs activities, agencies, and programs. (Budget functions are broad categories of the budget that Congress uses to view and allocate federal funds.) The world of international affairs is characterized by a dispersion of agencies and programs. This budget function includes the operations of the State Department in conducting diplomacy and public diplomacy and supporting international organizations (Chapter 2), foreign assistance programs that support economic objectives and humanitarian relief (Chapter 3), and foreign assistance programs that support the United States' strategic and security goals (Chapter 4).

Until recently, there was no central coordination of strategic planning or budgeting for the International Affairs category. The State Department, USAID, the Department of the Treasury, the Export–Import Bank, and the many other international agencies each prepared its own budget plan and submitted it directly to the White House. Even within the State Department, budget planning between foreign assistance programs and operations was uncoordinated. Moreover, the International Affairs agencies generally lacked formal mechanisms for long-term strategic planning or goal setting.

That has begun to change during the past decade and a half. State has established a strategic planning process for foreign assistance and has begun to connect these programs to its operational budgeting. The department increasingly asserts control over budgets for economic and humanitarian assistance and public diplomacy.

At the same time, however, the International Affairs arena has grown even more dispersed. With the creation of the new Millennium Challenge Corporation in 2002, there are now at least five distinct foreign assistance programs in the executive branch: Economic Support Funds (State), Development Assistance (USAID), Millennium Challenge Corporation, international development bank funds (Treasury), and Foreign Military Financing (State and Defense). Coordination of strategy and budgets among these programs or with the foreign policy goals articulated by the State Department or the White House almost never happens.

The Department of Defense and the Intelligence Community

The most widely studied and arguably the most coherent strategic planning and resource system within the executive branch is that of the DOD. Even in that department, the Planning, Programming, Budgeting, and Execution (PPBE) process is in flux, as discussed in Chapter 5. Initially designed during the 1960s to strengthen centralized control of the department by the Secretary of Defense, the process as practiced today emphasizes and encourages collaboration among the services and other stakeholders. Rather than helping a Secretary to set and enforce priorities, critics charge that instead it now helps the department's components reinforce the status quo. Big decisions, such as those made during the military drawdown of the 1990s about what forces to cut and which systems to cancel, are often made outside of the formal process. Nobody seems happy with the system, and the Obama administration appears poised to undo some of the most recent changes.

The lion's share of the intelligence budget, including that of the Central Intelligence Agency (CIA), is funded through the DOD, and the DOD plays a dominant role in planning and resource allocation for intelligence programs and activities. Nevertheless, 16 separate agencies and offices within the intelligence community collect, analyze, and disseminate intelligence. As discussed in Chapter 6, the missions and responsibilities of these organizations frequently overlap, leading to complex management, planning, and budgetary challenges.

Beginning with the creation of the CIA in 1947, national leaders have worked to organize the intelligence institutions and their budgeting in a more centralized and coordinated way. Those efforts culminated in the creation of the Office of the Director of National Intelligence (ODNI) in 2004. Turf struggles among the agencies continue, however, and it remains unclear whether the new ODNI architecture will succeed in improving the coherence of planning and budgeting across the intelligence community.

Planning and Resource Allocation for Homeland Security

In January 2003, the Bush administration drew 22 disparate agencies and some 170,000 employees into the new DHS. Even so, the DHS in FY 2009 spends only about half of the federal homeland security budget. Another one-quarter of the homeland security budget goes to the DOD, and the remainder is spread among nearly all of the other departments and independent agencies of government.

Proponents of establishing the DHS believed that a single department under a single Cabinet Secretary would be able to achieve what the White House Office of Homeland Security could not: unity of effort across the bulk of federal activities related to domestic security. The most important engine of such unity would be the control of the budget that the new Secretary of Homeland Security would enjoy.

To establish control, the department's early leaders created a PPBE modeled loosely on the one in operation within the DOD. Other departments with large roles in homeland security also took steps to consolidate or at least coordinate their internal planning and budgeting for the prevention of terrorist attacks, protection of people and infrastructure within the United States, and preparations to handle domestic emergencies should they arise.

As Chapter 7 discusses, the effectiveness of the new systems in forging unity of effort is not yet obvious. Within the DHS, the components generally continue to set their own agendas. Their shares of the DHS budget are not significantly different from what they were before the department was created, suggesting that strategic priorities have not been set or enforced. Coordination of planning and budgets across departments also appears weak, even in important areas like biological defense.

Resource Planning in the White House

With so many executive branch agencies involved in national security, the coordination of planning and budgeting falls to the White House. Two organizations within the Executive Office of the President bear most of the responsibility: the National Security Council (NSC) (which now includes the Homeland Security Council) and the Office of Management and Budget (OMB). The NSC coordinates national security strategy, advises the President on national security issues, oversees policy implementation through the interagency process, and integrates the White House response to national security crises. The NSC does not have a formal role in the federal budget process, but nearly every policy decision made in the NSC framework has resource implications.

OMB is the manager of executive branch budget processes. The organization sets requirements for the preparation and submission of budgets by all federal departments and agencies. Each year, it provides each agency with fiscal guidance that determines the size of the annual budget under consideration and constrains the agency's plans for future years. It works with the agencies to ensure that programs are linked to and consistent with the president's priorities. Increasingly in recent years, OMB also helps agencies to measure progress toward concrete outcomes, in an effort to improve the integration between budgets and performance. As Chapter 8 details, arrangements in both organizations are in flux, and interagency processes aimed at bringing coherence to the planning and resource allocation of the agencies involved in national security are still relatively immature.

Resource Allocation and Budgeting in Congress

Congress was instrumental in the security-related reorganizations and process reforms of the executive branch after 9/11. Yet as Chapter 9 discusses, one of the most striking features of federal resource allocation and budgeting for security and foreign engagement is the continued absence of a unified approach within the legislative body itself. In recent years, the House established a Homeland Security Committee. The Senate renamed its Governmental Affairs Committee as the Homeland Security and Governmental Affairs Committee and widened its jurisdiction to include some elements of homeland security. The Appropriations Committees in each chamber also established new subcommittees for homeland security and consolidated the subcommittees and appropriations within the International Affairs function.

Nevertheless, the responsibility for resource allocation and budgeting for national security remains divided among numerous committees and subcommittees. Several authorizing committees share jurisdiction for various elements of DHS, and even more get involved in the programs and budgets of other departments with roles in homeland security. Getting to a unified approach is probably not in the cards. But understanding how the system works in Congress can help one see how budgets for national security are ultimately made.

The Politics of National Security Budgeting

This book focuses on the machinery of planning, resource allocation, and budgeting in the executive branch and Congress. That machinery was generally designed to help leaders exert control over policy by aligning resources to strategic priorities and coupling budgets to performance. The organizations and processes discussed here are all built on the assumption that leaders can and do make rational decisions based on strategic priorities and program effectiveness.

In reality, budgets are shaped by a variety of forces. These include party politics, the tug of war between Congress and the executive branch, the bureaucratic interests and power of individual departments and agencies, and the abilities and preferences of individual leaders. Chapter 10 looks at such political factors and how they influence decisions about programs and budgets.

Finally, there are many efforts to reform this machinery and deal with the inadequacies the book reveals. In Chapter 11, we deal briefly with these efforts and proposals, many of which are designed to streamline agency processes, improve interagency coordination, strengthen the White House role in providing guidance on programs and budgets, and improve coherence in the way Congress handles national security resource decisions. It is increasingly important to long-term US interests to overcome agency stovepipes, reap the synergies of interagency activity, and make the congressional process more efficient. Many of these reform proposals are worthy of serious consideration.

Buying National Security

No simple formula can tell leaders how much the United States should spend on national security or how that spending should be allocated among departments and programs. Global engagement funded through the national defense and international affairs budgets serves multiple objectives: protecting national sovereignty and territorial integrity and sustaining a suitable level of global influence, supporting alliances, ensuring the safe conduct of international commerce, helping other countries to become more capable partners in the global economy, and lending a helping hand to those that need it. Many homeland security measures also serve multiple purposes: improving resilience in the face of naturally occurring disasters such as hurricanes or the global outbreak of pandemic disease as well as keeping citizens and infrastructure safe from the threat of direct attack.

The United States wants and needs a strong military and intelligence apparatus, vigorous civilian international engagement, and prudent homeland security. Achieving US objectives on the world stage and providing for security in the future will require continued substantial investment in all of those areas. Nevertheless, US resources are finite. The nation's current financial and economic woes will likely spark a tightening of the belt in every area of federal spending. Fiscal problems related to rising healthcare costs and the eligibility for retirement of large numbers of baby boomers make continued growth of national security budgets unlikely.

Setting priorities between guns and butter, and among the competing demands of national security, will be critically important to the nation's future. Federal arrangements for strategic planning and resource allocation for national security, across all the instruments of American security and statecraft, will be an important determinant of how well that is done.

Chapter 2

Resource Planning for International Affairs and State Operations

Introduction

While there is a large body of literature discussing US foreign policy, there is scarcely any on US foreign policy institutions and resource planning processes. This reality reflects both the disorganization of US foreign policy institutions and the high priority given to defense and defense planning as a major focus of US national security policy. In this and the following two chapters, we seek to remedy this imbalance of attention, discussing the dispersal of foreign policy institutions in American government and their planning and resource allocation processes. We focus first on the flagship organization of US foreign policy: the Department of State. In the next two chapters, we examine the large number of foreign and security assistance programs of the US government, in which State, USAID, and many other executive branch agencies play a role.

The Institutional Diaspora of US Foreign Policy

One naturally thinks of the Secretary of State as the institutional leader of US foreign policy. State is the oldest federal department, and the Secretary stands fourth in line in the order of presidential succession. Prior to World War II, it was clear that the State Department held primary responsibility for US international relationships.

After World War II, however, as US international responsibilities and activities grew, American statecraft became a far-flung enterprise, and the institutions that shape and execute US foreign and national security policy multiplied. As the United States became more engaged in the Cold War and in the global economy, other institutions and processes grew, assuming tasks and responsibilities that might have belonged to State. The National Security Act of 1947 created the National Security Council (NSC) to help the President oversee and coordinate a growing portfolio of programs and responsibilities. The Act also pulled the armed services into a single Department of Defense (DOD). The new DOD asserted and acquired a growing role in America's overseas engagement. Intelligence agencies also grew in importance for US national security planning and budgeting, both inside the DOD and in the new Central Intelligence Agency (CIA). Over time, the language of "national security" came to replace the language of "foreign policy" in the discourse of policymakers.

The State Department remained the source of Cold War institutional and policy innovation in the early years of the Cold War, with the Marshall Plan and the emergence over time of the national security strategy of deterrence and containment. The dominant early figures in national security policy were Secretaries of State: Cordell Hull, Dean Acheson, George C. Marshall, and John Foster Dulles. State's leadership over national security policy, however, was eroding. A large standing military and an expanding defense budget lent support to the growing voice of the Secretary of Defense. Competition for policy leadership emerged, as the storied battles between Dean Rusk and Robert McNamara, Henry Kissinger and William Rogers, Zbigniew Brzezinksi and Cyrus Vance, and Donald Rumsfeld and Colin Powell all indicate.

Institutional decisions made by foreign policy leaders contributed to this erosion. Over decades, State Department leaders, Presidents, and the Congress made a series of decisions about institutional development in the foreign policy world that led to the dispersal of civilian foreign policy and foreign assistance responsibilities. Each time a major requirement for funding emerged or a new policy initiative was undertaken, it seemed, a new institution was created to implement the program. As a result, unlike the military, no single department or agency is responsible for the full range of policymaking and budgeting in the area of foreign policy.

One important source of these institutional decisions was the reluctance of the State Department and the diplomatic community to expand the mission and role of the State Department itself after World War II. The State Department's dominant culture—the Foreign Service—takes pride in its traditional role as the home of US diplomacy. Diplomats represent the United States overseas, negotiate with foreign countries, and report on events and developments. Diplomats, from this perspective, are not foreign assistance providers, program developers, or managers. As a result, State did not organize itself internally to plan, budget, manage, or implement the broader range of US global engagement.[1] The civilian foreign policy and national security institutions and their budget planning processes have, as a consequence, emerged *ad hoc*, rather than as part of a strategic design. The resulting institutional structure covers traditional diplomacy (representation, negotiation, reporting), public diplomacy (exchanges, culture, and broadcasting), foreign assistance (security, economic, and development assistance), and international economic relationships (finance and trade).

The State Department is the home of traditional diplomacy and employs the largest part of the Foreign Service. Until 1999, public diplomacy was the responsibility of an independent United States Information Agency (USIA) and federally funded or operated broadcasting services (Voice of America (VOA) and the Broadcasting Board of Governors (BBG)). With the integration of USIA into State in 1999, only the broadcasting services remain independent of State. Security assistance programs are a shared responsibility between State and Defense. State also has some responsibilities for economic and development assistance, though USAID is the primary implementing agency. Over time, a number of other agencies and departments, including Treasury and Agriculture, also have taken on important economic development responsibilities (discussed in Chapters 3 and 4). Treasury, the US Trade Representative (USTR), and other departments have leadership roles in international financial and trade policy and the evolution of the international

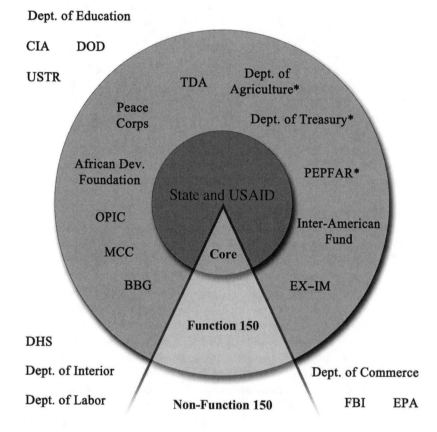

Figure 2.1 US foreign policy agencies.

Notes
* Partial Function 150.
EPA: Environmental Protection Agency; USTR: US Trade Representative; EX–IM: Export–Import Bank; DOD: Department of Defense; OPIC: Overseas Private Investment Corp.; BBG: Broadcasting Board of Governors; MCC: Millennium Challenge Corp.; PEPFAR: President's Emergency Plan for AIDS Relief.

economy. Moreover, over decades, an even larger number of agencies have extended their international engagement and their presence in US embassies, but with little linkage to overall US foreign policy and national security planning. Many of the continuing problems of coordination, mission overlap, turf conflict, and planning weakness in US foreign policy result from this diaspora.[2]

From a planning and budgetary perspective, these many civilian institutions and programs have not been connected. Each agency or department had its own separate planning and budget process, but there was no single "foreign affairs" budget or process for developing one.[3] In 1974, the Congress created an "International Affairs" budget function (Function 150). That act did not change any institutional boundaries, however. It simply grouped together for presentational purposes the programs and budgets of many, but not all of the civilian agencies with overseas activities. Until the early twenty-first century, there was very little effort to engage in coordinated planning and budgeting for foreign affairs.[4]

State Department Operations

As discussed further in Chapter 3, planning and budgeting for State Department operations were historically carried out separately from planning and budgeting for foreign assistance programs. During the George W. Bush administration, Secretary of State Colin Powell tried to integrate those functions to some extent by creating a new Bureau of Resource Management (S/RM) reporting to the Under Secretary for Management, containing offices that reviewed both operations and foreign assistance budgets. Secretary Rice separated the two in 2006, however, when she created the Office of the Director of Foreign Assistance. In 2009, the Secretary of State for the first time filled the position of the Deputy Secretary of State for Management and Resources, as the chief operating officer of the department, with responsibility for both State/USAID foreign assistance programs and State operations. The implications of this change for the integration of State Department planning and budgeting remain to be seen. In practice, planning and budgeting for State Department "Operations" remains the responsibility of the Under Secretary for Management (M),[5] reporting to the Deputy Secretary for Management and Resources.[6]

Plans and budgets for State Operations include the administration of the department, its human resources, physical infrastructure, communications and information technology, logistics, and consular operations. They also cover two specific areas of State Department activity: US payments to international organizations, including the United Nations and its family of organizations as well as assessed payments for UN peacekeeping operations, and public diplomacy and international broadcasting programs.

The bureaus and offices of the Under Secretary of State for Management work with the Office of the Secretary of State (S) and a number of the other

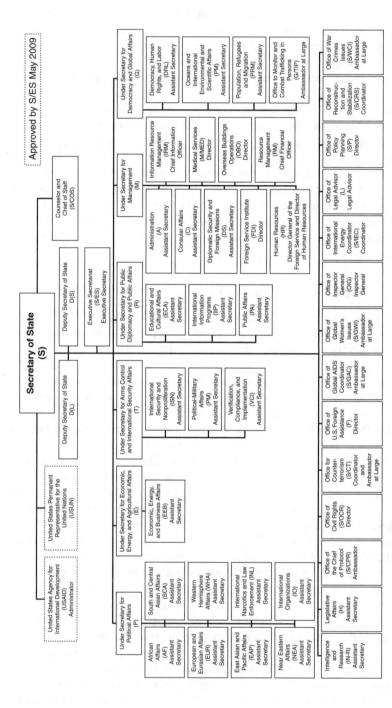

Figure 2.2 State Department organization chart (source: adapted from US Department of State).

State Department organizations in carrying out the budgeting for operations. Several bureaus and offices that report directly to the Secretary play important roles in this process.[7] The Secretary's Policy Planning Staff (S/P) sometimes participates in long-term strategic planning, though its work, at the request of the Secretary, can frequently be consumed by day-to-day crises and operations.[8] The Office of the Legal Advisor (S/L) provides the Secretary with views on the statutes that govern State planning and budgeting. The Bureau of Legislative Affairs office (S/H) is the principal liaison between State and the Congress, particularly with the department's "authorizing" committees (Senate Foreign Relations and House Foreign Affairs). S/H plays a key role in negotiating with the Congress on budgets and legislative language controlling spending.

The Under Secretary for Management is one of six Under Secretaries in the Department. The other Under Secretaries also play roles in M's planning and budgeting process. The most influential is the Under Secretary for Political Affairs (P), the fourth-ranking officer in the department after the Secretary and Deputy Secretaries. P assists in "the formulation and conduct of US foreign policy," as well as in the "overall direction, coordination, and supervision of interdepartmental activities," and provides "recommendations to the Secretary on all principal personnel appointments." This Under Secretary is also State's "crisis manager," and supports the "overall direction to the substantive functioning of the Department."[9]

The Under Secretary for Political Affairs (P) oversees the most central and dominant organizations in the State Department—the regional bureaus. The regional bureaus, each headed by an Assistant Secretary, are responsible for overseeing policymaking, reporting, and negotiations with respect to the bilateral relationship between the United States and the nations in that region. The regional structure has evolved over time, but its current form is typical: Africa (AF), Europe and Eurasia (EUR), Near East (NEA), Western Hemisphere (WHA), East Asia and the Pacific (EAP), and South and Central Asia (SCA). The Assistant Secretaries of these bureaus are key participants in operations planning and budgeting, since overseas posts are the heart of the State Department's infrastructure.

P also has responsibility for an important functional bureau that participates in the State Operations budget process.[10] The Bureau of International Organizations Affairs (IO) has responsibility for US diplomacy in international organizations, including the United Nations and its many affiliates. IO is also the principal liaison office with the US Permanent Representative to the United Nations (USUN) in New York. The US Ambassador to the United Nations, often an official with cabinet rank, reports to both the Secretary of State and directly to the President, and plays a critical role shaping US budget issues with respect to the United Nations and affiliated organizations.

State Operations has included budgets for public diplomacy programs since the USIA was absorbed into the State Department in 1999. That absorption created the position of Under Secretary for Public Diplomacy (R).[11] R is responsible for public diplomacy policy and the administration of exchanges, fellowships, and cultural programs.

The Under Secretary for Management also receives input on State Operations budgeting from the other Under Secretaries.[12] These include the Under Secretary for Arms Control and International Security Affairs (T), which is responsible for nonproliferation policies and programs (ISN); verification, compliance, and implementation of arms-control agreements (VCI); and the Bureau of Political-Military Affairs (PM). The Under Secretary for Economic Affairs (E) is responsible for State's role in trade and policymaking, US economic sanctions, and economic reporting. It has only a small impact on State Operations budget planning. The sixth Under Secretary position, Democracy and Global Affairs (G) was created in 1994 to bring together a number of functional activities at State, with responsibilities for activities that cut across regions. G has responsibility for policy oversight and coordination over democracy promotion, environment, human rights, international crime, migration, labor, oceans, science, and refugees.[13]

Under Secretary for Management Responsibilities

The Under Secretary for Management (M) is the central manager of State Operations planning and budgeting, and is the "principal adviser to the Secretary of State on all matters involving the allocation of State Department resources in support of the President's foreign policy objectives."[14] These responsibilities are carried out by a number of bureaus and offices that report to the Under Secretary.

The Bureau of Human Resources (HR) carries out personnel planning at State, a key element in State Operations budgets. It is overseen by the Director General of the Foreign Service, the highest ranking position in the Foreign Service. The bureau is in charge of recruitment, training, assignment, evaluation, promotion, discipline, career development, and retirement policies and programs for State Department personnel. Budgets for State personnel are contained in the Diplomatic and Consular Programs (D&CP) account.

The Bureau of Information Resource Management (IRM) draws up State's information technology strategic plan, which has important budgetary implications. The Bureau of Overseas Buildings Operations (OBO) manages State's sizeable portfolio of overseas property, with responsibilities for construction, rental, acquisition, and maintenance. The Bureau of Diplomatic Security (DS) is the security and law enforcement arm of the department, with responsibility for international investigations, threat analysis, cyber security, building and technology security, and the protection of people, property, and information. The Bureau of Resource Management (S/RM) has a key role in the State Department's planning and budgeting processes. Its Assistant Secretary, who also reports to the Secretary of State, is the Department's Chief Financial Officer. The Bureau was created in 2002 to prepare the department's strategic plan, integrate mission planning done in the field, and execute the department's responsibilities for evaluating program performance.

The Bureau of Administration (A) supports State operations in the United States and the embassies and consulates overseas. It has responsibility for facilities management, procurement, logistics, transportation, and diplomatic pouch and mail services. This bureau is also responsible for setting allowance rates for US government personnel assigned abroad, providing support to the overseas schools educating Foreign Service dependants, overseeing safety and occupational health matters, supporting White House travel abroad and special conferences called by the President or Secretary of State.

State Operations Budget Accounts

The largest accounts in the State Operations budget are those for diplomatic and consular personnel; property acquisition, construction, and management; diplomatic security; and communications and information technologies.[15] In addition to these management accounts, State Operations budgeting includes assessed payments to the United Nations and other international organizations (including UN-sanctioned peacekeeping operations), and public diplomacy (other than broadcasting).

Diplomatic and Consular Programs

Human resources are at the heart of State Department operations. Roughly 58,000 people work for the department in 267 embassies, consulates, and other facilities overseas and in the United States. Some 35 percent are US nationals; 65 percent are Foreign Service Nationals (FSN) working mostly overseas.[16] Of the US citizen employees, 55 percent are Foreign Service Officers and 45 percent are civil servants.[17] Pay and benefits for this staff, costing typically $7 billion to $9 billion a year, are funded with appropriated funds in the Diplomatic and Consular Programs (D&CP) account, which is planned and managed by M.

D&CP funds several different categories of activities and personnel. The most significant are pay and benefits for senior officials[18] (6 percent), Foreign Service Officers (FSOs) and other staff involved in diplomatic activity[19] (12 percent), consular relations[20] (20 percent), diplomatic security/counterterrorism/worldwide security upgrades[21] (19 percent), information resource management (13 percent), overseas and domestic infrastructure and program support[22] (16 percent), and public diplomacy[23] (6 percent).[24]

The Foreign Service, which numbered over 11,000 by mid-2008, is at the heart of State Department culture. FSOs are recruited for a potentially lifetime career and, following initial training at the Foreign Service Institute, enter "cones," or specific career paths: political, economic, consular, or administrative. While there is some movement across the cones over a career, the initial placement often shapes the long-term career path of an FSO. The "political" cone is the most prestigious, and political officers tend to dominate the senior ranks of the State Department.[25] FSO training, which takes place at the initial stage in a career, focuses on foreign languages and cultures and the skills of representation, reporting, and negotiating.

The size of the Foreign Service has become a major issue in State Department budgeting.[26] From FY 1994 to FY 2000, funds for D&CP shrank from $5 billion (1996 dollars) to $3.6 billion, as both the White House and the Congress cut the State Department budget.[27] Between 1994 and 1997, the department could replace only 53 percent of the employees lost through retirement, resignation, or death.[28] In 2001, the independent Hart–Rudman Commission noted that State Department recruitment and retention were growing problems. There had been a 25 percent decline in people taking the Foreign Service exam and attrition rates were climbing, driven by slow advancement, insufficient autonomy, inattention to human resource issues, and problems with family situations under the stress of rotating assignments.

The Commission urged a 10–15 percent expansion of the Foreign Service, at a cost of $200 million, to provide a training "float" similar to that for the military.[29] It also urged attention to the need to change the Service to reflect the new international agenda:

> This Commission believes that the US overseas presence has been badly short-changed by shortsighted budget cuts to the point where the security and prosperity of the American people are ill-served. But it also believes that the US presence must be adjusted to new and prospective economic, social, political, and security realities. Only with such changes will Congressional confidence be restored, and the necessary funding provided, to support these critical activities.[30]

Internal and external analyses focused on the need for increases in the size of the Foreign Service, greater flexibility in the diplomatic corps, an expanded presence in countries and regions that posed the greatest challenges, and revised training to focus on more unusual languages, the management of programs, and the emerging agenda of transnational security issues.[31] Both a larger Foreign Service and more training throughout a career were seen as important changes that could help meet these new needs.[32]

Secretary of State Colin Powell focused on this problem, announcing a "Diplomatic Readiness Initiative" to expand the Foreign Service by roughly 2,000 officers in order to fill the staffing deficit. Even this increase proved inadequate, given the demands from new crisis areas like Iraq and Afghanistan. In addition, training at the Foreign Service Institute was expanded 25 percent by 2004, with upgraded courses, a focus on critical languages, and new training in management and leadership.[33]

Progress was made in expanding the Foreign Service, but State continued to face difficulties in coping with the challenge of the emerging international agenda: failed states; stabilization and reconstruction efforts in post-conflict states; financial and economic crises of a globalized economy; terrorist organizations; trafficking in arms, people, and drugs; infectious disease; and climate change. Foreign Service Officers increasingly have responsibility for program planning, budgeting, and implementation, tasks for which they receive minimal training. Moreover, many of these issues involve other federal agencies and skills, which have begun to expand their overseas engagement (discussed in Chapter 4). Foreign Service training does not fully cover this range of engagement or the need for interagency coordination in Washington, DC or on the diplomatic platform overseas.[34]

Secretary of State Condoleezza Rice took further steps to adapt the US diplomatic presence to this agenda, announcing a "Transformational Diplomacy" agenda in January 2006.[35] The agenda began relocating the US diplomatic presence from European posts to countries of higher priority, such as India, China, and Brazil, and focusing on transnational issues such as terrorism, proliferation, disease, and drug trafficking. She also expanded a diplomat's job description to include responsibilities for program implementation:

> To succeed in [hardship] posts, we will train our diplomats not only as expert analysts of policy but as first-rate administrators of programs, capable of helping foreign citizens to strengthen the rule of law, to start businesses, to improve health and to reform education.[36]

Despite these initiatives, many of the Foreign Service personnel problems identified after the end of the Cold War persisted into the new century. Funds for personnel continued to be inadequate, Foreign Service expansion remained an objective, and adaptation to the new agenda continued to require attention.[37]

Consular Affairs

Roughly 20 percent of State Department's budget supports its consular relations activities, administered by the Bureau of Consular Affairs (CA), reporting to the Under Secretary of State for Management. Consular Affairs issues passports to American citizens, screens and issues visas to immigrant and non-immigrant travelers to the United States, provides services to Americans overseas, and provides information to travelers.[38] In 2007, Consular Relations issued more than 18 million passports, scrutinized 8.5 million non-immigrant visa applications, and processed 680,000 applications for immigrant visas.[39] Long considered a less attractive career path in the Foreign Service, consular officers, as one observer put it, "do the dirty work of the Department."[40] Consular offices are also the most public face of the State Department, both in the United States (13 regional passport offices) and overseas (200 embassies and consulates).

US consular programs became significantly more important, visible, and better funded after the September 11, 2001 terrorist attacks. The Al Qaeda group had received visas for entry into the United States through the consular system. After 2001, a major effort was made to upgrade the consular system and provide for greater security in the visa system outside and at the border (in cooperation with the immigration and border services in the new Department of Homeland Security).[41]

Consular Affairs plans, budgets, and administers a Border Security program that brought a significant expansion of Consular Affairs staff and technology.[42] The program includes new passport services and technologies, additional consular staff and support to handle increased demands for security, and information technology. New investments have been made in fingerprint and digital photo technologies, such as biometric technology, for all visas issued for travel to the United States. New software and connectivity systems allow information sharing with data bases in other departments, particularly Homeland Security.[43]

Despite this expansion of programs and budgets, the Bureau was unprepared and understaffed for the Western Hemisphere Travel Initiative, which took effect in 2007. The initiative required US travelers to have passports to reenter the United States after traveling in the Western Hemisphere. The surge in passport applications that resulted overwhelmed Consular Affairs, requiring a reassignment of other State personnel to temporary passport duty.[44]

Budgets for Consular Affairs and Border Security are unique among State Department accounts in being funded largely through fees. Until the 1990s, much of State's fee income was deposited into the general revenue fund of the federal government. Increasingly, however, State has been allowed to retain the revenues from passports, accelerated passport generation, and machine-readable visas, which virtually fully fund the personnel and activities of the Bureau.

Information Technology

Throughout the 1980s and 1990s, the State Department coped with an aging and increasingly obsolete information technology system, purchased from Wang Laboratories.[45] Most embassy personnel lacked desktop computers until well into the 1990s, and no State Department personnel had Internet access. There was little communication across State offices in Washington, DC or in embassies, and virtually none with personnel from other agencies. State was operating four information technology systems and had "simply not pursued information technology effectively," largely for lack of funding.[46]

Since the late 1990s, State has made major investments to correct this problem. The department's Capital Investment Fund was expanded, in part, by a larger appropriation and, in part, by a redirection of expedited passport fees dedicated to modernizing State's information technology.[47] The department created the position of Chief Information Officer, responsible for IT programs and the Bureau for Information Resource Management. By 2000, all State employees had email access, 75 percent had access to the Internet, and 20,000 desktop computers had been deployed to overseas posts.[48] By 2004, State's IT system hardware had been completely replaced and was on a four-year replacement cycle, a new system for transmitting the department's internal messages (known as "cables") was being tested, and the consular database was accessible globally and across agencies.[49] State also began to test a State/USAID intranet and was giving priority to "greater integration and collaboration among the more than 40 civilian agencies" in the embassies. State had also developed a five-year IT strategic plan, jointly with USAID.[50] Overall, nearly one-third of IRM's programs were funded through fees in FY 2008.

International Cooperative Administrative Support Services

For most of the twentieth century, the administrative costs of overseas diplomatic posts were funded in the State Department budget, with other agency personnel treated as "free riders." The Ambassador or Chief of Mission (COM) was the "country team" leader and State was the principal provider of administrative support, embassy transportation, and building maintenance and most of the personnel were State employees. As the US overseas presence expanded after World War II, this subsidy became more expensive. DOD personnel, intelligence officers, and foreign assistance providers expanded overseas from 1945 to 1990, but their logistical support and services continued to be provided by State.

In 1982, President Ronald Reagan signed National Security Decision Directive 38 (NSDD-38), giving the COM authority over the size and mission of other agencies' presence on the platform:

> All agencies with staffs operating under the authority of Chiefs of Mission will ensure that, in coordination with the Department of State, the Chiefs of Missions' approval is sought on any proposed changes in the size, composition, or mandate of such staff elements. Departments and agencies wishing to initiate changes should transmit their proposals to Chiefs of Missions in consultation with the Department of State. [Other departments should] keep the Department of State informed as to current and projected overseas staffing authorizations for each diplomatic post.[51]

These principles are routinely restated in the Letter of Instruction a new Ambassador receives from the President, which states: "I charge you to exercise full responsibility for the direction, coordination, and supervision of all

Executive branch US offices and personnel in [country X]." All other agency personnel overseas have the "responsibility to keep [the Ambassador] fully informed at all times of their current and planned activities." In addition, "every agency under [his/her] authority, including the Department of State, must obtain [his/her] approval for any change in the size, composition, or mandate of its staff," according to this letter.[52]

The administrative costs implied by this authority became even more of a budgetary burden with the end of the Cold War. As the foreign policy agenda expanded, even more federal agencies, such as the Federal Bureau of Investigation and other elements of the Department of Justice, the Centers for Disease Control and Prevention, and the Department of Homeland Security, deployed personnel overseas.[53] This growing overseas US presence coincided with the "government reinvention" effort led by Vice President Al Gore. State proposed reforming the administrative support system by creating the International Cooperative Administrative Support Services (ICASS) architecture.

The ICASS system, legislated in 1997, "allocates to each department and agency the full cost of its presence outside the United States."[54] ICASS is intended to ensure that

> all agencies should pay the true costs of their presence abroad. Service providers who are not reimbursed fully for their services subsidize their customers who therefore have no incentive to make rational choices on the level of services they receive. Customers have a vested interest in reducing costs and a greater voice in how shared administrative services are managed and delivered.[55]

ICASS was planned as a locally-controlled system for administrative support. Posts determine how the services are to be delivered, by whom, and at what cost. The service provider is accountable to the customers and is paid through a no-year working capital fund.[56] An embassy-wide local ICASS Council sets priorities, selects providers, approves the ICASS budget and personnel, defines the algorithm for cost sharing, and assesses performance.[57] While State might be the normal services provider, the system explicitly leaves open the possibility that other agencies with strong local capabilities might be the providers. The rules for such interagency competitive bidding are set at the post level.

The ICASS Executive Board in Washington, DC consists of senior representatives of the participating cabinet agencies and is chaired by the Assistant Secretary of State for Administration. The Board meets twice a year, along with monthly meetings of an interagency Working Group, representing all agencies in the ICASS system. The ICASS Service Center in State's Resource Management Bureau operates the ICASS Service Center, which is also staffed on an interagency basis.[58] This bureau oversees the ICASS system, oversees training, and provides instructions on the preparation and timing of ICASS budgets.[59] Budgets for overseas posts are prepared by the local ICASS Councils and transmitted as part of the State Department Mission Strategic Plan process. They are reviewed by the ICASS Working Group and Executive Board and briefed to the Office of Management and Budget (OMB). Agencies are then to include these costs in their budget proposals to OMB.[60]

Overseas Buildings Operations

As of 2007, the State Department owned and operated more than 15,000 facilities in more than 265 locations, worth approximately $14 billion.[61] Its embassies, consulates, and housing, along with rental properties, are managed by the Bureau of Overseas Buildings Operations (OBO), with a budget well over $1 billion a year.

Before the era of terrorist attacks, buildings were not a high priority in State Operations budget planning. OBO was primarily concerned with the deterioration of its overseas infrastructure and related working conditions. By the end of the 1990s, the Kaden Commission on US Overseas Presence noted that "the overseas facilities of the wealthiest nation in history are often overcrowded, deteriorating, even shabby."[62] The panel described the department's system for financing and managing buildings as "bureaucratic and inequitable," lacking a strategic plan or adequate funding. It urged the department to provide more funds and find a mechanism for "equitable sharing of costs" among the agencies on the diplomatic platform.[63]

The reality of a terrorist threat in the 1980s and 1990s did not change this relative neglect of State Department buildings. Following the attacks on the Marine Corps barracks and embassy annex in Lebanon (1983 and 1984), Secretary of State George Schultz convened an Advisory Panel on Overseas Security, chaired by retired Admiral Bobby Inman. The Inman panel recommended replacing buildings at roughly half of the department's overseas posts.[64] By 1991, however, the "Inman Program" had fallen short, thanks to "funding shortfalls, construction delays, and costs increases." Only 24 of the planned 57 new buildings had been completed.[65] Funding for the Program continued to be scarce through the 1990s, with only $134 million appropriated for security-related projects between 1994 and 1998.[66]

The August 1997 attacks on the US embassies in Tanzania and Kenya were a turning point for the organization and funding for buildings operations. A new Accountability Review Board, chaired by retired Admiral William J. Crowe, recommended installing urgent upgrades to security at existing diplomatic posts and placing high priority on a construction program for new, more secure facilities.[67]

Until 1997, buildings had been the responsibility of an "Office" level organization—Foreign Buildings Operations (FBO). After the attacks and the Crowe panel report, FBO was upgraded to a Bureau, renamed the Bureau of Overseas Buildings Operations, and given full responsibility for both the construction and the management of State Department overseas facilities.[68] This elevation in status and responsibilities put OBO on equal footing with State's regional bureaus, giving it new budgetary clout, according to the General Accounting Office:

> Prior to this reform FBO often subordinated its own responsibilities to the needs and desires of regional bureaus and posts. For example, many of the delays and cost overruns during the Inman program occurred because FBO did not reject change requests from regional bureaus and overseas posts. As a coequal, however, OBO can and does enforce a more disciplined process that discourages change orders that result in delays and cost increases. In fact, OBO considers project budgets to be locked once project funds are requested from Congress, and OBO will not request additional funds from Congress for those projects.[69]

OBO introduced new performance-based management principles for strategy and project planning, created a standardized embassy design and a "design-build" approach to construction, and set quantifiable strategic goals in a six-year Long-Range Overseas Buildings Plan drawn up in 2002. The plan is updated annually "to ensure that future construction plans align with changing priorities and budget actions."[70] A 2004 OMB review praised the impact of these changes on OBO, which it described as "free from significant flaws." OMB noted that

> The program's growth, the need to respond to the increase in the terrorist threat, and the improvement in OBO's organizational capabilities have combined to produce a program that is highly visible, meticulously planned, closely scrutinized, and precisely targeted ... Dramatic increases in capital projects in construction, substantially lower project costs, accelerated schedules, and superior products have all flowed from the better program design.[71]

In 2005, OMB, together with OBO, developed a program to ensure cost-sharing among agencies on the embassy platform, which, the budget office argued, would "ensure adequate capital funding and promote right-sizing of mission staffing."[72] The Capital Security Cost-Sharing program (CSCS) extended the ICASS cost-sharing principle to embassy construction, significantly increasing the resources available for the construction of new embassy compounds. The Crowe panel and Congress had called for the co-location in new, secure diplomatic facilities of all US government staff at overseas posts. With more than 80,000 US personnel in 324 embassies and other buildings, this posed a fiscal challenge to the State Department, which argued that agencies with overseas staff should share in the costs of new facilities.[73]

The CSCS program set out a 14-year projection for capital construction to replace 150 facilities overseas at a cost of $17.5 billion, with all agencies, including State and ICASS, sharing the costs in proportion to their overseas presence, using an algorithm to be developed by the State Department. Data for this plan are gathered through a common software system among the agencies, while planning and budgeting are done in Washington, DC. OBO prepares an annual construction budget based on these data, and each agency includes the CSCS costs in its budget request. This process gives agencies an incentive to restrain overseas personnel growth to hold down their shares of construction costs.[74]

OBO is a striking example of successful strategic planning and management reform at State. The office continues to be concerned about the operating and maintenance costs of overseas facilities, however. In part, this is due to the need to meet higher security requirements and employ more skilled technical staff. It also reflects a lack of clarity about operation and maintenance spending, due to the allocation of those costs among several accounts, rather than being a single line item in the State Department budget.[75]

OBO carries out its own internal planning through a Planning and Development office (including a Project Planning Division) and an Office of Resource Management, which advises the Director on budget and financial planning (including a Financial Management Division that "formulates and directs preparation of documentation for the annual budget").[76]

Diplomatic Security

The State Department devotes growing resources to the physical security of diplomatic personnel (both US and foreign in the United States), the prevention of terrorist attacks against buildings and personnel, and protection against visa and passport fraud. The Bureau of Diplomatic Security (DS) is responsible for these missions.

Although there have been State Department offices responsible for security since World War I, the Bureau of Diplomatic Security was not created until 1985, following the recommendations of the Inman panel calling for improvements in protective intelligence, threat analysis and alerts, and improved contingency planning at diplomatic posts.[77] By the 1990s, DS responsibilities included passport and visa fraud; building inspection, security planning, and protection; courier services; and the protection of foreign dignitaries in the United States. After the 1998 embassy attacks and the Crowe panel findings, the protection of US personnel and facilities overseas became a priority DS mission, funded by a $1.4 billion emergency supplemental appropriation for FY 1998.[78] The DS counterterrorism mission, in particular, has grown. DS carries out this mission, in coordination with other law enforcement organizations, through overseas agents, monitoring the international travel system, and training through State's Antiterrorism Assistance Program (discussed in Chapter 4).

By 2007, DS had become one of the fastest growing staffs at State, with roughly 500 DS Special Agents overseas in 159 countries.[79] The funds for DS salaries and programs are allocated in different parts of the State and foreign assistance budgets. After the 1998 embassy bombings, this funding rose quickly, including $1.5 billion for security overall in the 1998 emergency supplemental appropriation. By FY 2001, security-related appropriations in the regular State Department budget surpassed $1.1 billion, split between the Embassy Security, Construction and Maintenance, and the D&CP accounts.[80]

Assessed and Voluntary Contributions to International Organizations and Peacekeeping: CIO, CIPA and IO&P

Funding for the US-assessed share of dues for the United Nations and its affiliated organizations and for UN Security Council peacekeeping operations are provided through the State Operations budget.[81] The Contributions to International Organizations (CIO) account covers organizational dues, while the Contributions to International Peacekeeping Activities (CIPA) account funds the United States' obligation for peacekeeping.

CIO funding covers US obligations to 50 international organizations, the largest being the United Nations and its 15 affiliated organizations.[82] It also funds ten regional organizations, including the North Atlantic Treaty Organization (NATO) and the Organization of American States (OAS) and another 25 international institutions of which the United States is a member.[83]

Assessments to these organizations are generally negotiated as part of the treaty creating the organization and then adjusted over time. The algorithm is typically based on the relative size of the member countries' economies and their "capacity to pay."[84] With the largest economy, the United States is generally the largest contributor, with its share typically ranging from 20 to 25 percent of the total budget. The US share of the general United Nations budget has been roughly 22 percent in recent years. Overall, the annual US budget for CIO can be around $1.5 billion.[85]

US support for UN peacekeeping operations voted by the UN Security Council is funded through the CIPA account.[86] More than 60 UN peacekeeping operations have been stood up since 1948; 18 were underway in 2008. The largest of these were the UN–African Union mission in Darfur, and the UN missions in the Democratic Republic of the Congo, Sudan, Lebanon, Liberia, and Haiti. Smaller missions were deployed in Georgia, Yugoslavia, Timor-Leste, and Rwanda, among others.[87]

UN peacekeeping operations and funding have been the subject of significant international and domestic political controversy over the years.[88] US military forces rarely participate in UN peacekeeping missions, but the US pays a significant share of their costs according to a formula negotiated separately from that for UN dues. The larger UN member states bear a large share of these costs, with the US share fluctuating over the years from a high of nearly 32 percent to a 25 percent level early in the twenty-first century.[89]

The overall costs of these operations are hard to predict. The UN peace-keeping budget fell from a high of $3.8 billion in 1995, to a low of $900 million in 1999, only to rise again to $3 billion in 2002, and $7 billion in 2008–09.[90] This year-to-year fluctuation means that State Department budget requests for a projected set of operations may overstate or understate the actual costs of existing operations and fail to include costs for missions that arise unexpectedly.

The CIO and CIPA budgets have been the focus of controversy since the mid-1980s, when the United States decided to make its payment of assessed UN dues early in the new US fiscal year (which begins October 1), which was late in the UN fiscal year (which begins January 1). This decision, which deferred US budget costs, meant that as much as 25 percent of the UN budget would not arrive until late in the organization's fiscal year, creating fiscal turbulence and the occasional need to borrow funds to support the organization.[91] This turbulence increased in the 1990s when the United States began providing funding below the official assessed rate for its dues. In the 1990s, the Congress arbitrarily restricted US payments to a rate of 25 percent, well below the previously agreed assessment rate of 30 percent.

Peacekeeping costs and assessment rates were also part of this controversy. In 1993, the Congress demanded that the State Department project peace-keeping costs over a three-year period and in 1994 Congress froze the US peacekeeping share at 25 percent. In 1996, Congress prevented the United States from spending CIPA funds on a new or expanded UN mission unless the authorizing and appropriating committees were notified 15 days ahead of the UN Security Council vote about the estimated costs, length, and exit strategy for the mission, and the source of funds in the State Department budget.[92] The net result of the UN funding controversy was rapid growth in US "arrears" to the United Nations, which by the mid-1990s reached over $1 billion, putting fiscal stress on the organization.

Only a complex negotiation between the State Department and the Congress could resolve this budgetary issue (discussed in Chapter 10). As part of this agreement, an international negotiation was necessary to reduce the US rate of assessment for the general UN budget to 22 percent. Even then, the unpredictability and rising costs of UN peacekeeping in the twenty-first century led to the growth of new US arrears.[93]

Beyond its assessed dues, the United States also makes voluntary contributions to a number of international organizations through the International Organizations and Programs (IO&P) account.[94] Funding through IO&P account, which generally runs around $300 million a year, supports a wide number of multilateral activities such as the preservation of natural resources (e.g., tropical timber), maritime and aviation security, and response to natural disasters.[95] The largest recipients of support are the United Nations

Development Program (UNDP) and the United Nations Children's Fund (UNICEF), to each of which the United States contributes over $100 million a year.

Institutionally, the CIO, CIPA, and IO&P accounts are overseen and planned by the Bureau of International Organizations Affairs (IO), created in 1949, which reports to the Under Secretary of State for Political Affairs. The Bureau's Office of Management Policy and Resources monitors the budgets and finances of these many international organizations and works with State's Resource Management Bureau (reporting to M) to plan the CIO and CIPA budgets. IO's Office for Economic and Development Affairs is responsible for the funding for international economic organizations, coordinating with other agencies involved in those issues, including USAID, Treasury, USTR, Commerce, Agriculture, and Health and Human Services.[96] For several larger UN agencies, the IO Bureau works with other federal agencies to plan budget requests. The Department of Agriculture is a central player in US involvement in the Food and Agricultural Organization (FAO); the Department of Labor in the International Labor Organization (ILO), and the Department of Health and Human Services in the World Health Organization (WHO). The IO Bureau also works with the US Mission to the United Nations in New York (USUN) in planning US contributions to the UN budget.[97]

Public Diplomacy and International Broadcasting

Public Diplomacy

The term "public diplomacy" was coined in the 1960s to describe US government programs that engage publics and "civil society" in other countries. Such engagement is to provide perspectives on US policy, society, and culture, with the goal of improving understanding and affecting the climate for US overseas engagement. Public diplomacy programs range from exchanges of teachers, students, professionals, and citizens, to polling on overseas attitudes toward the United States, to government-funded international radio and television broadcasting.[98]

US public diplomacy has been a part of American statecraft since the 1950s. From 1953 to 1999, public diplomacy (including VOA broadcasting) and exchanges were developed, funded, and managed separately from the State Department by the USIA.[99] The Fulbright Act of 1946 and the Smith–Mundt Act of 1948 created peacetime international exchange programs and an overseas information program at State. Broadcasting and information programs were moved to the new USIA in 1953, while exchanges moved there in 1978.

USIA was an independent agency, with a Senate-confirmed Director, a budget well over $1 billion, and 6,300 employees. More than 500 of its 900 Foreign Service Officers served in 190 overseas embassies and cultural centers.[100] USIA provided the Public Affairs Officers (PAO), spokespersons, and Cultural Affairs Officers for US embassies and managed exchanges and cultural activities overseas. The USIA mission was to explain and advocate US policies to foreign cultures, provide information about the US people, values, and institutions, strengthen international linkages between US citizens and overseas citizens, and advise the President on the impact of foreign attitudes on the effectiveness of US policy.[101] At its peak, the USIA was the largest public diplomacy operation of any nation in the world.

As part of the 1999 reorganization of foreign policy agencies, USIA was absorbed into the State Department, moving most of its activities under the new Under Secretary for Public Diplomacy and Public Affairs (R).[102] The new Under Secretary also allocates public diplomacy resources to the regional and functional bureaus and oversees their use in those bureaus. In 2006, State appointed a Deputy Assistant Secretary for Public Diplomacy in each regional bureau, dual-reporting to the Assistant Secretary for the region and to R.[103] At embassies, the Public Affairs Officer is in charge of public diplomacy programs, overseeing Information Officers (directing the Information Resource Centers) and Cultural Affairs officers (who handle exchanges and programs).[104]

Today, public diplomacy is budgeted at around $1 billion. Administrative support for these activities has been integrated into the broader account for Diplomatic and Consular Programs. Polling activity and analysis were absorbed in State's Bureau of Intelligence and Research (INR). Broadcasting, including the VOA, was consolidated under a restructured, independent Broadcasting Board of Governors.[105]

The integration of USIA into State and its impact on US public diplomacy has remained controversial, especially as non-American views of the United States deteriorated in the wake of the terrorist attacks of 9/11 and the US invasions of Afghanistan and Iraq.[106] The State Department response to rising anti-American attitudes was to create new public diplomacy programs focusing on the Middle East and South Asia, including a Partnership for Learning Program, additional Fulbright, Citizen Exchange, and international visitor programs, public diplomacy elements in a new Middle East Partnership Initiative (MEPI), Arabic and Persian language websites dedicated to the region, and reports, fact sheets, and video documentaries on shared values.[107] The budgets for these new activities contributed to a rapidly growing overall public diplomacy budget, which rose to just over $1 billion in FY 2009.[108]

State also began to come to grips with the lack of strategic focus, inadequate funding, and low staffing levels for its public diplomacy activities. In September 2004, the department created an Office of Policy, Planning, and Resources in the office of the Under Secretary to provide long-term strategic planning and program performance measures, and to coordinate "with all affected bureaus within the department and developing resource allocation recommendations to support the Under Secretary's strategic vision and priorities."[109] This planning office was to focus "resources on the most urgent national security objectives, and provide realistic measurement of public diplomacy's and public affairs' effectiveness," and to coordinate State's efforts with those of other agencies.[110]

State has continued to struggle with public diplomacy resource and staffing issues. In 2005, 15 percent of the 834 overseas public diplomacy positions were not filled. For both security and budgetary reasons, some publicly accessible American Centers and libraries were closed.[111] In 2008, the Secretary of State's Advisory Committee on Transformational Diplomacy recommended that a semi-autonomous public diplomacy agency be created, reporting to the Secretary of State, which would be a move back toward the USIA model.[112]

State's public diplomacy has also had to deal with the growing number of public communications and public diplomacy programs being created across the government, especially in the wake of the 9/11 attacks and the US military presence in the Middle East. This increasing diversity of programs has created problems for the coordination of the US message overseas. In particular, Defense Department public information, strategic communications, broadcasting, and other forms of outreach to publics in Iraq and Afghanistan, Iran, and the wider Middle East grew substantially, but proved difficult to track and synchronize with State and White House efforts.[113] In addition, public information activities of the National Endowments for Democracy (NED), USAID, and the Broadcasting Board of Governors have expanded but are not closely coordinated with State's programs.[114]

International Broadcasting

US international broadcasting, which began in World War II, has been an important part of public diplomacy since the beginning of the Cold War, but its structure has changed significantly over time. The 1948 Information and Educational Exchange Act (Smith–Mundt) called for enhanced public dissemination of information overseas, and created exchange programs and the VOA within the State Department. In 1954, VOA was moved to a new United States Information Agency separate from the State Department. VOA was to be a "consistently reliable and authoritative source of news [which was] accurate, objective, and comprehensive." It would "represent America not any single segment of American society;" and would "present the policies of the United States clearly and effectively," along with "responsible discussions and opinion on these policies."[115] VOA continued to operate through USIA until the agency was absorbed into the State Department in 1999.

Separately, the United States created two "surrogate" radio services which provided alternative broadcasting into countries behind the Iron Curtain. Unlike VOA, surrogate radio services covered local news and events in these countries, using a staff composed of exiled nationals. Radio Free Europe (RFE), broadcasting to Eastern Europe was created in 1949, and Radio Liberty

(RL), broadcasting to the Soviet Union, in 1951. Both services were covertly funded by the CIA until 1972, when Congress voted to fund them overtly through a government corporation, the Board for International Broadcasting (BIB), which was created independent from USIA to establish clear independence from US foreign policy guidance.[116]

In 1994, RFE and RL were again reorganized under a new Broadcasting Board of Governors (BBG), with reduced budgets and a new location in Prague, Czech Republic. The BBG took over Radio Marti (created in 1983) from USIA, and later absorbed the new Asian service, Radio Free Asia (created in 1996). The Act also created an office in USIA—the International Broadcasting Bureau (IBB)—to handle construction and operation of transmission services for all official US government international broadcasting.[117]

In 1999, this structure was again changed with the absorption of USIA into the State Department.[118] The 1998 Foreign Affairs Reform and Restructuring Act removed all broadcasting services from State, including VOA, and consolidated them under the BBG, which it restructured as an independent federal agency whose members were appointed by the President.[119] The BBG directly administers or grants funding to all broadcasting services. In addition to VOA, Radio and Television Marti, Radio Free Asia, and RFE/RL, the BBG supports the Middle East Broadcasting Network, which operates Radio Sawa (2002) and Alhurra television (2004), both of which broadcast into the Middle East.[120] All US government international broadcasting is now consolidated under BBG, with an annual budget of roughly $700 million.

The relationship between international broadcasting and US foreign policy has been problematic. The BBG is sensitive about preserving its independence from overall US foreign policy and the State Department, though its board includes the Secretary of State.[121] Despite this separation, however, US international broadcasting grew quickly after the terrorist attacks and the US invasions of Afghanistan and Iraq, particularly in the Middle East and Gulf regions. Radio Sawa, Radio Farda (to Iran, through RFE/RL), and Alhurra Television were created and rapidly expanded. Arabic-language services consumed over 30.2 percent of the BBG broadcasting budget for FY 2008, second only to broadcasting for Europe, Eurasia, and Central Asia (37.1 percent).[122] In addition, the BBG Office of Policy receives State Department views with respect to editorials VOA must carry as an official government view. BBG also receives State input with respect to the language services it should broadcast.[123]

The BBG board, a nine-person bipartisan body, defines the broadcasting mission, oversees broadcasting operations, manages VOA and the Cuban services, administers grant funding for RFE/RL, RFA, and MBN, and makes the critical decisions about languages being broadcast. The Office of the Chief Financial Officer at the BBG, through its Budget Office, develops and oversees the implementation of the BBG budget for the services and grantees.[124]

Other State Operations Support

The State Operations budget also provides funding for a number of smaller institutional grants. Many of these are research or outreach institutions or provide support for democracy efforts in other countries.

National Endowment for Democracy

The United States began funding private organizations supporting democracy early in the Cold War. Some of that early support was provided covertly, through the CIA, to support anti-communist trade union and political organizations, especially in western Europe and Latin America. The revelation of that covert funding led Congress to decide to provide overt funding to support democratic institutions, political parties, and civil society in countries that were non-democratic, emerging into democracy, or struggling to strengthen democratic practices and governance.[125]

The National Endowment for Democracy (NED) was created in 1983, reflecting this decision.[126] NED is a private, non-profit organization, governed by a bipartisan board. Its mission is "to strengthen democratic institutions throughout the world through private, non-governmental efforts."[127] NED makes grants to other organizations, particularly four organizations that reflect NED's public/private, Democrat/Republican character: the American Center for International Labor Solidarity (affiliated with the AFL/CIO), the Center for International Private Enterprise (affiliated with the US Chamber of Commerce), the National Democratic Institute for International Affairs (affiliated with the Democratic Party) and the International Republican Institute (affiliated with the Republican Party).

NED also maintains an internal research center (the International Forum for Democratic Studies), a fellowship program, and a Center for International Media Assistance. NED funding supports elections and parliamentary training, participation in the political process, skills training, election support, policy institute support, legal education, production of written and visual materials, research grants, and meetings and conferences.[128]

NED receives its funding from a line item in the State Operations budget. In addition, in the 1990s, as US support for democracy overseas expanded, other US assistance programs were created for this purpose. These included the Freedom Support Act (Russia and the former Soviet Union), Support for East European Democracy (central and southeastern Europe), USAID (governance support and the Office of Transition Initiatives), and the State Department (Economic Support Funds and the Bureau of Democracy, Human Rights, and Labor). (These programs are discussed in Chapter 4.) These other programs sometimes supply funding to NED, which, in turn, grants the funds to non-government groups and organizations overseas. NED makes approximately 900 grants a year, with a total budget of roughly $80 million.

Conclusion

The State Department has operated for decades with a budgeting and planning system that separates its operations and administration from its program responsibilities. The dominant culture in the organization is not a strategic planning culture, which has made long-term budget planning difficult. Recent management changes, notably the appointment of a Deputy Secretary for Management and Resources, provide a new opportunity for the department to give greater priority to management issues and to a more integrated approach to budgeting. These changes are recent, however, and untested.

The State Department has also faced management challenges for decades. Budgets and Foreign Service personnel have not grown commensurate with the department's responsibilities, while internal management and administrative systems have fallen behind the curve of advances in information and communications technology. Since the mid-1990s, however, there has been considerable progress in modernizing State's management systems. A strong emphasis on embassy security has led to significant increases in investment in buildings and diplomatic security. Dedicated funding has made it possible for the department to modernize its information and communications systems on a global basis. New agreements with agencies hosted on the embassy platform have improved embassy administrative operations and increased funding for embassy repairs and construction.

Starting with Secretary of State Colin Powell, and continuing with Secretaries Rice and Clinton, there is a strong push to overcome the personnel and budgetary limits on State's personnel and activities. There may still be a significant underinvestment in public diplomacy and continuing shortfalls in funding for the United States' role in the United Nations and other international organizations. And it is difficult, for political reasons, for the State Department to increase its funding to the degree it would like (discussed further in Chapter 10).

Chapter 3

Foreign Economic Assistance Budgeting and Programs

Introduction

Most of the International Affairs budget is devoted to foreign and security assistance programs.[1] Between fiscal year (FY) 1977 and FY 2007, US bilateral and multilateral foreign assistance budgets totaled nearly $500 billion.[2] Annual budgets, however, have varied, due usually to unanticipated requirements.[3]

The management and implementation of foreign assistance programs is dispersed through the executive branch in roughly 20 budget accounts administered by several departments and agencies. Some are planned, budgeted, and implemented by the State Department. Some are planned by State, but

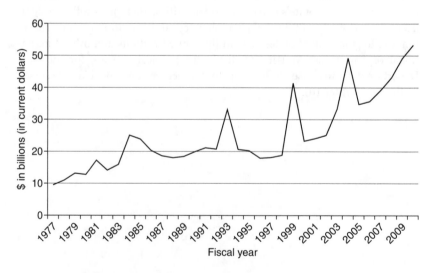

Figure 3.1 International Affairs (Function 150) budget (source: OMB Public Budget Database).

Note
Figures in current dollars.

implemented by the US Agency for International Development (USAID). Some are the direct responsibility of USAID. Still others are planned, budgeted, and implemented by other departments and agencies (see Figure 3.2). In addition to the accounts included in the International Affairs budget (Function 150), most other federal departments and agencies conduct foreign assistance like activities overseas. The result is a complex architecture of foreign assistance planning and implementation which has not been centrally planned or coordinated throughout much of US post-war history. This chapter begins with a discussion of the continuing search for a coherent planning and budgeting process for US foreign assistance programs included in the International Affairs budget function (Function 150).

We then move to a discussion of the different programs themselves. In this and in the following chapter, we divide US foreign assistance programs into four categories, defined by their objectives: economic assistance aimed primarily at achieving "development" objectives; humanitarian assistance; foreign assistance linked to US strategic and foreign policy goals; and security assistance to strengthen the security forces of other countries.[4] In this chapter, we discuss the executive branch organizations and budget accounts involved in the first two categories: economic assistance (sometimes referred to as "development" assistance) and humanitarian assistance. In the next chapter we

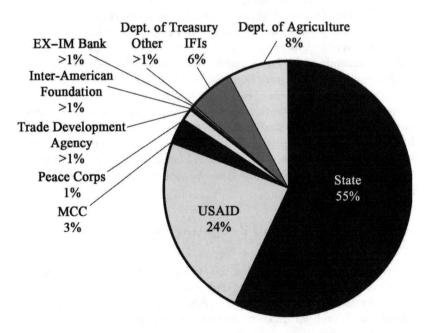

Figure 3.2 Function 150 diaspora: FY 2009 estimate (source: US Department of State, *FY 2010 Congressional Budget Justification* (Washington, DC: May 2009)).

review the programs and accounts that are closely linked to US foreign policy goals and security assistance.

Economic development programs and accounts are defined here broadly as funding that focuses principally on "long-term poverty reduction and economic growth."[5] We include in this discussion the programs and accounts at USAID, the nation's largest bilateral development assistance agency. We also examine the new Millennium Challenge Corporation (MCC), created in 2003, the President Emergency Program for AIDS Relief (PEPFAR), Treasury Department development and international financial programs (International Monetary Fund (IMF), World Bank, regional development banks, debt relief, and technical assistance), the Peace Corps, Export–Import Bank, the Overseas Private Investment Corporation, the Trade and Development Agency, the Inter-American Foundation, and the African Development Foundation. All of these agencies, programs, and accounts are part of the International Affairs budget function. Together, their funding reached a 30-year peak in constant dollars in the early 2000s, reflecting primarily growth in funding for the MCC and PEPFAR programs.[6] In FY 2005, funding in this category constituted over 40 percent of all US foreign assistance.[7]

We then discuss programs that provide humanitarian and disaster assistance, including the State Department's Migration and Refugee Assistance (MRA) and Emergency Migration and Refugee Assistance (ERMA), USAID's Office of Foreign Disaster Assistance (OFDA), and emergency food assistance the United States provides through Title II of PL 480. US funding for humanitarian and disaster response has been consistently high, with supplemental funding frequently added for natural disasters, such as the 2005 Indian Ocean tsunami and Pakistani earthquake.[8] In FY 2004, humanitarian funds amounted to over 10 percent of overall US foreign assistance.[9]

The chapter concludes with a brief discussion of the even wider US international engagement reflected in the programs and activities of agencies and departments whose budgets are not included in the International Affairs budget function: Commerce, Health and Human Services, the Environmental Protection Administration, Education, Agriculture, and the United States Trade Representative.

Strategic Planning and Budgeting for Function 150

Although it might be expected that the State Department would be responsible for foreign assistance planning and budgeting, there has been no integrated planning process for foreign assistance since these programs were created after World War II. Until the 1990s, State made little effort to coordinate strategy and resources; each agency and department did its own planning and submitted its budget request directly to the Office of Management and Budget (OMB). Since then, there have been gradual steps toward a more integrated and disciplined process, but this evolution is still very much a work in progress.

State Department culture focuses on diplomacy, not planning, program development and implementation, which are characteristic of foreign assistance. Within the State Department, foreign economic and security assistance budgets were planned separately from State Operations. Policy decisions, country selection, and overall budgets were prepared by the department's regional bureaus and the Bureau of Political–Military Affairs, and transmitted to the Secretary and Deputy Secretary. Implementation was the responsibility of USAID and the Department of Defense (DOD), respectively, with State itself having a minimal role. USAID prepared development assistance budgets separately, as did Treasury for multilateral bank and financial programs. The smaller international affairs agencies did the same.

As the US foreign policy agenda expanded, however, a number of new foreign assistance programs were created to deal with such areas as counternarcotics, terrorism, international crime, nonproliferation, peacekeeping, democracy support, and, most recently, post-conflict reconstruction. Because these programs were linked to foreign and national security objectives, the State Department role in program planning and budgeting also expanded, adding to the complexity of the foreign assistance budget process.

Secretaries of State have made intermittent efforts to cope with this dispersal of foreign assistance providers, budget accounts, and programs and to assert a more central role for the Secretary of State in providing more coordinated strategic and budgetary planning for overall foreign assistance.[10] In the late 1980s, Secretary of State James Baker created a Mission Program Plan/Bureau Program Plan (MPP/BPP) process to coordinate foreign assistance (and operations) planning starting at the embassy level, working its way through regional bureaus to the Secretary's office. However, this process did not generate useful budget information and did not lead to effective coordination within State. It also had minimal impact on the other international affairs agencies.[11] Secretary Warren Christopher created an office of Resources, Plans, and Policy (S/RPP) reporting to the Secretary to coordinate internal strategic and budgetary planning for foreign assistance, and to develop the Secretary's recommendations for the overall International Affairs budgets.[12] S/RPP developed a "budget hearings" process, chaired by the Deputy Secretary to review internal State budget requests and options and make recommendations for decisions to the Secretary. While the Secretary had no clear statutory authority over the budget planning carried out by other international affairs agencies, S/RPP held hearings to review USAID, the Arms Control and Disarmament Agency (ACDA), and the United States Information Agency (USIA) plans and budgets, and urged the other Function 150 agencies to present in such hearings, as well.[13]

The relationship between State and USAID was the most problematic part of this coordination effort. The development agency was created in 1961 to distinguish US foreign assistance with a "development" objective from assistance that was linked to the goals of US foreign policy and national security strategy. USAID's relative autonomy from State gradually eroded between the 1970s and the 1990s, but its strategic and budgetary planning processes for its own "development assistance" funds remained largely separate from State until 2005. However, USAID's role in implementing State's Economic Support Fund (ESF) programs made this relationship even more complex. ESF programs are linked to US foreign and strategic goals, making country choice and the size of the program a State responsibility, with development playing a secondary role. However, State had no implementation capability, giving USAID an important role in shaping individual country programs and field implementation from a development perspective. In the 1990s, USAID took on a similar role in program planning and implementation for assistance to Eastern Europe and the former Soviet Union, programs clearly linked to US foreign policy goals. By FY 2000, USAID had direct responsibility for a portfolio of over $12 billion in foreign assistance, the majority of these funds linked to US foreign and national security goals.

Secretary of State Colin Powell replaced S/RPP with a more institutionalized Resource Management Bureau (RM), headed by a new Assistant Secretary, reporting both to the Secretary and the Under Secretary for Management and responsible for both strategic and budgetary planning.[14] For the first time in State's post-war history, both State operations and foreign assistance budgets were the responsibility of this bureau. In principle, RM directed the department's overall budget process, prepared budgets for OMB and the Congress, was the department's principal witness at congressional hearings on State's budgets and management, allocated appropriated funds to the department's bureaus and offices, and oversaw implementation of the budget.[15]

A Deputy Assistant Secretary for Foreign Assistance within RM took on the role S/RPP had played in administering foreign assistance budget hearings and creating budget options for the Secretary, preparing the foreign assistance budget documents for the Congress, and developing legislative strategy to acquire the requested funds.[16] This foreign assistance office based its work on the Mission and Bureau Program Plans prepared in the embassies and the regional bureaus, and made sure the estimates were correct, could be executed, reflected the Secretary's priorities and initiatives, fell within resource constraints, and could be "marketed."[17] Each bureau then held hearings with State's senior leadership to review the budget recommendations, after which RM coordinated the budget documents for OMB and the Congress.[18]

Secretary Powell and Deputy Secretary Richard Armitage gave priority attention to State's management and budgeting processes, conducted detailed hearings and reviews through this process. In particular, as part of the restructured process, State and USAID developed a shared strategic plan for foreign assistance. The goal of the plan was to "move forward together, instead of pursuing this priority area as separate organizations," by developing "a joint methodology to allocate resources by strategic goal."[19]

Secretary of State Condoleezza Rice built on the Powell architecture, but split foreign assistance planning and budgeting away from the RM office and elevated its importance by creating a new Office of the Director of Foreign Assistance (State-F or S/F), at the level of a Deputy Secretary of State. This Director was to "develop a coordinated US Government (USG) foreign assistance strategy, including developing five-year country specific assistance strategies and annual country-specific operation plans."[20] The new position further integrated USAID planning into State, as the USAID Administrator was dual-hatted as the director of F.[21] In addition, the F staff of 80 to 100 employees was created by combining the small foreign assistance staff from RM with the much larger USAID Bureau for Policy and Program Coordination (PPC), and locating the new office at State.

The F office was given budget planning responsibility for all the State and USAID programs and accounts discussed in this chapter.[22] However, although Secretary Rice intended the office to "provide overall leadership to foreign assistance that is delivered through other agencies," it did not integrate the budget planning of the new HIV/AIDS program (PEPFAR) or the MCC and had even less authority to do so with the other independent departments and agencies in the International Affairs budget, such as elements of Treasury and the Peace Corps.[23] Nor could it coordinate the programs carried out by agencies and departments outside the International Affairs account. As a result, its budget planning authority covered only 55 percent of all US foreign assistance.[24]

The goal of the F process was to link State and USAID programs with the strategic goals of US foreign assistance in the recipient countries. The process took its guidance from the overall strategic goal of "helping build and sustain democratic, well-governed states that will respond to the needs of their people and conduct themselves responsibly in the international system." F developed a matrix which arrayed all State and USAID foreign assistance programs and accounts in two ways.

First, they were arrayed by US objectives: peace and security (preventing, mitigating, and recovering from internal or external conflict); governing justly and democratically (making governments accountable to their people by controlling corruption, protecting civil rights, and strengthening rule of law); investing in people (health, education, and environment); economic growth (reduction in barriers to entry for business, suitable trade policy, fiscal accountability); and humanitarian assistance (emergency relief and rehabilitation following catastrophes).[25]

Second, without naming specific countries, the matrix created categories for countries receiving US foreign assistance: rebuilding countries (emerging from internal or external conflict); developing countries (low or lower-middle income, not meeting governance criteria set out by the MCC); transforming countries (low or lower-middle income, meeting the MCC criteria); sustaining partnership countries (upper-middle income partner countries);[26] and restrictive countries (states of concern where there are significant governance issues).[27]

This process was controversial, especially with USAID's missions in the field. For FY 2008, F set an overall budget level for each country, combining all State and USAID accounts in that country, then reduced that level by 20 percent to provide a reserve which F and the Secretary could use to ensure that priorities were funded and to resolve appeals. The office then set objectives and budget planning levels for each country top-down in Washington, DC, which were then communicated as guidance for the embassy's MPP process.[28] F then created "core groups" in Washington, DC, which brought together regional and functional bureaus and relevant outside agencies (principally DOD on security assistance). These groups allocated the resources by country and by major program objectives. These recommendations were then reviewed by the Director and were the basis for a "senior review" with the Secretary or Deputy Secretary of State.[29]

Though controversial, the F process was a step forward for strategic and budgetary planning at State and USAID.[30] It was the first detailed effort at State to link overall foreign policy objectives to specific foreign assistance programs and dollars on a country-by-country basis. It combined the efforts of the two leading foreign assistance providers—State and USAID. It also had severe weaknesses. It was excessively top-down, leaving missions feeling they played too small a role and were overburdened in reporting requirements. The country categories were too inflexible. The Congress did not feel consulted in the process and did not understand the results.[31]

With the transition to the Obama administration, the process began to change even further. For the first time, the State Department named a second Deputy Secretary of State for Management and Resources, with responsibility for foreign assistance and State operations budgets, as well as for strategic planning. This position was not dual-hatted as USAID Administrator, but assumed all of the State-F responsibilities. In addition, the new Deputy Secretary assumed responsibility for strategic planning, for the preparation of the State Operations budget discussed in the previous chapter, and for overall State Department management. These are important steps in the direction of a more formal, institutionalized strategic planning and budgeting process at State and USAID. They do not yet, however, fully incorporate planning for the other agencies with foreign assistance programs in the International Affairs budget function, nor do they reach to the other non-150 federal agencies with a growing international engagement. The integration of US foreign affairs planning and budgeting remains a work in progress.[32]

US Agency for International Development

History, Missions, and Budgeting

The US Agency for International Development (USAID) was created in 1961 as a separate agency responsible for administering US bilateral assistance to developing nations, many of which were emerging from colonial domination. Their development was seen, in part, as a moral obligation of wealthy nations. It was also seen as in the interests of the United States. Continued poverty in the southern hemisphere provided an opportunity for the expansion of communism and Soviet power, while development would promote economic prosperity.[33] As President John F. Kennedy put it: "the economic collapse of those free but less-developed nations which now stand pointed between sustained growth and economic chaos would be disastrous to our national security, harmful to our comparative prosperity and offensive to our conscience."[34]

The decision to create a separate agency for development assistance reflected a desire to put a distance between development assistance and US military assistance programs, which were clearly driven by security interests. USAID would

> make clear the peaceful and positive purposes of this program,... emphasize the new importance this Administration places on economic and social development quite apart from security interests,... and ... make clear the relation between the Military Assistance Program and those interests.[35]

The ambiguous links between moral obligation and self-interest and between security and developmental goals has led to programmatic and institutional tensions that continue to affect the structure, content, and budgets of US bilateral foreign assistance.

The bureaucratic rationale for creating a separate agency also reflected a realization that US government economic assistance programs were dispersed and poorly coordinated by the State Department.[36] The Kennedy language, which resonates today, described foreign aid programs as "bureaucratically fragmented, awkward and slow," having an administrative structure that was "irrational," covering numerous departments and programs that were "obsolete" "inconsistent," and "unduly rigid." This had led to a "fall in morale and efficiency" among foreign assistance employees, who were frustrated by "overlapping agency jurisdictions and unclear objectives."[37]

The new agency combined several foreign assistance tools: a loan fund, a development grant fund, an investment guarantee program (later converted into the Overseas Private Investment Corporation), and a contingency fund. Reflecting the internal tension in US foreign assistance, however, the new agency was also given responsibility for US economic assistance focused on economic and political stability, which became the strategically driven ESF, over which State had policy and budgetary control. ESF recipients were not selected with development objectives in mind. It was designed to provide budget and commodity import support to countries with which the United States had important strategic and political relationships in the Cold War context.

Growing criticism of USAID's links to security objectives, especially in Latin America and Vietnam, combined with concern about the effectiveness of bilateral development assistance, has led to continuous efforts to redesign the agency and restructure its programs.[38] These reform efforts also reflect the continuing tensions in US bilateral foreign assistance between political/strategic goals and developmental goals, and the ambiguity of the relationship between State and USAID.

Because USAID continues to be both the bilateral development assistance flagship of the US government and the implementer of significant amounts of foreign policy driven funds (through ESF and other programs), the agency's structure and budget processes are complex and continue to evolve. The 1998 Act that consolidated USIA and ACDA into the State Department made it clear that, while the USAID Administrator was a principal advisor to the President and the Secretary of State on international development, this person was also "under the direct authority and foreign policy guidance of the Secretary of State."[39] The creation of the Office of the Director of Foreign Assistance in 2006 reflected a strong desire to reintegrate the different dimensions of US foreign assistance, including USAID, under the authority of the Secretary of State:

> In keeping with USAID's status as a distinct agency and recognizing that the Administrator is under the Secretary's direct authority and foreign policy guidance, the Secretary shall review USAID's strategic plan and annual performance plan, annual budget submission and appeals, allocations and significant (in terms of policy or money) reprogrammings of development and other economic assistance.[40]

Overview of USAID Accounts

The core mission of USAID is to plan, implement, and administer bilateral US development assistance. The Development Assistance (DA) and Child Survival and Health (CSH) accounts are the most important sources for this assistance. DA is used to support projects "designed chiefly to foster sustainable broad-based economic progress and social stability in developing countries."[41] DA funds, which are appropriated for two years, have covered a wide range of US commitments to assistance for agriculture, education, energy, economic growth, the environment, democracy, and human rights. DA consumes roughly 47 percent of the funds USAID directly controls.[42]

In the mid-1990s, Congress carved the CSH fund out of DA to support projects and programs "that expand basic health services and strengthen national health systems to significantly improve people's health, especially that of women, children, and other vulnerable populations."[43] CSH funds, which are appropriated for three years, support a broad range of health programs, including basic health services, immunization, sanitation, and control of infectious diseases. They also support family planning and reproductive health, which has been a controversial issue in the Congress in the 1990s and early 2000s. CSH funding has, in recent years, consumed roughly 34 percent of USAID's direct foreign assistance funding. In the FY 2010 budget request, the Obama administration eliminated the separate CSH account and combined its programs with a broader Global Health and Child Survival (GHCS) account that includes the PEPFAR program.

USAID also administers several food aid programs, most authorized under PL 480, the "Food for Peace" program, legislated in 1954. Food for Peace was designed to expand export markets for US agricultural products, to combat hunger and malnutrition, and to support economic development primarily by distributing large US agricultural surpluses.[44] This program has a natural base of political support in the agricultural industry, shippers, and nongovernmental organizations that distribute or sell the surplus commodities in developing and poor countries.[45] As a result, funding for US food aid programs has been significant for more than 50 years, at levels near $2 billion a year. The food aid program that began as PL 480 has expanded into six programs that distribute or sell agricultural commodities, provide humanitarian donations, or stockpile surpluses for these purposes.[46] Most of these programs are administered by USAID, though their funding is appropriated by Congress's agriculture subcommittees.

In 1994, the Clinton administration created a new rapid-response capability at USAID—the Office of Transition Initiatives (OTI). Because DA and CSH funds support longer-term development projects, the administration sought a more rapid capability to support government transitions in fragile or conflict-prone countries. OTI targets riskier, quick-response projects that promote reconciliation among parties in conflict, stimulate local economies, or support independent media and the democratic process. OTI funding is small—roughly $40 million a year—but is only partly allocated in advance, with the remainder available for contingencies as they arise. OTI funds are also known as "no year" funding, as they remain available until expended.[47]

USAID also administers a small credit program, guaranteeing credit that would provide private investment in local businesses and projects, such as banking, energy, housing, and small business in countries that lack available and affordable capital. During its first 30 years, USAID provided significant credit and loan guarantees. With growing debt in poorer countries, however, defaults rose and USAID credit programs ended. The new credit program is smaller, with appropriated funds available for four years.[48] Much of the debt was forgiven in the 1990s.

In addition to its own development assistance, food aid, rapid response, and credit programs, USAID is the principal implementing agency for economic assistance programs linked to US foreign policy and strategy goals, whose policies and budgets are determined by the State Department (discussed in Chapter 4).[49] USAID implements these programs with economic development goals in mind, but has little say with respect to countries or budget levels. Because of this broader implementing role, however, USAID can have responsibility for more than $12–14 billion in annual US foreign assistance in roughly 150 countries.

The administration of this portfolio is the responsibility of a Foreign Service and civil service staff at USAID that has shrunk significantly since the 1980s to 2,200 government employees, who work in overseas missions or manage private contractors working on USAID contracts and grants. Staffing and administrative costs for buildings, technology, and communications are funded through USAID's Operating Expenses (OE) account, which generally comes to $600–700 million per year. OE and some program funds also support more than 1,000 private Personal Service Contractors (PSC), who work directly at USAID.[50]

USAID Structure and Budgeting

USAID is directed by an Administrator and Deputy Administrator. Until much of its staff was absorbed into State's F process, USAID's Bureau of Program and Policy Coordination (PPC) was responsible for strategic and budgetary planning and oversight over program implementation and evaluation.[51] Today only the personnel budgeting and evaluation functions continue in this office.

USAID's Management office (M) provides central support for USAID's worldwide operations including personnel, accounting and finance, management policy, control and audit, administrative services, procurement policy, information resources, and business systems modernization. This office also administers all the financial controls and reporting requirements for funds appropriated to the agency.[52]

USAID has regional bureaus for Sub-Saharan Africa (AFR), Asia (A), the Middle East (ME), Latin America and the Caribbean (LAC), and Europe and Eurasia (E&E), each directed by an Assistant Administrator. The regional bureaus "recommend regional and country resource requirements, including operating expenses and food aid, within the Agency's overall budget process."[53] There are also "functional" or "pillar" bureaus responsible for programs that cut across regional bureaus and programs: Global Health (GH) for population and HIV/AIDS programs, Economic Growth, Agriculture, and Trade (EGAT), and the Democracy, Conflict, and Humanitarian Assistance

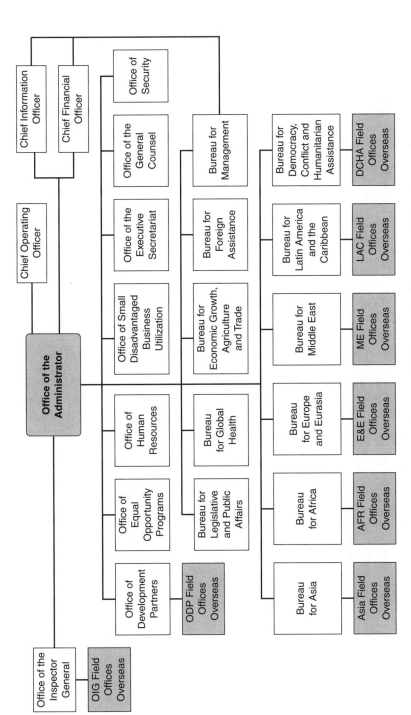

Figure 3.3 US Agency for International Development (source: US Agency for International Development).

(DCHA) bureau, which administers USAID's Office of Transition Initiatives (OTI), Office of Foreign Disaster Assistance (OFDA), and Office of Food for Peace (OFFP).[54]

The USAID planning and budgeting process has traditionally been "bottom-up," with the overseas missions playing a central role. Within the framework of the overall State/USAID strategic plan, bilateral country missions and offices and humanitarian assistance coordinators in roughly 150 countries shape local programs and plans, negotiate agreements with the local government and the private sector, and prepare planning and program recommendations. They provide those recommendations directly to the Washington, DC headquarters and, through the Mission Strategic Plans, to the State Department.[55] The recommendations take the form of a "Strategy Statement," which describes the country program's goals and rationale and the expected results and outlines the "aggregate levels of foreign assistance resources—program, OE, and staff—needed to produce these results."[56] Starting in 2006, the USAID missions also contribute to a separate Mission Operational Plan (MOP) for the entire embassy, which is a budget and personnel allocation of already appropriated funds for the entire foreign assistance program being carried out in that country.[57] The MOP provides the starting point for future budget planning and requests.

For USAID in particular, the mission's strategic plan and strategic objectives are reviewed in Washington, DC, to determine the longer-term implications of the proposed programs and projects. This review leads to a Management Agreement which "establishes a life of SO funding level for each Strategic Objective." This is an important feature of USAID budgeting. While the agreement cannot commit future funding, which must be obtained annually from the Congress, it creates the "expectation" of assistance for a given country or program beyond the initial fiscal year. In terminology unique to USAID, this expectation is described as a "mortgage."[58] The mortgage reflects an institutional commitment to a particular strategic objective in a country and can reduce the year-to-year flexibility of budget planners as needs or programs change.[59]

These budget requests are subjected to scrutiny through the regional bureaus at USAID and at State, and the "hearings" process administered by the Office of the Director of Foreign Assistance. Final budget decisions are made in August and September and then forwarded to the Office of Management and Budget.

USAID Planning Ambiguities

The evolution of USAID's relationship with the State Department has led to a "crisis of identity." The complexity of this relationship grows, in part, out of the role USAID plays as the implementing agency for foreign-policy-driven assistance programs appropriated to the State Department. This responsibility dilutes the "long-term development" character of USAID's mission and links its work more closely to the overall objectives of US foreign policy. The creation of the Office of the Director of Foreign Assistance further integrated the missions, planning, and budgeting of the two agencies. The USAID Administrator once held final authority over budget decisions for the DA and CSH accounts, but that responsibility migrated first to the Director of Foreign Assistance and, more recently, to the second Deputy Secretary of State for Management and Resources. At the field level, USAID mission planning is part of the broader Mission Strategic and Mission Operational planning processes in the embassies.

USAID has struggled to maintain a separate identity and to defend its development mission and funding, its signature activity, from this integration. At the same time, USAID's broader role brings political support because of its association with broader US foreign policy goals, and its interaction with State and other agencies providing foreign assistance. USAID planning in the early 2000s reflected this increasing ambiguity.[60] Its 2004 strategic review made a case both for the separate integrity of development assistance (DA and CSH) and for USAID's contribution to the administration's foreign policy priorities. Two of the agency's "core operational goals"—"transformational development" and "humanitarian relief"—have always been core agency activities. The other three, however—"strengthening fragile states," "supporting US geo-strategic interests," and "mitigating global and transnational ills"—reflect the growing connection between the agency's programs and the US foreign policy agenda, particularly the high profile of the problem of fragile states in the Bush administration's National Security Strategy.[61]

For USAID, "fragile states" posed a new foreign assistance challenge and required a new, separate strategy and funding. The strategy distinguished such states from those eligible for "transformational development" assistance and recognized that the agency's existing programs were not well designed to deal either with the complexity of the failed state problem or the need for rapid, near-term response.[62] USAID also noted that the response to this problem was interagency in nature. It required a close working relationship with the new State Department Office of the Coordinator for Reconstruction and Stabilization (S/CRS), created in 2004.[63] The agency argued vehemently, however, that the fragile state responsibilities should not divert USAID from its development focus and should draw on new, additional resources, rather than use existing DA or CSH funds.[64]

The same was true of USAID's responsibilities for managing "support for strategic states," such as Iraq, Afghanistan, Pakistan, Jordan, Egypt, and Israel. The agency noted that State and the National Security Council (NSC) determined the recipients of such assistance. Though the resulting programs might have a developmental focus, funding should come exclusively from "ESF or ESF-like resources," not from DA or CSH.[65] Equally, funds for meeting the challenges of "global/transnational issues and other special concerns," including HIV/AIDS and other diseases, climate, trade, international trade in narcotics or humans, and the environment were "frequently associated with earmarks, directives, and initiatives that entail relatively restrictive program guidance." From USAID's perspective, "separate resources should be identified for this goal," such as the PEPFAR program.[66]

USAID's ideal vision was to create a budgeting structure with separate funding for each of these other objectives, to avoid diverting DA and CSH resources or having "complex and confusing budget and strategy guidance."[67] By 2006, however, the Agency conceded that such a budget structure was unlikely. Reflecting the new foreign assistance framework and the closer integration with State that resulted from the creation of the new foreign assistance budget office, the new USAID strategy noted that it would "align budgetary resources with the goal they primarily support, and will manage them accordingly."[68] This was similar to the strategic and budgetary planning focus developed under State's new F framework.

Millennium Challenge Corporation

The Millennium Challenge Corporation (MCC) is the most recent addition to the government's dispersed foreign assistance architecture. MCC was designed to respond to the frequent criticism that US foreign assistance programs failed to reduce poverty or lead to economic growth because of corruption and weakness in the governance of recipient countries.[69] Rather than reorient USAID with governance objectives in mind, an interagency team of NSC, USAID, State, Treasury, and OMB designed a new organization that would link foreign assistance commitments to the performance of the foreign governments receiving support.[70]

The result was the MCC, an independent government corporation created in 2003. The MCC is managed by a CEO appointed by the President and is overseen by a Board of Directors, chaired by the Secretary of State, with the Secretary of Treasury, the Director of OMB, the Administrator of USAID, the US Trade Representative (USTR), and four Senate-confirmed non-government directors as members. The organization was intended to be small, with a staff of fewer than 100, but once operational in 2004, the ceiling was raised to 300, reflecting a more realistic assessment of the likely workloads.[71]

The MCC rapidly became one of the largest bilateral programs in the US foreign assistance portfolio. The administration initially proposed an annual funding level of $5 billion for MCC's Millennium Challenge Account (MCA), which would have made that account larger than USAID's bilateral DA and CSH accounts. While Congress has never appropriated the administration's full budget request for the MCA, its annual funding has been significant, rivaling USAID's DA account (see Table 3.1).

MCC funding was explicitly linked to recipient government performance

Table 3.1 MCA appropriations: FY 2004–FY 2009 (in $ millions)[1]

	FY 2004	FY 2005	FY 2006	FY 2007	FY 2008	FY 2009
Request	1,300	2,500	3,000	3,000	3,000	2,225
Appropriation	994	1,488	1,752	1,752	1,486[2]	1,544[3]

Notes
1 Curt Tarnoff, Millennium Challenge Account, CRS Report RL32427 (Washington, DC: Congressional Research Service, October 8, 2008), 24
2 Original appropriation was $1.5 billion. $58 million was rescinded in Supplemental Appropriations Act, 2008 PL 110-252 (June 30, 2008).
3 Funding availability through: Consolidated Security, Disaster Assistance, and Continuing Appropriations Act, 2009, PL 110-329 (September 30, 2008), effective through March 6, 2009.

in three areas: ruling justly (promoting good governance, fighting corruption, respecting human rights, and adhering to the rule of law), investing in people (providing adequate healthcare, education, and other social services), and economic freedom (fostering enterprise and entrepreneurship).[72] Countries could qualify for MCC "compacts" by meeting these goals, as measured through a number of detailed performance indicators.[73] The prospect of an MCC compact should create an incentive for recipient countries to take concrete steps to reduce corruption, improve governance, and strengthen democratic institutions. US national security goals were explicitly excluded from the MCC criteria.[74]

To become eligible, countries must fall below an annual per capita income standard.[75] MCC then combines the quantitative performance measures with a qualitative evaluation of the country in question.[76] A potential recipient country must score above the median relative to their peers on at least half of the indicators in each category and above the median on the indicator for combating corruption. The discretionary component of the evaluation takes into account the degree to which the country is addressing significant shortcomings, as well as other supplemental information.

Eligible countries are invited to submit proposals for an MCC compact. The compact contains program objectives, specific projects, project funding, and a program implementation framework. Following a country visit by the MCC staff, compact proposals are reviewed by the MCC board. Once it has approved, the board notifies the Congress of its intention to obligate funds. Compact funding is fully obligated from the start, to support projects and programs lasting three to five years. Compacts remain in force and the funds available for up to five years. By April 2009, MCC had signed compacts with 18 countries.[77]

Up to 10 percent of MCC funding can be used to support a "threshold program" for candidate countries seeking to qualify for a compact. To be eligible, countries must submit concept papers identifying why they fell short of specific MCC performance indicators, proposing reforms, and requesting assistance over two years to implement the reforms.[78] MCC staff members consult with USAID on these papers and submit a specific Threshold Country Plan (TCP) to the board for approval. Because USAID has a field staff, it is responsible for implementing these plans, using MCA funds, for which it charges a 7 percent administrative fee.[79]

The early years of MCC were somewhat controversial. Although 16 countries were declared eligible in FY 2004 and FY 2005, Congress raised questions about the decision to exclude other countries.[80] There was also concern about the decision to include Georgia as a compact country, which some felt was influenced by security policy considerations, as it did not appear to meet the MCC performance criteria.[81] Congress was also concerned about MCC operations and the slow rate at which MCC was signing compacts and committing funds, which led to congressional reluctance to approve the full MCC budget request.[82]

There has also been concern in Congress and in the foreign assistance community about the continued institutional dispersal of foreign assistance agencies, represented by the creation of MCC. Although the MCC Act requires consultations between USAID and the MCC, and provides a board seat for the USAID Administrator, the extent of coordination between the two development assistance organizations was unclear.[83]

MCC budget planning is done internally, in the Department of Administration and Finance, based on the number of countries eligible for compacts or threshold agreements, and the anticipated size of an average compact. Budget plans are vetted and approved by the Board of Directors. MCC discusses this budget with USAID and the Office of the Director of Foreign Assistance at State, but there is not a formal process for planning State/ USAID assistance budgets together with the MCC. In the long run, uncertainty remains about the survival of MCC as a separate institution, with one option being to fold the corporation into a reformed US foreign assistance architecture.[84]

The President's Emergency Plan for AIDS Relief

The President's Emergency Plan for AIDS Relief (PEPFAR) was created in 2003. The goal of committing $15 billion over five years to the prevention and treatment of HIV/AIDS was fully met by the Congress in FY 2008, leading to a new presidential commitment to another $30 billion in funding through FY 2013 and a congressional authorization of nearly $50 billion over the same period.[85] The PEPFAR program adds to the institutional diaspora of responsibilities for US foreign assistance programs, but has been innovative in its approach to interagency budget coordination and foreign assistance budgeting.[86]

As Table 3.2 shows, PEPFAR built on an extensive array of pre-existing US multilateral and bilateral efforts to combat HIV/AIDS globally. The PEPFAR

Table 3.2 US global health funding (in $ millions)

Program	FY 2004 actual	FY2005 actual	FY 2006 actual	FY 2007 CR	FY 2004–FY 2007 total	FY 2008 request
USAID HIV/AIDS (excl. Global Fund)	513.4	382.8	373.8	464.5	1,734.5	346.3
USAID Tuberculosis	100	87.8	91.5	–	279.3	89.9
USAID Malaria	100.9	98.2	102	248	549.1	387.5
USAID Global Fund contribution	397.6	247.9	247.5	247.5	1,140.5	0
State Dept—GHAI—OGAC	488.1	1,373.5	1,775.1	2,869	6,505.7	4,150
FMF	1.5	1.9	1.9	–	5.3	–
FY 2004 Global Fund carryover	-87.8	–	–	–	0	–
GHAI—Global Fund contribution	–	87.8	198	377.5	575.5	–
Subtotal, Foreign Operations Appropriations	1,519.5	2,279.9	2,789.8	4,206.5	10,795.7	4,973.7
CDC Global AIDS Program	291.8	123.8	122.7	120.8	659.1	121.2
NIH International Research	317.2	370	373	372	1,432.2	373
NIH Global Fund Contribution	149.1	99.2	99	99	446.3	300
DOL AIDS in the Workplace Initiative	9.9	1.9	–	–	11.8	–
Subtotal, Labor/HHS Appropriations	768	594.9	494.7	591.8	2,449.4	794.2
DOD HIV/AIDS prevention education	4.2	7.5	5.2	–	16.9	–
Section 416(b) Food Aid	24.8	24.8	24.8	–	74.4	–
Total	2,346.9	2,907.1	3,414.5	4,798.3	13,466.8	5,767.9

Source: Tiaji Salaam-Blyther, US International HIV/AIDS, Tuberculosis, and Malaria Spending: FY 2004–FY 2008, CRS Report RL 33485 (Washington, DC: Congressional Research Service, March 2007), 4, Table 1.

initiative provided funding for many of the existing bilateral HIV/AIDS programs and for multilateral efforts, and created a new program targeting 15 countries with severe infection problems.[87]

The structure and process for the PEPFAR program are innovations in interagency coordination and budget planning. The Office of the Global AIDS Coordinator (OGAC), which reports to the Secretary of State, was given statutory responsibility for government-wide planning and budget coordination for HIV/AIDS programs. The Coordinator was given unprecedented broad authority across agencies, having "primary responsibility for the oversight and coordination of all resources and international activities of the United States Government to combat the HIV/AIDS pandemic."[88] This included the authority "to transfer and allocate funds to relevant executive branch agencies," in order to "avoid duplication of effort," as well as the responsibility for "resolving policy, program, and funding disputes among the relevant government agencies."[89] The first Coordinator made it clear he would use this authority to "oversee and direct all US Government international HIV/AIDS activities in all departments and all agencies of the Federal Government."[90] .

The Coordinator leads an interagency process for global HIV/AIDS planning, policy development, and program implementation, relying on interagency coordinating committees, task forces, and working groups.[91] An interagency "Policy Group," including OGAC, USAID, Health and Human Services (HHS), DOD, the Department of Labor, the Peace Corps, the NSC, and the White House, meets weekly to oversee the program. While OGAC coordinates PEPFAR-related activities among the agencies, it does not implement individual agency programs. Procurement, project management, and oversight are the responsibility of the departments of State, Health and Human Services, Commerce, Defense, Labor, USAID, and the Peace Corps.

The Coordinator also created a unique strategic and budgetary planning process for the 15 focus countries of the program, using a five-year perspective and specific program performance goals for each country.[92] Details of the program for each country are developed by the country team, including all involved US government agencies, under the leadership of the ambassador. Consulting with the host country, NGOs, corporations, and multilateral institutions, the country team reviews existing resources and programs, needs, gaps, other potential international partners, objectives, and performance measures.[93] It then creates a five-year country strategy and an annual Country Operational Plan (COP) for AIDS prevention, treatment, and care services. The COPs are submitted to the Coordinator's office for review by interagency technical and program teams, which make recommendations to an interagency principals committee chaired by the Coordinator.[94] The Coordinator makes the final decision on the plan and determines final funding levels.[95] Once the plan is approved, the Coordinator allocates funds, which are released to implementing agencies.[96]

Funds for pre-existing agency HIV/AIDS programs are directly appropriated to those agencies. For the 15 focus countries, PEPFAR receives an appropriation to the GHCS account, controlled by the OGAC.[97] Once funding levels have been set in the planning process, OGAC transfers funds from its account to implementing agencies and departments. Since PEPFAR's inception, funding levels for pre-existing HIV/AIDS accounts have remained static, while while funds for the 15 countries targeted by the Global HIV/AIDS Initiative (GHAI) account have increased.[98]

Since FY 2004, the United States has contributed approximately $3 billion to the multilateral Global Fund to Fight AIDS, Tuberculosis, and Malaria, exceeding the $1 billion originally committed in 2003. Supporters of larger US contributions to the Global Fund refer to the fund's innovative features and multilateral coordination mechanisms. Since FY 2004, approximately 16 percent of PEPFAR funding has consisted of contributions to the Global Fund.[99]

Department of the Treasury: International Programs

The Treasury Department manages that part of the International Affairs budget that focuses on international economic and financial policies and institutions. Treasury's Office of International Affairs, headed by an Under Secretary, directs four international accounts: US participation in the International Monetary Fund (IMF), contributions to multilateral development banks (MDBs), restructuring and forgiveness of debt owed the United States by other countries, and technical assistance for foreign governments in the area of finance. Treasury's Assistant Secretary of International Affairs supports the Under Secretary and oversees seven Deputy Assistant Secretaries (DAS), each responsible for a "deputate" focused on a regional or functional area.[100]

The International Monetary Fund

The Secretary of Treasury, under authority delegated from the President, draws up US policies and instructs the US representatives to the IMF.[101] US participation in the Fund is managed by the Office of International Monetary Policy in the Office of International Affairs.[102] The IMF was created in 1946 as the institutional centerpiece of the post-war effort to prevent a recurrence of the Great Depression. It promotes economic stability and intervenes in international financial crises through surveillance of international financial flows, technical assistance, and lending programs.[103] The fund is responsible for international cooperation on monetary issues, facilitates the expansion of international trade, helps achieve exchange rate stability, supports the multilateral system of payments, and makes funds available to member countries experiencing balance of payment problems.[104]

As one of the largest participants, the United States held 16.77 percent of the Fund's total votes as of April 2009. IMF decisions are made through a weighted voting system. Each of the IMF's 185 member countries has a representative on the Board of Governors. Member countries provide resources to the Fund through a "quota" system, based on the size of its national economy and the level of its participation in the global economy. Quotas are denominated in Special Drawing Rights (SDRs), measured as a basket of currencies consisting of the euro, Japanese yen, pound sterling, and US dollar. The size of a country's quota determines a member's voting power.[105]

The budget for US participation in the Fund is treated in an unusual way. Until 1980, Treasury argued that US transfers to the Fund were simply an "exchange of assets," with dollars being swapped for SDRs, which the United States or other members could draw on, and then replenish to the Fund. From a budgetary point of view, once a new US quota had been authorized by the Congress, assets were "exchanged," without need for a congressional appropriation. Congress, however, argued that an appropriation was required by the US Constitution.[106]

Under a 1980 agreement resolving this disagreement, Congress would pass an appropriation and authorization for the Fund before the United States subscribes to a new quota.[107] The appropriation, however, consisted only of budget authority, without any associated outlays. The IMF could then draw against the US quota using the "exchange-of-assets" method. When the IMF restored funds drawn against the US quota, it could reuse the funds rather than return them to the Treasury. This arrangement avoided any need for a new appropriation every time the IMF wishes to re-draw on the US quota. It also permitted the Congress to appropriate the quota outside of any caps that might limit International Affairs budgets. The Fund rarely draws down the entire US quota (which was $37.1 billion in April 2009), but when it does, Treasury finances the amount by selling federal debt.[108] This agreement was amended, again, in 2009, to score IMF funding as a budget cost, but to the extent that there was a calculable risk that some of the funding would not be repaid by the borrowing country.

Multilateral Development Banks

The United States is a member of eight multilateral development banks (MDBs) and related institutions (see Table 3.3).[109] Treasury's deputate for International Development Finances and Debt, working with the regional deputates, manages US participation in these institutions. There is also an interagency Working Group on Multilateral Assistance (WGMA), consisting of Treasury, State, Agriculture, Commerce, USAID, the Federal Reserve Board, and Export–Import Bank, which meets before an MDB Board plans to act on contribution levels or new loans. The WGMA determines whether the proposed loan complies with US policy and laws, and communicates its views through Treasury to the US representative on the board.

Table 3.3 US voting shares and contributions to MDBs

	US voting share (as of 2008) (%)	US voting share rank
World Bank Group		
International Bank for Reconstruction and Development (IBRD)	16.4	1
International Development Association (IDA)	11.51	1
Multilateral Investment Guarantee Agency (MIGA	15	1
International Finance Corporation	23.7	1
Regional MDBs		
Asian Development Bank	12.9	1
African Development Bank	6.5	2
European Bank for Reconstruction and Development	10	1
Inter-American Development Bank	30	1
Similar agencies		
International Fund for Agricultural Development (IFAD)	7.90	1
North American Development Bank (NADB)	Mexico/ United States	No weighted voting
Global Environment Facility (GEF)	N/A	No weighted voting

Source: US Department of Treasury, *Treasury International Programs: Justification for Appropriations, FY 2009 Budget Request* (February 2008).

These financial institutions provide market rate and concessional rate lending and loan guarantees to developing countries. For market-based loans, the International Bank for Reconstruction and Development (IBRD) and the regional MDBs borrow money in world capital markets at market rates and re-lend the money to the borrowing country with a marginal markup.[110] To support these loans, members subscribe "callable capital," in the form of a guarantee that allows the MDBs to borrow at lower rates on the commercial market.[111] Concessional loans and guarantees are provided to the poorest countries at lower interest rates and with longer repayment periods than market-based loans. Member government funding for the International Development Association (the World Bank's concessional window) and the other MDBs are known as "replenishments," and are provided by appropriated funds.

The World Bank Group is the largest of these financial institutions. The IBRD, the original World Bank institution, was created in 1944 to support post-war reconstruction in Europe. The IBRD provides loans at market-based rates to middle- and lower-middle income countries to finance economic reforms, capital projects, and poverty reduction. The United States provided its last replenishment to the IBRD in FY 1996.[112]

The International Development Association (IDA) was created in 1960 to provide concessional loans and grants to the poorest developing country members. IDA is financed primarily through donor replenishments, with additional funding from borrower repayments, investment income, and direct transfers of World Bank net income.[113] In FY 2008, Congress appropriated $942.3 million for the US contribution to IDA, the first of three US payments for the most recent replenishment.[114]

The Multilateral Investment Guarantee Agency (MIGA) was created in 1988 to promote foreign direct investment in developing countries by providing investment insurance against non-commercial risks such as political violence or currency inconvertibility. The United States has not made a recent contribution to MIGA.

The International Finance Corporation (IFC) was created in 1956 to invest in private sector development, privatization, and efficient financial markets in developing countries. Since its establishment, the IFC has committed over $56 billion to finance investment projects in developing countries. In FY 2008, the IFC committed $11.4 billion in IFC funds to investment projects.[115]

The four regional MDBs provide both loans and grants. The Asian Development Bank (AsDB) was established in 1966 and added a concessional lending window, the Asian Development Fund, in 1973. In 2006, the AsDB approved $7.97 billion in loans, $654.8 million in credit enhancements, and $241.6 million in technical assistance operations.[116]

The African Development Bank (AfDB) was established in 1964 and the United States has been a member since 1983. Its concessional window, the African Development Fund, was created in 1973.[117] The European Bank for Reconstruction and Development (EBRD) was created in 1991 to support the transition of states in Eastern Europe and the former Soviet Union to market economies. Since its founding, the EBRD had financed approximately $40 billion in loans and equity investments in these countries.[118]

The three other international financial institutions provide loans and grants in specific functional areas or a more narrowly focused region. The International Fund for Agricultural Development (IFAD) funds projects in developing countries to alleviate poverty and increase agricultural production. The North American Development Bank (NADB) is a joint US–Mexican financial institution created in the North American Free Trade Agreement (NAFTA) to fund environmental projects in the border region between the two countries. The Global Environment Facility (GEF) is a trust fund of the World Bank that funds global environmental projects implemented by international organizations such as the World Bank, United Nations, and RDBs.

In most of these institutions the size of a member country's contribution determines its voting power on the bank's executive board. "Replenishments," or increases to the bank's capital, are generally negotiated at international conferences every three to four years.[119] These negotiations are typically conducted well in advance of congressional appropriations, creating some risk that the

Congress will provide funding below the agreed US replenishment level.[120] This occurred in the 1980s and 1990s when the Congress provided funds below the replenishment level to encourage reforms in these institutions and to reduce overall federal spending, leading to substantial "arrears" in US commitments to the banks. These backlogs were made up as part of the broader agreement on international organization reform in the late 1990s, which included funding to make up arrears to the United Nations (discussed in Chapter 2).

The congressional appropriation is only gradually transferred to these institutions. Treasury pledges the funds, which are transferred according to a schedule arranged between the donor countries and the MDB. The MDBs also rarely transfer the entire amount of a loan, but disperse it gradually as projects are completed; drawing down member contributions to provided the needed funding. As a result, only part of the US funding is actually counted as an outlay during the fiscal year for which it is provided.

Although Congress cannot directly affect bank decisions on specific loans, it has directed Treasury to instruct US representatives to push for certain reforms and policy changes. Congress has also made bank appropriations contingent on certification by the Secretary of the Treasury that policy changes have taken place or will take place in the future.[121]

Debt Restructuring

Treasury manages US policy with respect to the forgiveness or restructuring of debt owed to the United States by other countries. Debt restructuring and debt forgiveness reduce the fiscal burden of poorer countries, so that they can focus their own spending on poverty reduction and economic growth, rather than debt service. Restructuring can also provide an incentive for the recipient country to make structural and fiscal reforms.[122] Since 1990, the federal budget must compensate for the estimated costs of debt restructuring and forgiveness through additional appropriations, since lower future debt repayments lead to lower than anticipated federal revenues.

Debt forgiveness has become a major element of US foreign assistance policy since the mid-1990s, with the creation of the bilateral program for Heavily Indebted Poor Countries (HIPC), the HIPC Trust Fund, and the Tropical Forest Conservation Act (TFCA). The 1996 HIPC initiative was a joint effort by the World Bank and the IMF to provide deeper, broader, and faster debt reduction programs for those countries committed to economic reform and poverty reduction.[123] From FY 2000 until FY 2007, Congress provided more than $273.6 million in appropriations for bilateral HIPC debt reduction costs.[124] An additional $674.6 million was appropriated to the HIPC Trust Fund, an IDA account providing grants to eligible countries to relieve debt owed the participating multilateral organizations.[125] The TFCA of 1998 provides debt forgiveness in exchange for the recipient government's agreement to take steps to conserve endangered forests.[126]

Technical Assistance

The Treasury Department implements a small (roughly $20 million) technical assistance program, providing financial advisors to developing and transitioning countries to improve fiscal and budgetary competence and implement reforms. The program was first established in 1989 through the Support for East European Democracy Act (SEED), which provided assistance first to Central and Eastern Europe and later to the former Soviet Union.

Treasury established its Office of Technical Assistance (OTA) in 1991. From FY 1990–98, the program was funded by a transfer of funds from USAID. In 1999, Congress provided $1.5 million directly to the Treasury Department to fund technical assistance programs beyond the Central European and Eurasian region.[127] Treasury created the Treasury International Affairs Technical Assistance (TIATA) program to expand these operations to reform-oriented countries in Asia, Africa, Central and Latin America, and the Greater Middle East. TIATA funds have also been used to implement technical assistance programs in post-conflict countries such as Iraq, Afghanistan, Haiti, and Liberia.

Peace Corps

The Peace Corps was created in 1961 as an independent federal agency. It has sent nearly 200,000 American volunteers to 189 countries in the developing world and Eastern Europe and Eurasia, to work for two years on projects in such areas as education, youth outreach, community development, business development, agriculture, environment, health and HIV/AIDS, and information technology. The goal of the program has been to help meet the needs of developing and transitioning countries for trained personnel related to various aspects of development, help promote a better understanding of America, and help Americans understand other peoples.[128]

The Peace Corps was well funded during the Kennedy administration, with a budget in FY 1966 of $114 million supporting over 9,200 volunteers. The number of volunteers has declined, but the Corps continues to support a goal of at least 10,000 volunteers a year. In FY 2008, the Peace Corps budget was $333.5 million, supporting 7,886 volunteers in 74 countries.[129]

Though it is a small fraction of total International Affairs spending, the Peace Corps is highly visible. It is independent of State and the other foreign affairs agencies because it was considered important for the credibility and security of the volunteers that they be seen as independent of official US foreign policy. Because of this independence, while the Peace Corps communicates its budget information to the State Department, its request is transmitted directly to OMB. On occasion, the Corps does coordinate its work with other foreign policy agencies. For example, the Corps' Office of AIDS Relief, created in 2005, works with the US Global AIDS Coordinator, to ensure effective cooperation as part of the PEPFAR effort.[130] The Peace Corps reimburses the State Department for administrative and financial management support overseas, through the ICASS system (discussed in Chapter 2).

Peace Corps budget planning is done through its Integrated Planning and Budget System (IPBS). The Director issues overall planning guidance in the spring and internal offices set goals and objectives over a three-year time frame, linked to specific tasks, which are aligned with the planning guidance. These are submitted to the Director's budget office for review. If the eventual Congressional appropriation differs from these initial projections, plans are adjusted accordingly through an annual update of the three-year plan.

Export–Import Bank

The US Export–Import Bank (Ex–Im Bank) is also an independent agency, established in 1934 under a renewable charter to facilitate trade with the Soviet Union.[131] The Bank is the official export-credit agency of the United States, supporting "the financing of US goods and services in international markets." It assumes credit and country risks that the private sector is unable or unwilling to accept.[132] Ex–Im Bank provides working capital guarantees (pre-export financing), export credit insurance, loan guarantees, and direct loans to small and large US businesses. The Bank's lending and guarantees are seen as a way of "leveling the playing field," for US exporters to compete with those of other countries that are supported by similar export credit agencies.[133] The Bank also sees its programs as compensating for "market failures" in the private credit market, when private lending institutions may not be prepared to take the risk of supporting particular exports. Since its founding, the Ex–Im Bank has supported more than $400 billion in US exports.[134]

The Bank has supported exports of heavy equipment sectors such as aircraft, oil drilling, and nuclear power equipment.[135] Its authorizing statute and charter explicitly prohibit it from financing defense articles and services. Dual-use exports, that may have both military and civilian applications, are supported "if there exists convincing evidence that the item is non-lethal in nature and will be used primarily for civilian activities," conditions that the exporter may need to certify.[136]

The Bank protects the independence of its funding decisions from broader US foreign policy goals. However, it is regularly pressured by the State and Treasury Departments to link guarantees and lending to such broader policy goals as support for the emerging free market economies in Central Europe and the former Soviet Union. The Bank has increased its support for exports to these areas in response.[137]

Bank decisions on lending are made by a seven-person board, including the President and First Vice President of the Bank, the Secretary of Commerce, the US Trade Representative (USTR), and three outside directors, appointed by the President of the United States. They are supported by a

17-member outside Advisory Committee, representing major sectors of industry and the trade unions.

Budgets for the Bank are prepared between the offices of Policy and Planning and Resource Management and submitted directly to OMB. The Bank budget provides subsidy funding, supporting the value of Bank lending, and funding for personnel and administration. Prior to FY 2007, both the subsidy value and administrative costs were appropriated by Congress. In FY 2008, the Bank began to fund its budget using its own receipts. The $68 million in subsidy value for FY 2008 was estimated by the Bank to support $18.7 billion worth of American exports.

Overseas Private Investment Corporation

The Overseas Private Investment Corporation (OPIC) was established in 1971 as an independent agency to provide financing and risk insurance to support US investment in more than 150 developing countries and emerging market economies. OPIC investment guarantees stimulate private sector lending and investment to support large and small US businesses. The guarantees and insurance have covered such industries as infrastructure, telecommunications, power, water, housing, airports, hotels, high-tech, financial services, and natural resource extraction.[138] OPIC risk insurance can protect firms from currency inconvertibility, expropriation, and political violence.[139]

Although OPIC's decisions are largely market-driven, the Corporation does note that its "economic development mission is guided by the US foreign policy objectives," established by the Secretary of State.[140] It has been urged to orient its financing and insurance programs toward developing countries and newly emerging market economies, both important to overall US foreign policy, which has led to increased funding for such areas as Eastern Europe and the former Soviet Union.

OPIC financing and investment decisions are made by a 15-person board, seven from the government and eight from the private sector, appointed by the President. The government representatives include the USAID Administrator, the USTR, and other agencies such as Labor, State, Commerce and Treasury. The private sector representatives include industry, small business, labor, and cooperatives representatives.

Budgets for OPIC are prepared in OPIC's Office of the Chief Financial Officer and submitted directly to OMB. OPIC, like Ex–Im Bank, funds the subsidy value of its guarantees and insurance, as well as its administrative expenses, through its receipts rather than an appropriation of new funds. For FY 2009, OPIC expected to collect $249.6 million, which would more than cover $50.6 million in administrative expenses and $29 million in subsidy value.[141]

Trade and Development Agency

The US Trade and Development Agency (TDA) was established in 1981 as an independent agency providing technical assistance and funding feasibility studies, training, orientation visits, and business workshops in developing countries.[142] The agency builds "partnerships between US companies and overseas project sponsors to bring proven private sector solutions to developmental challenges."[143] Since its creation, TDA claims to have linked its funding to more than $28 billion in US exports.

TDA's charter does not prohibit close cooperation with other foreign policy agencies. It coordinates its mission and activities with USTR, State, Commerce, Homeland Security, Transportation, Ex–Im Bank, and OPIC. Project and program decisions are made internally in the organization, not by an outside board of directors.

TDA budgets have been around $50 million per year, covering projects and activities in 51 countries. The average grant size is around $400,000. Budgets are prepared internally by the financial office and presented directly to OMB.

Inter-American Foundation

The Inter-American Foundation (IAF) was created in 1969 outside the USAID framework to provide small grants to non-profit and private sector "self-help" programs and cooperatives at the grass-roots level in Latin America.[144] The Foundation works directly with the non-governmental sector, promoting entrepreneurship and local democracy. The recipients include agricultural cooperatives, small urban enterprises, and organizations that provide credit, training, technical, and marketing assistance to such cooperatives and businesses.[145]

Since it was created, IAF has provided more than 4,500 grants. It is governed by a nine-member Board of Directors, appointed by the President, six of whom come from the private sector. The other three are from government or international entities concerned with inter-American affairs, typically the Inter-American Development Bank (IADB) and the State Department.

The Foundation prepares its own budget, which it submits directly to OMB. It outsources its procurement, accounting, budget, and information technology support services to the Bureau of the Public Debt in the Treasury Department. The IAF annual budget is roughly $20 million a year in appropriated funds.[146] In addition, the Foundation receives funding from the IADB Social Progress Trust Fund, which has resources from repayments on loans made to Latin America in the 1960s.

African Development Foundation

The African Development Foundation (ADF) was created in 1980 as an independent public corporation with a mission to promote the participation of local African populations in economic and social development programs that "enlarge opportunities for community development" and "build sustainable African institutions that foster grass-roots development."[147] Its funding, in the form of grants smaller than $250,000, is provided to private organizations at the local level.

ADF is governed by a six-person board, drawn largely from the private sector, but including the Assistant Secretary of State for Africa. Its budget is roughly $20–30 million a year from congressionally appropriated funds, which it leverages to obtain private support and funding from African governments, sometimes over $10 million. It prepares its budgets internally, and submits them directly to OMB.

Humanitarian and Disaster Assistance

The United States has consistently had a significant capability to respond globally to natural disasters and humanitarian crises. The responsibility for this response is spread across several agencies, notably USAID and the departments of State and Defense.[148] There have been repeated proposals to combine the civilian response programs into a single humanitarian and disaster response capability.[149]

The Office of Foreign Disaster Assistance (OFDA), USAID's humanitarian response organization created in 1964, is housed in the Bureau of Democracy, Conflict, and Humanitarian Assistance. OFDA deploys Disaster Assistance Response Teams (DART), drawn from across the government, and frequently coordinates the government-wide response to life-threatening natural and human disasters.[150]

OFDA's response programs are funded through its International Disaster and Famine Assistance (IDFA) account, which typically receives an annual appropriation around $200–250 million. This funding is frequently increased through supplemental appropriations for specific crises. IDFA is one of the few International Affairs accounts that contain "contingency" funding with "no-year" status, meaning that the funds are not earmarked for specific countries or projects and are available until expended.

For disaster response, OFDA can also use USAID's "Food for Peace" program, authorized under PL 480, Title II, which provides emergency food assistance in response to crises and famines. USAID's Office of Food for Peace (FFP) administers this assistance, drawn from US agricultural surpluses. Some of this assistance is distributed through the UN's World Food Program (WFP). Some of this is contingency funding, since famines cannot always be anticipated.[151]

The State Department also responds to humanitarian disasters, through its migration and refugee programs. The United States has consistently been one of the world's largest donors of assistance for migration emergencies and refugee resettlement. Funding for these programs are managed by State's Bureau of Population, Refugees, and Migration (PRM), which reports to the Under Secretary of State for Global Affairs. PRM is responsible for US contributions to and participation in international refugee operations and organizations through the Migration and Refugees Assistance (MRA) and Emergency Refugee and Migration Assistance Fund (ERMA) accounts. PRM "determines the level of US contributions to international organizations for humanitarian assistance and protection-related programs" and has an Office of Policy and Resource Planning, which prepares the annual program budget for MRA and ERMA and determines how ERMA funds will be spent.[152]

Funding for migration and refugee programs can reach more than $900 million a year. MRA funding of roughly $800 million a year is contributed to inter-governmental and non-governmental organizations that provide services to migrants and administer refugee camps.[153] MRA budgets are driven by the costs of ongoing operations, but migration emergencies are common. In 1962, Congress created ERMA to respond to "unexpected urgent refugee and migration needs," whenever it is "important to the national interest."[154] ERMA is another "no-year" contingency fund, not allocated in advance and available until expended. ERMA has a permanently authorized ceiling of $100 million a year, frequently augmented by supplemental funding for emergencies.

Foreign Assistance outside the International Affairs Budget

One of the core realities of US engagement in the twentieth and twenty-first century is the growth of international activity in virtually every federal agency. Many of these programs are part of US foreign assistance, though they are planned and budgeted outside the International Affairs budget and are largely beyond the reach of the Secretary of State. According to the Organization for Economic Cooperation and Development (OECD), more than 25 other US agencies have foreign assistance programs of some type.[155] The General Accounting Office (GAO) estimated that in FY 1998, non-150 agencies spent roughly $7.6 billion on programs ranging from criminal justice to control of nuclear materials.[156] GAO noted that assistance programs for the former Soviet Union in the 1990s involved 23 departments and agencies carrying out 215 aid projects funded out of 11 different budget accounts.[157] A 2006 Congressional Research Service (CRS) review of US foreign assistance programs found that the funds and programs administered by State and USAID constituted only 55 percent of total aid disbursements in FY 2005.[158]

There is no mechanism in State, USAID, the White House, or the Congress for coordinating these activities and programs, determining overlaps and duplications, or filling the gaps. We briefly inventory some of the larger programs.

Department of Commerce

The US Department of Commerce promotes US foreign and domestic commerce, economic development, and technology.[159] Commerce has significant international engagement through the International Trade Administration and the Bureau of Industry and Security.

The International Trade Administration (ITA) promotes US trade and investment and ensures compliance with trade laws and agreements.[160] It also manages the United States and Foreign Commercial Service (USFCS), part of the US diplomatic service. USFCS provides businesses with counseling and free market research, screens foreign business partners, and builds relationships with host country officials. In 2006, USFCS had 108 offices within the United States and 150 international offices in 82 countries, largely in the US embassies.[161] ITA's Market Access and Compliance unit develops strategies to help US businesses expand in international markets, overcome market barriers, and resolve trade complaints from American corporations. Its Import Administration enforces US unfair trade laws, such as the anti-dumping and countervailing duty laws.[162]

Commerce's Bureau of Industry and Security (BIS) administers the Commerce Control list, which regulates the export of dual-use technologies.[163] BIS's Nonproliferation and Export Control Cooperation program helps other countries develop effective export control regimes, funded by the State Department's Export Control and Related Border Security (EXBS) program.[164]

Department of Health and Human Services

Three Health and Human Services (HHS) organizations have significant international activities. The Centers for Disease Control and Prevention (CDC) supports international research and disease prevention programs through global partnerships and global health programs (see Table 3.4). CDC is one of the implementing agencies for PEPFAR, supporting HIV/AIDS prevention, care, and treatment programs in over 50 countries.[165] CDC also provides epidemiologic, laboratory, and programmatic support to WHO and UNICEF, assigning staff overseas to implement immunization programs and provide technical assistance. CDCP's Global Disease Detection (GDD) program operates responses centers throughout the world to detect and respond to outbreaks of infectious diseases. CDC also operates a Field Epidemiology Training Program and a Sustainable Management Development

Table 3.4 CDC global health programs (in $ millions)

	FY 2004	FY 2005	FY 2006	FY 2007	FY 2008
Global AIDS Program	124.9	123.8	122.65	121	118.9
Global Immunization Program	137.9	144.3	144.3	142.3	139.9
Global Disease Detection	11.6	21.4	32.4	32	31.4
Global Malaria Program	9.21	9.1	9	8.9	8.7
FY 2005 Avian Flu Supplemental	0	15.00	0	0	0
Other global health	2.4	3.4	71.4	3.3	3.5
Total	286.0	317.2	380.0	307.5	302.4

Source: CDC Financial Management Office, FY 2005–2009 *Congressional Budget Justifications.*

Program to assist developing countries in building effective public health programs.

The Food and Drug Administration's (FDA) Office of International Programs (OIP) has negotiated 50 Memoranda of Understanding with foreign governments to ensure that FDA food safety standards are met before products leave the exporting country.[166] OIP also provides technical assistance to train regulatory counterparts in other countries and coordinates FDA's efforts in international organizations to strengthen international standards.

The National Institutes of Health (NIH) John E. Fogarty International Center, created in 1968, supports research and training programs to build a cadre of scientists in low- and middle-income countries who can collaborate in solving health issues.[167]

Environmental Protection Agency

The Environmental Protection Agency's (EPA) Office of International Affairs (OIA) collaborates on bilateral and regional environmental projects in Mexico, Canada, the Caribbean, Central America, Europe, Russia, Africa, Thailand, China, and India.[168] OIA coordinates with State, USAID, and DOE in developing regional and foreign country air-quality programs.[169] It also provides technical assistance to partner countries and international organizations to strengthen their capacity for policymaking on environmental compliance and emergency issues.[170] OIA's Environment and Trade program integrates environmental objectives in international trade agreements and investment projects. The Persistent Organic Pollutants (POPs) implementation program provides technical and financial assistance to such programs in Mexico, Central America, South America, Russia, Asia, and Africa.[171] EPA's international activities are budgeted at roughly $200 million per year.[172]

Department of Education

The Department of Education administers 14 International Education and Foreign Language Studies programs, with a budget of $109 million.[173] These programs fund language study centers in the United States, research and curriculum development, grants for American scholars to study abroad, and activities to increase the number of underrepresented minorities in international service.[174]

Department of Agriculture

The Department of Agriculture (USDA) promotes US agricultural exports through direct export subsidies, foreign market development, export credit guarantees, and food assistance.[175] USDA's international programs are largely administered by the Foreign Agricultural Service (FAS), with offices in 97 countries. Its Market Access Program (MAP) reimburses participating organizations for a portion of the costs associated with overseas marketing and promotional activities. In FY 2008, Agriculture's foreign market development programs had a $248 million budget, $200 million of which supported MAP.[176] The Commodity Credit Corporation (CCC), a government corporation owned and operated by USDA, administers export credit guarantee programs, which facilitate exports to foreign markets by providing payment guarantees for commercial financing. In FY 2008, the CCC provided $2.3 billion in export guarantees.[177]

The FAS also has responsibility for Agriculture's role in food aid. PL 480 funds are appropriated to Agriculture, though some are implemented by USAID. Title I, which FAS administers, provides long-term, low-interest loans to developing countries and private entities for purchases of US food. Title I programs have not been active since 2006.

US Trade Representative

The US Trade Representative (USTR), which was created in 1963 in the Executive Office of the President, is the US government's chief trade negotiator and spokesperson.[178] USTR also chairs the interagency process that coordinates US international trade policy, bringing together 19 agencies and departments. USTR also maintains an office in Geneva, Switzerland to support its work with World Trade Organization activities. USTR budgets are roughly $45 million a year.

Conclusion

The greatest challenge facing the Secretary of State and the White House is how to bring planning and budgetary coherence to this wide array of foreign economic assistance programs, provided by many agencies. The gradual emergence of a more central planning and budgeting office at State shows both the difficulty of achieving such coherence, and the importance of doing so.

The many agencies and departments providing foreign assistance resist central planning and coordination, arguing that they have different missions and different statutory charters. In some cases, such as USAID, the smaller agency worries about losing its long-term focus and mission if it is absorbed into the State Department.

Successive Secretaries of State have struggled to overcome this resistance, with limited success. Managing foreign assistance programs is not core to the State Department's diplomatic culture, which has made it difficult to create the strategic planning, budgeting, and program development capabilities to carry out such coordination. At the same time, the Secretaries have recognized that a dispersed and incoherent US foreign economic assistance program may serve neither the needs of economic development nor the goals of American statecraft. The initial steps, taken gradually over the past 25 years, have drawn USAID closer to State, with a more integrated budget process. This trend is likely to continue.

While the two large foreign assistance providers are more integrated, the broader US assistance agenda remains relatively untouched. The Secretary of State cannot direct Treasury or the financial and trade institutions, let alone cabinet departments outside the International Affairs budget function. That coordinating task may only be possible at the White House level. As will be seen, however, the National Security Council and the Office of Management and Budget are not currently structured or staffed for such planning and coordination. Coherence in US foreign economic assistance may only be possible if such a capability is created.

Chapter 4

Political and Security Assistance Budgeting and Programs

Introduction

Nearly half of all US foreign assistance is linked to US strategic and foreign policy goals. Some is in the form of economic assistance, provided to countries with which the United States has important political relationships. The remainder is security assistance in the form of weapons, services, and training for countries of strategic importance to US national security policy. The State Department is responsible for setting policies for these programs, choosing the recipient countries, and planning the budgets. Other agencies, notably the US Agency for International Development (USAID) and the Department of Defense (DOD) play a major role in their implementation. USAID's role in implementing policy-driven foreign economic assistance has created an internal tension between its development mission and its policy-driven responsibilities, as noted in Chapter 3. The growing role of DOD in providing security and economic assistance has created institutional friction between State and DOD, as discussed below.

This chapter reviews these programs. The largest economic assistance program linked to US national security goals is the Economic Support Fund (ESF), but the United States also provides significant policy-driven assistance through separate programs for Eastern Europe and the former Soviet Union, to support democracy, stem the flow of narcotics and combat international crime, confront terrorism, prevent the proliferation of nuclear and other weapons of mass destruction, and remove landmines. Budgets in this category rise and fall in response to major international events and changes in US interests, though funds focused on the Middle East have been consistently high over recent decades. Funding for such economic assistance accounts for roughly 23 percent of overall US foreign assistance.[1]

Security assistance includes a long-standing portfolio of State Department accounts that support foreign militaries; help them purchase US defense equipment, services, and training; finance education for foreign officers in the United States; and provide training for peacekeeping operations. These traditional security assistance programs constitute roughly another 14 percent of

US foreign assistance.[2] Since 2001, the Defense Department has developed a sizeable portfolio of security assistance programs under its own authorities, which parallel some of the State Department accounts. We discuss both sets of programs in this chapter.

State Department Economic Assistance Programs

Despite its culture that resists taking on program operations, the State Department has experienced substantial "mission creep" over the years with respect to policy-driven economic assistance programs that provide political support for allies, enhance regional stability, combat proliferation, support democracy, and confront terrorist organizations and international crime. State, working with the Congress, is responsible for setting the strategic goals for these programs, choosing the countries that receive assistance, and setting the overall funding levels.[3]

These programs have emerged incrementally, in response to specific policy goals, rather than as part of an overall strategic plan. Moreover, the management and implementation of many of these programs has been dispersed to other federal agencies such as USAID, Justice, Commerce, and Treasury, and to the private sector. This absence of a strategic vision and program dispersal (both internal and external) was a major stimulus for the creation of the Office of the Director of Foreign Assistance, discussed in Chapter 3.

Economic Support Fund

The Economic Support Fund (ESF) is one of the oldest foreign assistance accounts. Through ESF, the United States provides economic support for political and strategic reasons. Annual budgets for ESF are generally in the $4–5 billion range, larger than USAID's Development Assistance and child Survival and Health accounts combined. Funds appropriated for ESF are available for two years.

The origins of ESF go back to the post-war Marshall Plan, which provided emergency financial assistance to allied and friendly countries in war-torn Europe whose economic and political stability was important to the United States. In the early years of the Cold War, economic support was provided (through the "Security Supporting Assistance" program) to some NATO countries, as well as such key allies as Taiwan, Vietnam, and South Korea.[4] ESF became a central element in the Middle East peace process in 1979, supporting the Camp David peace agreement between Egypt and Israel.[5]

The ESF budget account was formally created in the International Security Assistance Act of 1978 (PL 95-384). Congress's intent was clearly strategic:

The Congress recognizes that, under special economic, political, or security conditions, the national interest of the United States may require economic support for countries in amounts which could not be justified solely [by economic development goals elsewhere in this Act].[6]

Administration justifications for ESF funding have continued to focus on the evolving national security agenda of the United States. In the 1980s, the focus of the program was to support peace in the Middle East (the lion's share of the funding), economic reform, and to assist countries that had US bases on their soil.[7] In the post-Cold War era, ESF has been refocused to provide support for Iraq and Afghanistan, counterterrorist operations, and democracy and free markets.[8] For FY 2010, for example, the administration requested $6.5 billion in total funding for ESF. Of that total, 77 percent ($5 billion) was for countries at the heart of US regional policy, principally Afghanistan

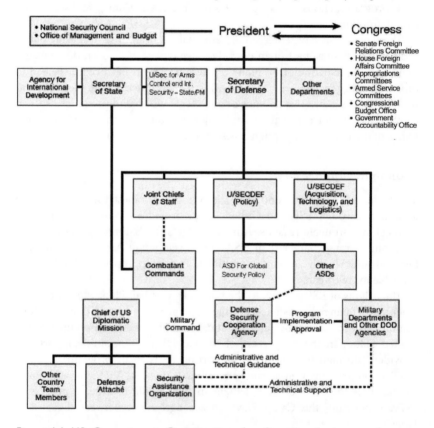

Figure 4.1 US Government Organization for Security Assistance (source: Defense Institute of Security Assistance, *Online Greenbook*, ch. 3, http://disam.mil/pubs/DR/greenbook.htm. Chart modified by authors to account for updates).

Table 4.1 Top ten recipients of ESF 1962–2007 *($ in current millions)*

Israel	31,931
Egypt	24,576
Afghanistan	4,766
Jordan	4,714
South Vietnam	4,352
Pakistan	4,079
Turkey	2,695
El Salvador	2,197
West Bank/Gaza	1,707
Costa Rica	1,034

Source: USAID Overseas Loans and Grants (USAID Greenbook).

($2.2 billion), Pakistan ($1.1 billion), Iraq ($415 million), the West Bank and Gaza ($400 million), Jordan ($363 million), Egypt ($250 million), and Lebanon ($109 million).[9] State describes ESF as "economic support for countries in amounts which could not be justified solely [for developmental purposes]."[10]

ESF is not used to support foreign military forces. However, one study suggests, a substantial share of ESF funds in the 1980s (between 45 and 60 percent) took the form of budget subsidies, which can free the recipient country to devote its own resources to meeting military needs. A smaller fraction of the funds (25–35 percent) was directed to development assistance projects. A still smaller share (10–20 percent) provided support for commodity import programs, making it possible for the recipient country to import American goods shipped on American carriers.[11]

ESF Planning and Budgeting

Embassies and regional bureaus have the key role in planning and budgeting the ESF program, particularly the regional bureaus for the Near East (NEA) and for South and Central Asia (SCA). The major country budgets are set by senior regional bureau or State Department officials, with input from the embassies. For critical countries such as Iraq, Afghanistan, and Pakistan, ESF funding is determined by senior policy officials at State. In the early 2000s, much of the ESF funding for these countries has been provided through supplemental budget requests, outside the core ESF budget. Smaller ESF requests will be projected by embassies as part of the Mission Strategic Plan process discussed in Chapter 3. Under the new State/USAID budget planning process, ESF funds have been pooled with other foreign assistance spigots at the planning stage and an overall assistance program, including ESF, is drawn up for the country in question.

Democracy Support[12]

The State Department and USAID implement a number of programs to promote democracy and governance around the world. One of the largest is the State Department's Human Rights/Democracy Fund (HRDF), administered by State's Bureau of Democracy, Human Rights, and Labor (DRL). HRDF was established in 1998 to give the State Department a way to "respond rapidly and decisively to democratization and human rights crises and deficits."[13] The mission of HRDF is to support "innovative programming designed to uphold democratic principles, support democratic institutions, promote human rights, and build civil society in countries and regions of the world that are geo-strategically critical to the US."[14] HRDF is funded with ESF dollars and has grown from $7.8 million in FY 1998 to nearly $70 million in FY 2007.

The Middle East Partnership Initiative (MEPI), established in December 2002, supports "democratic reform and vibrant, prosperous societies in the Middle East and North Africa," through political, economic, and educational reform and the empowerment of women.[15] MEPI makes small grants to non-governmental groups and citizens as a way to build a grass roots movement that increases the strength of civil society in the Middle East and North Africa. Through FY 2009, MEPI spent over $530 million on more than 600 projects in 17 countries and territories.[16] MEPI is managed by the Bureau of Near Eastern Affairs (NEA) and funded by ESF resources.[17]

Support for East European Democracy (SEED) and Freedom Support Act (FSA)

The SEED and FSA assistance programs were created after the fall of the Berlin Wall in 1989 to respond to the end of the Warsaw Pact, the emergence of democracies in Eastern Europe, and the collapse of the Soviet Union, all changes of strategic importance to the United States.[18]

In response to these events, Congress enacted the Support for East European Democracies (SEED) Act of 1989, and the Freedom Support Act (FSA) of 1991, creating two new foreign assistance programs. From 1989 to 2008, these two programs provided nearly $17 billion in assistance to these regions, focusing on projects and activities that would strengthen democratic governance and free markets.[19]

Initially, SEED funds were concentrated on northern European countries, initially Poland, Hungary, and Czechoslovakia, and later on the Baltic republics of Estonia, Latvia, and Lithuania. As these countries "graduated," funding focused on Bulgaria and Romania and the countries emerging from the breakup of Yugoslavia. Program activities also shifted from governance and free market support to conflict prevention and the development of civil society. By the early 2000s, SEED funding was helping "ensure that local and regional instability—particularly in South Central Europe—does not threaten the security and well-being of the United States and its allies."[20]

SEED funding has gradually declined from $674 million in FY 2001 to a request for $276 million in FY 2009, focused entirely on the Balkans.[21] Funding for Bulgaria, Croatia, and Romania ended in FY 2006. Reflecting the transition in the region, 60 percent of the FY 2009 budget request was committed to Kosovo and Serbia.[22]

FSA funding covers a broad region of importance to overall US national security strategy—Russia, the Caucasus, and Central Asia—where a number of new, transnational security challenges have emerged, including terrorism, proliferation, and energy.[23] FSA programs support democracy and independent media, promotion of trade and investment, energy development, education and healthcare reform, environmental reform, proliferation prevention, counternarcotics, international crime and human trafficking, and humanitarian assistance. Congress has also earmarked FSA funds for such functional areas as health and nuclear reactor safety.

Initially, FSA focused on Russia and Ukraine, but attracted congressional earmarks for Armenia and Georgia. Congress has also imposed restrictions on funding for governments that violate human rights or arms control agreements or permit the transfer of dangerous materials to other countries, and has encouraged increases in funding for democracy in Central Asia and civil society organizations in Belarus, Russia, and Uzbekistan.[24] Support for Russia has declined over time as US relations with Russia deteriorated and a government emerged that frustrated the effectiveness of a foreign assistance program.

Budgets for FSA have also declined, from a peak of nearly $1 billion in FY 2002 to a FY 2009 request for $346 million. Ukraine was the largest proposed recipient for 2009 at $70 million, followed by Georgia ($52 million), Russia ($47 million), and Armenia ($24 million). These four countries were projected to receive 56 percent of the total FSA budget.[25]

SEED/FSA Planning and Budgeting

Because these two programs were a policy priority in the 1990s, they were given an unusual administrative and budgetary structure and flexible authority. The statutes created two senior coordinator positions, both outside the relevant regional bureau. These high-visibility coordinators reported directly to the Secretary of State and had broad responsibility for bringing together the work of all agencies providing assistance in these regions, using their own or SEED/FSA funding.[26] In the late 1990s, reflecting a declining priority for these programs, the two coordinator positions were combined and placed inside the regional Bureau for European and Eurasian Affairs (EUR). In the FY 2010 budget submission, the State Department merged the two programs into a single account for Assistance for Europe, Eurasia, and Central Asia (AEECA).

Budget planning and authorities for these programs remain atypical, however. The Coordinator for US Assistance to Europe and Eurasia (EUR/ACE), unlike other regional bureaus at State, has direct program and budget planning responsibilities and a staff inside the regional bureau. The statute also provided the SEED and FSA Coordinator with significant latitude in planning and administering these programs. Unlike most foreign assistance programs, SEED and FSA funds have a "notwithstanding" and "no-year" status. This means the funds can be flexibly planned, spent regardless of other statutory provisions that may constrain program flexibility (including the Foreign Assistance Act itself), and remain available until expended.

International Narcotics Control and Law Enforcement

International narcotics and law enforcement are the focus of one of the larger State Department policy-driven assistance programs. In 1971 a new chapter—International Narcotics Control—was added to the Foreign Assistance Act (FAA), making the Secretary of State "responsible for coordinating all assistance provided by the United States Government to support international efforts to combat illicit narcotics production or trafficking," which were considered "an unparalleled transnational threat in today's world."[27] According to the FAA, "international narcotics trafficking poses an unparalleled transnational threat in today's world, and its suppression is among the most important foreign policy objectives of the United States." The Bureau of International Narcotics and Law Enforcement (INL) was created in 1978, headed by an Assistant Secretary reporting to the Under Secretary of State for Political Affairs.[28] The office was responsible for programs to suppress cultivation, manufacture, and trafficking of drugs, end money laundering and international criminal activities associated with narcotics trafficking, and assist producer and transit countries in halting the drug trade.[29] In 1986, President Ronald Reagan declared international narcotics a national security threat and tasked the Secretary of State and the Administrator of USAID with integrating counternarcotics efforts into US foreign assistance strategy.[30] These charters provide the framework for INL's responsibilities, which are funded through the budget account for International Narcotics Control and Law Enforcement.

Overall INL Programs and Funding

State's INL bureau plans, budgets, and manages programs in 150 countries, covering international narcotics, international crime, trafficking in persons, and law enforcement training.[31] Until FY 2010, INL also managed a separate Andean Counterdrug Program (ACP), discussed below. The two accounts were combined into INL's budget account for International Narcotics Control and Law Enforcement (INCLE) in the FY 2010 budget request to the Congress.

INL's budget and activities are quite broad, including counternarcotics operations, support for weak states, peacekeeping-related activities, and some counterterror operations. Budgets support "country and global programs critical to combat transnational crime and illicit threats, including efforts against terrorist networks in the illegal drug trade and illicit enterprises."[32] Funds have been used to strengthen law enforcement institutions that are weak or corrupt, implement the Sudan peace agreement, assist the Liberian police, support border security and law enforcement in Pakistan and Mexico, and train the Indonesian police. They also provide support for training at five international law enforcement academies in Thailand, Hungary, Botswana, El Salvador, and New Mexico, which have trained over 17,000 police and security officials.[33]

These responsibilities grew after the US invasions of Afghanistan and Iraq. Afghanistan became the world's largest source of heroin poppies.[34] In response, nearly $1 billion was appropriated for INL's Afghanistan program in FY 2005–06, covering programs to persuade Afghans to reject the heroin trade, discourage planting and eradicate poppy fields, and reform and train Afghani law enforcement and judicial officials to arrest, prosecute, and punish traffickers and corrupt officials, among other activities. Interdiction efforts funded through this program include support teams from the Drug Enforcement Agency (DEA) and DOD, supported by the State Department air wing and Afghan counternarcotics police.[35] Overall, INCLE budgets grew rapidly in the early twenty-first century, from $170 million in FY 2001 to $1.5 billion in FY 2009, including a new program of nearly $500 million for Mexico, and significant funding for Iraq and Afghanistan.[36]

Andean Counterdrug Program

INL's counternarcotics program in the Andean region is its largest responsibility, but its budget was requested and reported separately until FY 2010. Counternarcotics assistance to Colombia began in the 1970s and increased sharply in the 1989 "Andean Initiative," which provided Colombian security forces with equipment under Foreign Military Financing (FMF) and drawdown authorities. Funding declined during the 1990s, but increased sharply in FY 2000 as "Plan Colombia," which provided more than $765 million to train counternarcotics battalions, fund economic development, and support justice programs, among other activities.[37]

Plan Colombia moved to a regional focus in FY 2002 as the "Andean Counterdrug Initiative" (ACI) in FY 2003, and was renamed the Andean Counterdrug Program (ACP) in FY 2009. This separate budget supports programs implemented by several federal agencies, including USAID, DEA, and DOD, in Bolivia, Brazil, Colombia, Ecuador, Panama, Peru, and Venezuela. ACP's goal is to eliminate the cultivation and refining of coca and opium poppies, reduce the flow of drugs to the United States and strengthen law enforcement capacity to find, arrest, and prosecute drug traffickers. ACP activities include crop eradication, interdiction of drug flows, assistance for justice and legal systems prosecuting drug-related crime, air support (the State Department air wing), equipment for police and other security forces, and economic development projects (roads, bridges, schools, alternative crops).[38] From FY 2000 through FY 2009, the Andean program has received funding of more than $6.3 billion.[39]

INL Planning and Budgeting

Planning and budgeting for INL programs (including the ACP) are complex. Inside State, programs for counternarcotics "are developed on the basis of country strategies coordinated [in embassies] by the Country Teams and/or Law Enforcement Working Groups and host nation officials." These programs are "formalized through bilateral Letters of Agreement with key objectives, program priorities, performance targets, and funding levels." At the embassy level, country programs are coordinated in embassies by Narcotics/Law Enforcement Section Officers directly connected to INL. The proposed programs are transmitted to the Office of the Director of Foreign Assistance (F) and are the subject of hearings in the State Department. Funding to support these programs may also be drawn from other State Department accounts, including SEED, FSA, and Peacekeeping Operations (PKO).[40] The implementation of counternarcotics programs is also complex, because a number of agencies may receive INL support for their contribution, including USAID, Justice, FBI, DEA, DOD, IRS, CIA, Treasury, the Department of Homeland Security (DHS), the US Coast Guard, and the Department of Commerce.[41]

INL budget planning is further complicated by the role of the White House Office of National Drug Control Policy (ONDCP), which is responsible for coordinating both domestic and international narcotics programs with all agencies and for certifying that their budgets meet the requirements of national drug control policy. Agencies retain responsibility for internal budget planning.[42] INL notes that it coordinates with ONDCP, and plays a key role "by leading in the development and coordination of US international drug and crime programs."[43]

Nonproliferation, Antiterrorism, Demining, and Related Programs

The Nonproliferation, Antiterrorism, Demining, and Related Programs (NADR) account was created in 1996 "to give the executive branch more flexibility in administering funds for these kinds of activities."[44] NADR funding supports three program areas that are planned and budgeted in separate State Department offices and implemented by a broader set of agencies. Counterterrorism programs account for roughly 33 percent of the funds, nonproliferation 40 percent, and regional security/demining much of the remainder.[45] The account grew from roughly $150 million in 1997 to $530 million in FY 2009.

Counterterrorism Programs

The State Department's Office of the Coordinator for Counterterrorism (S/CT) not only manages State Department programs, but also has a cross-agency coordination role. The Office has its origins in the 1972 Office for Combating Terrorism, but did not exist in statute until 1994.[46] Its interagency authorities are not as extensive as those of the coordinators for PEPFAR or SEED/FSA, but its mission is broad: "[T]o develop and lead a worldwide effort to combat terrorism using all the instruments of statecraft: diplomacy, economic power, intelligence, law enforcement, and military. S/CT provides foreign policy oversight and guidance to all US Government international counterterrorism activities."[47] S/CT plays an important role in interagency counterterrorism planning. It sits on the White House Homeland Security Council, assists DOD in developing and implementing overseas counterterrorism operations, and leads the Foreign Emergency Support Team (an on-call rapid deployment team to advise US missions overseas in case of terrorist attacks). S/CT works with all other agencies involved in counterterrorism matters, including DOD, Treasury, Justice, DHS, the intelligence community (particularly the National Counterterrorism Center), USAID, and the White House.

The 1994 statute gives S/CT only an advisory role with respect to the counterterrorism budgets of other agencies. Inside State, S/CT does not control its own direct program budget, but has a formal role in planning and budgeting for the counterterrorism activities of other offices, as well as "policy oversight for all State Department counterterrorism programs, including training." S/CT works closely with the regional bureaus and the Bureau of Diplomatic Security in executing these responsibilities, but its own budget office prepares proposals and oversees implementation.[48]

S/CT oversees planning and budgeting for State's largest counterterrorism activity—the Antiterrorism Assistance (ATA) program. ATA was created in 1983 in the wake of the Marine barracks bombing near Beirut, Lebanon to enhance the ability of foreign law enforcement personnel to deter terrorist attacks by providing equipment and training.[49]

The ATA program has expanded over the years, assisting countries that lack resources to maintain infrastructure and training for counterterrorism operations.[50] With roughly $125 million in budget, it has supported training for more than 55,000 personnel in 150 countries in bomb detection, crime scene investigation, airport and building security, maritime security, counterterrorism management, and dignitary protection.[51]

ATA programs are developed in embassies and regional bureaus, but largely implemented by State's Bureau of Diplomatic Security, which assesses training needs, develops a curriculum, and contracts the training itself to police forces and private security companies.[52] The FAA prohibits funding to countries that violate human rights or sponsor international terrorism, but other FAA restrictions are waived.[53] ATA funds are flexible, with no geographic limitations, and are "no-year" money, expendable until exhausted.[54]

Nonproliferation Programs

The NADR account also funds State Department nonproliferation programs. State is the chief US negotiator on nonproliferation and has a small amount of funding for nonproliferation programs, which it can use to provide

> training services,... funds, equipment, and other commodities related to the detection, deterrence, monitoring, interdiction, and prevention or countering of proliferation, the establishment of effective nonproliferation laws and regulations, and the apprehension of those individuals involved in acts of proliferation of such weapons.[55]

The Under Secretary of State for Arms Control and International Security Affairs and the Assistant Secretary for International Security and Nonproliferation plan and execute State's nonproliferation programs, which have a small budget of roughly $100 million.[56] These include the Nonproliferation and Disarmament Fund (NDF), the Global Threat Reduction (GTR) program, export control and border security training, and voluntary US contributions to the International Atomic Energy Agency (IAEA) and the Comprehensive Test Ban Treaty's monitoring program.

The NDF was created in the 1992 Freedom Support Act because of growing concern about the safety of nuclear materials in the former Soviet Union.[57] It is one of the State Department's no-year contingency funds, a small ($30–40 million) fund designed to respond to urgent, unanticipated nonproliferation needs by preventing the spread of weapons of mass destruction and related materials.[58] The NDF budget is prepared in State's Bureau of International Security and Nonproliferation (ISN) and funds projects proposed and ultimately implemented by any executive branch agency.[59] NDF funds have been used to rapidly remove poorly secured nuclear materials from a number of countries, including Kazakhstan, Serbia, and Libya.[60]

The other nonproliferation programs support science centers in Russia, Ukraine, and other parts of the former Soviet Union, help foreign governments establish and operate export control systems through equipment and training, and provide voluntary US support to the IAEA and the Comprehensive Test Ban Treaty.[61]

Regional Stability and Humanitarian Demining Programs

The NADR account also includes no-year funds to support regional stability and demining assistance to a number of countries, programs which are planned and managed by State's Bureau of Political-Military Affairs (PM), in cooperation with regional bureaus. The major regional stability program, created through an international treaty in 2001, seeks to eliminate or secure small arms and light weapons. In addition, NADR funds support efforts to control Man-Portable Air Defense Systems (Soviet Strela and US Stinger) because of the threat terrorists could pose to aircraft and helicopters using such weapons.[62] The Humanitarian Demining Program, created in 1997, supports the location, clearing, and destruction of minefields around the globe. The goal of the program is to reduce landmine casualties, develop conditions that allow safe return to mined areas, and restore land to productive use.[63] Embassies endorse proposals from countries seeking assistance, which are then reviewed by a joint State/DOD committee. The program is managed by PM's Office of Weapons Removal and Abatement (PM/WRA). Contractors, NGOs, and international organizations implement funded proposals.[64]

Coordinator for Reconstruction and Stabilization

In 2004, the State Department created a new office to handle responsibilities for which it had been unprepared in Iraq and Afghanistan: the stabilization and reconstruction of post-conflict societies. The creation of the Department's Office of the Coordinator for Reconstruction and Stabilization (S/CRS) grew directly out of the post-conflict experience in Iraq, where it became clear that the US government lacked the civilian capacity, budgets, personnel, or institutional structures to plan and implement post-conflict stabilization and reconstruction (S&R) programs.

S/CRS was given government-wide responsibilities for managing interagency planning for reconstruction and stabilization in National Security Presidential Directive (NSPD-44) of December 2005. Its missions included creating a process to identify states at risk of instability or collapse, developing strategies and plans for the US response, and ensuring program and policy coordination among agencies. State was given primary responsibility for coordination with DOD, foreign governments, international organizations, and non-governmental organizations for these operations. The NSPD specifically charged State with the responsibility to "resolve relevant policy, program, and funding disputes" among government departments with respect to such operations. Other agencies were to coordinate with State in preparing their budgets for S&R.

S/CRS has developed a global monitoring program to identify states at risk of instability and developed a planning process that brings together all elements of US conflict response and facilitates coordination among civilian agencies and with the military for such operations. In addition, S/CRS has developed a detailed matrix of the tasks that need to be executed in a generic post-conflict reconstruction situation.[65] It is developing an inventory of skilled personnel in the government who could deploy early in a post-conflict setting and a small Active Response Corps for such deployments. It has also begun to create a civilian reserve for such missions. Finally, S/CRS has deployed a small number of people to assist in executing post-conflict stabilization missions, coordinate civilian capacities, or provide consultative advice in such places as Sudan, Haiti, Lebanon, Kosovo, Congo, and Nepal.

S/CRS Planning and Budgeting

S/CRS has struggled to establish its working relationship with the regional bureaus, the Office of the Director of Foreign Assistance (F), and USAID. As S/CRS responsibilities cover all regions, it may be active in the affairs of any particular region at any time and could be particularly active in the coordination of assistance programs. This relationship was particularly sensitive with the Near East Bureau and with F, concerning S/CRS's role in post-conflict Lebanon in 2006. Ultimately, State leadership for the Lebanon assistance program was given to F rather than S/CRS. In 2007, the S/CRS Office was moved into the F bureau.[66] S/CRS has not yet established a clear working relationship with USAID, which was given primary responsibility for civilian operations in Afghanistan in 2009.[67]

Through its first four years, S/CRS also had difficulty recruiting personnel or raising budget resources to fund actual operations.[68] For three years, State requested $75–100 million to create a Conflict Response contingency fund for operations, but those requests were denied. Because DOD felt it needed a stronger civilian assistance capability, it requested and received temporary authority under Section 1207 of the National Defense Authorization Act to transfer up to $100 million a year for two years to the State Department for such missions.[69] In 2009, Congress provided $145 million for stabilization and reconstruction programs, splitting the funding between S/CRS and USAID. It also authorized the creation of the Civilian Response Corps.

Security Assistance Programs

Assistance to the military forces of allied and friendly countries has been a part of US national security policy since World War II.[70] The Lend Lease Program, which was authorized by the Congress in 1941, provided roughly $50 billion of military equipment, food, and other aid to the United Kingdom, Russia, and other close allies. Since the creation of NATO in 1948, the United States has been the largest global supplier of military equipment, services, and training to other countries.

Security assistance was a crucial part of US support for the European, South Korean, and South Vietnamese militaries in the 1950s. It has been a continuing element of US policy in the Middle East, including military grant and sale programs for Israel, Egypt, and Jordan, and sales to Saudi Arabia, Iran, and a number of Gulf Cooperation Council States.[71] With the end of the Cold War and the challenges of terrorism, peacekeeping, post-conflict stabilization and reconstruction, failed states, and nuclear proliferation, US security assistance programs have taken new forms and reach into new regions around the globe.[72]

Because of the role of security assistance in meeting overall US foreign and national security policy goals, country selection, planning, and budgeting for such programs has traditionally been done under the auspices of the Secretary of State and funding has been part of the International Affairs budget. Since DOD and the military services have the requisite military expertise, equipment and services, and the global network of civilian and military connections with foreign militaries, however, DOD and the military services play an important role in that planning and implement most of the US security assistance programs.

The portfolio of security assistance programs under State's authorities includes FMF and related Foreign Military Sales (FMS), the International Military Education and Training Program (IMET), PKO, and smaller programs that distribute US defense equipment and services to other countries. In addition, State's counternarcotics, terrorism, and counterproliferation programs, discussed above, have security assistance dimensions.

The significant change in US security assistance over the past decade, however, has been the dramatic expansion of programs that are not carried out under the authority of the Secretary of State and are not included in the international affairs accounts. The most significant of these is the growing portfolio of security assistance programs planned, budgeted, and implemented directly by the Department of Defense. There are also security-related programs at the departments of Justice, Homeland Security, and Energy. The growing dispersal of security assistance programs has raised problems of coordinating budgeting and strategic planning.

Traditional Security Assistance Programs

Foreign Military Financing and Foreign Military Sales

Today's Foreign Military Financing (FMF) program and the related Foreign Military Sales (FMS) program grew out of the Military Assistance Program (MAP) created in the 1949 Mutual Defense Assistance Act. MAP grants and loans helped rebuild NATO militaries at the onset of the Cold War and provided assistance to the South Korean and South Vietnamese militaries.[73] FMF replaced MAP in 1989, as the program moved toward a focus on lending for Greece and Turkey, and, later, to grant assistance to countries in the Middle East and Southeast Asia.[74]

Between FY 1950 and FY 2007 MAP and FMF program budgets have totaled $151.3 billion.[75] In recent years, FMF budgets have ranged from $3.5 billion (FY 2001) to nearly $6 billion (FY 2003). Between FY 1950 and FY 2007, 55 percent of all MAP/FMF funds supported Israel ($52.9 billion) and Egypt ($30.7 billion). Of the FY 2010 FMF request of $5.3 billion, 88 percent went to Israel, Egypt, Pakistan, and Jordan.[76]

FMF Planning and Budgeting

FMF and FMS programs are authorized under the Foreign Assistance and the Arms Export Control (AECA) Acts. These statutes make the State Department the lead agency in the executive branch for determining which countries have FMF (as well as FMS and IMET) programs and what the funding levels should be, and making final decision on all transfers and sales.[77] At the same time, DOD and the military services play a major role in both planning and implementing the FMF programs. The planning, budgeting, and decision-making structure for these programs is, therefore, a complex interagency partnership.

At State, security assistance programs are managed by the Bureau of Political-Military Affairs (PM). The Deputy Assistant Secretary for Regional Security (PM/RS) in that Bureau prepares the annual FMF and IMET budgets, with significant input from the embassies, DOD, and the regional military commands. PM oversees planning and budgeting, maintains State's liaison with DOD, and ensures that FMF programs are consistent with arms export controls and other statutes. The State Department infrastructure for this responsibility, however, is relatively small.[78]

DOD plays a role in FMF planning and budgeting through both the military services and the Defense Security Cooperation Agency (DSCA), which reports to the Under Secretary of Defense for Policy, through an Assistant Secretary. DSCA is the institutional memory bank for FMF, develops the

Table 4.2 Top recipients of MAP/FMF: FY 1950–FY 2007 (*$ in millions*)

Israel	52,991
Egypt	30,779
Turkey	5,217
Pakistan	2,842
Jordan	2,363
Afghanistan	1,218
Philippines	1,054
Colombia	664

Source: Defense Security Cooperation Agency, Foreign Military Sales, Foreign Military Construction Sales, and Military Assistance Facts (as of September 30, 2005); US Agency for International Development, Overseas Loans and Grants (USAID Greenbook); and US Department of State, *FY 2009 Foreign Operations Congressional Budget Justification* (February 2008).

program's databases and manuals, and executes the program.[79] In contrast to State, DSCA crafts long-term strategic plans for security assistance, including FMF, covering policy, program, and management goals.[80] DSCA and the military services determine what equipment and services are available, make recommendations on funding levels, and procure the equipment, using the military services as agents.[81] DSCA also oversees negotiations with buying countries and manages interagency coordination and liaison with industry.[82] In many ways, DOD and the services are the dominant agencies in FMF (as well as FMS and IMET) planning and budgeting, despite State's statutory authority.

The DOD role is also dominant in the field, the starting point for an FMF (and FMS) "case," as it is called. These cases originate in the field, where DOD and the military services have significant staff and contacts with local militaries. Recommendations on recipient countries, the shape of the program, and the projected cost all originate with an embassy's Security Assistance Organization (SAO), which is staffed largely by military personnel who report to the ambassador and to the regional Combatant Commander (COCOM) and DSCA. State Department political and military officers are also part of the SAO. The SAO evaluates host nation military capabilities and requirements, prepares the cost and budget estimates, and manages the implementation of FMF/FMS cases.[83]

The COCOMs also play a role in this planning and budgeting process.[84] The COCOM, such as the Commander of the US Central Command, develops his own view of regional security assistance needs, coordinates with the SAO, evaluates the proposed FMF cases, and makes direct recommendations both to the SAO and directly to the Joint Staff and the Secretary of Defense.[85]

Overall, three chains of command plan and budget FMF simultaneously: the State Department, starting with political officers in the embassy up through PM (in coordination with regional bureaus); the DSCA; and the regional military command structure.

Foreign Military Sales

FMF funding is typically used by recipients of grants and loans to purchase US military goods, services, and training. The United States is also the world's largest exporter of military equipment and services. With appropriate export licenses, some governments buy US military equipment directly from manufacturers. The US government frequently acts as the manager for these transactions through the Foreign Military Sales program.[86]

From 1950 to 2007, the FMS program has provided or arranged to provide over $400 billion worth of military equipment and services to foreign countries.[87] The vast bulk of these sales have been to US NATO and Middle East allies and participants in the Middle East peace process (see Table 4.3).

Table 4.3 Top 15 recipients of FMS FY 1950–FY 2007

Rank	Country	FMS agreements ($ in millions)
1	Saudi Arabia	70,597
2	Egypt	28,988
3	Israel	28,909
4	Taiwan	18,266
5	Turkey	17,349
6	South Korea	16,732
7	Australia	16,742
8	Japan	16,087
9	United Kingdom	16,054
10	Germany	15,097
11	Iran	10,767
12	Netherlands	10,311
13	Kuwait	10,124
14	Spain	8,888
15	Pakistan	8,139

Source: Defense Security Cooperation Agency, *Historical Facts Book* (as of September 30, 2007).

FMS Planning and Budgeting

Countries seeking to purchase equipment and services through FMS provide a Letter of Request to the embassy SAO. State PM and the military evaluate the request and draw up a Letter of Offer and Acceptance, describing the equipment, cost, and delivery date. State and DSCA are required to notify the Congress of most of these proposed sales.[88] If Congress does not object, the purchasing country makes a funding deposit in the United States for the purchase. The equipment may come from US military stocks if they are in excess to the military's needs, or the military service may negotiate a contract with a private supplier. FMS sales can have a budgetary impact if they are funded through an FMF grant or loan. In addition, the United States receives a 3.8 percent administrative fee for acting as the agent for an FMS sale.[89]

International Military Education and Training

The traditional security assistance portfolio also includes a small (roughly $90 million) program which has funded professional training and military education to foreign military officers from more than 100 countries since 1947.[90] The initial goals of International Military Education and Training (IMET) were to further regional stability through military-to-military relationships, transfer critical skills to foreign militaries, and train militaries for combined operations with the United States. These goals were expanded in 1991 to include educating foreign military and civilian defense personnel in democratic values and civilian control, assist cooperation with law enforcement personnel in counternarcotics operations, and reform military justice systems.[91] The program has been controversial over the years, given the role the military has played in political developments in other countries.[92]

IMET Planning and Budgeting

The State Department decides on the eligibility of countries for IMET funds and on the overall level of support, but (as with FMF) DOD's Defense Security Cooperation Agency, the embassy SAO, and the COCOMS provide program recommendations and DSCA manages the program. The average country program is small, at less than $1 million. Largest recipients in FY 2009 included Turkey ($3.2 million) and Jordan ($3.1 million), but funds are spread widely across the regions of the globe.[93]

Peacekeeping Operations

The State Department manages the Peacekeeping Operations (PKO) account, created in 1978, which supports non-UN multilateral operations and a growing military training program for peacekeepers.[94] The statutory language for the PKO account is rather broad:

> The President is authorized to furnish assistance to friendly countries and international organizations, on such terms and conditions as he may determine, for peacekeeping operations and other programs carried out in furtherance of the national security interests of the United States.[95]

Through the PKO account, the United States has been able to support non-UN multilateral peacekeeping initiatives and operations, assist countries less able to pay for their participation in peacekeeping operations, train and encourage other militaries to provide peacekeepers, strengthen regional organizations to support peacekeeping, and enhance the interoperability of military forces.[96]

The PKO account has grown over time, as the United States became more involved in peacekeeping and regional stability after the end of the Cold War. Before 1989, funding tended to be in the $30–50 million range, but grew in the 1990s to $75–120 million. It grew again after the genocide in Rwanda. The United States did not intervene in that crisis, but the administration sought to strengthen African capabilities to provide regional peacekeeping for future crises by creating a peacekeeping training and operational support program, the African Crisis Response Force. The Bush administration developed this program further into the African Contingency Operations Training and Assistance Program (ACOTA), overseen by a joint board representing State, DOD, and the NSC. This program was further expanded into the Global Peacekeeping Operations Initiative (GPOI), increasing PKO funding to over

$500 million, including supplemental funding. Nearly 80 percent of the FY 2009 PKO budget request was for training and regional stability operations in Africa.[97]

A number of smaller, but important operations are funded through this account, including the Trans-Sahara Counterterrorism Partnership (a border control training and equipping program created in 2002 to assist Mauritania, Mali, Niger, and Chad security forces), and a multilateral (United States, Egypt, Israel) patrol operation ensuring security in the Sinai Peninsula—the Multinational Force and Observers (MFO).[98] PKO has also been used to provide emergency supplemental funding as peacekeeping crises occur, including African Union operations in Darfur, Sudan in FY 2006 and FY 2007 and in Liberia.

The GPOI is the most ambitious PKO-funded program, consuming roughly 40 percent of the account. GPOI provides resources, training, and equipment for the militaries of recipient developing countries, in order to "increase worldwide capacity to provide the appropriate personnel needed to conduct peace operations, including UN peacekeeping missions."[99] Created following the 2004 G-8 summit in Sea Island, Georgia, the goal of GPOI is to train, equip, and exercise 75,000 troops worldwide by 2010 for peacekeeping capabilities and to increase training of gendarme-like forces for policing responsibilities in failed states. It also included a clearing house on peace operations, a global transportation and logistics support arrangement for peacekeeping operations, and equipment purchases.[100]

PKO Planning and Budgeting

Planning and management of the PKO account is the responsibility of the Office of Plans, Policy, and Analysis in State's Bureau of Political-Military Affairs (PM/PPA). Specific programs are defined with the appropriate regional bureau at State and moved forward to the F budget office. The GPOI program is managed by a dedicated team in the PM/PPA Office in partnership with the DOD Office of the Assistant Secretary for Stability Operations and Low-Intensity Conflict (OSD SO/LIC), and the Joint Staff's Stability Operations and Security Assistance Office. GPOI program and budget proposals are reviewed by an interagency Coordinating Committee composed of State PM, SO/LIC, the regional bureaus, and the NSC and transmitted to State PM as part of the broader security assistance budget process. GPOI activities are implemented by these offices and the military's regional COCOMS. Once appropriated, PKO funds are available for one year.[101]

Excess Defense Articles and Drawdowns

The United States can also supply other countries with its own military equipment through two other programs, administered under State Department authorities. The Foreign Assistance Act (Section 516) allows the President to supply foreign countries with defense articles that are excess to the US military. They are generally sold at a discount price, but can be transferred without cost if there is a foreign policy benefit and no adverse effect on the US technology and industrial base. The Secretary of State initiates the request for an Excess Defense Articles (EDA) delivery. From FY 2001 through FY 2008 total EDA transfers came to more than $2 billion, roughly half of that for countries in the Middle East and South Asia.[102]

The United States can also transfer US military equipment to another country through "drawdowns" under the Foreign Assistance Act (Sections 506(a)(1) and (a)(2), and Section 552(c)). These authorities allow the transfer, at no cost, of US military equipment and services which may not be in excess of US military needs. Section 506(a)(1) permits a drawdown of up to $100 million in equipment for emergencies. Section 506(a)(2) permits a drawdown of up to $200 million for counternarcotics, disaster assistance, antiterrorism, or counterproliferation purposes.[103] Section 552(c) allows a $25 million drawdown for peacekeeping emergencies.

The White House initiates a request for a drawdown, but State's PM office prepares the package in consultation with the Joint Staff and the military services.[104] In all three cases, the FAA authorizes the President to seek an appropriation of funds to reimburse the agencies whose assets or resources have been drawn down.

The Changing World of US Security Assistance

The dispersal of foreign economic assistance programs outside of the International Affairs budget, noted in Chapter 2, is mirrored in the world of security assistance. The Defense Department and the military services have the most extensive overseas engagement of any federal department outside State/USAID. DOD's security assistance activities, already large, have expanded significantly since the terrorist attacks of 9/11 and the invasions of Afghanistan and Iraq.

Other federal agencies have also expanded their overseas activities, especially since the end of the Cold War and 9/11. The Department of Energy's nonproliferation programs grew significantly with the end of the Cold War and are now budgeted at over $1 billion a year. The US response to terrorist attacks has accelerated the overseas engagement of the DHS and the Department of Justice/Federal Bureau of Investigation (FBI).

Serious problems of planning, budgeting, and coordination result from this dispersal of activity. The Secretary of State does not have the authority to coordinate all security assistance programs and there is no coordination at the White House. Given the expansion of DOD programs, in particular, there is also growing concern about the imbalance of authority between the two departments.[105]

Department of Defense

The Defense Department and regional military commands have been directly engaged in security assistance activity for decades. DOD policy offices routinely conduct negotiations with countries over basing rights, force planning, defense technologies, joint weapons programs, and defense trade issues. DOD has been a major player in counternarcotics activity for over three decades and plans, budgets, and implements the Nunn–Lugar Comprehensive Threat Reduction (CTR) program, which has prevented the proliferation of nuclear materials from the former Soviet Union and reduced the size of the former Soviet nuclear arsenal. DOD also manages the Partnership for Peace training program for former Warsaw Pact militaries. The Joint Chiefs of Staff and regional commands support joint training and military exercises with allied countries. The regional COCOMS are, in many respects, military/diplomatic representatives of the United States to the countries in their respective regions.[106]

The attacks of 9/11 and US experiences in Afghanistan and Iraq gave rise to a major expansion of DOD's security assistance portfolio.[107] A number of new DOD authorities and programs were created, all of which are implemented under DOD's statutory resources and resourced in the DOD budget. This new DOD security assistance portfolio has received funding of over $50 billion between FY 2002 and FY 2009. It includes new programs to train and equip foreign security forces, to reimburse foreign governments for support provided to US forces, to carry out reconstruction programs in Iraq and Afghanistan. State has a minimal policy or oversight role in these programs, though many of them parallel the existing portfolio of traditional security assistance.

These new authorities and activities were created in large part because DOD viewed the traditional portfolio of security assistance programs as inadequate to meet emerging security needs in the dynamic environment of counterterror and complex contingency operations. FMF and ESF were seen as excessively earmarked and legislatively constrained, leaving such key countries as Pakistan ineligible for assistance. The State Department was seen as incapable of raising adequate resources or providing a flexible and agile response to emerging security assistance needs.[108]

DOD's new set of programs provided the flexibility, agility, and funding the department felt it needed to conduct counterterrorist operations, train indigenous security forces, and establish security in combat zones. As the programs have developed, moreover, DOD has sought to expand their coverage to a global application, legislate them as a part of DOD's permanent law, and increase their funding levels significantly (see Table 4.4).[109]

DOD is responsible for the budget planning, funding, and implementation of these programs, though in some cases, they do so with the "concurrence" of the Secretary of State. Many of these new authorities clearly parallel those

Table 4.4 New DOD security and foreign assistance programs FY 2002–09

Name	FY 2002–FY 2009 total ($ in millions)	FY 2010 request ($ in millions)	Parallel traditional security assistance programs
Train and Equip for Afghan and Iraqi Forces	37,300	7,500	PKO, FMF, IMET
Section 1206	1,350	400	PKO, FMF, IMET
CERP	4,913	1,500	USAID-OTI/OFDA and State MRA
Coalition Support Funds	8,900	1,900	ESF
Combating Terrorism Fellowship Program	135	0	IMET

Source data: Defense Appropriations Acts, FY 2002–FY 2009, Supplemental Appropriations FY 2002–FY 2009.

of the State Department, raising problems of overlap and potential conflict with State's policy agenda and the overall foreign policy goals of the United States.

Train and Equip (T&E) Funds for Afghan and Iraqi Forces

The largest new DOD security assistance supports the training and equipping of the new military and security forces in Iraq and Afghanistan. DOD's FY 2004 emergency supplemental budget request sought authority for DOD, with the concurrence of the Secretary of State, to use up to $200 million of defense-wide operation and maintenance funds for the "training and equipping" of military forces in Iraq, Afghanistan, and "other friendly nearby regional nations."[110] The Act, as passed, limited this authority to the Iraqi and Afghan armies. DOD is responsible for planning and budgeting for these programs, which have received nearly $35 billion in appropriations since they were created.[111]

Global Train and Equip: Section 1206 Authority

Broader US military counterterror operations led to the creation of a global DOD T&E program, supporting training for security forces in any country cooperating with the United States in combating terrorism. In 2005 Secretary of State Condoleezza Rice agreed that DOD could seek authority to create and implement such a global program, which was provided in Section 1206 of the National Defense Authorization Act for FY 2006. The State Department retains a role in the program, since projects are to be "jointly formulated" by the two departments and require the concurrence of the Secretary of State.[112]

However, according to a 2007 Government Accountability Office report, coordination did not occur consistently at the field level between combatant commands and embassy country teams.[113] The initiative for projects and the funding, however, are in DOD's hands.

Through FY 2008, Section 1206 funding provided over $850 million in training and military equipment to at least 33 countries around the globe.[114] Although initially funds for Section 1206 were drawn from DOD's operations and maintenance accounts, up to a legislated ceiling, in FY 2009 Congress directly appropriated $300 million for the program, further establishing it as a core DOD activity. Congress, however, concerned about the growing State–DOD imbalance with respect to security assistance programs, has resisted making the program permanent law.[115]

Coalition Support Funds

DOD's Coalition Support Funds (CSF) budget also grew out of the Iraq, Afghanistan, and counterterrorism operations. Lacking an infrastructure in the region, the DOD asked Pakistan and Jordan, among others, to provide basing, logistics, and other assistance. The emergency supplemental appropriation for FY 2002 provided $100 million to the Secretary of Defense to "reimburse ... Pakistan and Jordan for logistical and military support provided, or to be provided, to US military operations in connection with Operation Enduring Freedom."[116] Subsequent appropriations broadened these CSF funds to allow reimbursement to "other key cooperating nations."[117] Through FY 2009, CSF has provided more than $7.5 billion to reimburse other countries for logistical and other support for the Afghanistan campaign and counterterrorist operations.[118]

Although CSF funds ostensibly reimburse military activities, as a budget support program they also provide indirect foreign economic assistance, as they can free up resources the recipient government can use for non-defense purposes. The utility of these funds in meeting counterterrorist goals has been questioned, particularly in the case of Pakistan, which received more than $5.5 billion in CSF funding through FY 2008.

Congress has also begun to question whether it made sense to continue to fund the Pakistan program through DOD, given the similarities between this program and ESF.[119] As with Section 1206, CSF requires the concurrence of the Secretary of State, but the proposals to use the funds originate with the Defense Department and they are appropriated to DOD, which oversees the reimbursement process.

Combating Terrorism Fellowship Program

DOD's Combating Terrorism Fellowship Program (CTFP) grew out of a 2001 request by regional COCOMS for a military education program that could quickly and flexibly provide counterterrorism training and education to foreign military partners. Pacific Command hoped to use this program to offer training programs in Indonesia, where IMET programs had been suspended because of restrictions in the Foreign Assistance Act. CTFP was created in DOD to avoid those restrictions. It is funded at $35 million a year through the defense budget, but is similar to IMET and uses DOD's IMET implementation process and regulations.[120]

Africa Command

As part of the expansion of DOD security and foreign assistance programs, the COCOMS have also begun to broaden their missions to include humanitarian and economic assistance and the broader coordination of US assistance programs in a given region. The new regional command for Africa (AFRICOM) began operations in 2008 to bring together the growing military counterterrorism effort in that region with its humanitarian and evacuation operations and African peacekeeping training programs.[121] AFRICOM was explicitly designed to include US civilian agency participation through the appointment of a Foreign Service Officer as a Deputy to the Commander.[122] The goal is to coordinate State and USAID assistance programs more closely with the military's assistance activities, which include military security force training, humanitarian food distribution, and small-scale development projects.[123] However, there has not been joint program building or budget coordination in Washington between State, USAID, and ARICOM.

Commander's Emergency Response Program

DOD has extended its role into economic assistance, particularly in Iraq and Afghanistan, through the Commander's Emergency Response Program (CERP). CERP was created first in Iraq, then extended to Afghanistan, and, in 2008, to the Philippines to provide rapid, small-scale emergency assistance at the local level, as part of the process of "winning the hearts and minds" of populations in zones of insurgency and civil strife where the American military was deployed. Its origins were based on the military's sense that the civilian US agencies were poorly staffed and insufficiently agile to provide rapid-response assistance to meet local social, economic, and governance needs. In addition, because these activities were taking place in combat zones, civilian providers from State and USAID could not meet these needs safely.[124]

CERP was initially funded using Iraqi currency assets seized during the US invasion and occupation.[125] As these assets dried up, DOD requested a congressional appropriation. Congress has provided $6.4 billion for CERP through FY 2009, largely through emergency supplemental appropriations. CERP funds are extremely flexible, allowing local commanders to decide on projects, rather than requiring a formal contracting action.[126] Commanders have a list of permissible areas of expenditure and dollar limits on the amounts they can commit without higher approval. Projects have overlapped considerably with the mission of civilian assistance agencies, including improvements to water and sanitation infrastructure, food production and distribution, healthcare, education, telecommunications, installation or restoration of irrigation systems, and funds for day laborers to perform civic cleaning.[127] They have also been used to support the work of the Provincial Reconstruction Teams (PRTs), which combine military and civilian assistance providers in Iraq and Afghanistan.[128]

Budgeting for CERP is straightforward. DOD estimates the financial need and requests the funds from its appropriators. State has no concurrent authority over the program, despite the similarity in projects and the fact that the military and civilian agencies are often working side by side. As a result, there has been a growing issue about the lack of coordination between CERP and the broader reconstruction efforts in Iraq and Afghanistan.[129] DOD has sought permanent statutory authority for the CERP program, as well as its expansion on a global basis. Congress has deferred these requests because of the apparent overlap with State/USAID authorities and programs and the absence of coordination mechanisms.[130]

Department of Justice/Federal Bureau of Investigation

The Department of Justice has had an overseas Legal Attaché program in more than 50 countries for decades. The attachés, who are coordinated through the Office of International Operations, coordinate international investigations and FBI police training programs.[131] The 9/11 attacks led to an expansion of the department's international activity as it began to focus more attention on terrorists and international criminal organizations. The FBI's National Security Branch and its Counterterrorism Division seek to "neutralize terrorist cells and operatives here in the US and to help dismantle terrorist networks worldwide," including coordination programs with international partners. The Branch and this Division increased its efforts to coordinate intelligence and programs with international partners.[132]

The DEA at Justice pursues international narcotics traffickers and works closely with other federal agencies in the Organized Crime and Drug Enforcement Task Force (OCDETF) to attack drug trafficking and money laundering organizations. It is deeply involved in counternarcotics operations in Colombia and the Andean region, as well as in Afghanistan. Its international work is supported both by direct appropriations and by funds transferred from State Department INL accounts.

Department of Homeland Security

The Department of Homeland Security (DHS) also has several security-related international activities. Throughout the Container Security Initiative (CSI) of the Customs and Border Protection office (CBP), forward-deployed officials work with host country customs officials to establish security procedures for identifying and screening high-risk containers before they are shipped to the United States. As of March 2008, CSI was operating in 58 international ports shipping the largest volume of containers to the United States.[133]

Through its Office of International Affairs and Trade Relations (INATR), CBP maintains overseas field offices to facilitate and secure international trade. INATR provides targeted countries with training and advisory support through the Capacity Building and Export Control and Border Security (EXBS) program.

DHS also administers the Federal Law Enforcement Training Center (FLETC), an interagency law enforcement training center in Glynco, Georgia, with training sites in New Mexico and South Carolina. In addition to providing counterterrorism training to federal agencies, FLETC oversees the International Law Enforcement Academies (ILEAs) in Gaborone, Botswana and San Salvador, El Salvador and supports training services in Hungary, Peru, and Thailand and in Roswell, New Mexico.[134] Training at ILEAs for non-American police forces are funded through the State Department's Bureau for International Narcotics and Law Enforcement Affairs, which also provides policy guidance to the ILEA Directors.[135]

Budget planning for these programs is carried out through the DHS budget process, described in Chapter 7.

Department of Energy

The Department of Energy (DOE) also has a large, security-related international program through its National Nuclear Security Administration (NNSA).[136] NNSA, created in 2000, is a semi-autonomous agency, with responsibility for US nuclear weapons, naval reactors, and nuclear nonproliferation policies and programs.[137] Its Office of Defense Nuclear Nonproliferation (ODNN) manages a significant Nonproliferation and International Security program of roughly $1.1 billion, which has grown with the collapse of the Soviet Union and the increasing threat of the proliferation of nuclear weapons.[138]

The Nonproliferation and International Security program addresses sensitive exports, supports international safeguards, partners with foreign governments to design and implement proliferation controls, monitors the reduction in nuclear stockpiles and materials, and provides policy and technical analysis to foreign governments. It also funds programs that redirect former weapons scientists in Russia and other countries in the region to non-military research and commercial ventures. To execute these activities, ODNN partners with more than 100 countries and the IAEA.

The International Nuclear Materials Protection and Cooperation program assists Russian and other efforts to secure and eliminate nuclear weapons and material. The Elimination of Weapons-Grade Plutonium Production program supports the discontinuation of production of weapons-grade plutonium by replacing nuclear power plants with fossil-fueled power plants. The Fissile Materials Disposition program works with Russia to dispose of surplus weapons-grade fissile materials. The Global Threat Reduction Initiative seeks to reduce and protect nuclear and radiological materials located at international civilian sites. Several of these programs are partially funded through DOE's national labs—Los Alamos, Sandia, and Lawrence Livermore.

Planning and budgeting for these programs is carried out through the department's budget planning machinery, which uses a Planning, Processing, and Budgeting System-like process. There are no formal mechanisms, however, for coordinating this planning and budgeting with DOD or State Department activities in overlapping program areas.

Conclusion

Strategic economic and security assistance are a major funding priority for US national security policy. The State Department plans and budgets a number of assistance programs focusing on global security issues, from strategic support for allies to foreign military sales, military training and education, assistance for counterterrorism, counternarcotics, and counterproliferation, and support for regional peacekeeper training. Because State is not a strategic planning organization, these programs are only loosely coordinated. Implementation of the programs is largely the responsibility of other organizations, principally USAID (for economic assistance) and DOD (for security assistance).

As a result, there is a lack of overall planning for strategically-driven economic assistance programs, and a growing coordination problem in the area of security assistance. Because State's security assistance programs are thinly staffed, relatively inflexible, and lack agility, and because it is difficult for State to raise resources for these programs, the Defense Department has developed a substantial portfolio of its own security assistance programs. While some of these require Secretary of State concurrence, they are initiated, budgeted, controlled, and implemented at DOD. This growing imbalance in security assistance funding, programs, and authorities has created problems of coordination between the two departments.

The executive branch has not yet focused policy attention on the need for greater strategic and budgetary coordination of security assistance programs. Nor has it yet sought from Congress the flexibility that would be required to strengthen State Department staffing, planning, and oversight capacity with respect to these programs.

Chapter 5

Planning, Programming, Budgeting, and Execution in the Department of Defense

Introduction

Of all the departments and agencies involved in national security, the Department of Defense (DOD) arguably has the strongest, most mature, and most forward-looking processes for planning and resource allocation.[1] The DOD's procedures may also be the most complex of those processes in federal government today.

The complexity is no surprise. With some 1.4 million active-duty personnel, 850,000 paid members of the Guard and Reserve, and 700,000 civilian employees, DOD is by far the largest employer in the United States and the biggest department in the US federal government. The department spends roughly one-half of all of the funds appropriated by Congress from year to year and one-sixth of the total federal budget.[2]

Important features of DOD's current planning and resource allocation system were put in place as the Planning, Programming, and Budgeting System (PPBS) by Secretary of Defense Robert McNamara during the early 1960s. The PPBS was DOD's first formal process for integrating the long-term plans, programs, and budgets of all the armed services into a unified whole.[3] At the time, PPBS was a revolutionary innovation. The new system modernized DOD's resource allocation arrangements consistent with the best industrial practices of the time. In addition, it put teeth into the authority for cross-service integration granted to the Secretary of Defense under the National Security Act of 1947, which consolidated the nation's armed services into a single department.

The point of the new system was to help the Secretary of Defense make decisions about the future size of the military, its force structure, weapons programs, operations, sustainment, military pay and benefits, and infrastructure based on explicit criteria of national strategy. Secretary McNamara and his staff saw PPBS as a tool of executive management that would help to unify the department and strengthen civilian control of the military.[4] The process ensured that key decisions about priorities and resource allocation would be made centrally within the department, rather than left solely to the individual services or to the compromises they might be able to strike among themselves.

The idea was to provide top-down national and departmental guidance early in the process—the planning phase; give the services the opportunity to develop their desired programs consistent with that guidance, and then have the Secretary make adjustments based on a program review run by the Office of the Secretary of Defense (OSD)—the programming phase; and finally, tune the programs to account for problems related to budget execution, and translate the department's databases into the categories and formats required for submission to Congress—the budgeting phase. The PPBS considered military requirements and costs simultaneously, and considered both the five-year costs and the future consequences of present decisions.[5]

Since the 1960s, the PPBS has undergone substantial modifications. The Goldwater–Nichols Act of 1986 introduced the voices of combatant commanders and the chairman of the Joint Chiefs of Staff (JCS) explicitly into the process. In 2003, DOD modified the system again and gave it a new name: the Planning, Programming, Budgeting, and Execution process (PPBE).[6] The Quadrennial Defense Review (QDR), first mandated by Congress in 1996 and now required near the beginning of each presidential term, is now an integral part of the planning phase of the process.[7] The process is likely to continue to change in the future.

This chapter describes the workings of the PPBE as of May 2009. It begins with a discussion of the organizations involved in the process. It then outlines in turn the activities involved in planning, programming, budgeting, and execution. The chapter ends with a brief concluding section that highlights some problems with the current arrangements.

Organizations Involved in DOD's Planning, Programming, Budgeting, and Execution Process

DOD is a massive and complex organization, with numerous players involved in the various aspects of control, leadership, planning, acquisition, operation, and sustainment of the nation's military (see Figure 5.1). The Army, Navy, Marine Corps, and Air Force—the armed services themselves—are the department's force providers. They organize, train, and equip the military units that make up the nation's fighting force. The services are organized into three military departments, each of which reports to the Secretary of Defense: the Department of the Army, Department of the Navy (which includes the Marine Corps), and the Department of the Air Force. In addition, the chiefs of the four services, together with a chairman chosen from one of the services, comprise the Joint Chiefs of Staff—which in turn is served by its own joint staff.

DOD military operations are conducted by the combatant commands, each headed by a combatant commander, or COCOM, who reports directly

Department of Defense

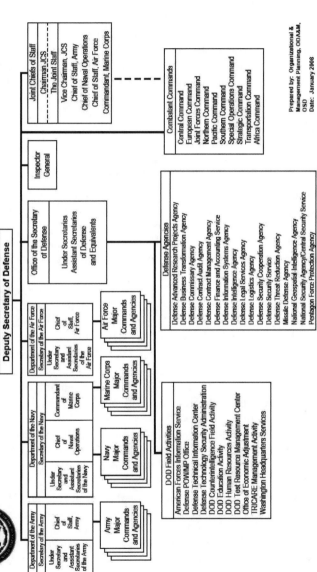

Figure 5.1 Organization of DOD as of January 2008 (source: US Department of Defense).

to the Secretary of Defense. In addition, 17 defense agencies and 11 field activities report through various Under Secretaries to the Secretary of Defense. The Secretary and Deputy Secretary of Defense are served by an internal staff of their own, the OSD.

OSD manages the PPBE for the Secretary and Deputy Secretary of Defense. The individual services, agencies, and field activities, the component commands, and the JCS also play important roles. As discussed in Chapter 8, DOD is unique among federal departments in that for decades, the White House Office of Management and Budget (OMB) has also participated directly in the programming and budgeting phases of Defense's internal process. This section discusses each of those entities in turn and highlights their respective roles in the system.

The Office of the Secretary of Defense

OSD is the staff of the Secretary of Defense. The office develops and articulates DOD policies and oversees their implementation by the services, agencies, and combatant commanders. OSD administers the PPBE. Most of OSD is organized into the offices of five Under Secretaries (see Figure 5.2). This section describes key offices within OSD and explains the parts they play in the PPBE.

Three OSD players hold especially important responsibilities in the PPBE: the Under Secretary of Defense for Policy (USD(P)), the Director of Program Analysis and Evaluation (D(PA&E)), and the DOD Comptroller (USD(C)). As the chief advisor to the Secretary of Defense on the formulation of national security and defense policy, USD(P) starts the PPBE ball rolling by articulating the defense strategy that resources are meant to support and by drafting the planning guidance that will serve as input to programming and budgeting. USD(P) also represents DOD on matters of policy in the White House and in the interagency processes.

PA&E plays multiple, crucial roles in the PPBE: it conducts analyses of alternatives to the programs proposed by the services and agencies; it prepares the fiscal guidance that allocates DOD's expected total budgets among the three military departments and the various defense agencies and field activities; it manages part of the planning phase that results in Joint Programming Guidance (JPG) to the services and other defense components; it leads the program review phase; and it designs, maintains, and populates the database that constitutes the Future-Years Defense Program, or FYDP.[8]

PA&E was established during the McNamara years as the Office of Systems Analysis, staffed by operations research analysts who came to be known as the Secretary's "whiz kids." PA&E still conducts cost–benefit analyses and trade-off studies to identify alternatives to service plans, programs, and budgets for consideration by the Secretary and Deputy Secretary of Defense.[9] PA&E is also the home of the Secretary's Cost Analysis Improvement Group (CAIG),

Office of the Secretary of Defense

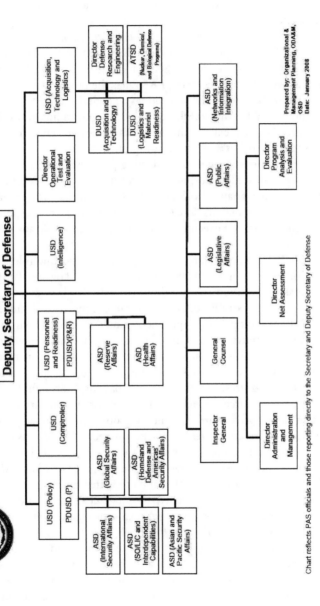

Secretary of Defense

Deputy Secretary of Defense

- USD (Policy)
  - PDUSD (P)
    - ASD (International Security Affairs)
    - ASD (SO/LIC and Interdependent Capabilities)
    - ASD (Asian and Pacific Security Affairs)
    - ASD (Global Security Affairs)
    - ASD (Homeland Defense and Americas' Security Affairs)
- USD (Comptroller)
- USD (Personnel and Readiness)
  - PDUSD(P&R)
    - ASD (Reserve Affairs)
    - ASD (Health Affairs)
- USD (Intelligence)
- Director Operational Test and Evaluation
- USD (Acquisition, Technology and Logistics)
  - Director Defense Research and Engineering
  - ATSD (Nuclear, Chemical, and Biological Defense Programs)
  - DUSD (Acquisition and Technology)
  - DUSD (Logistics and Materiel Readiness)
- Inspector General
- General Counsel
- Director Net Assessment
- ASD (Legislative Affairs)
- ASD (Public Affairs)
- ASD (Networks and Information Integration)
- Director Administration and Management
- Director Program Analysis and Evaluation

Chart reflects PAS officials and those reporting directly to the Secretary and Deputy Secretary of Defense

Prepared by: Organizational & Management Planning, OD A&M, OSD
Date: January 2008

Figure 5.2 Organization of OSD as of January 2008 (source: US Department of Defense, Office of the Secretary of Defense).

which develops independent estimates of the future costs of individual defense systems and programs.[10]

The director of PA&E serves as the executive secretary of two important cross-DOD governance committees: the Senior Leader Review Group (SLRG) and the Deputy's Advisory Working Group (DAWG). The SLRG is chaired by the Secretary of Defense, assisted by the chairman of the JCS; it advises the Secretary on the strategic priorities and directions of the department.[11] The DAWG is chaired by the Deputy Secretary and is the main review body for the PPBE.[12] As executive secretary, PA&E has the power of the pen: the office records the SLRG and DAWG meetings and drafts the Program Decision Memoranda (PDMs) that result from the programming effort. PDMs are binding directives that express the decisions of the Secretary and Deputy Secretary to add, cut, or reshape specific programs.

The Comptroller manages the budgeting phase of the PPBE and leads the fiscal accountability effort during the execution phase. The Comptroller is the department's chief financial officer and the Secretary's principal advisor on budgetary and fiscal matters. The Comptroller holds overall responsibility for budget formulation and execution and for the control of funds after budgets are approved.

Other OSD Under Secretaries play important supporting roles. The Under Secretary of Defense for Acquisition, Technology, and Logistics (USD(AT&L)) is the defense acquisition executive and runs the DOD's acquisition system, which intersects the PPBE but is not the same thing. The ultimate decisions about which technologies the department should pursue and which systems it will develop and purchase, on what schedule, are made through the acquisition system. Such decisions have important repercussions for the PPBE, and vice versa: even if a major system gets the green light through the acquisition system, it still needs to secure the money to pay for it through the PPBE; conversely, even if resources are allocated to a major system through the PPBE, the system cannot go forward without the proper acquisition approvals.

The Under Secretary of Defense for Personnel and Readiness (USD(P&R)) advises the Secretary on readiness and on the requirements for and management of personnel across the active-duty military, the Guard and Reserve, and DOD's civilian workforce. USD(P&R) participates in all phases of the PPBE to ensure that the number, quality, training, healthcare, and readiness of DOD personnel are consistent with national security and defense strategy.

The Under Secretary of Defense for Intelligence (USD(I)) is the Secretary's principal advisor on intelligence, counterintelligence, and homeland security. As discussed in Chapter 6, USD(I) is also the director of defense intelligence and the principal advisor to the director of national intelligence on intelligence matters in DOD. USD(I) participates in all phases of the PPBE to ensure that DOD's intelligence and counterintelligence resources match the national security and defense strategy.

Services, Agencies, and Field Activities

The armed services, defense agencies, and field activities—sometimes referred to as the components of DOD—participate in all phases of the PPBE. As will be described in the next section of this chapter, all are invited to make their wishes known as the defense strategy develops and as the planning and programming guidance are drafted during the planning phase. Each component draws up its own preferred five- or six-year plan, called a Program Objective Memorandum (POM), for defense programs under its purview. It also draws up its corresponding two-year budget plan, called a Budget Estimate Submission (BES). The collective POMs and BESs become the starting point for the DOD-wide development of programs and budgets that result during the programming and budgeting phase. The components also hold the first line of responsibility for program execution.

The Joint Chiefs of Staff

As the senior uniformed member of the armed forces, the chairman of the JCS has important roles in planning and programming. The chairman develops the National Military Strategy that feeds into the strategic planning guidance. He prepares a Chairman's Program Recommendation (CPR), which informs the joint programming guidance that ends the planning phase and kicks off the programming effort. During the programming phase, he has the opportunity to assess the service POMs through a Chairman's Program Assessment (CPA), provided to the Secretary of Defense and the SLRG.[13]

The joint staff participates throughout the PPBE. Within the joint staff, the directorate for force structure, resources, and assessments (J-8) coordinates the internal PPBE effort and serves as the main conduit into OSD, the services and defense agencies, and the combatant commands throughout the process. J-8 analyzes the COCOMs' integrated priority lists for the chairman of the JCS, with an eye toward recognizing shared concerns and identifying the top priorities among the COCOMs.

Like PA&E in OSD, the J-8 office conducts studies and tradeoff analyses to assess the potential costs and capabilities inherent in alternatives under consideration and to explore the consequences of potential changes to the budget. The J-8's tradeoff studies and risk assessments typically inform the National Military Strategy, the CPR, and the CPA.

The Combatant Commands

DOD's Unified Command Plan assigns a specific collection of missions and an area of geographic responsibility to each combatant command. For example, Northern Command is responsible for homeland defense of the United States; Central Command conducts exercises, coordination, and military operations in the geographic arc that runs from Egypt to Kazakhstan—including operations in Iraq, Afghanistan, and Pakistan.

The COCOMs provide input to every phase of the PPBE. Their most direct routine contributions are the Integrated Priority Lists (IPLs), which each COCOM submits individually each year. The IPL indicates the commander's top priorities and serves as input to the planning and programming phases. The COCOMs are also invited to prepare issue papers during the program review process, and can be invited to participate in meetings of the SLRG and the DAWG.[14]

In addition, the COCOMs make their wishes known through the chairman of the JCS as the National Military Strategy, strategic planning guidance, and joint programming guidance are developed. As the services develop their POMs, the COCOMs work through the service components of their own commands to promote the programs they want the services to undertake to organize, train, and equip the forces that the commands will use. The COCOMs also submit to the services the anticipated budgets for their own operations.[15]

The White House Office of Management and Budget

As discussed in Chapter 8, OMB's examiners participate side by side with OSD in the PPBE's program and budget reviews. The practice has advantages and disadvantages for both OMB and DOD, as that chapter details.

It goes without saying that each of the many civilian and military players has its own institutional preferences regarding the program and budget that result from the PPBE. The next section discusses the broad outlines of the PPBE.

The PPBE Process

A fundamental purpose of PPBE is to bring defense programs and budgets into line with national strategic goals. When Secretary McNamara introduced PPBS into the department, the National Security Council and the Secretary's OSD policy advisors were the main arbiters of strategy. The services were directed to develop their programs consistent with that guidance. PA&E (then called the Office of Systems Analysis) and the Comptroller conducted the program and budget reviews that brought potential alternatives to the attention of the Secretary, and the Secretary made decisions based on those alternatives.[16]

As highlighted in the previous section, numerous DOD players have important stakes in the outcome of the PPBE. As in any organization, there is always a tension between decisions made from the center and the achievement of compliance and cooperation in the execution of those decisions by the rest of the department. Over the years, successive Secretaries of Defense have modified PPBE to expand the roles of other key players in every phase.

Those who favor those modifications say that the current process helps DOD's leaders build consensus by considering the concerns of key organizations. Other observers argue that the push for consensus defeats the purpose of the system as initially envisioned; what was once a top-down process to provide information and alternatives to the Secretary is now a service-driven process that promotes logrolling among the components and reinforces the status quo. To be sure, nobody seems happy with the process as currently practiced. Participants from both OSD and the components complain that the process is complex and time-consuming and its results unimpressive.[17]

To get ready to play in the PPBE, the services, defense agencies, and combatant commands typically begin their programming and budget formulation well before OSD sends them the policy or fiscal guidance meant to shape their choices. Thus each organization in the process has its own view of where and when the process begins. This section looks at PPBE from the point of view of OSD.

In recent years, OSD has generally run PPBE on a two-year cycle.[18] The process that will lead to the program and budget for an even fiscal year (FY), such as FY 2012, is called the on-year process. The process that will result in an odd-year budget is denoted off-year. In the on years, DOD runs a complete PPBE that results in a six-year program and budget, called the Future-Years Defense Program. (The schematic in Figure 5.3 illustrates the broad outlines of the PPBE aimed at an on-year budget.) The off-year process is leaner, making adjustments to the previous year's on-year programs and budgets only where they are necessary to reflect unforeseen events or new information. The next four sections describe in turn the activities and products of planning, programming, budgeting, and execution for the PPBE directed at an on-year program and budget.

The Planning Phase

The planning phase represents the first step in the PPBE.[19] Its purpose is to provide all of the actors in the process with the strategic, policy, and fiscal guidance they will need to develop and tune the programs and budgets that are the fundamental products of the PPBE.

The overall planning, programming, and budgeting parts of the process can take nearly two years. Congress typically takes another eight months to pass the associated authorization and appropriation measures. Thus, the planning phase in DOD typically starts nearly three years before the budget year in question (see Figure 5.3 and Table 5.1). For example, the planning phase for FY 2008, which began on October 1, 2007, started early in 2005.

The USD(P) is the Secretary's principal advisor for this phase of the process. His or her office runs the planning process and drafts the strategic and policy guidance that the Secretary will sign. PA&E and the Comptroller develop the fiscal guidance that sets limits on the size of the budget that each

On-year PPBE process

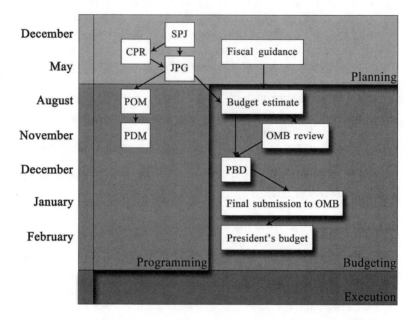

Figure 5.3 DOD's PPBE process directed toward a one-year (even-year) budget (source: Graphic by Miranda Priebe, based on DOD and CRS sources).

Notes
CPR: Chairman's program recommendation; JPG: Joint Programming Guidance; OMB: Office of Management and Budget; PBD: Program Budget Decision; PDM: Program Decision Memorandum; SPG: Strategic Planning Guidance.

service and defense agency will be permitted to submit. All of the DOD organizations discussed in the previous section play some role in the planning phase.

Defense Planning in the White House

Defense planning actually begins in the White House, with the development of the National Security Strategy of the United States by the National Security Council (see Chapter 8).[20] The National Security Strategy is meant to articulate the nation's "worldwide interests, goals, and objectives"; outline its foreign policy commitments and defense capabilities; explain how the administration proposes to use the various tools of statecraft, including political and economic tools as well as military ones, to achieve its security aims; and evaluate the balance among those tools.[21]

Table 5.1 DOD's PPBE for FY 2008: planning phase

Completion dates	End product	Key players
December 2005	Strategic Planning Guidance: strategy, priorities, broad guidance for capabilities (consistent with National Security Strategy, QDR, National Military Strategy)	SLRG and COCOMs (working together as the Strategic Planning Council); signed by Secretary of Defense
April 2006	Fiscal guidance to services	OSD PA&E, with Comptroller
May 2006	Joint Programming Guidance: fiscally constrained, detailed guidance on capabilities and programs (consistent with QDR, Strategic Planning Guidance)	SLRG and COCOMs (working together as the Strategic Planning Council); signed by Secretary of Defense

Source: Table by Miranda Priebe based on DOD and CRS sources.

DOD Strategy Documents and the QDR

Within DOD, the planning phase begins with development of the National Defense Strategy and the conduct of the Quadrennial Defense Review (QDR) in OSD and the preparation of the National Military Strategy in the JCS (see Table 5.1). The DOD documents ostensibly flow from the National Security Strategy.[22] The White House strategy is often late, however, in which case DOD develops its documents without benefit of the overarching national strategy.[23]

The National Defense Strategy is prepared by the office of USD(P) and signed by the Secretary. It generally does at the department level what the National Security Strategy does at the national level. It describes the strategic environment and DOD's objectives and explains in broad terms how DOD hopes to achieve those objectives.

Congress mandated the first QDR in 1996 and now requires that a report on the review be submitted concurrent with the budget in the February following the first year of each presidential term.[24] The QDR is meant to spell out the full chain from strategies to budgets—starting with the threat environment and strategic priorities, articulating the force structure, programs, and infrastructure that will be needed, and estimating the resources that will be required to sustain them—for a period of two decades. Of the three QDR reports submitted to Congress between 1997 and 2009, however, only the first one discusses the level of resources needed to carry out the planned strategy.[25]

The Strategic Planning Guidance

Using those documents as a foundation, the office of USD(P) works with members of the SLRG and the COCOMs to draft the Strategic Planning Guidance (SPG), which provides more specific policy guidance for the coming six-year period than the QDR or the National Defense Strategy.[26] The SPG communicates the Secretary's top priorities, information about risk tolerance in the department's various theaters and mission areas, and broad guidance related to the military and business capabilities that the upcoming program and budget are meant to support.[27]

The SPG is intended to be "resource informed"—meaning that it should not call for capabilities that would be unaffordable in the context of likely future defense budgets and numbers of personnel, and that the risk levels it identifies should be generally consistent with realistic budgets. It is not "resource constrained"—meaning it does not tote up the full costs of its strategic choices and limit them for each service based on an estimated topline. The official schedule calls for the SPG to be signed by December, about two years before the start of the fiscal year in question, but it is often late.[28]

Fiscal Guidance to the Components

To develop their proposed programs and budgets, the components need to know how much money they will have to work with. The fiscal guidance communicates to each service and defense agency the topline to which it should program for a six-year period.

PA&E and the Comptroller develop the fiscal guidance based on the topline guidance DOD receives from OMB early in the calendar year. Preparing the guidance is an art, because those who develop it are squeezed between the White House on the one hand and the DOD components on the other. The guidance is meant to reflect national and departmental priorities that may have changed significantly, yet the services scrutinize it closely for any change in the share of the budget they will receive.

The Joint Programming Guidance

With the SPG and the fiscal guidance in hand, the department is ready to prepare the Joint Programming Guidance (JPG). The JPG is more specific and more direct than the SPG. It instructs the services and various OSD players to include work on specific capabilities within their programs and to fund them in their budgets. The JPG may highlight areas of special interest to the Secretary. It may also establish metrics and goals for individual capabilities and programs, and call upon the services and other entities to work toward and report on them.[29] The JPG is fiscally constrained in the sense that each component should be able to carry out its guidance within the budget it anticipates.

To be effective, the resource allocation process for a complex organization needs to include opportunities for leaders at the center to consider alternatives to the status quo as well as tradeoffs among the various preferences of the organizational components. Who conducts the alternative studies and at what point their results enter into the process are important questions in the design of any resource allocation system.

A single office at the center, like PA&E in OSD, is in a good position to conduct analyses that are coherent and relatively free of the institutional biases of the components. On the other hand, such an office often lacks the detailed information available at the component level, and the components may be so skeptical of its results that achieving their compliance with the resulting decisions becomes an uphill battle. In organizations where the top leaders have the final say, that might not be a problem; the central decision-maker can fire those who do not comply and move on. In the DOD, firing is clearly an option, but disaffected components have multiple opportunities to get decisions overturned by the White House or Congress, or simply to wait for a new Secretary of Defense to come along. Since the inception of PPBS in the 1960s, DOD has increasingly drawn the components and ultimately the COCOMs into the conduct of such analytic studies.

The timing of tradeoff studies has also shifted. For decades, the tradeoff studies meant to inform decisions at the Secretary's level were conducted as part of the program review, rather than during the planning phase. The advent of the QDR and its institutionalization as part of the PPBE changed that. The QDR was positioned as part of the planning process, and tradeoff studies were meant to inform the Secretary's decisions during that review. Tradeoff studies continue as an important part of the programming phase.

Between 2002 and 2006, Secretary of Defense Donald Rumsfeld further changed the PPBE to shift much of the assessment of alternatives to the front end of the PPBE. To inform the JPG, OSD instituted a continuous analytic process for identifying and assessing alternatives and tradeoffs. That analytic process was organized around nine broad "capability portfolios," namely command and control, battlespace awareness, network-centric operations, logistics, building partnerships, force protection, force support, force application, and corporate management support.

Each capability portfolio had a pair of civilian and uniformed Capability Portfolio Managers (CPMs), who co-managed the portfolio.[30] The work of the CPMs was reviewed by the DAWG, generally made up of the principal deputies of the members of the SLRG. In theory, recommendations from the CPMs feed into the JPG.

Decisions on the various capability portfolios can be made throughout the year as analytic results become ready. The portfolio management process appears not to have worked well, however. Recommendations developed through the process were not timely or significant enough to play a useful role in shaping the programming guidance. Early indications are that the Obama administration may end the practice of organizing analyses around these portfolios.[31]

The USD(P) and PA&E draft the JPG. The Chairman of the JCS may also offer separate advice regarding the JPG to the Secretary through the Chairman's Program Recommendation. The JPG is reviewed by the SLRG and the COCOMs and then prepared by USD(P) and PA&E for the Secretary's signature.

The Secretary is meant to sign the JPG by May, some nine months before the budget will be delivered to Congress and 16 months before the beginning of the fiscal year to which the guidance pertains. This guidance is often several months late, however, thus shortening the time available for the programming and budgeting activities discussed in the next sections. Finally, OSD prepares detailed instructions for the next phases of the PPBE, including data formats and due dates for the services to provide their programming and budgeting requests.

Programming Activities

DOD uses the programming process to turn guidance into a five-year (in the off years) or six-year (in the on years) program, the FYDP.[32] The FYDP lists DOD's programs line by line, and identifies the funds it will request on each line for each of the five or six years.

Until Secretary of Defense Rumsfeld changed the PPBS and renamed it the PPBE, programming and budgeting were largely sequential processes that together took about eight months. In the PPBE as practiced today, programming and budgeting are meant to occur in parallel during a far shorter period. Nevertheless, their products and processes are still largely distinct (see Table 5.2).

Programming by the Services and Defense Agencies

In theory, programming begins after the services and defense agencies receive their fiscal guidance and the Secretary signs the JPG. In practice, if the components wait for those products of the planning phase to be signed, they will not have time to accomplish all the work that goes into preparing their requests. Instead, they start building their program and budget databases as early as October, about two full years before the start of the fiscal year in question and ten months before it is scheduled for submission to OSD—in other words, months before the formal guidance arrives. The components then adjust them as needed after they receive the guidance and instructions from OSD.

The components each build two databases: a Program Objective Memorandum (POM) and a Budget Estimate Submission (BES). The POM includes six years of data, organized by program—the format in which OSD reviews

Table 5.2 DOD's PPBE for FY 2008: programming and budgeting phases

Completion dates	End product	Key players
August 2006	Program Objective Memoranda, Budget Estimate Submissions	Services, Defense Agencies, Field Activities
December 2006	Budget Review, Culminating in Program Budget Decisions (PBDs) to Services	OSD Comptroller; Secretary of Defense
December 2006	Program Review, culminating in Program Decision Memoranda (PDMs) to Services	OSD PA&E, JCS; Secretary of Defense
January 2007	President's Budget and Future Years Defense Program (FYDP) to OMB	OSD
February 2007	President's Budget and Future Years Defense Program (FYDP) to Congress	OMB

Source: Table by Miranda Priebe based on DOD and CRS sources.

the program. The BES includes only two years—the budget year and one year beyond—and is organized by appropriation title and account, the format in which Congress will ultimately view the President's request.

The line-item unit in the program (or POM) view is referred to as a program element (PE). For example, one program element for the Air Force is PE 0207138F, F-22A Squadrons; it is the upgrade program for already-purchased F-22 fighter aircraft. Another Air Force example is 0604800F, Joint Strike Fighter Engineering and Manufacturing Development, which is the development program for the F-35 Joint Strike Fighter.[33] The program elements are grouped into 11 major force programs, or MFPs (see Table 5.3).

Units in the appropriations (or BES) view are the appropriation titles and accounts that Congress requires and uses as it considers the budget. For example, the F-22A squadrons in the example above fall into Appropriation 3600F: Research, Development, Test, and Evaluation, Air Force.[34] The appropriation accounts are grouped into appropriation titles (see Table 5.4).

In its POM, each service typically rank-orders its program elements, based on its own preferences as well as the strategic and programming guidance expected from the Secretary of Defense. When that guidance arrives, the service makes adjustments as it sees fit. After OSD's fiscal guidance arrives, the component chops the POM into two stacks: the higher-ranking programs that can be afforded under the fiscal guidance, and those at the bottom of the

Table 5.3 DOD FY 2008 base budget request by program

Program number	Program name	FY 2008 defense request ($ in billions)
01	Strategic forces	10.4
02	General purpose forces	189.1
03	C3, intelligence, and space	72.1
04	Mobility forces	13.4
05	Guard and Reserve forces	36.0
06	Research and development	49.9
07	Central supply and maintenance	21.5
08	Training, medical, and other	63.5
09	Administrative and associated activities	14.2
10	Support of other nations	2.1
11	Special operations forces	9.2
	Total	481.6

Source: Author's table based on *National Defense Budget Estimates for FY 2008* (also called the Green Book), DOD Office of the Undersecretary (Comptroller), Table 6.1, www.defenselink.mil/comptroller/Docs/fy2008_greenbook.pdf.

Notes
C3 is command, control, and communications.
Budget figures reflect total obligational authority (TOA).
Figures may not add to total due to rounding.

Table 5.4 DOD FY 2008 base budget request by appropriation account

Appropriation title	FY 2008 defense request ($ in billions)
Military Personnel	116.3
Operation and Maintenance (O&M)	164.7
Procurement	101.7
Research, Development, Testing, and Evaluation (RDT&E)	75.1
Military Construction	18.2
Family Housing	3.1
Revolving and Management Funds	2.4
Total	481.6

Source: Author's table based on *National Defense Budget Estimates for FY 2008* (also called the Green Book), DOD Office of the Undersecretary (Comptroller), Table 6.4, www.defenselink.mil/comptroller/Docs/fy2008_greenbook.pdf.

Notes
Budget figures reflect total obligational authority (TOA).
Figures may not add to total due to rounding.

rank-ordered list, which it cannot afford unless OSD revises the fiscal guidance. The top stack of programs is often referred to as "above-the-line," and the residual stack as "below-the-line." The service keeps track of the below-the-line programs in case more money becomes available later.

The Program Review

These days, the components submit their POMs and BESs electronically, feeding them directly into databases run by the Comptroller and PA&E. PA&E then begins a program review, and the Comptroller runs a budget review. Current arrangements call for these reviews to take about ten weeks. In recent years, however, tardy guidance documents and late POM and BES submissions by the services shortened even further the time allotted for the reviews.

PA&E leads the program review and drafts the PDMs that result from it. Any member of the SLRG can identify an issue for discussion. Issues enter the discussion as issue papers. The chairman of the JCS may also provide his own Chairman's Program Assessment (CPA) at this stage, indicating whether service programs comply with guidance and meet the needs of the combatant commands. As discussed in Chapter 8, OMB budget examiners may also participate during this stage of the process.

Issues can be raised because a POM appears not to support the SPG or JPG, or because another office identifies a more cost-effective alternative to delivering a capability similar to one that is offered in one of the POMs. Sometimes issue papers offer ways to deal with emerging threats or opportunities.

Each issue paper includes a discussion of the advantages and disadvantages of the proposed alternatives as compared with the POM. It also includes an estimate of the costs of the alternative as compared to the POM over the six-year period that the POM covers. Alternatives that would increase spending typically require offsets whose costs total to the amount added, so that each issue paper is internally budget-neutral.

Sometimes an issue can be settled between the office that raises it and the component whose POM is involved. In that case, the concerned office and the component write up and sign a deal, and the issue is resolved as a so-called "out of court settlement."[35] Issues that cannot be settled out of court are distributed to issue teams whose participants are drawn from offices of SLRG members with an interest in the issue. (OMB examiners may also be invited to participate.) The issue teams refine the analyses and options that underlie the issue paper. The costs, benefits, and risks associated with those options are then presented at a meeting of the SLRG.

At an SLRG meeting on the program review, members have an opportunity to make their cases to the Deputy Secretary, who typically runs the meeting. The group deliberates, and the Deputy Secretary makes a decision, which is recorded by PA&E in a draft PDM. The components get an opportunity to challenge PA&E's write-up, after which the final version goes to the Deputy Secretary for decision and signature.

SLRG meetings on program issues are meant to be held relatively early in the fall, giving OSD a few months to complete development of the program and budget before the submission to Congress in February. In recent years, they have often been deferred until late in the calendar year, with PDMs deferred until November or December.

During the first year of Secretary McNamara's PPBS, the program review took up matters of great national consequence and resulted in a substantial shift of resources among the services' nuclear programs.[36] In the decades since, the issues treated in the program review gradually narrowed, and the resulting resource shifts shrank. Participants in the process complain that the program review has devolved to much ado about nothing—a lot of work on issues of low import, resulting in small shifts of funding.[37]

Budgeting Activities

Through the budgeting process, DOD finishes its work on the two-year budget and prepares it for submission to Congress. As arranged by Secretary of Defense Rumsfeld, budgeting runs concurrently with programming. As with programming, the process begins within the services and defense agencies. The OSD Comptroller and OMB then run a budget review. The budget review is meant to begin during August and to end early in December, two months before the budget is submitted to Congress in February. Budgeting results in the budget itself and in multiple Program Budget Decisions (PBDs) prepared by the Comptroller or OMB and typically signed by the Deputy Secretary of Defense.

Budgeting in the Services and Defense Agencies

As discussed in the previous section, the components develop two-year BESs—their budgeting products—as they prepare their five-year or six-year POMs. In contrast to the POMs, which are organized by program, the BESs are organized by appropriation title and account, the format in which Congress will view the President's budget. The components submit their BESs electronically to OSD at the same time that they transmit their POMs.

The OSD/OMB Budget Review

With the BESs in hand, the office of the DOD Comptroller leads a budget review. As the PPBS was designed during the 1960s, the program review focused on policy issues, while the budget review concentrated on financial matters. The budget review turned to policy matters only when a new threat or other new information arose. Over the years, that distinction was blurred, and many of the issues raised during the budget review fell into the policy realm.

A modern example was Secretary of Defense Rumsfeld's decision to increase DOD's effort in the area of biological defense. During the PPBE for FY 2006–11 (conducted in 2004), the Secretary directed the expansion of such work. The decision was one of major policy import that affected billions of dollars in spending. Yet the decision to expand and the program offsets needed to fund the expansion were formalized not in a program review PDM but in a budget review PBD.[38]

Although policy issues may be raised during the budget review, financial issues are its centerpiece. Budget analysts from the Comptroller's office, together with budget examiners from OMB, take particular interest in four aspects of the components' budgets.[39] The most important of these is budget execution—whether the program has spent the current year's money according to the schedule anticipated.[40] Other important areas of review are program pricing—whether the budgets for individual programs reflect their most likely costs; program phasing—whether the budgets for those programs are properly matched to the acquisition schedules that were approved through the acquisition process; and compliance with funding policies—whether the budget reflects current congressional, White House, and DOD guidance related to the funding in the various appropriation categories.[41]

The budget review begins with a round of "advance questions" to the services and defense agencies from the office of the Comptroller.[42] Based on the written responses to those questions, the Comptroller's budget analysts may conduct hearings with appropriate staff members from the components and OSD.[43] The Comptroller's budget analysts then draft Program Budget Decisions (PBDs) recommending adjustments to the two-year BESs. The services and defense agencies are offered a brief window in which to disagree, or "reclama," after which the budget analyst prepares the final version for decision and signature by the Deputy Secretary.[44]

Pulling the Data Together

As things currently work, the services and defense agencies must then adjust their program and budget databases to reflect the changes made during the program and budget reviews. They translate the various adjustments as needed into appropriation figures for Congress and program elements for internal use, and prepare final versions of their detailed budget justification documents. Upon receipt of the components' electronic transmissions, PA&E and the Comptroller staff develop the FYDP based on the POMs and the President's Budget (PB) based on the BESs.

OSD is working on a new data-collection system that will automate and combine some of the steps that today are handled in piecemeal fashion at the component level. Each service and defense agency will provide its POM and BES data through a single submission, before the program and budget reviews begin. OSD will then keep track of all adjustments made during the two reviews and update the database as needed to complete the preparation of the FYDP and the PB.[45]

Transmittal to the White House and Congress

After OSD completes the preparation of the PB, it sends it electronically to OMB. As discussed earlier in this chapter, White House oversight at this point differs substantially from the practice vis-à-vis other departments and agencies. Because OMB's budget examiners participate side by side with OSD in DOD's internal processes, OMB typically forgoes the reviews and passbacks (instructions for adjustments) that are key tools of White House oversight for other federal entities.

As a result, in recent decades OMB has generally permitted DOD to submit its budget request late in December, rather than in September as is common for other agencies. OMB's budget examiners are not entirely happy with that arrangement, however. In recent years, OMB has instructed DOD to submit its program and budget earlier, with the expectation of a subsequent review and passback.[46] As of May 2009, DOD's practice has not changed: the PB is passed electronically into OMB's database late in December, just in time to be folded into the President's budget request to Congress.

By the first Monday in February, about eight months before the beginning of the first fiscal year at which the budget is directed, the White House sends the President's request for the entire federal budget to Congress. Finalizing the FYDP is more complex, and DOD has until April to submit it to Congress.[47]

The Execution Phase

Execution encompasses all of the program and budget activities that follow the appropriation of funds by Congress. The first year of execution is the fiscal year for which the budget was developed. Execution activities continue in later years, as the services carry out the programs for which Congress allotted those funds.

The point of renaming the PPBS as the PPBE in 2003 was to shine a light on the performance of DOD's programs as they are executed. The management directive that formalized that reform calls for the development of performance metrics that will become the "analytical underpinning" by which the department's functions and programs will be judged.[48] The goal is to establish measures indicative of the degree to which strategy and objectives are actually achieved—so-called outcome measures—rather than the level of effort devoted to them—so-called input measures. This section describes

DOD's execution review in the context of wider federal reforms aimed at improving the links between performance and budget. It ends with a brief discussion of the financial side of execution and some accounting terms that come up during execution.

The Execution Review

Once such metrics are in place, the services and defense agencies are meant to collect information and report periodically on progress toward the goals that they establish. The 2003 management directive calls for the Comptroller and PA&E to run an execution review, concurrent with the budget and program reviews. The budgets of programs that fail to meet their performance goals are then meant to be adjusted.

DOD's emphasis on execution performance is in part a response to a broad push within government to link budgets more closely to performance. To illuminate the ideas behind the recent DOD reform, the next section briefly describes the wider federal effort.

Recent Federal Initiatives to Improve Budget-Performance Integration

Improving the links between performance and budgets was a major area of emphasis during the administrations of George H.W. Bush, Bill Clinton, and George W. Bush. As discussed in Chapter 8, the first Bush administration pushed for the Government Performance and Results Act (GPRA), which was introduced in Congress during the late 1980s and then championed by the Clinton administration.[49] Passed in 1993, GPRA requires all federal agencies to prepare five-year strategic plans, annual performance plans, and annual performance reports.[50] The performance reports are meant to explain how well actual performance measures up to the plan and what the agency will do to narrow the gap between plans and performance.[51]

The George W. Bush administration undertook its own reforms, including the Program Assessment Rating Tool (PART), a rating system built around a collection of questionnaires that elicit information about the purpose, strategic planning, management, and results of efforts in all federal departments and agencies.[52] During the Bush administration, budget examiners in OMB worked with the agencies, including DOD, to develop the metrics based on which programs would be judged and conduct the PART assessments. Early indications are that the Obama administration will continue to use PART in some form.[53]

Early assessments of progress by other organizations toward such integration are mixed. Observers generally find that the choice of outcome measures can be politicized;[54] information about genuine outcomes can be hard to come by;[55] and even when such information is available and well documented, budgets may not be adjusted to account for it.[56] Clearly, information about performance during execution is not a miracle cure for all budget ills, and performance information cannot be used mechanistically to translate into resource allocation decisions.[57] Nonetheless, performance measurements can be an important source of information to be weighed together with the strategic and political considerations that go into the development of programs and budgets.

DOD's emphasis on performance is in part a response to the GPRA and PART requirements and the wider push toward budget-performance integration in management circles. Participants and observers say that the hopes for such integration have not been realized.[58] It is not clear whether any defense programs have been adjusted through the execution review—either by adding money to fix their performance problems or reducing budgets and canceling programs because they are underperforming—in the context of the non-financial side of the execution review.

The Financial Side of Execution

As discussed in the section on the budget review, the Comptroller is also deeply interested in the financial performance of programs as they are executed. The Comptroller looks at financial execution through a variety of lenses and works with the services to translate between them.

The annual appropriation acts provide the DOD with Budget Authority (BA), that is, the authority to enter into obligations for the department's various programs.[59] The amount DOD actually has available may differ from what Congress provides for a given year, however. This can happen when BA lapses before the department incurs the obligations associated with it, when Congress extends the period during which funds may be used through a reappropriation, and for other reasons.[60] In recognition of the fact that the direct funding authority that DOD has may differ from what Congress provided in annual BA, the department uses an internal accounting term, Total Obligational Authority (TOA).[61] In most years, TOA and BA are nearly the same.

Obligations can take the form of contracts, orders, hiring agreements, or other commitments.[62] The actual spending of the obligated funds is called expenditure, and the funds expended are referred to as outlays (see Table 5.5 for a comparison of DOD TOA, BA, and outlays in the President's budget request for FY 2009).

Outlays typically lag BA, because many programs take multiple years to complete. For example, the BA to build a Navy ship typically results in outlays over a six-year period. For a ship that Congress authorized for FY 2009, DOD expects to expend only about 18 percent of the BA in FY 2009. The department expects outlays for that ship in FY 2010 to come to 25 percent of the total BA, and to spend most of the remaining 57 percent of BA between FY 2011 and FY 2014.[63]

Table 5.5 DOD FY 2009 budget request by title *(FY 2009 dollars in billions)*

Title	TOA	BA	Outlays
Military Personnel	125	129	129
Operation and Maintenance	180	180	213
Procurement	104	104	113
RDT&E	80	80	76
Military Construction	21	21	14
Family Housing	3	3	3
Revolving and Management Funds	3	2	2
Trust and Other		−1	−1
Total	517	518	551

Source: US Department of Defense, Office of the Undersecretary of Defense (Comptroller), *National Defense Budget Estimates for FY 2009* (Greenbook), updated September 2008.

One of the most important challenges in execution is to ensure that programs obligate and expend their BA as anticipated. When obligations or expenditures fall below expectations, the problem may be outside the control of the program manager. For example, new information about threats may obviate the requirements that underlie the program, or a production contract might be put on hold because of a natural disaster or a labor strike. Often the failure to obligate and expend on schedule signals a problem, however. Thus the components' own financial managers and the Comptroller's budget analysts keep a close eye throughout the year on both of these measures. Any problems in these two areas become fodder for the budget review for the next fiscal year.

Conclusion

DOD arguably has the strongest, most mature, and most forward-looking processes for planning and resource allocation of all the departments and agencies involved in security and international affairs. The DOD's procedures may also be the most complex of those processes in federal government today.

The PPBE as practiced today gives a department whose programmatic and budgetary decisions could otherwise be completely unwieldy an orderly way to think about its top priorities, to tie programs and budgets to strategies, to draw the links between requirements and costs, and to consider the performance of existing programs before sending more money their way. It provides mechanisms to consider the multiple-year costs of immediate decisions. These are all positive features.

The process is centralized in the sense that the Secretary and Deputy Secretary of Defense make the final decisions about strategy, forces, programs, and budgets. It is decentralized in the sense that the services, defense agencies, and field agencies—the department's components—take the first crack at their own programs and budgets, and their decisions generally stand. The system is highly consensual. The main OSD players, joint staff, service chiefs and secretaries, defense agency heads, and COCOMs have multiple opportunities to contribute to planning documents and to the program, budget, and execution reviews. Even after the Secretary or Deputy Secretary voices decisions during a meeting of the senior leader review group, nearly everyone involved gets a final chance to lodge a formal protest about the decision or the way it is written up.

Nevertheless, the system as practiced today raises some concerns, as discussed briefly in the following sections.

Problems with the Planning Process

The planning process is meant to lay the strategic foundation for defense programs and budgets. DOD's planning should flow from the National Security Strategy, but that document is often released too late to have an effect. That makes it all the more important that the DOD's own strategic documents—including the National Defense Strategy, the National Military Strategy, and the report of the Quadrennial Defense Review—reflect national priorities as well as the constraints of the real world.

The National Defense Strategy and National Military Strategy do not consider the resources that will be required for implementation. The QDR, in contrast, is meant to spell out the full chain from strategies to budgets for a period of two decades. The law specifically mandates that the review address the resources that will be required to carry out the strategy and programs envisioned. The QDRs conducted during the George W. Bush administration did not do that. Lacking at the outset of the process any clear understanding of the future costs of its policy choices, the department has little incentive to set genuine priorities and make the tough choices that are a hallmark of sound strategy. The QDR could help the Secretary of Defense establish firm, long-term linkages from strategic priorities into programs and budgets—but only if future Secretaries restore its mandated resource component.

In the National Defense Authorization Act for fiscal year 2003, Congress changed the timing of the QDR from September during the first year of a presidential term to the February of the second year. The adjustment made sense at the time. QDRs are a lot of work, and a new administration may not even have all of its staff in place until the summer, leaving only a few months to complete the review and write the report.

Unfortunately, the February delivery makes the QDR too late to affect policy and budgetary choices during the first year of the administration; and the first year often sets the tone for the Secretary's relationship with the components throughout the presidential term. During the first year of the Obama administration, Secretary of Defense Robert Gates made key decisions about the department's future force structure, equipment, and infrastructure outside of the QDR or the formal PPBE. For the QDR to have its intended effect in integrating strategy, programs, and budgets, it probably makes sense to restore a September due date.

To inform the JPG, OSD now runs a continuous analytic process, organized around nine "capability portfolios," to identify alternatives and tradeoffs for filling gaps and meeting the needs of the department. The practice of organizing the front-end analytic work around capability portfolios also seems not to be working well, and it appears that the Obama administration will change it.

The programming guidance is often several months late, thus shortening even further the time available for programming and budgeting. To be effective, the capability analyses need to be brought to conclusion in time to affect the guidance, and the programming guidance must be signed by the Secretary and delivered to the components in time for them to build their POMs and BESs around it.

Problems in Programming and Budgeting

During the first year of Secretary McNamara's PPBS, the program review took up matters of great national consequence and resulted in substantial shifts of resources. In the decades since, the issues treated in the program review gradually narrowed, and the resulting resource shifts shrank. Participants in the process complain that the program review has devolved to much ado about nothing—a lot of work on issues of low import, resulting in small shifts of funding.

Shortening the programming and budgeting phases and running them concurrently, as DOD did beginning in 2003, makes sense in theory. The tighter schedule for the back end could free time at the front of the cycle to conduct the tradeoff studies and elicit key policy choices from the Secretary early in the game, so that all participants in the PPBE march to the same drummer through programming and budgeting.

In practice, things are not working as well as they should. The capability-based alternative studies meant to inform the JPG have not teed the ball up for key decisions by the Secretary. The late delivery of the JPG means that the services and defense agencies make most of their own decisions before they receive the guidance meant to shape their plans. The program and budget reviews are compressed even further than envisioned, leaving very little time for the development and analysis of alternatives. Insiders say that running the program and budget reviews concurrently leads to an inefficient and confusing cycle that feeds budget decisions back into program deliberations and vice versa.[64] SLRG meetings on program issues are deferred until late in the calendar year, leaving no time for White House review.

Both the level of import of the issues considered and the time to review them need to be raised if the PPBE is to be effective in the future. Expanding the time for program and budget review will require trimming the time allotted to planning. Raising the import of the alternatives under consideration will be harder, and may require moving to a less consensual process than the one in place today. Such a move may be crucial if defense budgets are tightened in the future to help reduce federal deficits and alleviate the mounting federal debt.

Little Gained from the Focus on Performance

DOD ostensibly established the execution review to improve budget-performance integration. The hopes for such integration do not seem to have been realized, however. It is not clear that any major defense programs have been adjusted through the execution review—either by adding money to fix their performance problems or reducing budgets and canceling programs because they are underperforming—in the context of the non-financial side of the execution review.

The Obama administration has made program performance a centerpiece of its management agenda. The FY 2010 budget request put forward by Secretary Gates calls for canceling several weapon systems and trimming others based on their poor track records in acquisition. If the PPBE is to have any teeth in the future, it needs to be adjusted so that such decisions can be made routinely in the context of the execution review.

The PPBE Can Be Improved

DOD's PPBE may be one of the better planning and resource allocation systems in use in the federal government, but there is much room for improvement. Participants from both OSD and the components generally say that the system creates huge amounts of work for everyone involved, but results in few significant changes to component plans.[65] In its current collaborative form, it seems better suited to preserving the status quo than to changing policy through the budgetary tool.

For decades, the department has made most of its big decisions about programs and budgets outside of the PPBE structure. Most of the decisions about what to cut during the post-Cold War downsizing of the military during the late 1980s and early 1990s were made through informal compacts between the services and OSD and later justified through JCS and OSD reviews conducted outside of the PPBS. Secretary Rumsfeld made the decision to expand DOD's role in biological defense largely outside of the PPBE, though he used the PPBE to refine the plan and identify programs that could be reduced to offset the cost of the new initiative. Secretary Gates made crucial decisions about the FY 2010 budget—the first for the Obama administration—before the PPBE or the QDR got under way in earnest.

As discussed in Chapter 10, the nation's security choices are often shaped not through rational processes like the PPBE but by political and institutional forces. This is to be expected. Nevertheless, a disciplined, rational process can help leaders establish priorities and make important choices among the alternatives they face. If strengthened and valued, PPBE can be such a tool.

Chapter 6

Intelligence Planning and Budgeting

Introduction

Intelligence planning and budgeting is complex. The complexities grow out of the dispersed institutional architecture of the Intelligence Community (IC), the overlap in responsibilities among these institutions, and the dominant role played by the Department of Defense (DOD). There are 16 agencies and offices in the IC that collect, analyze, or disseminate intelligence. This includes agencies that manage intelligence collection and dissemination, as well as agencies that analyze their own intelligence along with that gathered by others.[1] Some of the organizations engage in similar intelligence gathering activities, but for different clients.[2] The missions and responsibilities of these organizations frequently overlap, leading to complex management, planning, and budgetary challenges.[3] At the same time, the majority of intelligence programs and roughly 80 percent of the budgetary resources are concentrated in the DOD, giving that organization a dominant role in mission and resource planning.

Over the decades since the creation of the Central Intelligence Agency (CIA) in the National Security Act of 1947 there have been numerous efforts to organize the IC institutions and budgeting in a more centralized and coordinated way. These efforts culminated in the creation of the Office of the Director of National Intelligence (ODNI) in 2004, in the wake of the terrorist attacks of 9/11. It remains unclear whether the new ODNI architecture will succeed in bringing more coherence to the structures and processes in the IC.[4]

Intelligence responsibilities and budgets are grouped into two major categories, relating to the focus of the agency's intelligence activity and the customer being served: the National Intelligence Program (NIP) and the Military Intelligence Program (MIP). The NIP supports national policy priorities and includes national-level collection and analysis of national security intelligence, whether the source of the intelligence is foreign or domestic. The customer is primarily the broad national security and foreign policy community in the government. The Director of National Intelligence (DNI) is the overall

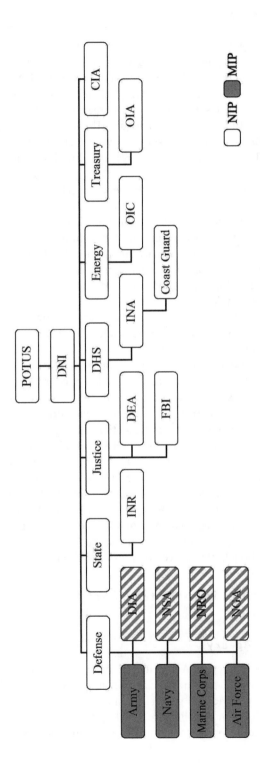

Figure 6.1 US Intelligence Community.

Notes
DIA: Defense Intelligence Agency; NSA: National Security Agency; NRO: National Reconnaisance Agency; NGA: National Geospatial-Intelligence Agency; INR: Intelligence and Research; DEA: Drug Enforcement Agency; FBI: Federal Bureau of Investigation; OIC: Office of Intelligence and Counterintelligence; OIA: Office of Intelligence and Analysis; CIA: Central Intelligence Agency; NIP: National Intelligence Program; MIP: Military Intelligence Program.

manager of the NIP. The MIP focuses on defense missions and covers intelligence with respect to military issues and missions. This intelligence is collected and analyzed by DOD and military service organizations. The Secretary of Defense is the overall manager of the MIP.[5] There is some overlap of mission between these categories. Further, the IC's organizational structure is not necessarily aligned with its budgetary structure. The Defense Intelligence Agency (DIA), for example, carries out some activities that fall in the NIP, and some in the MIP, and consequently receives funding from both programs.[6]

Another way of organizing intelligence is by what are called "disciplines," the various activities of the intelligence community. These "disciplines" frequently cut across agencies and organizations in the IC. Geospatial Intelligence (GEOINT) focuses on physical features of the earth, primarily through space, air-borne, and ground sensors. Signals Intelligence (SIGINT) involves the interception of communications and other signals. It can be subdivided into Communications Intelligence (COMINT) and Electronic Intelligence (ELINT).[7] Measurement and Signals Intelligence (MASINT) covers a variety of activities that collect data that help identify the characteristics of targets. Human Intelligence (HUMINT) is intelligence collected by human agents, operating clandestinely or overtly.[8]

The organizational and definitional complexity of the IC has contributed, over time, to serious problems of institutional cooperation, coordination, and intelligence sharing. There is a history of turf tension between the organizations, especially between DOD and the civilian intelligence organizations. In part, this stems from the difference between the national policy focus of many intelligence organizations and the military mission focus of DOD and the military services. The history of US intelligence repeatedly reveals these problems.[9] The intelligence community's failure to foresee the terrorist attacks of 9/11 led to a renewed effort to reform IC planning, coordination, and budgeting.[10] The position of Director of Central Intelligence (DCI), who was dual-hatted as the Director of the CIA, was replaced by a new Office of the Director of National Intelligence, who was given responsibility for coordinating, planning, and budgeting of the National Intelligence Program throughout the IC.

The 16 Organizations in the Intelligence Community

Central Intelligence Agency

The Central Intelligence Agency (CIA), created in the 1947 National Security Act, is one of the oldest elements in the IC.[11] When it was established, the agency was given a fairly broad and general mission: to advise the National Security Council (NSC) on intelligence, make recommendations for coordination of intelligence in the government, correlate and disseminate intelligence, and perform other duties the NSC might request.[12] The CIA has interpreted this charter broadly, expanding its activity in both analytical and operational directions.

Today the CIA is one of the three all-source analysis entities in the IC, along with the DIA and State's Bureau of Intelligence and Research. The agency carries out a broad array of intelligence activities, including a significant analytical capability, covert operations, technical research and development, human intelligence collection (HUMINT), as well as targeted analytical analysis focused on WMD proliferation, international crime and narcotics, and terrorism.[13] The CIA has approximately 20,000 employees and its annual budget may exceed $5 billion.[14] The agency develops its own budget, which is classified and is included in the DOD budget.[15]

Given its range of responsibilities, the Director of the CIA was also, until 2004, the Director of Central Intelligence (DCI), the head of the entire Intelligence Community. As DCI, the Director coordinated and managed, in principle, "the entire national Intelligence Community as well as running the CIA," and had specific oversight responsibilities for all intelligence budgets.[16] Although not a member of the Cabinet, the DCI reported directly to the President, participated in NSC Principals meetings, and had a significant role in national security policymaking.[17]

National Security Agency

The National Security Agency (NSA), created in 1952, carries out and analyzes "signals intelligence" (SIGINT), which results from intercepting foreign communications and electronics activity to support national intelligence requirements.[18] NSA is also responsible for "information assurance" (IA), or creating the communications procedures and codes for government agencies with national security functions, including the State Department, the Defense Department, the CIA and the FBI. It creates security communications networks for strategic weapons systems and protects the overall communications system of the US national security apparatus.[19]

The NSA is an organization within the DOD, but with significant responsibility over signals intelligence for the federal government and the IC.[20] It has "operational control" over government SIGINT activities, provides technical guidance for such operations, and produces and disseminates the intelligence that results from communications intercepts. As part of its SIGINT and IA capabilities, the NSA Director heads the Central Security Service, a military intelligence unit that conducts worldwide SIGINT and IA and provides Cryptologic services for the military.[21]

NSA employs more than 20,000 people and has a classified budget estimated in excess of $7 billion.[22] NSA draws up its own budget, covering military and civilian personnel, communications support, and research and development. NSA submits its NIP budget to the ODNI for review and its

MIP and IA budget to the Office of the Secretary of Defense (OSD). As a DOD agency, its budget is included in the overall DOD budget.

Defense Intelligence Agency

The Defense Intelligence Agency (DIA), created in 1961, collects and disseminates military intelligence, supporting the requirements of the Secretary of Defense, the Joint Chiefs of Staff, and military commanders. DIA's mission is to "provide timely and objective military intelligence to warfighters, policymakers and force planners."[23] It also oversees the activities of defense attachés on the embassy platform around the world. It was created to bring together non-SIGINT, non-IMINT military intelligence that was not "organic" to military units, as a way of centralizing military intelligence that had been dispersed and duplicated through DOD.

Today, DIA focuses on six areas of intelligence support for the DOD: (1) targeting and battle damage assessment; (2) weapons proliferation; (3) warning of impending crises; (4) support to peacekeeping operations; (5) maintenance of databases on foreign military organizations; and (6) support to US allies and UN operations.[24] DIA employs more than 7,000 people worldwide and has a classified budget estimated at more than $1 billion. DIA develops its budget as part of the overall DOD planning, programming, and budgeting process. As with NSA, DIA submits its NIP budget to the ODNI for review and its MIP budget to OSD.[25]

National Reconnaissance Office

The National Reconnaissance Office (NRO), which was also created in 1961, is responsible for imagery intelligence (IMINT)—acquiring, launching, and maintaining satellites, and disseminating the product of US satellite intelligence-collection hardware.[26] NRO's origins go back to the mid-1940s when the US government first began to examine aerial and space reconnaissance requirements. Over the next 20 years, aerial and spatial reconnaissance capabilities developed in the Air Force, ranging from the U-2 program to early satellite monitoring of the Soviet Union in the 1950s. The responsibility for these systems was moved from the Air Force to the NRO as a joint CIA–Air Force operation in 1961. Despite the creation of an organization, the NRO was largely an umbrella over the reconnaissance efforts of the CIA, Air Force, and Navy. Reconnaissance activities were a "federation of intelligence and military organizations that maintained their separate identities while being part of the NRO."[27]

In 1992, the NRO was restructured to create a more functional organization. The separated Air Force, Navy, and CIA reconnaissance programs in the organization were replaced with three new functional directorates: (1) the Communications Systems Acquisition and Operations Directorate; (2) the IMINT Systems Acquisition and Operations Directorate; and

(3) the SIGINT Systems Acquisition and Operations Directorate. Each directorate is responsible for the research and development and procurement of systems relevant to its functions. Later, two more directorates were added, the Advanced Systems and Technology Directorate to explore the feasibility of small satellites for reconnaissance, and the Directorate of Systems Integration and Engineering, to establish standards for systems engineering and architecture.[28]

As of 1997, NRO had close to 3,000 employees assigned from the parent organizations: Air Force (53 percent), CIA (24 percent), NSA (15 percent), Navy (8 percent), DIA and Army (<1 percent). NRO's classified budget is estimated to be roughly $9 billion, making it one of the larger elements of the intelligence community. Given its responsibilities for acquiring hardware and technology, this is to be expected.[29] The organization has a Deputy Director for Business, Plans, and Operations, who is responsible for budget planning and oversight. The office was created in 1996 after it was revealed that NRO had retained something like $3.8 billion in its accounts, as a result of slower than expected acquisition and deployment of new satellites. The previous generation of satellites had surpassed their anticipated life span, making the expenditures less urgent than projected.[30]

As with the other DOD intelligence agencies, the NRO submits its NIP budget to the ODNI for review and its MIP budget to OSD; however, given the nature of satellite programs, the NRO's budget receives the most coordinated review in the Intelligence Community.

National Geospatial-Intelligence Agency

The National Geospatial-Intelligence Agency (NGA) was created in 1996 as the National Imagery and Mapping Agency (NIMA) to rationalize intelligence responsibilities for interpreting imagery and mapping.[31] NGA provides geospatial intelligence support to military forces and national policymakers through analysis of imagery and geospatial information that can "describe, assess and visually depict physical features and geographically referenced activities on the Earth."[32] NGA describes its mission as providing "imagery and map-based intelligence solutions for U.S. national defense, homeland security and safety of navigation."[33]

The NGA has three major directorates: (1) Analysis and Production; (2) Acquisition; and (3) Source Operations and Management. The Analysis and Production Directorate is responsible for the interpretation of IMINT with a focus on regions or functions and topics like counterproliferation. The Acquisition Directorate procures systems and equipment used by the NGA. The Source Operations and Management Directorate handles imagery and target requests from US government military and civilian organizations and provides tasking for US satellites.

When the consolidation was first under discussion, there was concern in Congress in that an integrated agency bringing CIA personnel into the

Defense Department risked subordinating the needs of national imagery intelligence (as defined by the White House and the CIA) to purely military requirements (as defined by DOD and the military services). The issue was overcome by ensuring in the legislation that the DCI would "retain tasking authority over national imagery systems and that the Secretary of Defense needed to obtain the DCI's concurrence before appointing the [NGA] Director."[34]

NGA employs roughly 9,000 people. Its classified budget, which may be as much as $2 billion, is drawn up in the agency. As with other DOD intelligence agencies, NGA submits its NIP budget to the ODNI and its MIP budget to OSD.[35]

Department of Justice (DOJ)

Federal Bureau of Investigation

Since it was founded in 1908, the FBI has been primarily a law enforcement organization, focusing on criminal prosecution, with only a limited role in crime prevention and intelligence gathering.[36] The latter mission had slowly expanded in the 1990s with an increase in the Bureau's legal attaché program dealing primarily with liaison on investigations of terrorism, drug trafficking, and organized crime. At that time, this expansion made the FBI one of the fastest growing presences in US embassies.

The Bureau's role changed significantly in the wake of the 9/11 terrorist attacks. The 9/11 Commission recommended a major transformation, urging the creation of a "specialized and integrated national security workforce … consisting of agents, analysts, linguists and surveillance specialists."[37] In 2005, the Bush administration directed the FBI to "combine the missions, capabilities, and resources of the counterterrorism, counterintelligence, and intelligence elements of the FBI … [co-create] a national security workforce."[38] In September 2005, the FBI established a National Security Branch (NSB), including a Directorate of Intelligence, to handle its growing responsibilities for counterterrorism and intelligence.[39] It also significantly increased its overseas presence. By 2009, the FBI had legats, as they are known, in 75 US embassies and consulates overseas, covering more than 200 countries, territories, and islands.[40] The National Security Division is the component of the FBI that is part of the Intelligence Community and its mission is to proactively investigate threats to the United States and provide intelligence to national policymakers and homeland security and law enforcement communities.[41]

The goal of these changes is to transform the Bureau into a "major partner within the Intelligence Community," with an emphasis on "threat-based, intelligence-driven investigations and operations, especially in the areas of counterterrorism and counterintelligence, and on internal and external information sharing."[42]

The FBI is authorized to conduct intelligence activities against foreign targets within the United States, and occasionally overseas, in cooperation with other US intelligence agencies. Executive Order 12333 permits the FBI to "conduct within the United States, when requested by the officials of the intelligence community designated by the President, activities undertaken to collect foreign intelligence or support of foreign intelligence collection requirements of other agencies within the intelligence community."[43] The Bureau is also an active participant in cross-agency intelligence fusion efforts with respect to counterterrorism, notably through the National Counterterrorism Center.

The FBI intelligence budget is developed as part of the Bureau's overall budget, overseen by its Finance Division and Resource Planning Office. It is not easy to separate intelligence spending out of that budget. The Bureau requested $4.4 billion in FY 2009 for its efforts to "prevent terrorism and promote the nation's security," which would likely include intelligence operations.[44] The intelligence budget is prepared as part of the overall Justice/FBI budget planning process and is included in the Justice Department budget.

Drug Enforcement Administration

Although the Drug Enforcement Administration (DEA) Intelligence Division (ID) has long been an active part of US intelligence operations, it was not a formal part of the IC until 2006, when its Office of National Security Intelligence (ONSI) was included.[45] ONSI is not the only DEA office responsible for intelligence on drug trafficking organizations, but it is responsible for providing drug-related intelligence to the rest of the IC.[46] In addition, ONSI manages a centralized database of requests for analysis relating to DEA's drug enforcement activities.[47] DEA has one of the largest overseas presences in the IC with 86 offices in 63 countries.[48]

Department of State

The State Department's Bureau of Intelligence and Research (INR) originated from the wartime Office of Strategic Services, whose research functions were transferred to State after it was dissolved at the end of World War II.[49] It took its present name in 1957. Its functions are primarily analytical, in support of the diplomatic community, based on gathering all-source intelligence together.[50] Its role is to ensure "that intelligence activities are consistent with US foreign policy, and that other components of the intelligence community understand the information and analysis needs of senior foreign policy decision-makers."[51] INR's primary "customer" is the Secretary of State. It also supports US embassies around the world by providing assessments, guidance, and support.[52]

INR participates externally in the preparation of National Intelligence Estimates and Special Estimates (produced by the National Intelligence Council, part of ODNI), and internally produces regional and functional reports, considered by many to be among the more analytical intelligence products.[53] Its structure, in part, mirrors the Department's regional bureaus, with an office for each region. In addition, it has functional offices focusing on economic issues, global issues, terrorism and crime, and proliferation.[54]

INR employs just over 300 people, nearly half of whom have doctoral degrees.[55] Its budget is $55–60 million, which largely supports its personnel and IT systems.[56] The budget is prepared as part of overall State budget planning, through the Bureau of Resource Management, reporting to the Under Secretary for Management, and is included in the overall State Department budget.

Department of Homeland Security

Office of Intelligence and Analysis

The Department of Homeland Security (DHS) was established in January 2003. One of its tasks is to coordinate and analyze intelligence relating to direct threats to the United States. This responsibility was initially given to the Directorate for Information Analysis and Infrastructure Protection.[57] Subsequently, a reorganization of the Department included the creation of the Office of Intelligence and Analysis (OIA). The mission of the OIA is to "provide homeland security intelligence and information to the Secretary, other federal officials, and our state, local, tribal, and private sector partners."[58] The Office's budget is included in the overall DHS budget.

Coast Guard

Coast Guard Intelligence (CGI) is one of the oldest intelligence offices in the United States, though it only became a member of the US intelligence community in 2001.[59] CGI was first established in 1915 when Coast Guard *Regulations* "provided for the establishment of a Chief Intelligence Officer who was to be attached to the Office of Assistant Commandant."[60] Today, the Coast Guard provides intelligence to support counternarcotics missions, port security, immigration interdiction, search and rescues, and maritime safety.[61] CGI is the only IC member whose parent agency is both an armed force and an enforcement agency.[62]

Department of Treasury

The Department of Treasury's intelligence office has for some time overtly collected foreign financial and economic data to support the work of the IC. The 9/11 attacks led to a restructuring of Treasury's intelligence operations and altered its core mission. Since 2004, the Assistant Secretary for Intelligence and Analysis (OIA), working under the Office of Terrorism and Financial Intelligence (OTFI), has had responsibility for the Treasury Department's intelligence and financial crimes enforcement. In addition, the office is responsible for tracking the finances of terrorist organizations and individuals. More broadly, OIA is responsible for the "receipt, analysis, collation and dissemination of foreign intelligence and foreign counterintelligence information related to the operation and responsibilities of the Department of Treasury."[63] The budget for Treasury's intelligence programs is developed as part of overall Treasury budget planning and is included in the Department's budget.

Department of Energy

The Department of Energy's (DOE) intelligence activities date back to 1947. At that time, the predecessor organization—the Atomic Energy Commission (AEC)—was responsible for all civilian and military nuclear technology in the United States. AEC was also given some responsibilities to carry out foreign intelligence gathering on the nuclear activities of other counties.[64]

These responsibilities were folded into the DOE when it was created in 1977. Throughout the 1990s and 2000s, DOE intelligence activities were reorganized several times until they were consolidated in 2006 in the Office of Intelligence and Counterintelligence (OIC). OIC has five bureaus: Collection Management, Nuclear Intelligence Analysis, Counterterrorism, Energy Security, and Science and Technology.[65] The budgets for these programs are prepared as part of overall Energy Department budget planning and are included in the Department's budget.

DOE is also responsible for intelligence conducted through the Z Division of Lawrence Livermore National Laboratory's Directorate for Nonproliferation, Homeland Security and International Security.[66] This division was created in the 1960s to work jointly with the CIA in analyzing the Soviet and Chinese nuclear weapons programs. Its agenda has since expanded to focus on nuclear proliferation in general, as well as chemical and biological weapons proliferation.

Military Intelligence

Army

Army intelligence includes two entities responsible for tactical, operational, and strategic intelligence support to the Army and joint force commanders: US Army Intelligence and Security Command (INSCOM) and the Army Deputy Chief of Staff for Intelligence (G-2). Created in the years following the Vietnam War, INSCOM is tasked with planning and conducting "intelligence, security, and information operations for the US Army and its military commanders, as well as for the president and other national decision-makers."[67] After transferring its HUMINT activities to DIA, it began to concentrate on supporting treaty verification, counter drug operations and other non-traditional military intelligence activities.

INSCOM consists of eight directorates and smaller offices with a staff deployed to more than 180 locations worldwide. These include the Foreign Liaison, Plans and Operations, ISR Integration, Foreign Intelligence, HUMINT, Resource Integration, Management Services, Intelligence Community Information Management directorates and the Army Intelligence Master Plan and Intelligence Personnel Management Offices.[68] Subordinate to INSCOM is the 900-member National Ground Intelligence Center (NGIC) which creates general military intelligence along with scientific and technical products.[69] INSCOM was active in the development of J-STARS and other battlefield intelligence platforms.[70]

The Deputy Chief of Staff, Intelligence (G-2) is the Army's Chief Intelligence Officer. This office is responsible for policy formulation, planning, programming, budgeting, management, evaluation, and oversight for Army intelligence activities. Each service has its own Chief Intelligence Officer responsible for management and budgeting of intelligence.[71]

Navy

Naval Intelligence was first established in 1882, making it the oldest continuously operating intelligence unit in the United States.[72] Like the Army, Naval Intelligence consists of two entities to conduct intelligence activities and manage its operations. The Director of Naval Intelligence (N-2) is the service's Chief Intelligence Officer and the Office of Naval Intelligence (ONI) is responsible for the Navy's intelligence activities. Within the ONI, the NMIC (National Intelligence Maritime Center) is the largest intelligence unit. NMIC consists of the intelligence operations of the three maritime defense arms. At the end of the Cold War the Navy downsized its seven intelligence organizations, eventually putting the resulting structure under the aegis of the NMIC. The ONI is the largest of the NMIC agencies and has a diverse mission.

ONI is tasked with organizing and training intelligence personnel, maritime naval analysis including war-game and scenario development, and oversight for intelligence and security manpower issues; serves as a liaison between DOD and non-department agencies; supports foreign liaisons; and conducts long-term foreign navy analysis. Additionally, ONI is charged with acquiring intelligence systems and scientific, strategic, and technical trade analysis.[73]

Marine Corps

Marine Corps intelligence activities are organized under the Director of Intelligence (DIRINT). The director, a position created in 2000, manages the

Intelligence Plans/Policy Division and the Intelligence Operations Division. Also under the DIRINT is the Marine Corps' component of the NMIC, the Marine Corps Intelligence Activity (MCIA), which focuses on supporting Marines on the ground.[74] Following the Marine's expeditionary nature, the 1,000-strong MCIA supports tactical intelligence requirements and works with its sister intelligence agencies to provide combatants with threat, technical, and terrain analysis.[75]

Air Force

Newly reorganized into the Air Force Intelligence, Surveillance and Reconnaissance (ISR) Agency in 2007, the former Air Intelligence Agency (AIA) is administered by the Air Force deputy chief of staff for Intelligence, Surveillance and Reconnaissance. As a "field operating agency," the Air Force ISR Agency expanded from its base of SIGINT into other areas of field operations.[76] The agency now includes 12,000 members of the 70th Intelligence Wing, Air Force Cryptologic Office, National Air and Space Intelligence Center, and the Air Force Technical Applications Center (AFTAC), among other units.[77]

The 1,000-member AFTAC is subordinate to Air Force ISR. AFTAC is responsible for "operating and maintaining a global network of nuclear event detection sensors, the US Atomic Energy Detection System (USAEDS)."[78] Serving the entire intelligence community, AFTAC focuses on high-tech collection and analysis methods to track nuclear development and detonations.[79]

Intelligence Community Management and Budgeting

The Intelligence Budget Structure: The National Intelligence Program

Intelligence budgeting is structured through the two categories described earlier—the National Intelligence Program (NIP) and the Military Intelligence Program (MIP).[80] Funding appropriated to each of these categories is distributed across the military and civilian organizations discussed above.

NIP budgets support national policy and intelligence needs and priorities, supplying intelligence to national policy officials. This budget is overseen by the DNI, but each of its components is prepared and implementation overseen by a "Program Manager." The Program Manager is responsible for drawing up the budget proposal for the programs, allocating the funds to the organizations participating in that program, and overseeing the execution of the funds, all subject to the guidance of the DNI. NIP funds are noticeably "fenced," in that they are meant for national intelligence purposes and cannot be reprogrammed, transferred, or affected by across-the-board budget reductions without the approval of the Program Manager and, in the end, the DNI.[81]

The NIP includes the Central Intelligence Agency Program (CIAP). This program funds CIA operational and analytical activities. The Program Manager is the Director of the CIA, who draws up its budget proposal and oversees its execution.

At least five NIP programs fund DOD intelligence agencies and activities, which are the bulk of the NIP, including the Consolidated Cryptologic Program (CCP), the General Defense Intelligence Program (GDIP), the DOD Foreign Counter-Intelligence Program (DOD FCIP), the National Geospatial-Intelligence Program (NGP), the National Reconnaissance Program (NRP), and other programs "designated ... as national foreign intelligence or counterintelligence activities."[82] These programs cut across organizations and appropriations accounts.[83]

The CCP covers the activities of several agencies involved in SIGINT missions. The bulk of this activity is in the NSA, but a fair amount is also carried out by cryptologic elements of the military services. The Director of NSA is the Program Manager for the CCP, who must balance the needs of the services with those of NSA in preparing the CCP budget, which is transmitted to the DNI.[84] CCP funding is appropriated directly to the organizations carrying out the activity, but the DNI and CCP Program Manager can ensure that NIP funding is not reprogrammed to other purposes.[85]

The GDIP element of the NIP covers a broad range of national intelligence activities carried out by military organizations. It covers much of the budget of the Defense Intelligence Agency (DIA), but also significant funding for the military services' intelligence programs and the Joint Intelligence Operations Centers (JIOCs) of the Combatant Commands (COCOMS). It is not the only source of intelligence funding for these organizations, but covers "general military intelligence needs of its consumers for all-source intelligence."[86] The Director of the DIA is the Program Manager for the GDIP, who is in charge of budget preparation and submission to the DNI, setting fiscal guidance, funding allocation, and oversight. To ensure that conflicts are resolved and that the program has a common agenda, the GDIP also has an oversight board—the Defense Intelligence Resources Board—and a Chief Financial Executive (GDIP-CFE), who oversees a management office.[87]

The NGP covers primarily NGA activities, whose Director is the Program Manager. The NGA Director provides guidance to the geospatial intelligence community, which includes some military service and COCOM elements. He draws up the budget, which is transmitted to the DNI. All NGP funding is appropriated to NGA, and the Director allocates funds both inside and outside the organization.[88]

The NRP covers much of the activity of the NRO, whose Director is the Program Manager.[89] Budget requests for this program are prepared by the

NRO Director and transmitted to the DNI. Appropriated funds are allocated inside the organization by the Director.

There are NIP elements in the programs of other agencies in the IC. The OIA and the CGI program, both at the DHS, are part of the NIP. The FBI National Security Division and the DEA's Office of National Security Intelligence, both at the Department of Justice, are also included. Other NIP elements include the State Department's Bureau of Intelligence and Research, the Energy Department's Office of Intelligence, and the Treasury Department's Office of Intelligence and Analysis. Each of these departments and agencies acts as the Program Manager for its element of the NIP. The budgets are prepared in the department and agency budget offices and transmitted both to the DNI and directly to Office of Management and Budget (OMB) and the Congress. Finally, the DNI himself is the Program Manager for the Community Management Account (CMA), which funds the Office of the DNI's management responsibilities and activities, including the National Intelligence Council, National Counter Terrorism Center, National Counter Intelligence Executive, and the National Counter Proliferation Center, discussed below.[90]

The Intelligence Budget Structure: The Military Intelligence Program

Military Intelligence Programs (MIP) include programs and activities that are carried out exclusively within one military service (formerly known as TIARA, for Tactical Intelligence and Related Activities), and programs and activities that crossed services, providing intelligence to multiple users (formerly known as the JMIP, for Joint Military Intelligence Program). MIP intelligence is developed primarily for the use of military commanders. Oversight over these programs was previously divided between service managers (for TIARA) and joint Program Managers (for JMIP). Because budget planning for both was done within the military services and included in the service Program Objective Memorandum to the Secretary of Defense, JMIP Program Managers had only limited impact on joint program budgets.[91]

The creation, in 2003, of the position of Under Secretary of Defense for Intelligence (USD(I)) gave higher visibility to and more central control over DOD intelligence programs and investments. As a result, TIARA and JMIP were merged in 2005 into the new MIP, whose policies and budgets are managed by the new Under Secretary.[92] The MIP covers a wide range of activities, from tactical intelligence capabilities carried into the field by military units, to defense-specific communications, reconnaissance, and counterintelligence programs.[93] These activities are carried out entirely within DOD by the OSD, the military services, the Special Operations Command, as well as the DIA, NGA, NRO, and NSA.

MIP program budgets are submitted to DOD and budget planning is carried out through the DOD Planning, Programming, Budgeting, and

Execution (PPBE) process in an integrated way with the rest of defense budget planning. While ODNI can and does participate in that process with regard to the MIP, the USD(I) is the ultimate manager of MIP budget planning and execution. The USD(I) participates actively in the PPBE process, proposing programs, making budget estimates, and overseeing program implementation.[94] MIP funding is not as seriously "fenced" as NIP programs, but they may not be reprogrammed without the approval of the USD(I).

Office of the Director of National Intelligence

Roles and Responsibilities

The intelligence failures revealed in the 9/11 terrorist attacks gave impetus to proposals for major reform of the IC's structures and processes. The 9/11 Commission investigating the attacks focused on long-term problems in managing and coordinating US intelligence assets, particularly the weak authority of the Director of Central Intelligence (DCI) with respect to the budgets and activities of the IC agencies:

> The episode [the terrorist attacks] indicates some of the limitations of the DCI's authority over the direction and priorities of the intelligence community, especially its elements within the Department of Defense. The DCI has to direct agencies without controlling them. He does not receive an appropriation for their activities, and therefore does not control their purse strings. He has little insight into how they spend their resources ... [T]he vision of central management clearly has not been realized.[95]

The Commission pointed out that the DCI had only the authority to coordinate budget requests from the intelligence agencies in order to prepare a single document for the Congress, which then became separate documents for each agency.[96] He had no authority to hire or fire senior IC managers, though he concurred in the hiring of directors of the DOD intelligence agencies.

The Commission tackled this management problem directly, proposing the creation of a National Intelligence Director, separate from the CIA Director, who would be in charge of the entire national intelligence program, oversee the agencies involved, and be directly responsible for cross-agency centers focused on specific subjects of interest to the US government, such as a proposed new National Counterterrorism Center.[97] The Director would be empowered to submit a unified intelligence budget, which would be appropriated to his or her office. The Director would give his views on OMB's apportionment of funds and would have the authority to reprogram funds among the agencies to meet new priorities. The Director would be a confirmation position. He or she and a small staff would be part of the Executive Office of the President. The Commission strongly recommended that the total intelligence budget be declassified.

The 9/11 Commission's recommendations led directly to the passage of the Intelligence Reform and Terrorism Prevention Act (IRTPA) of 2004, which created a new overseer of the IC, replacing the role of the DCI. The new Director of National Intelligence (DNI) would

> serve as the head of the intelligence community; [and] act as the principal advisor to the President, to the National Security Council, and the Homeland Security Council for intelligence matters related to the national security; [and] ... oversee and direct the implementation of the National Intelligence Program.[98]

The Intelligence Reform Act did not consolidate existing IC agencies, did not locate the DNI in the Executive Office of the President, and fell short of giving the DNI all of the authorities the 9/11 Commission had recommended. It renamed the National Foreign Intelligence Program as the National Intelligence Program (NIP) to indicate that the DNI's responsibilities included foreign intelligence that was gathered domestically (notably by the FBI).[99] It moved cross-agency intelligence centers into this new office.[100] It gave the DNI expanded authority to concur in the appointments of major IC department and agency heads. And it made the DNI a decision-maker over major acquisition programs, an authority that is shared with the Secretary of Defense, with respect to defense systems.[101]

As the Office of the Director of National Intelligence (ODNI) has expanded its size and activity, concern has also grown that the new office has become "what intelligence professionals feared it would: an unnecessary bureaucratic contraption with an amazingly large staff," according to one retired CIA official.[102]

ODNI and the Intelligence Budget

The Intelligence Reform Act specifically addressed the issue of the DNI's authority over intelligence budgeting. The DCI had the authority to "facilitate" the development of the NFIP budget. The Act gave the new DNI the authority to provide "guidance" to NIP agencies for budget preparation. He would then "develop and determine an annual consolidated National Intelligence Program budget," based on the agency submissions.[103] This authority fell slightly short of the 9/11 Commission's recommendation, since the NIP budget would continue to be composed of budgets developed within the various IC agencies and would not be appropriated to the DNI.[104] Nevertheless, it was a significant expansion in authority over that possessed by the DCI, because the DNI would provide guidance, review and approve the budgets prepared by the agencies, and assemble the results into a single consolidated budget that would be transmitted to the President.[105]

As a result of these statutory changes, the DNI's authority over the NIP budget is considerably greater than the authority the DCI possessed previously. NIP budget submissions go to the DNI, who oversees a budget review, in coordination with DOD. ODNI also participates in the MIP budget review, which is part of the PPBE budget planning process at DOD.[106]

The DNI was also given a number of authorities over budget execution, which also went well beyond the previous authority of the DCI. Significantly, under the IRTPA, once NIP funds are appropriated, OMB's apportionment of those funds to the NIP agencies by the Director of OMB is to be done "at the exclusive direction" of the DNI.[107] Although this authority does not allow the DNI to determine the specific details of an agency's budget, it does allow him to specify how the funds being apportioned can be spent and to set conditions that must be met as they are expended. IRTPA also gives the DNI the authority to direct the allocation or allotment of apportioned NIP funds; the DNI can withhold final allotment as a way of enforcing the DNI's spending priorities.[108] The Director is to monitor the execution of the program by the agencies and report to the President and the Congress within 15 days if that execution is inconsistent with law or with the directions he has given the agency.[109]

The DNI was also given stronger authorities with respect to transfers and reprogrammings in the NIP account. He is authorized to transfer or reprogram funds within and across agencies in the NIP, but only with the approval of the Director of OMB and after consultation with the agency head.[110] These transfers and reprogrammings are limited to not more than $150 million of an agency's annual NIP funds, cannot exceed 5 percent of those annual funds, and cannot result in the termination of an acquisition program.[111] In addition, no other agency can transfer or reprogram NIP funds without his prior approval.[112] The extent to which the DNI has tested the edges of these broad budgetary, apportionment, and reprogramming authorities remains unclear.[113]

The ODNI responsibilities for these budget planning and execution functions are carried out under the Deputy DNI for Management (DDNI/M). The Deputy's Chief Financial Officer (CFO) is responsible for preparing the DNI's budget decisions and consolidating the agency budget submissions, working with the DOD Under Secretaries for Intelligence and for Comptroller. This office also prepares the congressional justification books, working with the NIP agency offices, oversees NIP budget execution, and processes the reprogramming actions described above.[114]

The key relationship for the DNI, and the restraint on broader budget authority, continues to be that with the Secretary of Defense, since DOD controls roughly 80 percent of all intelligence activities, assets, and budgets.[115] DOD resisted the 9/11 Commission's recommendations on budget authorities for the DNI. DOD was concerned about giving a non-defense official control over DOD budget decisions and the risk that DOD's intelligence assets might be diverted from military to national intelligence missions. The Congress underlined the sensitivity of this relationship in the statute, which states that the DNI

> shall, after consultation with the Secretary of Defense, ensure that the National Intelligence Program budgets for the elements of the intelligence community that are within the Department of Defense are adequate to satisfy the national intelligence needs of the Department of Defense, including the needs of the Chairman of the Joint Chiefs of Staff and the commanders of the [combatant] commands, and wherever such elements are performing Government-wide functions, the needs of other Federal departments and agencies.[116]

DNI authorities with respect to the Military Intelligence Program are more constrained. While ODNI participates in DOD's MIP budget development process to ensure that there is no overlap with the NIP, his role in the process is purely consultative.[117] Should the Secretary of Defense wish to transfer or reprogram MIP funds, he must notify the DNI.[118] The primary responsibility for the MIP programs and budgets remains with the USD(I).[119]

The budget process developed by ODNI continues to evolve as the DNI seeks to define a more authoritative role. For the first few years, the DNI provided budget guidance on the NIP to all 16 agencies in the IC. Over the succeeding months, the DNI, DOD, and the other agencies coordinated budget planning, fitting the ODNI priorities into the agency budget planning processes. The resulting NIP budget was transmitted to the Congress in a classified annex to the broader budget transmittal.[120] In 2008, ODNI began to develop a more streamlined version of this lengthy process, adopting elements of the PPBS process used by DOD. This plan, known as the Strategic Enterprise Management system (SEM), would "align strategy, budget, capabilities and performance" in the IC.[121]

The goal of this planned reform is to link a more proactive overall intelligence strategic plan to intelligence missions and to the objectives of each element in the IC through the planning, programming, and budgeting process. Leadership would be provided by an Intelligence Resources Board, consisting of senior agency officials. In the planning phase, an inter-IC Planning Committee would seek IC and non-IC input to define intelligence needs, identify gaps and shortfalls, set priorities, and draft an intelligence planning guidance. In the programming phase, a Programming Committee would translate those needs into a five-year "intelligence capability programming guidance," shape options, and draft program decision memoranda for the ODNI. In the budgeting phase, a Budget Committee would review IC agency budget submissions for compliance with the guidance and the decision memoranda and draft decision documents for ODNI. These final decisions would lock down an overall NIP budget to be transmitted to OMB.[122]

National Counterterrorism Center

The IRTPA institutionalized the new National Counterterrorism Center (NCTC), an interagency-staffed organization with a dual mission: the integration of all government intelligence on terrorism, and strategic planning for counterterror operations.[123] Reporting to the DNI, the NCTC is to serve as "the primary organization in the United States Government for analyzing and integrating all intelligence possessed or acquired by the United States Government pertaining to terrorism and counterterrorism, excepting intelligence pertaining exclusively to domestic terrorists and domestic counterterrorism."[124] Reporting directly to the White House, the NCTC was given an even more expansive authority:

> to conduct strategic operational planning for counterterrorism activities, integrating all instruments of national power, inducing diplomatic, financial, military, intelligence, homeland security, and law enforcement activities within and among agencies ... [including the authority] to assign roles and responsibilities ... to lead Departments or agencies for counterterrorism activities.[125]

Using the latter authority, NCTC was tasked with drawing up a National Implementation Plan for the War on Terror.[126] From 2005 to 2006, the NCTC coordinated a government-wide planning effort to develop this plan, leading to a classified document setting out more than 500 individual tasks for agencies to undertake as part of a coordinated counterterrorism effort. While the planning effort was quite detailed, it did not formally include the OMB or provide clear budgetary guidance to agencies to support the strategy. Agencies were somewhat reluctant to follow the externally determined priorities and alter internally driven resource decisions.[127]

National Counterproliferation Center

The reform act also established a National Counterproliferation Center (NCPC) under the DNI.[128] The NCPC grew out of the CIA's interagency Counterproliferation Center. Under the DNI, it was made responsible for coordinating and integrating intelligence on proliferation.[129] Like the NCTC, the NCPC conducts net assessments and warnings about threats to national security, but it does not have the strategy and planning functions of the NCTC.

Declassifying the Intelligence Budget

For at least a decade, there has been a debate over declassifying the intelligence budget. Proponents argued that the disclosure of the total NIP budget would not compromise national security, but would provide greater transparency over the level of the nation's investment in intelligence and is, in any case, consistent with the constitutional requirement to publish government accounts. Opponents argued that disclosure of the total budget would set a precedent, opening the door to pressures to disclose further budgetary details, leading to a security problem. In 1997, DCI George Tenet disclosed that FY 1998 national intelligence (NFIP) spending was $26.6 billion, as a one-time response to a Freedom of Information Act request.[130]

The 9/11 Commission strongly recommended formalizing such disclosures.[131] This recommendation was legislated in the 2007 Act implementing the Commission's recommendations. It requires the DNI to disclose the aggregate total of the National Intelligence Program (NIP) for the prior year 30 days after the end of the fiscal year.[132] While this figure does not include the MIP, it provides some visibility on the nation's overall intelligence spending. For FY 2007, the DNI disclosed an NIP budget of $43.5 billion.[133] In October 2008, the DNI disclosed the FY 2008 NIP budget as $47.5 billion.[134] If DOD receives roughly 80 percent of all US intelligence spending, this would suggest that DOD's NIP funding came to roughly $38 billion. A significant part of that funding would go to such technologically intensive agencies as NSA and NRO.[135] In 1996, the Commission on Roles and Capabilities of the US Intelligence Community estimated that the NIP includes roughly two-thirds of the entire intelligence budget of the United States.[136] If true, this suggests MIP funds may come to roughly $23 billion, for an overall intelligence budget total of roughly $70 billion. These funds are largely concealed in the DOD budget.[137]

Congress and the Intelligence Budget

The 9/11 Commission Report described Congressional oversight of intelligence as "dysfunctional."[138] Congressional responsibility for intelligence oversight is lodged in the House Permanent Select Committee on Intelligence (HPSI) and the Senate Select Committee on Intelligence (SSCI). These authorizing committees were created in 1976 and 1977, respectively, after congressional investigations uncovered massive abuses in the intelligence community. They were to "consolidate legislative and oversight authority over the entire intelligence community" by becoming hybrids of standing and select committees, able to report out legislation.[139] The committees have legislative authority over the CIA, DNI, and the NIP, but share authority over the rest of the IC with committees responsible for DOD, DHS, Justice, and other departments.

While these committees are the principal authorizers for the intelligence accounts, a number of intelligence programs are authorized by the congressional armed services committees. Each intelligence committee includes members of the committees with which it shares jurisdiction, such as Armed Services, Foreign Affairs/Foreign Relations, Homeland Security, and the Judiciary, as well as members of the Appropriations committees.

The actual appropriation of funds for the DNI and the parts of the NIP controlled by DOD is done by the defense appropriations subcommittees in each chamber. As a result, there has been ongoing tension between the authorizers, who are focused on intelligence requirements, and the appropriators, who are focused on the broad requirements of national defense.[140] The 9/11 Commission proposed resolving this tension by creating a single committee that would both authorize and appropriate the intelligence budgets.[141]

Neither chamber has adopted this solution. In the Senate, a 2007 memorandum of agreement allows staff of the SSCI and the Appropriations subcommittees to attend each other's hearings. It also permits the authorizing committee staffer for an appropriator to attend the appropriations markup as well, and lets the chair and ranking minority members appear before the other committee before markup of authorization or appropriations bills.[142] The House formed a new Select Intelligence Oversight Panel, separate from both committees, with three members from the Intelligence Committee and ten from Appropriations. The Panel cannot report a bill, but it does provide a report to the defense appropriations subcommittee making recommendations on the intelligence budget.[143]

Chapter 7

Resource Allocation and Budgeting for Homeland Security

The Homeland Security Act of 2002 launched the most extensive reorganization of US government since the creation of the Department of Defense (DOD) in 1947.[1] Under the terms of the legislation, the Bush administration in January 2003 drew 22 disparate agencies and some 170,000 employees into a new Department of Homeland Security (DHS).[2]

Proponents of the reorganization believed that a single department under a single Cabinet Secretary would be able to achieve what the White House Office of Homeland Security could not: unity of effort across the bulk of federal activities related to domestic security.[3] The most important engine of such unity would be the control of the budget that the new Secretary of Homeland Security would enjoy.

In addition to fostering unity of effort, that budget authority would allow the Secretary to establish and enforce priorities. A Secretary would be able to "weigh the benefit of each homeland security endeavor and only allocate resources where the benefit of reducing the risk is worth the amount of additional cost."[4] The first Secretary of Homeland Security, Tom Ridge, also believed that the new department would pay for itself through the elimination of redundancies.[5]

The record on these achievements to date is mixed.[6] The effectiveness of the system in forging unity among the department's operating components or keeping costs in line has not yet become obvious. The components generally continue to set their own agendas, and their individual shares of the budget do not shift much from year to year (see Table 7.1). There is also little evidence of cost savings based on the elimination of redundant activities.

One reason for the failure to forge unity or instill cost effectiveness is that the DHS captures only about one-half of total federal budgets for homeland security. For FY 2009, the Bush administration requested more than $500 million for homeland security programs at each of six federal departments outside DHS (see Table 7.2). With so many departments and agencies involved, it would be astonishing if the Secretary of Homeland Security were able to instill unity of effort across the full federal effort. Moreover, many of DHS's activities are not homeland security functions.[7] In FY 2009, about 35 percent of the DHS budget was devoted to non-homeland security

Table 7.1 Operating component shares of DHS budget, FY 2003–FY 2008[a] (percent)

	2003	2004	2005	2006	2007 estimate	2008 request
Secret Service	4	4	4	3	3	3
FEMA Operations, Planning and Support[b]	N/A	1	1	1	1	1
Coast Guard	20	19	19	19	19	19
Transportation Security Administration (Including Federal Air Marshals)[c]	17	15	16	15	14	14
Immigration and Customs Enforcement (Net of Federal Air Marshals)[c]	9	9	9	10	11	11
Customs and Border Protection	19	17	17	19	21	22
Citizenship and Immigration Services	5	5	5	5	4	6
Seven Components' Share of Total DHS	**73**	**69**	**70**	**72**	**73**	**76**

Source: Authors calculations based on US Department of Homeland Security, *FY 2004 to FY 2008 Budgets in Brief.*

Notes
a Figures based on total budgets, including discretionary, mandatory, and fee-funded activities. Figures exclude funding for Bio-Shield and emergency supplemental appropriations for disaster relief; they include supplementals for Global War on Terrorism.
b Figure is for core operations of FEMA; excludes most grants to state and local governments as well as disaster relief.
c Federal Air Marshals transferred from ICE to TSA in January 2006. For comparability, this table includes budgets for Federal Air Marshals in the TSA figures, rather than in the ICE row, for all six years.
Totals may not add due to rounding.

missions, such as marine safety and the mitigation of oil spills by the Coast Guard or preparations to deal with natural disasters by the Federal Emergency Management Agency (FEMA). This means that the Secretary's attention is often rightly focused on matters largely unrelated to homeland security.

Another reason why expectations have not been met may be DHS's arrangements for planning and resource allocation. If the budget is the route to a unified department, as proponents of a consolidated department believed, then planning and resource allocation processes should be the engine that pulls the players along that route. To date, however, even for the genuine homeland security functions that fall within DHS, department-wide programming and budgeting are still relatively immature.

Table 7.2 Homeland security budget request, FY 2009

Department or agency	Budget authority in ($ in billions)
Department of Homeland Security	32.8
Defense	17.6
Health and Human Services	4.5
Justice	3.8
State	2.5
Energy	1.9
Agriculture	0.7
National Science Foundation	0.4
Other Agencies	2.1
Total Homeland Security	66.3

Source: Office of Management and Budget, "Crosscutting Programs," in *Analytical Perspectives*, Budget of the United States for FY 2009 (February 2008).

The three federal departments with the largest budgets for homeland security are DHS, DOD, and the Department of Health and Human Services (HHS). Chapter 5 examined planning and resource allocation in DOD. This chapter looks at the arrangements in DHS and HHS. The next two sections take up each of those departments in turn. The chapter ends with a brief concluding section.

Planning and Resource Allocation in the Department of Homeland Security

The White House articulated its strategic goals for homeland security in *The National Strategy for Homeland Security*.[8] In addition, during this decade, the White House has developed several other strategy documents related to homeland security. These include:

- *The National Strategy for Combating Terrorism* (February 2003 and September 2006);
- *The National Strategy to Secure Cyberspace* (February 2003);
- *The National Strategy for the Physical Protection of Critical Infrastructures and Key Assets)* (February 2003);
- *The National Strategy for Maritime Security* (September 2005);
- *The National Strategy for Pandemic Influenza* (November 2005); and
- *The National Strategy for Aviation Security* (26 March 2007).

To establish strong links between strategy and resources within DHS, the department in its first year fashioned a Planning, Programming, Budgeting, and Execution (PPBE) system modeled after that of the DOD. As discussed in

Chapter 5, PPBE is a phased, disciplined process meant to help leaders explore tradeoffs and make decisions based on explicit criteria of national strategy, rather than compromises among institutional forces. Such a system can help bring programs and budgets into line with strategic goals. A PPBE can also serve as a management tool by revealing gaps and areas of duplication across the various components and programs of the organization and by fostering an outlook that considers the future costs and consequences of current decisions.[9]

As discussed in Chapter 5, when Secretary of Defense Robert McNamara established the Planning, Programming, and Budgeting System (PPBS) in the DOD in the early 1960s, he hoped the new mechanism would help achieve the promise of the National Security Act of 1947—the genuine integration of multiple armed services into a unified cabinet department.[10] The Secretary would take control of the reins of policy and budget across the armed services by making major decisions about how to allocate the department's resources among programs. To manage the new process, formulate policy alternatives, and conduct tradeoff studies of the costs and consequences of the various choices, Secretary McNamara created within the Office of Secretary of Defense a new systems analysis office, later renamed the Office of Program Analysis and Evaluation (PA&E).

Similarly, in 2003, the staff of the Secretary of Homeland Security hoped that a PPBE could help turn the loose confederation of 22 legacy agencies into a single department, with a coherent set of programs and activities organized around the goals of the homeland security strategy. Of particular interest were seven main operating components, which together account for about 83 percent of the department's budget in FY 2009: the Secret Service, FEMA, the Coast Guard, the Transportation Security Administration (TSA), Immigration and Customs Enforcement (ICE), Customs and Border Protection (CBP), and Citizenship and Immigration Services (CIS) (see Figure 7.1).

The Homeland Security Act of 2002 requires the DHS each year to submit a five-year plan, called the Future-Years Homeland Security Program (FYHSP), similar in its structure and level of detail to the DOD's Future-Years Defense Program (FYDP) (see Chapter 5). DHS was not required under the Act to establish a PPBE as the basis of its FYHSP, but the department's early leaders chose to make such a system the basis of planning and resource allocation. To manage the PPBE, the department's first chief financial officer set up within his office a PA&E, modeled loosely on DOD's.

The following subsections describe the various budget categories used by DHS, the organizations involved in the department's PPBE, and the PPBE process itself.

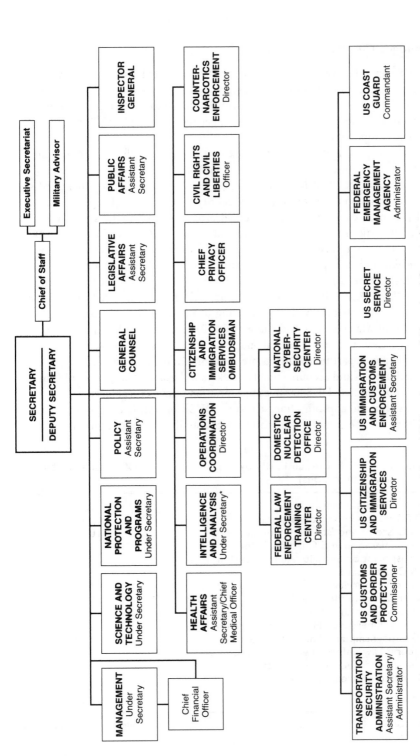

Figure 7.1 Organization of DHS (source: adapted from US Department of Homeland Security).

Budget Categories in DHS

DHS views its programs through a variety of budget lenses. The main budget break-outs are by organizational component, homeland security versus non-homeland security, homeland security mission category, and appropriation account. Table 7.3 displays DHS's budget request for FY 2009 by organizational component.

The department also keeps track of the amounts that its organizations budget for homeland security versus non-homeland security activities (see Table 7.4). The 2002 *National Strategy for Homeland Security* identified six critical mission areas for homeland security.[11] The DHS staff expected that the department could organize its budget around those missions, as DOD did with its major force programs during the 1960s (see Chapter 5). Early in 2009, the Obama administration combined those six missions into three categories: prevent and disrupt terrorist attacks; protect the American people, critical infrastructure, and key resources; and respond to and recover from incidents (see Table 7.5). All of the departments and agencies involved in homeland security report their budgets according to these mission categories, and the Office of Management and Budget (OMB) reports spending in the mission categories as part of the annual budget submission to Congress.[12]

Finally, department budgets are transmitted to Congress using the appropriation titles and accounts that lawmakers will examine and into which funds are appropriated. DHS has five appropriation titles (see Table 7.6).

Within the appropriation structure, DHS's operating components generally retain the same appropriation accounts that they inherited from their

Table 7.3 DHS budget authority by organization, FY 2009 President's budget ($ in millions)

Departmental Operations	1,086
Office of the Inspector General	101
US Customs and Border Protection	10,941
US Immigration and Customs Enforcement	5,676
Transportation Security Administration	7,102
US Coast Guard	9,346
US Secret Service	1,639
National Protection and Programs Directorate	1,286
Office of Health Affairs	161
Federal Emergency Management Agency	8,767
US Citizenship and Immigration Services	2,690
Federal Law Enforcement Training Center	274
Science and Technology Directorate	869
Domestic Nuclear Detection Office	564
Total	50,502

Source: US Department of Homeland Security, *FY 2009 Budget in Brief* (February 2008).

Table 7.4 FY 2009 budget request for homeland security activities in DHS, by mission category (budget authority $ in millions)

DHS homeland security activities	
Intelligence and warning	403
Border and transportation security	22,971
Domestic counterterrorism	2,454
Protecting critical infrastructure and key assets	3,768
Defending against catastrophic threats	1,236
Emergency preparedness and response	1,788
Other	197
Total, DHS homeland security activities	**32,817**
DHS non-homeland security activities	17,685
Grand total DHS	**50,502**

Source: Author's display based on Office of Management and Budget, *Analytical Perspectives*, Budget of the United States for FY 2009 (February 2008), 20–9, and US Department of Homeland Security, *FY 2009 Budget in Brief* (February 2008).

Note
Table reflects Bush administration mission categories.

legacy departments. For example, FEMA has a detailed account structure that includes some 17 accounts (see Table 7.7). In contrast, ICE has just four broad accounts.

Organizations Involved in DHS's PPBE

Every component and office of DHS is involved in some way in the PPBE (see Figure 7.1 for an organization chart). The individual components, including the seven main operating components and others, develop their own draft programs and budgets, based on policy and fiscal guidance drafted by the

Table 7.5 Mission categories for homeland security

George W. Bush administration	Obama administration
Intelligence and warning Domestic counterterrorism Border and transportation security	Prevent and disrupt terrorist attacks
Protecting critical infrastructures and key assets Defending against catastrophic threats	Protect the American people, our critical infrastructure, and key resources
Emergency preparedness and response	Respond to and recover from incidents

Table 7.6 Homeland security appropriation titles

Title	Organizations funded through the title
Title I: Departmental Operations	• Office of Management • Office of the Secretary • CFO • Analysis and Operations • CIO • Office of the Inspector General • Federal Coordinator for Gulf Coast Rebuilding
Title II: Security, Enforcement, and Investigations	• CBP • ICE • TSA • Coast Guard • Secret Service
Title III: Preparedness and Recovery	• National Protection and Programs Directorate • FEMA • Office of Health Affairs
Title IV: Research and Development	• CIS • Science and Technology Directorate • Federal Law Enforcement Training Center
Title V: General Provisions	

Source: Author's display based on the Congressional Research Service Report to Congress, Jennifer E. Lake *et al.*, "Homeland Security Department: FY 2008 Appropriations," CRS Report RL34004 (Washington, DC: Congressional Research Service, May 17, 2007), 2.

Secretary's central staff. Within the Secretary's staff, the Assistant Secretary for Policy oversees the planning phase. Two organizations reporting to the Chief Financial Officer (CFO) oversee the other aspects: PA&E manages the overall PPBE and oversees the programming phase; the budget division oversees budgeting and execution.[13]

During 2008, the department established a Program Review Board (PRB) to review and deliberate on issues raised during the programming and budgeting phases. The PRB is chaired by the Deputy Secretary and includes the top career official from each component or directorate together with the CFO, the deputy general counsel, and the Deputy Assistant Secretary for Strategic Planning.[14] Final decisions are made and signed by the Secretary or the Deputy Secretary.

DHS's PPBE System

DHS's PPBE process has four phases.[15] The first three, which unfold in sequence, are planning, programming, and budgeting. They are followed by

Table 7.7 Appropriation accounts of three DHS components

FEMA	• State and local program • Assistance to firefighter grants • United States Fire Administration • Operations, Planning, and Support • Readiness, Mitigation, Response, and Recovery • Administrative and Regional Operations • Office of the Under Secretary • Public Health Programs—national disaster medical system • National pre-disaster mitigation fund • Emergency food and shelter • Disaster relief • Cerro Grande fire claims • Flood map modernization fund • Direct assistance disaster loan program account • Biodefense countermeasures • National flood mitigation fund • Flood mitigation fund offsetting collections
Customs and Border Protection	• Salaries and expenses • Automation modernization • Construction • Border security, fencing, infrastructure, and technology • Air and marine interdiction, operations, maintenance, and procurement • Fee accounts and trust funds
Immigration and Customs Enforcement	• Salaries and expenses • Federal protective service • Automation modernization • Fee accounts

transmission of the budget and the five-year plan to the White House and Congress (see Table 7.8). After the budget is passed by Congress and signed into law by the President, the execution phase for that budget occurs. Programs funded by budgets passed in the current and previous years are in their execution phases while the planning, programming, and budgeting phases for future years are carried out. The Director (PA&E) is responsible for managing the overall process.[16]

Planning Phase

For each year's budget, the planning process in DHS begins more than two years before the start of the fiscal year. This phase is meant to provide crucial links from the national homeland security strategy, assessments of the security environment, and the Secretary's key priorities into the department's plans for future staffing, programs, and activities. The department's planning documents are generally unconstrained by resources.

Table 7.8 Planning, Programming, Budgeting, and Execution System (PPBE) for the FY 2011 budget in the Department of Homeland Security

End date	Event or product	Responsible office
Planning phase		
June 2008	Threat and Vulnerability Assessment	Office of Intelligence and Analysis, with Components
October 2008	Strategic Assessment Report	Director, Strategic Plans
November 2008	Integrated Planning Guidance (IPG)	Assistant Secretary for Policy, with CFO (PA&E and Budget), input from others
February 2009	Fiscal Guidance	Office of the CFO
Programming phase		
April 2009	Resource Allocation Plans (RAPs)	Components
July 2009	Program Review, culminating in draft Resource Allocation Decisions (RADs) to components: emphasis on resource allocation, priorities	PA&E, Secretary
August 2009	Final RADs signed	PA&E, Secretary
Budgeting phase		
September 2009	Budget Review, culminating in DHS budget and FYHSP: emphasis on pricing, phasing, performance, execution	CFO (Budget)
September 2009	DHS budget and FYHSP to OMB	CFO
November 2009	White House passback to department	White House Office of Management and Budget (OMB)
Transmission to Congress		
February 2010	DHS budget and FYHSP to Congress	OMB

Source: Author's display based on US Department of Homeland Security, PPBE Management Directive #1330 (February 14, 2005), and the presentation by DHS PA&E, "DHS Resource Allocation Process" (November 18, 2008).

The process begins with a threat and vulnerability assessment that projects the operating environment for homeland security for the coming five to ten years. The Assistant Secretary for Intelligence and Analysis works with the components and the science and technology offices to develop a picture of the world environment and identify high-priority threats and vulnerabilities.

The threat and vulnerability assessment is central to the approach to resource allocation articulated in the October 2007 *National Strategy for Homeland Security*. The strategy document identifies risk as a function of three elements: threats, which include natural disasters and catastrophic accidents as well as terrorist capabilities for and intentions to attack; vulnerabilities to those threats; and the consequences of such events. It calls for a risk-based framework to "identify and assess potential hazards…, determine what levels of relative risk are acceptable, and prioritize and allocate resources among all homeland security partners."[17] The assessment is meant to identify important security gaps and inform resource priorities by clarifying the risks associated with various policy choices.

Concurrent with the threat and vulnerability assessment, the Director of Strategic Plans works with the components and regional headquarters to develop the strategic assessment report.[18] That report, scheduled for publication in October, communicates strategy recommendations and requirements to be considered during programming. The report is intended to identify shortfalls and gaps, particularly those that cut across components and regions.

The planning process culminates with preparation of the Integrated Planning Guidance (IPG), which the Assistant Secretary for Policy prepares for the Secretary's signature with help from PA&E and the CFO's budget division. The IPG is meant to be sent to the components in November, some 15 months before the administration will submit its budget request to Congress. The IPG includes a discussion of strategic goals and objectives, a description of the projected operating environment, and a list of key program and policy priorities. For example, the fiscal guidance for FY 2010–14 emphasized border control and the detection of biological pathogens.[19] The IPG may provide specific guidance on issues like biological defense that cut across multiple components.

PA&E and the CFO's budget division also prepare fiscal guidance and a memorandum containing instructions for the preparation and submission of budget proposals and justification materials to be prepared during the programming phase. The fiscal guidance tells each component and directorate how much money it should budget for each year of the five-year FYHSP.

The Secretary or Deputy Secretary of Homeland Security is meant to sign the IPG and the instructions to components. In the first iterations of the process, those documents were transmitted to the components directly from the CFO's office, without the signature of a top leader. Those managing the process have worked in recent years to strengthen this step of the process by ensuring the attention and signature of the Secretary or Deputy Secretary, and the instructions for FY 2010–14 were signed by the Acting Deputy Secretary.[20]

The planning phase represents an important opportunity to align the department's programs with national strategy. In this regard, the process as practiced to date is weak. At the front end, the plethora of overlapping strategy documents related to homeland security can make it difficult to discern top priorities. Improved assessments of threats, vulnerabilities, and risks could help in this regard, but the department lacks tools to integrate such assessments across its components in a way that could help leaders to manage risks by shifting resources from one activity to another.

Another problem is that the department's risk-assessment mechanisms are still in their infancy. In the biodefense area, for example, DHS has developed a framework for assessing the risks associated with a variety of biological agents.[21] A review of that framework by the National Academy of Sciences found deep flaws. These include the lack of a mechanism for considering what information decision-makers would actually need to help allocate resources in a way that would reduce risk; the lack of mechanisms like red teaming that could bring in the potential moves of intelligent adversaries; and the absence of an approach to managing risk.[22]

Previously, DHS had no formal, periodic review of the long-term linkages between strategy, programs, and budgets. To rectify that problem, Congress in 2007 required the department to conduct a Quadrennial Homeland Security Review (QHSR) that draws long-term links from strategy to resources. The first review is due in 2009.[23] As with DOD's Quadrennial Defense Review, the QHSR should help the department to improve the integration of priorities and budgets, but only if it actually includes the assessment of required resources that the legislation mandates (see Chapter 5).

Programming Phase

During the programming phase, DHS components and the Office of the Secretary translate the policy and fiscal guidance provided at the end of the planning phase into the detailed allocation of resources for the five-year period under consideration. Between January and April, each component develops a Resource Allocation Plan (RAP). The RAP includes a program-by-program budget proposal and justification materials for the five-year period. The components enter their RAPs electronically into the CFO's databases.

After the components submit their RAPs, PA&E conducts a program review. The program review focuses on the components' compliance with strategic guidance and the Secretary's priorities and progress toward performance objectives. PA&E also reviews the components' compliance with funding targets provided with the IPG and the allocation of funding across homeland security mission categories.

During the summer of 2008, the department also instituted a review of alternatives as part of the program review. PA&E prepared "decision briefs" on several issues for the recently constituted PRB. Each brief included background information on the question under consideration, an examination of the RAP plan and other options, and a structured decision point for the PRB.

Following the briefings and deliberations by the PRB, the Deputy Secretary made the decisions.

PA&E also works with the components' planning and budgeting offices throughout the year to develop performance metrics that capture key effectiveness goals for DHS's major programs, and to assess those programs relative to the metrics. The performance assessments use OMB's Program Assessment Rating Tool (PART) and are an input to PA&E's program review. (Chapter 8 describes the PART in more detail. Chapter 5 discusses the use of the tool in DOD's effort to integrate budgets and performance.)

If the review surfaces differences between the RAPs and the Secretary's guidance, then PA&E drafts a Resource Allocation Decision (RAD) for the Secretary's signature. Decisions made by the Deputy Secretary following PRB deliberations are also recorded as draft RADs. Components are offered an opportunity to comment on the draft RADs, then PA&E prepares and the Secretary signs the final RADs. At that point the programming phase is complete.

In early iterations of the PPBE, the analytic underpinnings of the program review were weak. PA&E analysts spent much of their time helping the components develop and report on metrics used to track their performance using PART. In addition, DHS PA&E did not have the senior analysts with the breadth of experience and the perspective to conduct gap analyses and trade-off studies. As a result, PA&E did not conduct the analyses that could have provided the Secretary with information about the costs, risks, and benefits of shifting resources among programs. During the 2008 summer program review, PA&E did conduct such analyses, and the Secretary made decisions based on them. PA&E remains small compared with the size of its job, however, and many of its analysts still lack significant experience in conducting tradeoff studies and gap analyses.[24]

Budgeting Phase

Shortly before the programming phase is finished, the CFO's budget division begins its budget review, the heart of the budgeting phase. The budget review focuses on program pricing, adjustment of budget figures for expected rates of inflation, the proper spread of program content across the years of the FYHSP, and the question of whether the budget is financially executable. PART assessments continue in this phase, with an emphasis on financial performance.

During the budget review, the CFO also adjusts current and past budget figures for recent congressional action, as well as changes in the costs of systems being purchased or in development and other fact-of-life changes. Based on changed requirements, the CFO may recommend small adjustments to the figures in the RADs, but by that point in the cycle, any increase in funding is expected to be offset with a decrease of the same magnitude.

The budgeting phase ends with the transmission of the President's DHS budget (the single-year request on which Congress will act) and the FYHSP to OMB and then to Congress.

Execution

The execution of programs under budget authority granted during the current and previous years continues throughout the year, and thus overlaps the other three phases of the PPBE. Execution reviews include the PART performance reviews and the CFO's examination of obligations and expenditures. Execution also includes the CFO's administrative control of funds through apportionment to the components.

Planning and Resource Allocation for Homeland Security in the Department of Health and Human Services

A look at HHS's arrangements for the planning and budgeting of its homeland security activities offers a window into the challenges faced by other departments whose role in homeland security is small when compared with the other functions they undertake.[25] HHS has the third-largest share of the federal homeland security budget. (DHS and DOD have the largest and second-largest shares.) The President's budget request for FY 2009 included $4.5 billion for HHS, most of it related to countering biological terrorism or preparing to address the consequences of a possible pandemic.

The weight and distribution of the homeland security effort within HHS is far different from the weight and distribution in DHS. Not only is funding for homeland security much smaller in HHS than in DHS—$4.5 billion in contrast with $33 billion—it is also a much smaller fraction of the department's total. HHS's total budget for FY 2009 is more than $800 billion, most of which goes toward health entitlement programs like Medicare and Medicaid. Homeland security constitutes only about one-half of 1 percent of the department's budget. In contrast, while homeland security is not the only job of DHS, it is that department's main job, accounting for about 65 percent of the DHS budget. HHS's homeland security effort is split among multiple internal organizations, none of whose main jobs is homeland security.

The situation in HHS is representative of that in most of the other federal departments that play supporting roles in homeland security. DOD's homeland security effort comes to just 3 percent of the department's total non-war budget and is fragmented across multiple internal components. The Department of Energy spends less than 3 percent of its budget on homeland security.[26]

The next two subsections briefly discuss the organizations within HHS that have roles in homeland security and the various budget categories used in

HHS. The section then discusses the organizations involved in planning and resource allocation and the processes the department uses to plan and develop its budgets.

The Homeland Security Effort in HHS

The Office of the Secretary and three separate operating units—the National Institutes of Health (NIH), the Center for Disease Control and Prevention (CDC), and the Food and Drug Administration (FDA)—share responsibility for homeland security in HHS. Within NIH, much of the homeland security budget goes toward research and development of medical countermeasures such as vaccines, antibiotics, and antiviral drugs. NIH also spent more than $1 billion in recent years to build new biological defense research facilities or upgrade security at existing ones.

The CDC passes about one-half of its annual homeland security budget on to state and local governments as grants to help improve public health capacity. CDC also maintains the strategic national stockpile—a store of vaccines, medicines, and medical supplies that can be trucked to a community should a public health emergency exhaust the local supply. In addition, the CDC's biosurveillance initiative includes improvements in quarantine stations at US ports of entry, a laboratory response network to identify and report suspicious cases, and the BioSense program. BioSense aims to analyze and evaluate health data from emergency rooms, pharmacies, poison control centers, and other clinical settings to identify possible disease outbreaks.

Most of the FDA's homeland security dollars go to monitor food safety. The Office of the Secretary passes about one-half of its homeland security funds to local entities, to help hospitals prepare to handle public health emergencies.

HHS Budget Categories

Each of the HHS agencies with a major role in homeland security—the NIH, the CDC, and the FDA—has its own appropriation in Congress. In addition to the appropriation categories, HHS tracks its homeland security budgets according to the mission categories discussed in the section on DHS (see Table 7.9). Under the Bush administration mission categories for homeland security, almost all of HHS's funding was directed toward defending against catastrophic threats (in this case countering biological terrorism or naturally spread disease) or emergency preparedness and response. Using the combined mission categories of the Obama administration, HHS homeland security funding falls into two of the three categories, namely "protect the American people, our critical infrastructure, and key resources" and "respond to and recover from incidents."

Table 7.9 FY 2009 budget request for homeland security activities in HHS, by mission category (budget authority in millions of dollars)

Intelligence and warning	0
Border and transportation security	0
Domestic counterterrorism	0
Protecting critical infrastructure and key assets	200
Defending against catastrophic threats	2,219
Emergency preparedness and response	2,038
Total, HHS homeland security activities	4,457

Source: Author's display based on Office of Management and Budget, *Analytical Perspectives*, Budget of the United States for FY 2009 (February 2008), 20–9.

Note
Table reflects Bush administration mission categories.

Budget Categories at NIH

NIH includes 19 separate institutes and four research centers, most of which have their own appropriation accounts. Congress generally appropriates at the institute or center level, and there is no formal appropriation breakout below that level.[27] Most of NIH's homeland security budget goes either to the office of the NIH director or to the National Institute of Allergy and Infectious Diseases (NIAID).

Internally, NIH tracks its budgets by institute and center. It also tracks spending by so-called funding mechanism—for example, grants for research projects versus research and development contracts or intramural research.[28]

Budget Categories in the CDC and FDA

The CDC has multiple appropriation accounts, including one for Terrorism Preparedness and Emergency Response (TPER). The TPER appropriation currently breaks out into four subcategories (see Table 7.10).

The FDA's appropriation does not include a category for terrorism preparedness and emergency response, but the agency keeps a separate track of its

Table 7.10 CDC FY 2009 budget request for Terrorism Preparedness and Emergency Response (TPER) (budget authority in millions of dollars)

State and local capacity	609
Upgrading CDC capacity	139
Biosurveillance initiative	101
Strategic national stockpile	570
Total, CDC TPER	1,419

Source: Author's display based on US Department of Health and Human Services, *FY 2009 Budget in Brief* (February 2008), 28.

biodefense budgets in three categories: food defense; vaccines, drugs, and diagnostics; and physical security (see Table 7.11).

HHS Organizations Involved in Planning and Resource Allocation

As in other departments, HHS's planning and resource allocation processes start with its components, including the NIH, the CDC, and the FDA (see Figure 7.2). This section highlights the organizations within the Office of the Secretary of HHS that manage and oversee the integration of plans, programs, and budgets across the department. For the department's overall planning and resource allocation effort, two organizations play key roles: the Office of the Assistant Secretary for Planning and Evaluation (ASPE) and the Office of Budget.

ASPE was established during the 1960s to bring a systems-analytic perspective to departmental decision-making.[29] Like the PA&E offices in DOD and DHS, ASPE conducts independent analyses of the multiple-year costs and benefits of policy choices that face the department. ASPE manages the department's cross-cutting strategic planning activities and conducts studies to evaluate the effectiveness of HHS programs.

The Office of Budget, which resides in the Office of the Assistant Secretary for Resources and Technology, manages the department's budget formulation and execution processes. The office coordinates program performance assessments required under the Government Performance and Results Act (GPRA) of 1993 and the PART requirements of the Bush administration's President's management agenda, and pulls together the budget justifications and other budget documents required by OMB and Congress. (Chapter 8 discusses GPRA and PART more fully. Chapter 5 discusses them in the context of DOD's integration of budgets and performance.)

Both of those offices are typically consumed with other issues, however. HHS manages a vast array of healthcare programs, including Medicare, Medicaid, children's health insurance, and a sprawling medical research enterprise. It is a wide-ranging, diverse, decentralized institution.[30] Homeland security is just a tiny fraction of its effort.

Table 7.11 FDA FY 2009 budget request for biodefense (budget authority in millions of dollars)

Food defense	213
Vaccines, drugs, and diagnostics	67
Physical security	7
Total, FDA biodefense	287

Source: Author's display based on US Department of Health and Human Services, *FY 2009 Budget in Brief* (February 2008), 18.

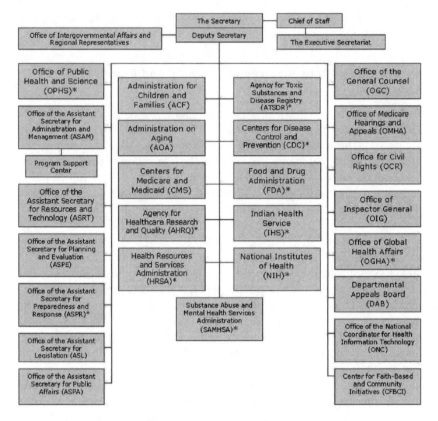

Figure 7.2 Organization of the Department of Health and Human Services (HHS) (source: US Department of Health and Human Resources).

Note

* Designates components of the Public Health Service.

To manage the integration of the department's strategies, policies, plans, and operations to deal with homeland security and public health emergencies, HHS in recent years created the position of Assistant Secretary for Preparedness and Response (ASPR). ASPR also represents HHS on homeland security matters in the interagency arena.

Within the Office of ASPR, the Office of Policy and Strategic Planning has a role in the homeland security and biological defense arena somewhat like the one that ASPE holds for all of HHS. ASPR's Office of Policy and Strategic Planning has a mandate to conduct gap analyses and studies of policy alternatives, manage the development of integrated, department-wide strategic plans and policy objectives for biological defense and public health preparedness, and serve as the homeland security focal point for HHS in the interagency policy arena.

Planning and Resource Allocation Processes in HHS

HHS uses a department-wide, cascading process to align the annual plans and budgets of all its operating divisions with the goals set forward in a departmental long-term strategic plan.[31] The process culminates in budget presentations by component agencies in a meeting with the Secretary and Deputy Secretary, which inform the Secretary's final resource allocation decisions.

The shift of budget shares among HHS's various agencies is consistent with the department's growing strategic emphasis on homeland security and biological defense. Between 1999 and 2007, NIH budgets nearly doubled, in part to fund the Institutes' growing role in homeland security. Within NIH, moreover, the share of spending devoted to the NIAID, where NIH's biological defense effort is concentrated, grew from 10 percent in 1999 to 15 percent in 2005, while shares for that agency's institutes and centers that lack roles in biological defense generally shrank.[32]

NIH's approach to allocating resources for the research conducted in its various institutes is in flux. There is a debate over whether centralized or decentralized resource allocation produces the most value for taxpayers. Some experts take the view that good science requires a freedom to explore that can be achieved only through decentralization and autonomy; others hold that centralized decision-making and collaboration will give taxpayers more bang for the research buck. The NIH Reform Act of 2006 (Public Law 109-482) moved the Institutes from a process that was decidedly decentralized toward a more centralized approach, by expanding the authority of NIH's director to allocate resources. The director set up an office of portfolio analysis and strategic initiatives to jump-start priority projects, and now holds back a "common fund for shared needs" to pay for such central projects.[33]

Within the medical countermeasures area, there are important choices to be made between research and acquisition aimed at individual diseases and the broad-spectrum research on medicines that might be used against a wider variety of threats. In 2006, HHS created a departmental public-health-emergency medical-countermeasures enterprise, led by the ASPR and including members from NIH, CDC, and FDA as well as partners from DOD, DHS, and the Department of Veterans Affairs.[34] The group is charged with integrating federal research on and acquisition of medical countermeasures. The group has developed a cross-cutting strategy, and HHS's budget request for advanced research and development of countermeasures identified in that strategy grew by 60 percent between FY 2008 and FY 2009.[35] It is not yet clear whether ASPR will have the budgetary clout to integrate countermeasures work across HHS or, through its non-HHS partners, across federal departments.

Conclusion

Of all the areas of security and foreign affairs discussed in this book, homeland security may be the most complex when it comes to planning and resource allocation. The establishment of DHS in 2003 made the job more manageable for the roughly 50 percent of homeland security activities (by budget) folded into the new department. Important homeland security functions still cut across departments, however, and DHS's own organizations and processes for planning and resource allocation seem only now to be coming into their own.

Leaders of the new department had important choices to make about the planning and resource system DHS would use. The justification for a new department rested heavily on the notion that a Cabinet Secretary could use his or her budget clout to unify the panoply of federal homeland security activities. Thus a relatively centralized system seemed in order, despite the diversity of missions and activities of the multiple components. The staff reached for a centralized model already operating as effectively as any in federal government: DOD's PPBE. They set up a PA&E with a mandate somewhat similar to that of DOD's and, consistent with the terms of the Homeland Security Act of 2002, created a Future-Years Homeland Security Program with a structure similar to DOD's FYDP.

The effectiveness of the system in forging unity among the department's components or keeping costs in line has not yet become obvious. The components generally continue to set their own agendas, and their individual shares of the budget did not shift much from year to year. There is also little evidence of cost savings based on the elimination of redundant activities.

It may not be realistic to count on centralized authority and systems to bring unity of effort across a department whose missions and components are as diverse as those of DHS. FEMA and the Secret Service are in completely different businesses; asking one to give up activities to free resources for the other may not make sense in the way that cross-service tradeoffs might make in DOD.

That said, to the extent that the goal of the department is to create unity of effort where little existed before, the department seems hampered by several elements of planning and resource allocation. The first two problems start in the White House and are shared by all of the departments and agencies with roles in homeland security: a proliferation of White House strategy documents and the immaturity of tools for risk and vulnerability assessment anywhere in the executive branch. The proliferation of strategies can create confusion regarding genuine priorities. The discipline of tying strategic goals to a long-term budget plan, as Congress now mandates for a QHSR, may help DHS to clarify and trim its own list of priorities—but only if realistic resource constraints are actually considered during the review.

Immature tools for risk and vulnerability assessment also cause problems. In this area, there may not be an obvious solution. In the United States, both the questions and the answers about risk and vulnerability are highly political and also politicized. Developing better tools may require a level of consensus about threats and vulnerabilities to attacks or public health emergencies that cannot be achieved.

The final problem reflects a weakness in the programming phase of DHS's initial PPBE. In 2008, DHS strengthened the programming phase by having PA&E develop alternatives to the components' plans during the summer program review. In addition, the Deputy Secretary and Secretary engaged directly at key points during the process—a change from previous practice. It is too soon to tell whether the revised arrangements will help the Secretary and Deputy Secretary to establish the degree of integration that proponents of the new department espoused during 2001 and 2002.

In any case, the Secretary of Homeland Security has virtually no authority over the one-half of federal homeland security funding that flows into other departments and agencies. Thus it would be unrealistic to expect him or her to wield the budget tool in any way that would create unity of effort or bring cost effectiveness across the overall federal effort. That job is left to the White House, as discussed in Chapter 8.

The Role of the Executive Office of the President in National Security Budgeting

Introduction

The federal budget is the President's budget; it is not transmitted by executive branch agencies, but by the Executive Office of the President (EOP).[1] While presidents have varied in the extent of their involvement in budget planning, this responsibility is one the White House office cannot ignore.

For the President, the budget is his most important tool for shaping the policy agenda and implementing policy goals. Budget planning and program execution are at the heart of the relationship between the White House and the executive branch agencies. The budget is generally the focus of policy disagreements and negotiations with the Congress. Consequently, the budget planning tools and processes in the White House are a crucial ingredient of national security budgeting.[2]

The EOP's responsibility for national security resources does not end with the submission of the budget to Congress. Once Congress has appropriated funds, the Office of Management and Budget (OMB) in EOP "apportions" appropriated funds and resolves a steady stream of budget and spending issues across the executive branch. Moreover, especially in the national security world, new requirements for funding often emerge between budget cycles. The White House and the agencies regularly need to react to events they do not control: international pledging conferences for emergency assistance, the outbreak of conflict, unanticipated war expenses, humanitarian and natural disasters, or terrorist attacks. The budgetary and fiscal responsibilities of the EOP require a year-round process.

The President's Office of Management and Budget is the critical EOP organization when it comes to budgets. In addition, a number of other White House offices become involved in the process. The President himself sets the broad parameters for his budget proposals. The National Security Council (NSC) is the crucible in which crisis decision-making is made, usually with implications for spending. The Office of the Vice President is regularly involved in the budget planning process. Other White House offices, such as the US Trade Representative, the Council on Environmental Quality, and the

Office of Science and Technology Policy, also play a role in the budget process. This chapter examines the roles played by these EOP institutions in national security budgeting.

Office of Management and Budget

OMB's Overall Functions

With roughly 490 professional and support staff, the President's Office of Management and Budget (OMB) is the only permanent civil service organization of significant size in the EOP.[3] It is at the heart of government planning and operations in the executive branch. OMB is the White House "memory bank"—the repository of knowledge and experience on budgeting and operations throughout the executive branch.[4] It is the "operator" of the executive branch budget process, setting requirements for the preparation and submission of budgets from all federal agencies. Finally, it is a hub, or "funnel" through which all budgets, program proposals, draft legislation, regulations, testimony, and communications between executive branch agencies and the Congress are expected to pass, in order to have presidential approval.[5] The OMB staff has the detailed knowledge of executive branch operations, budgeting and management that a president needs to shape and implement policy, ensure that resources support that policy, and control, to the extent possible, executive branch operations.

OMB is a relatively flat organization with only a handful of policy officials subject to Senate confirmation: the Director, Deputy Director, Deputy Director for Management, and the heads of three "statutory" offices—the Office of Information and Regulatory Affairs (OIRA), the Office of Federal Procurement Policy (OFPP), and the Office of Federal Financial Management (OFFM) (see Figure 8.1).[6] OMB's responsibilities for budget and legislation are in the hands of the Resource Management Offices (RMOs), each of which covers a specific set of federal agencies. Each RMO is headed by an Associate Director (commonly known as a Program Associate Director, or PAD), who is a non-confirmation but politically appointed policy official. Each PAD has at least two divisions reporting to him/her, headed by a career Senior Executive Service official known as a Deputy Associate Director (DAD). Each DAD, in turn, has two or more Branch Chiefs, each of whom has a staff of Program Examiners. The Program Examiners are the primary workforce, handling a specific set of government agencies or programs.

OMB's legislative clearance work is administered by an organization-wide Legislative Reference Division (LRD). Their work includes reviewing the proposals and circulating them to all agencies that might be affected. Working with the RMOs, LRD adjudicates disagreements over the language prior to transmitting the proposals to Congress. LRD and the RMOs also clear the written statements of department and agency officials called to testify as witnesses before the Congress, especially where programs and budgets are

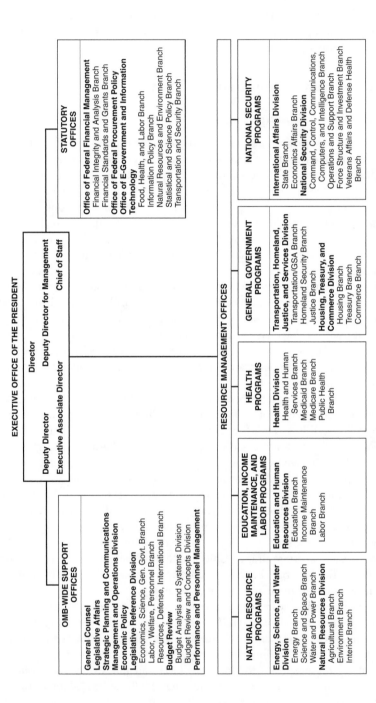

EXECUTIVE OFFICE OF THE PRESIDENT

Director
Deputy Director   Deputy Director for Management
Deputy Director   Chief of Staff
Executive Associate Director

OMB-WIDE SUPPORT OFFICES

General Counsel
Legislative Affairs
Strategic Planning and Communications
Management and Operations Division
Economic Policy
Legislative Reference Division
Economics, Science, Gen. Govt. Branch
Labor, Welfare, Personnel Branch
Resources, Defense, International Branch
Budget Review
Budget Analysis and Systems Division
Budget Review and Concepts Division
Performance and Personnel Management

STATUTORY OFFICES

Office of Federal Financial Management
Financial Integrity and Analysis Branch
Financial Standards and Grants Branch
Office of Federal Procurement Policy
Office of E-Government and Information Technology
Food, Health, and Labor Branch
Information Policy Branch
Natural Resources and Environment Branch
Statistical and Science Policy Branch
Transportation and Security Branch

RESOURCE MANAGEMENT OFFICES

NATURAL RESOURCE PROGRAMS

Energy, Science, and Water Division
Energy Branch
Science and Space Branch
Water and Power Branch
Natural Resources Division
Agricultural Branch
Environment Branch
Interior Branch

EDUCATION, INCOME MAINTENANCE, AND LABOR PROGRAMS

Education and Human Resources Division
Education Branch
Income Maintenance Branch
Labor Branch

HEALTH PROGRAMS

Health Division
Health and Human Services Branch
Medicaid Branch
Medicare Branch
Public Health Branch

GENERAL GOVERNMENT PROGRAMS

Transportation, Homeland, Justice, and Services Division
Transportation/GSA Branch
Homeland Security Branch
Justice Branch
Housing, Treasury, and Commerce Division
Housing Branch
Treasury Branch
Commerce Branch

NATIONAL SECURITY PROGRAMS

International Affairs Division
State Branch
Economics Affairs Branch
National Security Division
Command, Control, Communications, Computers, and Intelligence Branch
Operations and Support Branch
Force Structure and Investment Branch
Veterans Affairs and Defense Health Branch

Figure 8.1 OMB organization chart (source: adapted from Office of Management and Budget).

concerned. LRD, working with OMB's Legislative Affairs Office (responsible for Congressional relations), also drafts administration statements on legislation pending before the Congress, known as "Statements of Administration Policy" (SAPs), and advises the President on decisions to sign or veto legislation and appropriations bills.

OMB began as the Bureau of the Budget (BOB) at the Treasury Department. Before BOB was established, the War Department (for the Army) and the Navy Department submitted their budgets directly to the corresponding appropriations subcommittees in the Congress. Congress's intent in creating BOB was to provide for greater central scrutiny of agency budgets, in order to restrain federal spending and to limit separate agency lobbying of Congress.[7]

BOB's capabilities expanded with the growth of government in the Roosevelt administration, leading to a decision in 1939 to incorporate the office into the White House.[8] Its responsibilities for budget and management expanded after World War II. BOB became the budget and program analyst for the White House, the central clearing office for federal agency budgets, programs and legislation, the developer and steward of overall federal management practices, and the advocate for the White House budget, policy, and management agenda. With this expanding responsibility, BOB was reorganized in 1970 as the Office of Management and Budget.

The Budget and Impoundment Control Act of 1974 further enlarged OMB's responsibilities.[9] The Act created a more integrated congressional process for overall federal budgeting, led by new Budget Committees in each chamber and supported by the analytic capability of the new Congressional Budget Office (CBO). As Congress redefined its budgetary role, OMB expanded its role in tracking legislation and congressional engagement and its responsibilities for clearing agency legislative proposals.

The 1974 Act divided the federal budget into 19 "budget functions," and required the executive branch to provide its budget proposals not only by federal department and agency, but also distributed into these functions. There are now 21 such budget functions. Two of them are entirely national-security-related: Function 050 for "National Defense" (Department of Defense and the military nuclear programs—weapons and naval reactors—of the Department of Energy) and Function 150 for "International Affairs" (State Department, foreign assistance programs and international financial institutions). As discussed in Chapter 9, there is no budget function for homeland security.

OMB's responsibilities expanded again during the era of deficit reduction, from 1985 through 2002. Congressional efforts to reduce the federal deficit began with the passage of the Balanced Budget and Emergency Deficit Control Act of 1985 (Gramm–Rudman–Hollings).[10] The Act required OMB to estimate the federal deficit and, if it exceeded the deficit targets in the law, execute an across-the-board reduction of federal spending, known as a "sequester," including budgets for national security.

The weaknesses in the Act spurred further efforts to reduce the deficit, leading to the Omnibus Budget and Reconciliation Act of 1990. This legislation contained the Budget Enforcement Act (BEA) provisions, which broadened OMB's budget control responsibilities and had a direct impact on national security budgets. The most important provision called for a "cap," or limit, on total spending subject to appropriations (called "discretionary spending").[11] Although the spending caps were regularly renegotiated, they remained in effect through FY 2002. The caps made it necessary for OMB to press agencies for lower spending, including for defense and international affairs.[12]

OMB's responsibility under the BEA was to estimate the spending that would result from the executive branch's budget proposals (known as "scoring"). OMB's scoring would be the test of whether the deficit reduction goals had been met by the budget proposal. This task led OMB to become the executive branch's principal negotiator on budgets and spending priorities with the Congress. This role included negotiating on appropriations bills and, as Congress found it increasingly difficult to enact these bills on time, on Continuing Resolutions, which extended federal spending authority at prior-year levels until appropriations bills could be passed. (Chapter 9 discusses appropriations and continuing resolutions from the point of view of Congress.) As the only executive branch official who could propose cross-agency spending tradeoffs on behalf of the President, the Director of OMB during the 1990s became the executive branch's point person for negotiating with Congress on appropriations.

OMB's planning and management responsibilities also expanded during the 1980s and 1990s, in part in response to congressional action. The congressional Government Performance and Results Act (GPRA) of 1993 required OMB to work with agencies to develop strategic and performance plans. This OMB mission expanded in 2001 to include the regular evaluation of agency management, through the Bush administration's President's Management Agenda, and a systematic assessment of the effectiveness of agency programs through the Program Assessment Rating Tool (PART). These management and performance tools affect all of the national security agencies.

When they take office, a new President and his staff may view OMB as a legacy representative of the previous administration, because it carries out these functions on a permanent basis.[13] As Cabinet Secretaries begin to assert agency agendas, however, most White Houses come to rely on OMB to screen agency proposals and enforce the President's priorities. In 1993, for example, Vice President Al Gore created a separate White House organization—the National Performance Review (NPR)—to oversee the reform of executive branch management, including the reform of OMB itself. While OMB was modestly restructured, the NPR staff quickly realized that OMB's budgetary and management authorities could be a valuable tool for carrying out their reform agenda, and began working closely with the budget office.[14]

OMB can be a unique asset for presidents who wish to establish their priorities early in the administration. President Ronald Reagan's OMB Director David Stockman, for example, used the capabilities of OMB to draw up and implement the Reagan economic agenda of smaller government, lower spending, lower taxes, and increased defense spending right at the start of the administration. Within the first year, for example, he developed a budgetary and legislative package quickly and then exploited a device that was instituted in the Congressional Budget and Impoundment Control Act of 1974: reconciliation. The reconciliation procedure allowed congressional leaders to lower taxes and domestic spending, while increasing defense spending, through a single legislative act, using streamlined procedures that limit the amount of time allowed for debate and preclude filibusters.[15]

Similarly, President Bill Clinton's OMB Director, Leon Panetta, was the principal architect of and advocate for the administration's first budget plan, which aimed to reduce the federal budget deficit by half during Clinton's first term. The outgoing Bush administration had not prepared or transmitted a new budget.[16] Working backwards from an FY 1997 target of reducing the deficit by half, OMB and the White House carried out a rapid budget preparation process, resulting in a budget request that restrained domestic spending and also lowered projected defense spending by more than $100 billion over four years, consistent with the lower deficit target. Similarly, in 2009 the Obama OMB conducted a rapid process for the FY 2010 budget, setting agency budget totals early on that led to lower levels of defense spending than those anticipated in 2008 by the outgoing Defense Department.

The OMB staff has acquired significant expertise on agency programs and operations over long periods of time. It is known for its willingness to provide unvarnished advice to the President.[17] As OMB's functions have expanded to include shaping program and providing advocacy to the Congress, however, these more "politicized" roles have conflicted with the agency's "neutral" and more technical image.[18]

The OMB Structure and National Security

The national security responsibilities of OMB are concentrated largely in the RMO for National Security Programs. This organization has responsibility for all the Function 150 diplomacy and foreign assistance agencies and programs, the Department of Defense, the Department of Veterans Affairs, the National Nuclear Security Agency of the Department of Energy, and the intelligence agencies. It is organized into two Divisions: International Affairs and National Security. The International Affairs Division has two branches, one for State and one for Economic Affairs. The National Security Division has four branches: Command, Control, Communications, Computers, and Intelligence; Operations and Support; Force Structure and Investment; and Veterans Affairs and Defense Health.[19]

The National Security Budget Process

OMB's role in foreign policy budget planning and resourcing is similar to its broader role in overall federal budgeting and spending. Its role in defense budgeting is the same in many respects, but also includes some unique aspects. The OMB budget planning process starts roughly 18 months ahead of the fiscal year for which the administration is requesting funds.[20]

In the spring of each year, OMB deals with three budgets at the same time—the budget being implemented in the current fiscal year; the budget request for the next fiscal year, which the President has already submitted to Congress; and the budget request being prepared for the fiscal year after that. In April 2008, for example, OMB was overseeing the implementation of the FY 2008 budget, working with the Congress as it considered the FY 2009 budget request, and sending fiscal guidance to departments and agencies as the first step in preparing the FY 2010 budget request. This first step toward a new budget plan, the OMB fiscal guidance, is made in a context of uncertainty about how funds will be spent in the current fiscal year, and how much funding and what programs Congress will provide for in the coming fiscal year. OMB manages this uncertainty by basing its guidance on the multiple-year projections that were contained in previous budgets, any new presidential priorities that have emerged, agreements made with the Congress, the electoral setting, and emerging economic and fiscal realities such as economic growth rates, inflation, and deficit projections.

Thus the fiscal guidance that OMB gives to the departments and agencies involved in national security can be affected by broader fiscal, budgetary, policy, and political priorities that have little to do with national security requirements. In 1993, as noted above, the Clinton administration planned overall budget strategy to achieve a 50 percent reduction in the federal deficit by FY 1997.[21] That target resulted in a significant reduction in the growth of defense budgets compared with projections by the previous administration. It also led to reductions in real terms for International Affairs budgets.

Once it has provided this guidance to agencies, OMB generally leaves them to their own internal budget planning processes during the spring and summer. As discussed below and in Chapter 5, this is not the case for DOD, where OMB has for years carried out a "joint review," with budget examiners participating directly in the department's internal program and budget reviews. The OMB relationship with the State Department is also changing, as discussed later in this chapter. There is continuing contact, however, to identify major budget issues and conflicts that might appear during the fall OMB process. In the middle of the summer, OMB provides agencies with a more formal statement of the White House's budget requirements in the form of its annual Circular A-11.[22] A-11 describes in detail the types of data and information agencies must provide in their budget submissions.

A-11 is a key document.[23] It provides the format for agency submissions to OMB, covering applicable budget laws, terms, and process, and the types of data and information agencies should provide in their budget submissions. It sets the calendar for agency budget submissions to OMB (typically by mid-September).[24] It also describes any specific, unique data requests to which OMB and the White House want agencies to respond. These can include calls for data on agency non-proliferation programs, information technology spending, or management reports such as the agency's PART scores, strategic plans, or performance reports. A-11 also describes the materials agencies should provide to explain and support their budget requests, known as "justification" requirements.[25]

The annual A-11 circular also lays out requirements for the preparation of emergency supplemental budget requests. DOD and State/USAID emergency supplemental requests for operations in Iraq and Afghanistan and against terrorists grew in size and frequency after the 9/11 terrorist attacks.

OMB and International Affairs (Function 150) Budgets

OMB's role in budgeting for the foreign policy agencies is similar to its role with other agencies. There are, however, a number of departments and agencies involved in the International Affairs world, making the management of the overall Function 150 account more complex, as discussed in Chapters 2 and 3. Until recently, the budget for State Department operations (including personnel and overhead costs, public diplomacy, and UN-assessed dues) was prepared by State's Under Secretary for Management and submitted to OMB by mid-to-late September. USAID submitted its own development assistance budget request separately at roughly the same time, as did other foreign policy agencies whose budgets are not controlled by the Secretary of State.

State Department foreign assistance programs, however, were generally delayed. The Secretary of State, who was responsible for State's own foreign assistance program funds, often did not submit these budget requests until late October or even November. As the Secretary of State sought a more central role in overall Function 150 budget planning in the 1990s, State began to hold internal "hearings" both on the State Department budget and on the budget plans of other Function 150 agencies. These hearings further delayed the submission of foreign assistance budget requests to OMB, as the Secretary of State developed his/her views on other agency budgets.

As the State Department began to develop a more formal process for integrating parts of the foreign assistance budget, OMB officials began to participate directly in the internal State Department reviews. Early involvement gave OMB greater transparency into emerging budget plans and issues. At the same time, because these internal reviews could not make budget decisions for agencies other than State and USAID, OMB also continued to deal directly with the other international affairs agencies. Essentially, through 2008, overall budgets for Function 150 were only integrated at the OMB level.

That integration begins with the distribution of agency budget submissions to the appropriate program examiners in the State Operations and Foreign Operations branches at OMB. OMB staff review the budget requests internally and conduct a number of hearings—meetings lasting an hour to a full day with agency program and budget officials responsible for specific programs. The hearings might be conducted by the examiners, though Branch Chiefs, DADs, and occasionally the senior policy official (the PAD) might attend. In the 1990s, for example, assistance programs for Eastern Europe and the former Soviet Union were a high policy priority for the administration. As a result, a senior State Department assistance coordinator typically gave the briefing, and the OMB PAD chaired the session. The OMB hearings are designed to determine whether the agency request is adequately justified and priced, and to evaluate the performance of the program. Hearings also give OMB an opportunity to ensure that presidential policy priorities are reflected in the agency's request.

The OMB budget hearings lead to the next stage in the OMB process, the "Director's Review." On the basis of the internal "scrub" of the budget request and the results of the hearings, OMB staff prepares a lengthy briefing book for the OMB Director and senior staff. The Director's Review is carried out in November and early December in a lengthy closed session, sometimes restricted to OMB officials alone.[26] The Division's briefing book reviews recent State and USAID budgets and programs, provides a summary of the agency's budget proposal, and describes detailed options for changes, reductions, and additions for the Director to consider.

During the briefing, the Division's PAD, DADs, Branch Chiefs, and Examiners present these options. Options can be wide-ranging and may depart significantly from what the agency proposed. For example, in the 1990s, the OMB staff proposed "fencing" some of the State Department visa receipts in the Department's Capital Investment Fund, restricting their use to upgrading State's information technology. Or OMB might propose increasing funding above an agency request for a presidential priority, such as HIV/AIDS prevention. Overall Function 150 funding might be proposed at a level below that requested by State and the other 150 agencies, in keeping with broader presidential budget priorities. Or, as happened during the preparation of the first Obama budget, OMB might propose that funding for humanitarian programs such as PL 480 food aid and disaster assistance be included in the base State Department/USAID budget at full annual levels, rather than seeking a lower funding level that would be made up through a subsequent supplemental budget request.

The senior OMB leadership meets after the Director's Review and discusses final decisions and the contents of a letter to be sent to the agency head. This letter is known as the OMB "passback." It contains the Director's decisions and recommendations for the agency budget, including both funding and program activities, and is generally sent around Thanksgiving. The International Affairs agencies review this passback quickly, deciding which decisions they accept and which they wish to appeal.

If the Secretary of State or an agency head wishes to appeal the decision, this is communicated orally or in writing to the OMB Director. The PAD and the International Affairs Division staff work to resolve as many of the issues as they can. Any remaining disputes are taken to the senior OMB level for resolution.

The OMB Director has generally held back an allowance so that he or she can resolve appeals without having to go to a higher level in the White House. In the end, however, some budget appeals, usually few in number and highly significant, can be resolved only at the presidential level. The White House established a semi-formal process for presidential meetings to resolve such disagreements. In the Clinton administration, these meetings would take place in the Cabinet Room with the President, Vice President, OMB Director, and National Economic Council members attending, along with the cabinet official making the appeal. Secretaries of State Christopher and Albright regularly sought such meetings, disagreeing with OMB's overall budget level for Function 150 and wanting to meet face-to-face with the President. These meetings generally resulted in only slight increases above the OMB levels. During the George W. Bush administration, Vice President Cheney typically conducted the appeal meetings.[27]

Following the final presidential meetings and decisions, State/USAID and the other 150 agencies enter their budgetary data into OMB's "MAX" database, which "locks" in early January to allow for preparation of the President's budget. Even at this late stage, State may continue to appeal decisions to OMB. In 1994, for example, the Under Secretary of State for Management appealed the OMB decision to "fence" visa revenues and dedicate them to IT investments. Shortly before Christmas, the Under Secretary and the National Security Advisor phoned the OMB Associate Director to appeal the decision, but were denied. Post-appeal disputes can sometimes continue into January, compressing the time OMB has to complete the preparation of the budget.[28]

OMB and National Defense (Function 050) Budgets

While many of the traditional features of OMB's budget work apply to its relationship with DOD, there are also unique features in the DOD case. From the 1970s, with occasional interruptions, OMB staff has played an earlier, more integrated role in the DOD budget process through what has been called the "joint review." The DOD budget is roughly 13 times the size of that for International Affairs, and the DOD internal budget process—the Planning, Programming, Budgeting, and Execution (PPBE) system—is more formal, lengthy, and complex than that for International Affairs (see Chapter 5 for a discussion of DOD's PPBE).

In contrast to its relatively hands-off involvement in the early stages of the State and USAID process, OMB for decades has participated in the program and budget reviews of DOD's PPBE. During the program review, OMB's budget examiners get early insight into emerging DOD budget options. The joint process also gives the examiners an opportunity to make White House views known to DOD. Toward the end of the program review, the OMB PAD may participate in the decision meetings chaired by the Deputy Secretary or the Secretary.

The joint review has an uneven history, however, and mixed reviews from both sides. For OMB, the review has both advantages and disadvantages. Defense is the largest and most complex budget subject to annual appropriation by Congress. Waiting to review DOD decisions until September would put OMB's National Security Division's small staff of roughly 45 under intense pressure. Moreover, the DOD budget proposal would arrive at OMB with major compromises and program decisions already made, making a reversal of those decisions difficult at that late stage. Early identification of key issues and early participation by OMB staff make it possible for OMB to focus on priority programs and policies and disagreements. It also allows the White House to bring its preferences to the department early in the decision-making process. The chief disadvantage is that the joint review can disarm potential OMB disagreement early in the decision process, leading to approval of DOD programs and policies ahead of the other agencies and before OMB has conducted its own hearings and Director's Review.

The joint review also has advantages and disadvantages for DOD. The opportunity to gain OMB/White House approval of the department's decisions early in the process is clearly an advantage. Late OMB decisions could prove disruptive to the complex PPBE process. The chief disadvantage is the early insight into internal DOD budget disagreements that OMB obtains before the Secretary makes the final decisions. This transparency can provide OMB with views and evidence it can use later to critique the Secretary's final decisions.

Both sides have at times considered abandoning the joint review. During the first Clinton term, Secretary of Defense Les Aspin excluded OMB from DOD's internal process for his entire tenure, reportedly on the advice of former Secretary of Defense Harold Brown.[29] The Secretary's resistance to the OMB role was exacerbated by the early OMB decision to reduce the defense topline from the level projected by the previous administration (discussed in Chapter 10). When William Perry succeeded Secretary Aspin in January 1994, that decision was reversed, and the Joint Review was renewed. At the start of the Obama administration, OMB senior staff seriously considered abandoning the Joint Review unless it was more formally defined and institutionalized. The view of OMB staff was that the Bush administration had largely excluded OMB from internal defense deliberations and had routinely end-run the process with direct appeals for more resources to senior White House officials.[30]

Because of the joint review process, DOD does not submit a budget request to OMB in September. Instead, the OMB involvement in internal DOD deliberations continues through the fall budget review by the DOD Comptroller. As the Comptroller develops draft Program Budget Decisions (PBDs), OMB has an opportunity to review them. OMB can also prepare its own draft PBDs for the DOD budget review.

This interaction can be complex. During the Carter administration, for example, the President himself reviewed the PBDs and transmitted his preferences to DOD through the OMB Associate Director, a process that might have contributed to Secretary Brown's dislike of the joint review.[31] During the Clinton administration, the White House used PBDs to integrate its priorities into DOD budget plans, over DOD resistance. In one instance, after President Clinton asked DOD to create a Technology Reinvestment Program (TRP) to support defense firms that would apply their technologies to civilian uses, the department failed to fund it as the White House wished. OMB developed a PBD and set funding levels for the TRP through its own budget review.

DOD officials can also use this interaction to their advantage when the services fail to budget adequately for the projects the leadership desires. For example, in the 1990s the Joint Chiefs of Staff sought support for investments in defense technology that would improve inter-service connectivity for command, control, and communications. The services did not give these investments a high priority. Senior Joint Staff officials met with senior OMB officials and encouraged them to add funding through a White House PBD.

At the same time as this interactive Joint Review takes place, OMB also holds fall "hearings" with DOD offices to scrutinize specific budgets and programs. These hearings also lead to a Director's Review for DOD and a passback on decisions that were not resolved in the Joint Review or to ensure White House priorities are reflected in the final DOD budget. DOD generally appeals a relatively small number of major issues, often involving major programs or the overall level of the defense budget, through the OMB Director and frequently to the President himself.

OMB and Intelligence Budgets

Intelligence budgets are generally included in a classified way in the President's defense budget request. Roughly 80 percent of overall federal spending for intelligence is the responsibility of the Defense Department. OMB's role in intelligence budgeting, therefore, is the responsibility of the National Security Division's Command, Control, Communications, Computers, and Intelligence branch. This branch has a small staff, which generally has professional experience in the Intelligence Community (IC).

For many years, OMB's involvement in the IC's budget processes was minimal, as the elements of the IC resisted detailed, outside budget scrutiny and coordination, even at the level of the Director of National Intelligence.

Nevertheless, the OMB branch regularly received and reviewed budget requests from the various intelligence agencies. OMB worked particularly closely with the IC's Community Management Staff (CMS), which was responsible for overall IC budget coordination and planning.

In addition, OMB played a role in several key intelligence budget issues that became public in the 1990s. OMB was involved in examining the budget practices of the National Reconnaissance Organization (NRO) surrounding the construction of a major new headquarters building in Virginia. It was also involved in the scrutiny of NRO "forward funding" of satellite programs, which led to using roughly $1 billion in NRO funds as an offset for the costs of the military presence in the Balkans.[32] The growing number of intelligence budget issues in the 1990s led to closer OMB scrutiny of IC planning and budgeting and OMB agreement to increase CMS resources to strengthen the capacity of the Director of Central Intelligence to carry out cross-IC budget coordination. The intelligence budget system changed with the creation of the office of the Director of National Intelligence in 2004, who was given expanded authorities to coordinate IC budgeting across agencies (discussed in Chapter 6). OMB continues to work closely with the ODNI in this process.

OMB and Homeland Security Budgets

The homeland security budget process at OMB differs from defense and international affairs. As discussed in Chapter 7, the Department of Homeland Security (DHS) has responsibility for only about one-half of federal homeland security funding. Moreover, DHS does more than homeland security; about 35 percent of its FY 2009 budget goes toward non-homeland security activities like marine safety. As a result, White House involvement with homeland security budgets is complex.

OMB played a key role in the establishment of the Homeland Security Department in 2003, helping the White House planning team identify those parts of federal activity and spending that might be included in the homeland security budget. It remains a key actor for integrating the homeland security budget, as it is the only institution in the executive branch with the cross-agency perspective needed to pull all homeland security budget elements together.

However, budget examination for homeland security agencies and programs is not located in a single office at OMB. The Department of Homeland Security's budget is the responsibility of the "General Government" RMO, which has a Homeland Security Branch. A Deputy Associate Director at OMB is responsible for coordinating homeland security budgets more broadly across federal agencies and across the OMB divisions. The Department of Homeland Security transmits its budget request in September for the typical hearings and Director's Review process. At the same time, OMB reviews the homeland security-related budget requests from other agencies. OMB's homeland security Director's Review is conducted as a "cross-cut" review, examining all programs and including all relevant OMB staff.[33]

OMB Cross-Cut Reviews

In addition to its normal budget planning process, OMB also conducts reviews of programs and budgets that cut across agencies. These agency cross-cut reviews focus on particular policy areas and can occur during the regular fall budget process, or at any other time. The goal can be to gather data and program information on a policy area in which several agencies are involved, identify level of agency activity and gaps in coverage or duplications, or shape options for the Director to provide to agencies during the OMB passback. During the 1990s OMB agency cross-cuts covered such policy areas as counternarcotics, counterterrorism, and counterproliferation.

OMB Apportionment

Once funds have been appropriated by the Congress, they must be "apportioned" to the agencies, subject to the conditions of the Anti-Deficiency Act and the Congressional Budget Impoundment and Control Act, which ensure that agencies are not spending more funds than they had appropriated or are not withholding funds Congress intended be spent for specific purposes.[34] Agencies request such apportionment from OMB. The primary purpose of the apportionment process is to ensure that spending conforms to the appropriation and will "achieve the most effective and economical use of amounts made available."[35] Through the apportionment process, OMB, together with the agencies, defines the categories agencies should use to report on their spending, some of which are standard and some of which reflect particular programs for which OMB wishes to track spending.[36]

The apportionment process has occasionally been used by OMB to influence agency activities, through "footnotes." These footnotes seek agency responses to OMB questions or provide specific guidance for spending. On occasion, footnotes have grown out of congressional instructions with respect to the use of funds.[37] For example, in the early 1990s, OMB apportioned funds to the DOD revolving fund supporting depot maintenance (the Defense Business Operations Fund or DBOF) restricting DBOF spending to a month-by-month apportionment of funds. The DBOF had been making inaccurate estimates of monthly funding requirements, leading to closer OMB attention than normal to DBOF functioning before additional funding would be provided.

OMB has also on occasion been given responsibility for allocating funds that have been appropriated to the President, making decisions about which agencies should execute those programs. This was the case with respect to the first emergency supplemental appropriations responding to the 9/11 terrorist attacks and, again, in 2003, for the emergency funds appropriated for stabilization and reconstruction programs in Iraq.

OMB Responsibilities for Agency Management

The White House also has an impact on executive branch agency operations, largely through OMB. OMB has overseen agency management since it was created in 1921, but its responsibilities grew when it moved to the White House in 1939 and became involved in war mobilization planning.[38] In 1970, the organization was given a more formal structure for management issues.

In 1974, the Office of Federal Procurement Policy (OFPP) was created at OMB to oversee government-wide procurement policies and regulations. The OFPP Administrator chairs the Federal Acquisition Regulatory Council (FARC), composed of representatives from DOD, NASA, and the General Services Administration, which oversees the content and implementation of the Federal Acquisition Regulations (FAR). FARC issues are particularly important to DOD, which procures roughly two-thirds of all federal goods and services. The OFPP Administrator also chairs the Cost Accounting Standards Board, which sets mandatory federal standards for allocating costs to federal contracts.

A second major expansion of OMB's management role occurred with the passage of the Paperwork Reduction Act of 1980, which created the Office of Information and Regulatory Affairs (OIRA). OIRA was made responsible for reviewing all federal government policies on statistics, information technology, privacy, and data quality, with the objective of reducing and standardizing government information gathering.[39] Through the 1993 Executive Order on Regulatory Planning and Review, OIRA took on significant additional responsibility for overseeing agency regulatory activity.[40]

While neither DOD nor State/USAID is a regulatory agency, their information technology policies and investments are overseen by OIRA, as are their information-gathering activities. Occasionally, the regulatory activity of other agencies has an impact on DOD, in particular. For example, regulations from the Environmental Protection Administration or on land use from the Department of the Interior can have an impact on DOD's US basing structure and operations. If there are interagency disputes over such regulations, they are frequently adjudicated by the OMB RMO for national security and OIRA.

Despite these procurement and regulatory responsibilities, OMB's management role remained secondary to its budget role into the 1990s. As one observer pointed out, "the dominant budget side long had little regard or use for the management side's perspective in preparing budgets or evaluation programs."[41] The two sides of the organization had only a limited working relationship, as budget offices were too overloaded to carry out management oversight.

The organization's management role expanded in the 1990s, with the passage of the Chief Financial Officer's Act of 1990, the Government Performance and Results Act (GPRA) of 1993, and the creation of the National Performance Review (NPR) in the same year. The Chief Financial Officer's Act created the position of OMB Deputy Director for Management and the Office of Federal Financial Management (OFFM), which increased OMB's responsibility for overseeing agency financial systems practices.[42] The Act required all federal agencies to appoint a Chief Financial Officer who would administer agency financial management, produce "auditable" annual financial statements, and modernize accounting systems.[43]

The GPRA instituted a more formal agency strategic planning process than had previously existed. It called for an initial pilot program overseen by OMB, requiring ten agencies to draw up strategic plans linked to agency goals and objectives and to measures of performance to show how well programs actually met those goals and objectives. By 1997 all federal agencies were to draw up strategic plans and by 2000 all were to draft performance reports. OMB oversees the implementation of the GPRA process.[44]

The national security agencies participated in the GPRA process. OMB staff worked closely with USAID, in particular, to draft measurable performance objectives and with State to develop an overall State Department and International Affairs strategic plan. The USAID effort developed a large number of performance objectives and measurements, but these did not prove to be an effective management tool. The State Department strategic plan was a significant first step, but the plan was not connected to State or International Affairs budget planning processes and not well integrated into the Department's overall day-to-day management. DOD also participated in the process, but did not produce a usable strategic plan, relying instead on its PPBE process for planning purposes. Nonetheless, GPRA began a process of stimulating more formal planning and results orientation in all three agencies, which developed further in the first decade of the twenty-first century.[45]

The Vice President's NPR created by Vice President Al Gore also gave impetus to this process and gave further responsibilities to OMB. The NPR agenda was to "reinvent government," to make it more responsive and efficient. OMB's own NPR review—"OMB 2000"—led to a decision to more closely integrate the management and budget sides of the organization.[46] OMB's budget offices were renamed Resource Management Offices (RMO) and given responsibility for integrating management issues into their budgetary responsibilities. Previous efforts to link the two had foundered because they imposed a new burden on the existing budget staff. As a result, OMB 2000 also moved some management staff into the RMOs to provide both expertise and additional personnel.[47]

The Bush administration continued this trend. In 2002, OMB created the Performance Assessment Rating Tool (PART) in part because of dissatisfaction with the results of GPRA.[48] PART was intended to "strengthen and reinforce GPRA-mandated reporting" and the results "inform agency and OMB decision-making on resource allocation."[49] PART evaluations of federal programs were carried out from 2002 to 2008 by OMB staff, working closely with agency personnel. The PART questionnaire gathered data to measure whether the program's design and purpose were clear and defensible (20 percent of a PART score), whether agency strategic planning set valid annual and long-term goals for the program (10 percent), and the effectiveness of program management, including financial oversight (20 percent). Most important, the PART evaluation looked at program results, measured in outputs and outcomes in the target constituency, to ensure that the agency could report results accurately and consistently (50 percent). The PART reports included an independent evaluation of the program.

The result of these evaluations was a numerical score, translated into a qualitative rating ranging from "Effective," to "Moderately Effective," to "Adequate," to "Ineffective." Where performance measures or data did not exist, the program received a rating of "Results Not Demonstrated." These results were to be used in reviewing, reducing, or adding to an agency's budget request to OMB.[50] They were also published with the budget documents transmitted to the Congress and posted on a new website maintained by OMB.[51]

The PART process evaluated a number of national security programs.[52] Through 2006, 54 DOD programs had been reviewed, with 70 percent of them considered "Effective" or "Moderately Effective." Only 18 percent were rated "Adequate," while none were rated "Ineffective," and another 11 percent were rated "Results Not Demonstrated." Results were less positive for the Department of Homeland Security. Of 63 programs rated, only 43 percent reached the "Effective" or "Moderately Effective" rating, 24 percent of the rated programs were rated "Adequate," and another 33 percent fell into the "Results Not Demonstrated" category. International Affairs evaluations were also mixed. Overall the 72 percent of the 83 programs evaluated had ratings of "Effective" or "Moderately Effective," while only 24 percent were rated "Adequate." International assistance programs had lower ratings. Only a few economic assistance programs were rated "Moderately Effective," and many were considered only "Adequate." Significantly, no defense, homeland security, or international affairs programs were rated "Ineffective," which may suggest a wariness about providing a negative evaluation in the PART process.

In addition, the Bush administration created a broader President's Management Agenda (PMA) in its FY 2002 budget request. This agenda set out 14 major objectives for agency management, including human capital management, competitive sourcing, financial performance, electronic government, and budget and performance integration. Agency progress with respect to these 14 areas would be measured by OMB, which would provide overall agency ratings with each successive annual budget.[53]

The National Security Council, the Interagency Process, and Budgeting

The President's National Security Council (NSC) is responsible for coordinating national security strategy, advising the President on national security issues, overseeing policy implementation through the interagency process, and integrating the White House response to national security crises.[54] The NSC does not have a formal role in the OMB budget process, nor does NSC staff typically have expertise in resource planning. Virtually every policy decision made in the NSC framework, however, has resource implications. As a result, there is constant NSC/OMB interaction on resource issues.

The "Normal" Budget Cycle

NSC staff views and the interagency discussions held through the NSC frequently have important implications for the President's budget. Moreover, budget decisions made in the OMB process can facilitate or limit the policy options open to the NSC and interagency.[55] The program priorities of NSC staff often differ from those put forward by agencies in their budget submissions to OMB. NSC program and budget priorities reflect presidential priorities, or, at times, the policy preferences of senior NSC officials, which they present to OMB as presidential priorities, though the President may not have expressed a view on the issue. During the Clinton administration, for example, NSC staff sought higher funding levels for such activities as democracy promotion, assistance for Eastern Europe and the former Soviet Union, counternarcotics, counterterrorism, and international environmental programs. In the defense arena, NSC officials supported higher funding than DOD preferred for international cooperation programs, such as the MEADS cooperative anti-ballistic missile program (with Germany and Italy).[56]

The process for making NSC budget views known is not institutionalized; it varies from year to year and administration to administration. There is often no internal NSC coordination on these views; each Senior Director or Director may provide requests directly to OMB. At other times, one NSC Director may be asked to coordinate these views and, once approved by the Deputy National Security Advisor, provide a single set to OMB's National Security Programs RMO during the budget process.[57] In some years, NSC Directors and Senior Directors could be invited to Director's Review meetings to provide NSC views and ask questions.

The informal nature of this process means that differing, even contradictory views are often communicated to OMB. This is particularly true for International Affairs budgets, as NSC responsibilities for foreign policy are widely distributed within the organization. Regional desks have views about priority programs and spending levels within their region. Functional offices may have differing priorities with respect to such cross-agency programs as counternarcotics funding, democracy promotion, or post-conflict reconstruction and stabilization in a particular region. During the Clinton administration, for example, the NSC Senior Director for Global Affairs would commonly recommend a high level of funding for counternarcotics programs in Latin America, but lower support for democracy promotion in general, while the Senior Director for Democracy would recommend the reverse.

NSC actions can also create budget requirements of which OMB is unaware. In 1994, for example, the NSC Near East directorate coordinated the White House visit of a Middle East head of state, which led to a Presidential commitment to forgive that country's bilateral debt to the United States. The NSC staff was not aware that this commitment required an appropriation of funds, which had not been included in the President's budget submission to Congress. Several months later, preceding another state visit by that leader, NSC staff became aware of that budgetary requirement, requiring a hasty OMB amendment to the President's budget request, already pending before the Congress.

On occasion, an NSC office might seek to coordinate program and budget planning entirely outside the normal OMB process. In 1996, for example, the NSC Senior Director for Global Affairs made an effort to coordinate a supplemental budget request for counterterrorism programs without including OMB. Conversations at a senior level between OMB and NSC reversed this course, making OMB the coordinator of the budget supplemental planning effort.

The Homeland Security Council

Shortly after 9/11, President George W. Bush created a Homeland Security Council (HSC) to coordinate interagency efforts and provide advice on strategic and policy matters in areas related to homeland security.[58] The HSC was modeled to a degree after the NSC, and many of its members were also members of the NSC.

President Bush also created a White House Office of Homeland Security, headed by former Governor Tom Ridge. Many observers believed that without authority over budgets, the Office of Homeland Security would not have the leverage needed to integrate federal homeland security activities into a unified set of policies and programs. To remedy the situation, in 2002 Congress passed the Homeland Security Act that established DHS. The HSC continued, however, chaired by an Assistant to the President for Homeland Security and Counterterrorism.

The Office of Homeland Security and, later, the HSC prepared the Bush administration's strategy documents and executive decisions related to homeland security, sometimes in concert with the NSC. Thus, HSC for several years set the strategic priorities meant to inform homeland security programs and budgets at the department and agency level. The HSC also served as the main coordinating mechanism for homeland security efforts that cut across agencies.

In theory, the HSC advised the President on domestic security matters while the NSC continued to be concerned with international ones. In reality, the two sets of issues are often deeply intertwined, and crucial national security missions such as countering the threat of nuclear or biological terrorism require an integrated international and domestic approach. To improve the integration of domestic and international security planning, in May 2009 the HSC was folded into the NSC. The HSC still exists and is headed by the Assistant for Homeland Security and Counterterrorism, who now reports to the National Security Advisor. The HSC will continue to focus on setting homeland security priorities and coordinating homeland security efforts across agencies.

Reforming the Interagency Coordination Process

The NSC–OMB relationship is critical to planning and implementing the President's policy priorities, especially those that cut across agencies. Effective policy for dealing with major national security priorities such as terrorist attacks, nuclear proliferation, global economic and financial trends, fragile and failing states, climate change, or post-conflict reconstruction and stabilization require cross-agency planning, priority-setting, and budget allocation.[59]

When OMB and NSC communicate effectively and work in tandem, the White House can have considerable influence over agency planning and budgeting for such policy priorities. When they do not coordinate, however, agency budget decisions may not reflect presidential priorities, or the agencies may not be willing to accommodate presidential requirements. The informal, unstructured character of the NSC–OMB relationship has inhibited the development of a systematic capability to implement presidential national security priorities. Both organizations tend to operate in a short-term time frame, and there is no White House process to link budget decisions to long-term national strategy goals. While the NSC articulates a National Security Strategy, that document is disconnected from budget planning or guidance to agencies.[60]

Several studies and commissions have recommended reforms to the NSC and OMB that would change their roles in carrying out strategic planning and providing such guidance. These proposals include making the two organizations responsible for national security strategy planning, detailed guidance to agencies, and the preparation of a more integrated national security budget submission to the Congress. The strategy might be a quadrennial exercise, similar in form to the Quadrennial Defense Review carried out by the Defense

Department. The guidance could be a formal, biennial classified communication to the national security agencies laying out administration priorities, defining specific agency tasks, and providing detailed instructions for agencies to fund those priority tasks. Such guidance could be used to eliminate duplication and gaps among agency programs, define interagency synergies, and propose internal and cross-agency tradeoffs. An integrated budget document would bring together the budget requests for all of the national security agencies—DOD, the international affairs agencies, the Department of Homeland Security, and the intelligence agencies. It would integrate the presentation, describe the synergies among the budget requests, and focus attention on the key national security priorities.[61]

There are precedents for such a reform in efforts to coordinate strategic and resource planning for specific areas of policy, though the experience is mixed. The Clinton administration created a National Economic Council to coordinate economic policy across agencies and advise the President. Although the NEC was not institutionalized in statute, it did provide the framework within which the President and Vice President reviewed the administration's overall budget request and handled agency appeals at the end of the budget process.[62]

The Office of National Drug Control Policy (ONDCP) constitutes such a coordination effort with respect to counternarcotics programs. ONDCP was established in statute in 1988 to set drug policy priorities, implement a national strategy for narcotics, and to certify federal drug-control budgets. The strategy was to be "comprehensive and research-based; contain long-range goals and measurable objectives; and seek to reduce drug abuse, trafficking, and their consequences." ONDCP has a wide mandate on paper:

> [it] evaluates, coordinates, and oversees both the international and domestic anti-drug efforts of executive branch agencies and ensures that such efforts sustain and complement State and local anti-drug activities. The Director advises the President regarding changes in the organization, management, budgeting, and personnel of Federal Agencies that could affect the Nation's anti-drug efforts.[63]

The ONDCP Director is required to submit an annual, consolidated National Drug Control Budget. While he does not provide budget guidance to agencies, he does review and certify their budgets. That certification authority is rarely used to "decertify" an agency budget, however, given agency reluctance to allow the Director such a role in their budget planning.[64]

Counterterrorism policy has been the focus of one of the most ambitious efforts to coordinate national security agencies in a major area of national security policy. The Intelligence Reform and Terrorism Prevention Act of 2004 created a National Counterterrorism Center (NCTC). The statute gave NCTC the responsibility "to conduct strategic operational planning for counterterrorism activities, integrating all instruments of national power, including diplomatic, financial, military, intelligence, homeland security, and law enforcement activities within and among agencies." It was to report to the President in fulfilling this responsibility.[65]

The NSC/HSC directive on counterterrorism programs (NSPD46/HSPD15) tasked NCTC with preparing a strategic plan and guidance for counterterrorism, known as the National Implementation Plan on counterterrorism (NIP). The plan was to focus agencies on denying terrorists resources, preventing the proliferation of weapons of mass destruction, defeating terrorist organizations, countering state and non-state support for terrorists, and countering ideological support for terrorists. NCTC conducted an interagency planning process to write the NIP and provided agencies with program guidance in 2005–06, covering more than 500 detailed taskings to the agencies involved in counterterror operations.

The NIP effort was carried out by an agency that was not part of the Executive Office of the President, though the NSC's Deputy National Security Advisor and OMB did participate in the process. OMB's involvement was not mandated by statute, but was intended to see that agency budget planning incorporated the guidance. In the end, the NIP process had a minimal impact on agency planning and budgeting. Its plan was seen as having too many priorities and agencies resisted the guidance process, fearing the interagency priorities would require reductions in the budgets for other agency programs. NSC and OMB staff were few in number, making consistent follow-up difficult.[66]

The work of HSC has been another experiment in cross-agency planning at the White House level. HSC staff has carried out such coordination in direct contact with OMB's responsibilities for preparing homeland security budgets. However, the HSC does not have clear authority over agency budgets, and the OMB process continues to require coordination within OMB, given the dispersal of homeland security program responsibilities inside the agency.[67]

As these precedents suggest, an OMB–NSC effort to create a more coordinated and authoritative strategic and budget planning and guidance process in the White House faces significant obstacles. Agencies generally resist such guidance or act in ways that frustrate its implementation.[68] Some of the national security agencies, especially State, lack planning processes that could support such a White House effort. Agencies frequently "game" such processes, using presidential priorities as a basis to obtain additional resources, rather than setting internal priorities and making budgetary trade-offs.[69] They also "end-run" such processes, asking members or their committees in Congress to restore funding they have lost in such a process. Moreover, NSC and OMB lack the staff they would need to execute such a process. There is also widespread opposition to enlarging the planning role of NSC, based on the fear that it might become an "operational" rather than a coordinating agency.[70]

Coordination Case Study: Post-Conflict Stabilization and Reconstruction

The White House has regularly struggled, often unsuccessfully, with the problem of coordinating policy, programs, and budgets across agencies. It is especially acute when it comes to coordinating planning and resource issues relating to the use of military force in overseas contingency operations and the need for planning of post-conflict operations overseas by military and civilian agencies.[71] The recent history of post-conflict contingency operations is a classic case study in the difficulties the White House faces in coordinating across agencies.

US operations in Iraq and Afghanistan were preceded by a history of smaller operations in the 1990s in Haiti, Somalia, Northern Iraq, and Bosnia. The US experience in these earlier operations led the Clinton White House to realize that there was a need for a more effective interagency process for responding to such contingencies involving both military and civilian agencies. As a result, a Presidential Decision Directive—PDD-56—gave the NSC a new, lead role in overseeing a planning process for such operations:

> The PDD calls upon the [NSC] Deputies Committee to establish appropriate interagency working groups to assist in policy development, planning, and execution of complex contingency operations. Normally, the Deputies Committee will form an Executive Committee (ExCom) with appropriate membership to supervise the day-to-day management of US participation in a complex contingency operation. The ExCom will bring together representatives of all agencies that might participate in the operation, including those not normally part of the NSC structure.[72]

Resource issues were explicitly part of the process established in PDD-56. According to the directive, the ExCom was to include an agency-led legal–financial working group whose role was to consult with the ExCom to ensure that tasks assigned by the ExCom can be performed by the assigned agencies "consistent with legal and fiscal authorities." The Political-Military Implementation Plan that would result from ExCom work was to include "funding requirements," and the required "rehearsal" of a plan was to include resource allocation processes and decisions. After an operation, an "after-action review" would be conducted, including the identification of any "budgetary difficulties."

The NSC has difficulty implementing such a systematic process, however. The Clinton framework was not used in subsequent Clinton administration contingency operations. As one analyst of such operations has noted, "successive administrations have treated each new mission as if it were the first and, more importantly, as it if were the last."[73] Iraq and Afghanistan followed this pattern. Both operations faltered from the start because there was no White

House-directed interagency planning for post-combat programs. Instead, coordinating responsibility was handed *ad hoc* to one or another federal department. Before the Iraq war began, the Department of Defense, rather than the NSC, was given responsibility for post-war planning (NSPD-24). The DOD plan consisted largely of being ready for a short-term humanitarian and migration emergency after the invasion.

Since military planners anticipated a relatively rapid US withdrawal from Iraq, there was no other operational or budgetary planning for a post-war American presence, stabilization activities, or post-war reconstruction, especially not at the White House level. The administration assumed that economic activity would quickly resume and reconstruction needs would be handled by the Iraqi government and bureaucracy, funded by oil revenues. Only a minimally funded *ad hoc* military organization, the Office of Reconstruction and Humanitarian Assistance (ORHA) was put in place to meet the assumed short-term needs.

Still another coordinating architecture was created in 2003—the Coalition Provisional Authority (CPA) in Baghdad—as the administration grew to realize that post-conflict requirements would be more demanding than anticipated. The CPA continued to report, however, through the Secretary of Defense. It was succeeded, in turn, by the State Department's Iraq Reconstruction Management Office and the Iraq Transition Assistance Office.

The DOD lead for the Iraq operation did not work as a coordinating mechanism. The relationship between State/USAID and Defense was contentious and non-communicative for much of the first two years. Lacking training and expertise for the task, DOD struggled to deliver security and reconstruction assistance. Moreover, because they did not have the right legal authorities, flexibility, funding, and personnel, State and USAID underperformed in the field. Policies, programs, and projects for stability, reconstruction, governance, and military operations evolved constantly; personnel delivering those policies were often inexperienced and rotated frequently in and out of the country. Program implementation, especially for governance and reconstruction, was slow, chaotic, and largely ineffective.[74]

The absence of a strong coordinating process at the White House level was a major weakness in post-conflict operations in Iraq. Neither the NSC nor OMB played a planning and oversight role, and the two were not well connected to develop policy, plan resources, or authoritatively resolve interagency disputes. The NSC did not create an oversight working group until more than a year after the war started, and continued to change oversight structures thereafter. The administration had done no central budget planning for reconstruction before the invasion and a budget for this purpose was not transmitted until eight months later. Beyond the initial $18.4 billion appropriated for reconstruction in 2003, Congress only reluctantly provided a small amount of additional funds in the following years.[75] Rather than integrated coordination, there were consistent conflicts between DOD, USAID, and State over the implementation of these funds on the ground.[76] Without systematic interagency planning, budgeting for post-conflict operations in Iraq was done incrementally, with constantly shifting goals and objectives.

The many difficulties with Iraq planning and funding, which were mirrored in Afghanistan (with a much lower priority and level of funding), led to a renewed effort to create a more systematic approach to interagency coordination for "stabilization and reconstruction" (S&R) operations. Consistent with its Iraq planning, however, the administration did not put NSC or OMB at the center of the effort. Instead, each of the two major departments was given a role in such operations. In November 2005, DOD issued a directive putting "stabilization and reconstruction operations" on par with combat operations for the military.[77] At the same time, the NSC issued a National Security Presidential Directive—"Management of Interagency Efforts Concerning Reconstruction and Stabilization" (NSPD-44)—which gave the coordinating task to the State Department. NSPD-44 named a new State Department Office of the Coordinator for Reconstruction and Stabilization (S/CRS), not NSC or OMB, as the interagency coordinator for such operations, outside of Iraq and Afghanistan.[78]

The responsibilities for this new office were quite broad, including developing S&R strategies, coordinating the process of identifying states at risk of instability, leading interagency planning for conflict mitigation, developing contingency plans for S&R operations, providing options for the US response and coordinating that response, coordinating with other countries and international organizations, creating a civilian response capability, and identifying issues for resolution in the NSC interagency process.

The new directive explicitly superseded PDD-56 and sought to limit the coordinating responsibilities of the White House. S/CRS was "to recommend when to establish a limited-time PCC-level [NSC Policy Coordination Committee] group to focus on a country or region facing major reconstruction and stabilization challenges." While a standing PCC for Reconstruction and Stabilization Operations was created, it was to be chaired by the S/CRS Coordinator. Most importantly, S/CRS, not the NSC or OMB, was charged with resolving policy, program, and funding disagreements between executive branch agencies "consistent with the Office of Management and Budget's budget and policy coordination functions."[79]

S/CRS was initially established as an office reporting to the Secretary of State, but was absorbed into the foreign assistance budget office (F) in 2007. Because it was inside one department, and at a relatively lower level, it had limited authority to coordinate the interagency process. Outside the State Department, it was far from clear that the other departments of government, notably DOD, were prepared to accept S/CRS leadership in any specific contingency.[80] Inside State, the S/CRS mission overlapped with the responsibilities of State's regional bureaus and country desks. To the extent it actually had staff deployed overseas, moreover, S/CRS's mission seemed similar to that of USAID's offices of Transition Initiatives and Foreign Disaster Assistance (discussed in Chapter 3).

The weaknesses of the interagency process established by the Bush administration made raising funds for post-conflict civilian operations difficult. The request for a contingency fund at State for such operations was repeatedly rejected by the Congress, although the DOD was given authority to transfer up to $200 million to State for such operations. S/CRS budgets remained small, as did its staff size, which depended heavily on its ability to obtain detailees from other agencies. In 2008, the State Department was given additional funds for the "Civilian Stabilization Initiative" to be administered by S/CRS, which would include a 250-member Active Response Corps, a 2,000-member Standby Corps drawn from a number of agencies—State, USAID, Justice, Commerce, Treasury, Agriculture, Health and Human Services, and Homeland Security—to carry out actual reconstruction and stabilization operations, and a 2,000-member Response Corps, drawn from the private sector and universities.[81] Additional funding was provided in the FY 2009 budget.

S/CRS will find it difficult to act as the coordinator of interagency S&R actions. One federal department is hard pressed to coordinate the actions of another department or to resolve policy, program, or budgetary disputes. This is especially true, as the Iraq case suggests, between State and Defense, two of the most powerful agencies in the national security arena, but one significantly better funded than the other.

Only the White House level seems to have the authority to resolve the many disagreements and turf struggles that occur when such missions emerge.[82] In 2009, the new administration began, once again, to reconsider the role of the NSC as a coordinator for such operations.[83] In the end, only a clear and more centralized NSC–OMB process could ensure effective implementation of S&R operations, but the experience of the Balkans, Iraq, and Afghanistan suggests how difficult it is to create such a capability.[84]

Crisis and "Out of Cycle" Budget Decisions

As the Iraq and Afghanistan cases suggest, foreign policy and national security problems do not always conform to the schedule of the US federal budget. The White House is regularly seized with budget requirements for events and crises that occur at unpredictable times during the year. Planning for the September 1994 US invasion to restore President Jean Bertrand Aristide of Haiti, for example, began in January 1994, after the FY 1995 budget request had been transmitted to Congress. The August 1997 attacks on the US embassies in Kenya and Tanzania took place as the Congressional appropriations process was winding up; the budget contained no additional funding for embassy security or reconstruction. The terrorist attacks of September 11, 2001 occurred just before the start of a new fiscal year, with no counterterror or recovery funding in already-appropriated funds. The invasion of Iraq began March 19, 2003, but no funds had been requested for this deployment or for post-conflict assistance to Iraq.

The White House, particularly OMB, is forced to develop resource options to support policy decisions that are out of phase, whether for military operations, foreign assistance, security measures, or reconstruction at home or abroad. The OMB and NSC response to such decisions and events is generally *ad hoc* and differs from administration to administration, though resource needs are met using a number of existing tools, including seeking new funds or reallocating existing appropriated funds.

In some cases, such as Haiti, OMB is integrated into an informal interagency planning process, defining funding options for emerging policy options. As part of the Haiti coordination process, OMB conducted weekly interagency teleconferences to identify agency responsibilities, to "de-conflict" agency disagreements on budgets and funding authorities, and identify funding sources from existing appropriations to cover the new requirements. Similarly, in 1994, OMB, NSC, and State coordinated a six-month effort to develop a funding package to support the newly elected democratic government in South Africa. This planning was carried out before the elections and before any formal request had come from the White House for such a support package. It drew on existing agency resources, rather than seeking supplemental funding from the Congress.

In other cases, OMB is not initially involved in the decisions that define new policies or reactions to events. The interagency process in NSC, however, can frequently result in a stalemate about funding responsibilities for these decisions. NSC cannot authoritatively enforce resource decisions on agencies, but OMB has greater leverage to persuade agencies to find the needed resources.

The White House can have recourse to a number of mechanisms to meet such funding requirements, including agency contingency funds, reprogrammings, transfers within agency appropriations, and supplemental funding requests to the Congress. The national security and foreign policy agencies have some contingency funding capabilities. These are small at DOD, but DOD's Operations and Maintenance accounts are sufficiently flexible to be used for military contingencies, deferring spending on other planned programs which can be reimbursed later through supplemental funding.

State and USAID have several small contingency funds: the Emergency Refugees and Migration Account (ERMA), the USAID Office of Transition Initiatives (OTI), and the USAID International Disaster and Famine Assistance (IDFA) account, discussed in Chapter 3. The President also has authority under the Foreign Assistance Act of 1961 to transfer or reprogram relatively small amounts of foreign assistance funding to deal with "unanticipated contingencies," and to "draw down" services and equipment from agencies for emergencies, discussed in Chapter 4. The White House can also ask agencies to transfer funds to other agencies following specific statutory requirements. The most significant national security example is Section 1207 of the FY 2006 Defense Authorization Act, which permits DOD to transfer up to $100 million to the State Department to support stabilization and reconstruction operations.

OMB has the White House responsibility for requesting such reprogrammings, transfers, drawdowns, and contingency funding commitments. OMB typically asks the affected agency to prepare the paperwork for actions being taken under agency authorities, which the agency then notifies to the appropriate congressional committees or subcommittees (Armed Services, Foreign Relations/Affairs, and/or Appropriations Committees or subcommittees). In some cases, Congress is pre-notified of such an action to ensure it does not meet with congressional opposition. When the President's authority is involved, such as for a "draw down," OMB will draw up the documentation and request agency action.

Although the authorities for these budget actions are specified in statute, the *ad hoc* character of the system for handling "out-of-phase" funding needs identified in the interagency process has led to a number of initiatives to reform the NSC–OMB process. Late in the Bush administration, NSC staff developed a questionnaire for NSC Senior Directors and Directors to use as they considered new White House initiatives, programs, and crisis responses. The questionnaire was intended to make NSC staff aware of the resource implications of their decisions and to engage OMB early in the process of shaping policy. They were also directed to include OMB and agency budget officials in NSC interagency working groups.[85]

A White House coordination process such as that developed in the Bush administration generally does not survive the transition to a new administration. The Obama NSC will change the coordination guidelines, with some indication that they may engage in a more structured policy and resource planning process, in tandem with OMB.[86]

Budget Amendments and Supplemental Budget Requests

Unanticipated, out-of-phase funding needs can easily exceed the resources available through contingency funding, reprogramming, and transfers, especially when military operations take place. Federal budgeting also allows the White House to use broader funding mechanisms to meet such requirements, known as "budget amendments," and "supplemental funding." Budget requests are frequently amended by the White House, especially during a transition to a new administration. In July 2001, for example, the Bush administration transmitted to Congress a budget amendment for an additional $18.4 billion in defense funding for FY 2001, the fiscal year already under way, adding to what candidate George Bush had described as an insufficient defense budget. That budget amendment was prepared by DOD, but reviewed and transmitted by OMB. Budget amendments can change or add to the funding requested in the budget under consideration in Congress.

Supplemental budget requests are separate from the basic budget request made by an administration. They are intended to meet emergency funding needs for actions, programs, or operations that were unforeseen. If designated as an "emergency" and appropriated by Congress as such, these supplemental requests do not count against any caps or ceilings on discretionary spending.[87]

Emergency supplemental budget requests have been made frequently since the end of the Cold War and especially between 2001 and 2009. During the Clinton administration, there were 19 emergency supplemental budget requests including assistance to the newly created Russian Federation, air patrols over northern and southern Iraq, the deployment of American military forces and post-conflict assistance programs in Bosnia and Kosovo, counterterrorism programs, and embassy construction and security programs after the Al Qaeda bombings of the US embassies in Kenya and Tanzania. In general these requests ranged from several hundred million dollars to a 1998 request of $2.45 billion for military operations and assistance in Bosnia. The largest was $8.7 billion for operations and assistance in Kosovo, made in two parts in 1999.[88] The Republican Congress occasionally demanded that these requests be offset by reductions in spending elsewhere in the National Defense or International Affairs budgets, in order to stay within overall deficit reduction targets. Generally, however, these requests were granted emergency status by the Congress.

Emergency supplemental requests reached a new level following the 9/11 terrorist attacks and with the conflicts in Iraq and Afghanistan. From FY 2001 to FY 2009, through nine successive budgets, $864 billion was provided by the Congress to fund the conflicts in Iraq and Afghanistan, virtually all of it in the form of emergency budget requests. Of this funding, 94 percent was provided to the Department of Defense and 6 percent to State and USAID.[89] Such a use of the emergency supplemental mechanism for military operations, diplomacy, and foreign assistance was unprecedented. In general supplemental funding outside the regular budget process was provided for the first year or two of military operations, after which funding requests were generally prepared inside normal agency and OMB budget processes.[90]

This large, extended use of emergency funding for military, diplomatic, and foreign assistance programs has generally weakened internal budget discipline in the national security agencies. While the bulk of the funds have supported military and foreign assistance efforts in combat zones, the supplementals were also used to acquire weapons programs unrelated to the war effort and funding for foreign assistance programs in other areas.[91] Because these supplementals moved quickly through the executive branch process, they were not subject to the normally intensive OMB process of hearings and Director's Review that is applied to normal agency budget requests.[92]

Other White House Offices and the Budget Process

Other White House offices can have an impact on national security budgeting. The Office of the Vice President (OVP) can play a major role, depending on the administration. The OVP role has expanded since the vice-presidency of George H.W. Bush, with growing participation in the national security planning and budgetary process. Vice President Al Gore was actively involved in this process. His staff regularly communicated with OMB about the Vice President's budgetary priorities before and during the Directors' Review process.

President Clinton put Vice President Gore in charge of bilateral commissions dealing with US government programs and funding for Russia, Egypt, and South Africa. Gore convened regular interagency meetings to develop an agenda of bilateral cooperation, covering issues ranging from governance to health, energy, the environment, and nuclear clean up. OMB representatives typically attended those meetings, at which agencies would describe bilateral programs they were pursuing with counterpart ministries in that relevant country. The Vice President's staff would follow up with OMB to ensure that agencies included these programs in their budget submissions.

Gore also actively lobbied OMB on the budgets for international environmental policies and organizations such as the Montreal Protocol (an international treaty banning ozone-depleting substances), the Global Environmental Facility (an international fund to support environmental projects in developing countries), and programs to swap forgiveness of US loans for local investments in conservation in developing countries.[93] He also participated actively in budget appeals and final decision meetings with the President.

Vice President Dick Cheney played an even more central role in the White House budget process. He actively supported higher budgets for programs in which he had an interest, particularly Iraq and Afghanistan. He also played a central role in the overall budget process, particularly for national security, chairing the agency appeals process that followed OMB passback.[94]

Other EOP offices have also become involved in the White House process. The Office of National Drug Control Policy (ONDCP) sometimes participates in OMB cross-cut reviews of counternarcotics program budgets, making its own recommendations for funding. The United States Trade Representative (USTR), which is the White House office responsible for conducting trade negotiations, advocates for its own operating budget, and also has supported Treasury and OMB efforts to identify revenue options to use as offsets to compensate for the impact of trade agreements on projected federal receipts.[95] The White House Office of Science and Technology Policy (OSTP) regularly advocates for higher levels of funding for research and development than the budgets requested by DOD, NASA, NSF, and the Energy Department.

The President himself plays a direct role in the budget process, making the final budget decisions. Some presidents become highly involved in budget details. President Jimmy Carter was well known for his detailed budget reviews, particularly the DOD budget request. President George H.W. Bush was involved in final decisions, especially on national security issues and on overall budget policy. President Clinton chaired virtually every final appeal and decision-making meeting on his budget requests. The presidential office can also play an important role, acting on the President's behalf. Chief of Staff Leon Panetta, who had been OMB Director, continued to play an active role in budget decisions, holding frequent meetings on key budget issues and negotiating on budget items with members of Congress.

Conclusion

The White House, and particularly OMB, plays a central role in budgeting for national security. Budgets and legislation proceed through the White House; policy coordination is a White House responsibility. At the same time, there is a weakness in the White House capacity to deal with national security operations that cross agencies. While many planning and budgetary tools exist that can be used for such coordination, they do not fit into any concept of an overall coordination strategy or a systematic role for White House offices in providing guidance for agencies. As a result, the White House, OMB, and NSC can have considerable impact on agency planning and budgeting, but have not become central coordinating tools for a strategic national security agenda.

Chapter 9

Resource Allocation and Budgeting in Congress

Introduction

The Constitution enshrines competition between the executive branch and Congress on matters of foreign policy and defense.[1] The President negotiates treaties, but the Senate ratifies them. The Congress raises and supports the Army, provides and maintains a Navy, and makes "rules for the government and regulation of the land and naval forces"; but the President is commander-in-chief. As a result, in every aspect of national security, Congress has an institutional incentive to contest the power of the executive.[2] The Constitution grants Congress the power of the purse, and the budget is often the most obvious avenue for lawmakers to engage in the contest.

Lawmakers exercise their power through formal mechanisms, including hearings, confirmations of executive branch appointees, resolutions, and legislation—including the authorization and appropriation acts that establish organizational structure, policy, and budgets in federal departments and agencies. In addition, they often influence budgets through less formal mechanisms, such as meetings held with administration officials at the staff level.

This chapter describes the structure and processes through which lawmakers exercise the power of the purse in national security. The chapter begins with a brief discussion of the importance of politics and parochialism. It then provides a brief overview of three types of congressional committees and their roles in resource allocation and budgeting, followed by an introduction to three congressional support agencies—the Congressional Budget Office (CBO), the Library of Congress, and the Government Accountability Office (GAO)—that provide information essential to lawmakers as they exercise the power of the purse. The chapter continues with a discussion of the committees and mechanisms involved at each of the main steps in congressional resource allocation and budgeting for security and international affairs: the Budget Committees and the Concurrent Budget Resolution, the authorizing committees and authorization bills, and the Appropriations Committees and subcommittees and appropriations bills. It ends with a brief concluding section and a summary of several concerns raised by today's arrangements.

Politics and Parochialism on Capitol Hill

In the months and years following the terrorist attacks of 2001, Congress played an important role in reorganizing the executive branch to address the nation's security needs in a more integrated way. As discussed in other chapters, those reorganizations have important implications for planning, resource allocation, and budgeting on the executive side. The Homeland Security Act of 2002 established the Department of Homeland Security (DHS), putting the authority for about one-half of federal homeland security budgets into the hands of a single Secretary. In addition, Congress mandated the establishment of the 9/11 Commission and cast into law many of its recommendations, including the creation of the post of Director of National Intelligence and assignment of budgetary responsibility to that individual.

One of the most striking features of federal resource allocation and budgeting for security and foreign engagement, however, is the absence of a unified approach within the legislative body itself. Getting to a unified approach will be no easy task. As Chapter 10 describes, political and organizational forces are powerful factors in the shaping of budgets for security and international affairs. Such forces are the heart of the matter in Congress. Individual members jockey constantly for position and privilege. Committees and subcommittees jealously guard their jurisdictions. Bringing any bill to a final vote is a complex process that often ends in failure, and that process pales in comparison to the challenge of altering the committee structure or getting multiple committees to cede to others on matters they deem crucial.

Senior military officers sometimes joke that they have a board of directors with 535 members: the 100 members of the Senate and the 435 members of the House of Representatives. In the case of Congress, every member of the board has the interests of his or her own state or district to look after, and must do so to achieve re-election. Loyalty to party, chamber, and committee is also important. The multiple layers of parochialism can make it hard for outsiders to fathom what lies behind any vote.

Because the fundamental fact of congressional life is that each of its members must act parochially to achieve re-election, the institution has evolved in a way that all members generally defer to the parochial interests of the others. No member is expected to argue to cut the budget of a weapon system produced in his or her district. The norm is so strong that, generally, no one else will argue to cut it either. This parochialism influences every aspect of policymaking and budgeting in the legislative body. The role of parochial behavior is not an official part of the congressional budget process, but it is the basis of American democracy. Keeping this in mind can help one understand and appreciate the structures, processes, and challenges this chapter describes.

Overview of Congressional Committees and Budget Processes

Congress gets most of its work done through committees.[3] Three types of committee have important roles in planning, resource allocation, and budgeting for security and international affairs: the Budget Committees of the House and Senate, multiple authorizing committees in each chamber, and the Appropriations Committees of the two chambers. Each of the three types of committee holds hearings and prepares drafts and reports for one of the products of the process: the Concurrent Budget Resolution, authorization bills, and appropriations bills.[4] Figure 9.1 shows an overview of the process for the case of national defense. Table 9.1 shows the official target dates by which the products are meant to be completed. (Those target dates have shifted to the right over time and still are rarely met, however.)

After the White House submits the President's Budget to Congress in February each year, the House and Senate Budget Committees begin the planning and resource allocation process by drafting the Concurrent Budget Resolution. The crafting of the budget resolution represents a unique point during the congressional resource allocation process: it is the only time when lawmakers view the budget as a whole. Thus the budget resolution presents the main opportunity for lawmakers to consider any broad tradeoffs between spending cuts and higher taxes, between guns and butter, or among the various tools of national security.

Once agreed to by majority votes in both chambers, the budget resolution will become Congress's internal budget plan. It is not signed by the President, and does not have the force of law. The resolution does have compelling authority when it comes to authorization and appropriations, discussed next.

House and Senate authorizing committees have jurisdiction over authorization bills. These bills can establish or modify agencies and programs and stipulate how they are to operate. They may also set specific funding

Table 9.1 Official target dates for congressional budget products

First Monday in February	President's budget request submitted to Congress
April 15	Concurrent Budget Resolution completed
June 15 (or on timetable set by budget resolution)	Reconciliation bill enacted for mandatory spending and revenues (if required by Concurrent Budget Resolution)
September 30	Authorization Bill enacted (if required)
September 30	Appropriations Bill or continuing resolution enacted
October 1	New fiscal year begins

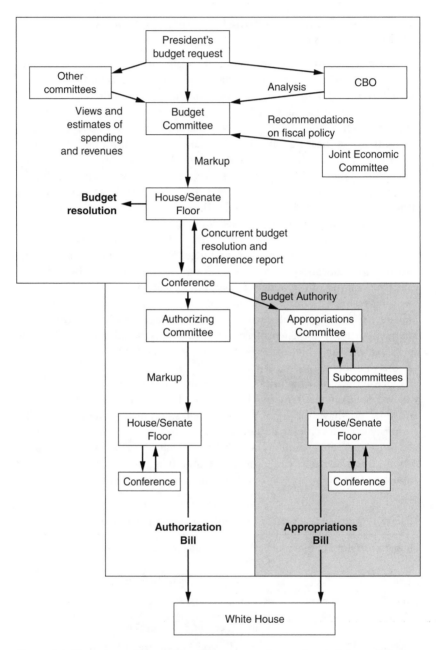

Figure 9.1 Overview of annual budget process for national defense (source: Graphic by Miranda Priebe, based on Senate Budget Committee, Minority Staff, *The Budget and Appropriations Process* (as of October 20, 2008), www.senate.gov/~budget/republican/analysis/ budget process.pdf).

guidance—or "authorize for appropriation" for the activities of those agencies and programs.[5] Some authorizations, for example the one for national defense, are required annually. Others are written to cover multiple years.[6]

Finally, most of the activities of national defense, homeland security, and international affairs get their funding through annual appropriation legislation drafted by the Appropriations Committees of the House and Senate and passed in both chambers. Later sections of this chapter discuss in greater detail the three types of committee and the budget resolution, authorization process, and appropriation process.

Members of Congress usually make their own appeals to House and Senate leadership for committee assignments. As a result, each committee is typically composed of members who have the strongest views about the areas under its jurisdiction or the greatest constituent interest in the activities it oversees. Defense committees tend to be pro-defense, with members representing states or districts with military equipment plants, shipyards, or bases.

Congressional Support Agencies

The members and committees of Congress have small staffs and large numbers of budget items to oversee. Thus they often depend on information and analyses provided by three nonpartisan support agencies: the CBO, the Library of Congress, and the GAO. CBO develops economic and budgetary projections, provides independent estimates of the costs of policy changes under consideration, and prepares reports that include descriptions of alternatives to current policies and detail their costs and potential consequences.

Within the Library of Congress, the Congressional Research Service (CRS) prepares reports on a wide variety of topics of interest to members. These include comprehensive descriptions of congressional resource allocation and budgeting arrangements and examinations of executive branch activities and programs. CRS views itself as the lawmakers' research librarian. It typically does not conduct independent critical analysis, but rather summarizes the analyses of others. Its reports are not distributed to the public or posted on the Internet. Nevertheless, CRS reports often find their way into the public domain. The Library of Congress also maintains extensive records of proposed and enacted legislation, including an online database and search engine called Thomas (Thomas.loc.gov) in honor of Thomas Jefferson. As the federal government's chief auditor, GAO prepares assessments of programs across government and makes recommendations for improvements.

Since 2001, CBO, CRS, and GAO have provided important reports on a variety of topics related to security and foreign engagement. These include past and current spending and projected costs of the wars in Afghanistan and Iraq, the organization of the executive branch and Congress, the performance and effectiveness of various agencies in carrying out individual programs, and interagency cooperation.

The Budget Committees and the Budget Resolution

The Concurrent Budget Resolution represents Congress's budget plan for the coming year and several years into the future. Developing it constitutes lawmakers' main chance to align federal budgets with anticipated revenues and broad national priorities. The Budget Resolution establishes limits over at least a five-year period (the fiscal year that will begin on October 1, plus the four years after that) on the total budget available for distribution among the committees. The resolution's limits on total spending have important implications for the ultimate budgets in every area of federal spending, including security and international affairs.

The House and Senate Budget Committees and the budget resolution framework were established through the Congressional Budget and Impoundment Control Act of 1974, which also created the CBO and generally strengthened Congress's role in resource allocation for the entire federal government.[7] In the House, the 1974 Act and the chamber's rules restrict the membership of the committee and the number of congressional terms during which a member may serve on the committee.[8] The Senate's Budget Committee membership is not limited in those ways.[9] The broad, government-wide perspective of the two budget committees can give them an advantage in examining broad national priorities and tradeoffs in matters that cut across multiple budget functions.

Following the submission of the President's budget in February each year, the Budget Committees start formulating Congress's budget plan (refer to Figure 9.1). They begin by gathering information and analyses about the nation's economic and fiscal picture and about broad national spending priorities. They formally solicit the views of the authorizing and appropriations committees. Those views become an important element of the Budget Committees' deliberations. Additional information and analyses come from hearings and from CBO's annual reports on the budget and economic outlook and the President's budgetary proposals.[10]

Each chamber's Budget Committee then prepares its draft, or markup, of the Concurrent Budget Resolution. The drafts are typically amended through floor action in each chamber. Differences between the two chambers are ironed out in a conference committee that brings together members from both chambers' Budget Committees.

The conferees prepare a Budget Resolution Conference Report that includes a Joint Explanatory Statement. Each chamber then votes to pass the conference report, the final step in the budget resolution process. The resolution and conference report provide guidance to the Congress itself. Since the resolution is not a law, it does not require the President's signature.

The text of the budget resolution includes recommended totals covering at least five years for federal revenues and spending and for Social Security revenues and spending. It also provides targets for dividing the total federal budget among 21 broad categories of federal spending known as budget functions (see Table 9.2).[11]

The joint explanatory statement that accompanies the conference report translates ("crosswalks") those functional allocations into spending targets for committees that have jurisdiction over spending, including the Appropriations Committee in each chamber. Those spending targets are called 302(a) allocations, named for the section of the Congressional Budget and Impoundment Control Act of 1974 that requires them.[12] The 302(a) allocations of the House and Senate Appropriations Committees serve as spending limits for total appropriations.

As will be discussed in a later section, the Appropriations Committees in turn develop sub-allocations, called 302(b) allocations, which divide funds—up to the 302(a) limits—among their subcommittees. Both chambers enforce the 302(a) and 302(b) limits through procedural devices, including "points of order" that can prevent consideration on the floor of legislation that would violate the spending limits.[13]

Table 9.2 Federal funding in the concurrent budget resolution for FY 2009, by budget function

Budget function	FY 2009 budget authority ($ in billions)
050 National defense	542.5
150 International affairs	37.2
250 General science, space, and technology	30.6
270 Energy	6.5
300 Natural resources and environment	40.5
350 Agriculture	22.6
370 Commerce and housing credit	9.6
400 Transportation	74.7
450 Community and regional development	15.2
500 Education, training, employment, and social services	94.3
550 Health	310.3
570 Medicare	420.2
600 Income Security	415.5
650 Social Security	21.3
700 Veterans benefits and services	93.3
750 Administration of justice	48.3
800 General government	24.0
900 Net interest	334.4
920 Allowances	−13.2
950 Undistributed offsetting receipts	−67.1
970 Overseas deployments and other activities	70.0
Total	2,530.7

Source: Author's display based on Concurrent Resolution on the Budget for FY 2009, House Report 110-659 (June 5, 2008), section 104.

National defense spending corresponds to budget Function 050. International affairs spending finds itself in budget Function 150. There is no single budget function for homeland security. Instead, bits of funding for homeland security show up in most of the 21 budget functions (see Table 9.3).

For national defense and international affairs, the budget functions ensure the involvement of the Budget Committees, with their broad overview of fiscal realities and national priorities. The absence of a budget function for homeland security means that the Budget Committees do not get involved in the annual allocation of total resources to homeland security through the resolution process. Yet the budget resolution constitutes lawmakers' principal opportunity to fill in the full fiscal picture of the federal government for the coming year. Lacking a budget function of its own, homeland security is never considered in its entirety during Congress's planning and resource allocation process.

The absence of a budget function may also inhibit Congress's ability to audit spending transparently and weakens the links between budgets as planned and as actually carried out. With no requirement on the part of the executive branch to keep a consistent record for overall homeland security spending, Congress depends instead on the administration's annual report of

Table 9.3 FY 2008 homeland security funding, by budget function

Budget function	Budget authority ($ in billions)
050 National defense	21.9
150 International affairs	2.0
250 General science, space, and technology	1.3
270 Energy	0.1
300 Natural resources and environment	0.3
350 Agriculture	0.5
370 Commerce and housing credit	0.2
400 Transportation	10.0
450 Community and regional development	3.3
500 Education, training, employment, and social services	0.2
550 Health	4.3
570 Medicare	0[a]
600 Income Security	0[a]
650 Social Security	0.2
700 Veterans benefits and services	0.3
750 Administration of justice	18.9
800 General government	1.2
Total	64.7

Source: Author's display based on Office of Management and Budget, *Analytical Perspectives*, Budget of the United States for FY 2009 (February 2008), 35.

Note
[a] Less than $50 million. Figures may not add to total due to rounding.

homeland security spending in the "Crosscutting Programs" chapter of the *Analytical Perspectives* volume of the federal budget (see Chapter 7 for further discussion of homeland security budgets). That report provides no consistent historical audit of spending.

Authorizing Committees and Authorization Legislation

Congress generally exercises its oversight of the executive branch through authorizing committees of the House and Senate (see Table 9.4). The authorizing committees develop authorizing legislation, which can establish or modify agencies and programs and stipulate how they are to operate. By authorizing to appropriate, such legislation can also set guidance for funding those agencies and programs.[14]

In the 110th Congress, three committees in each chamber held primary jurisdiction for oversight and authorization in the areas of national defense, international affairs, and intelligence: the House and Senate Armed Services Committees, the House Foreign Affairs Committee and Senate Foreign Relations Committee, and the House Permanent Select Committee on Intelligence and Senate Select Committee on Intelligence (see Table 9.5). In recent years, the House and Senate created authorizing committees for homeland security, but those committees share jurisdiction with several others (see Table 9.6).

Table 9.4 Some authorizing committees of the 110th Congress

House	Senate
• Agriculture	• Agriculture, Nutrition, and Forestry
• Armed Services	
• Education and Labor	• Armed Services
• Energy and Commerce	• Banking, Housing, and Urban Affairs
• Financial Services	
• Foreign Affairs	• Commerce, Science, and Transportation
• Homeland Security	
• Judiciary	• Energy and Natural Resources
• Oversight and Government Reform	• Environment and Public Works
	• Finance
• Science and Technology	• Foreign Relations
• Small Business	• Health, Education, Labor, and Pensions
• Transportation and Infrastructure	
• Veterans' Affairs	• Homeland Security and Governmental Affairs
• House Permanent Select Committee on Intelligence	• Small Business and Entrepreneurship
• House Select Committee on Energy Independence and Global Warming	• Veterans' Affairs
	• Indian Affairs
	• Senate Select Committee on Intelligence

Table 9.5 Authorizing committees in the 110th Congress with substantial jurisdiction for security and foreign affairs

House		Senate	
Committee	Jurisdiction	Committee	Jurisdiction
Armed Services	National defense budget function generally, including DOD and the DOE's nuclear weapons activities;[a] selective service system	Armed Services	National defense budget function, including DOD and the DOE's nuclear weapons activities; selective service system
Foreign Affairs	US foreign relations generally, including most of the international affairs budget function (Export–Import Bank is an exception)	Foreign Relations	US foreign relations generally, including most of the international affairs budget function;[b] advice and consent on treaties
House Permanent Select Committee on Intelligence	Intelligence community staff and Director of National Intelligence; CIA; intelligence-related activities of and authorizations for the Defense Intelligence Agency, National Security Agency, and other DOD agencies;[a] intelligence activities in other departments	Senate Select Committee on Intelligence	Intelligence activities and programs of the United States

| Homeland Security | Overall homeland security policy; organization and administration of DHS; and functions of DHS relating to the following: border and port security (except immigration policy and non-border enforcement); customs (except customs revenues); integration, analysis, and dissemination of homeland security information; domestic preparedness for and collective response to terrorism; research and development; and transportation security | Homeland Security and Governmental Affairs | DHS except for the following: Coast Guard, TSA, Secret Service, Federal Law Enforcement Training Center, the immigration and customs enforcement functions of CBP and ICE, and revenue functions of CBP |

Source: US Congress, "Organization of Committees," Rule X, Rules of the House of Representatives, 110th Congress (March 11, 2008), 6–16; US Congress, "Standing Committees," Rule XXV, Standing Rules of the Senate, 100th Congress (September 4, 2007), and websites of the relevant House and Senate committees, including web pages on jurisdiction, oversight plans, and archives of hearings and nominations.

Notes

a The House Armed Services Committee and House Permanent Select Committee on Intelligence share jurisdiction over the tactical intelligence and intelligence-related activities of the DOD. The Senate Energy and Natural Resources Committee and the House Energy and Commerce Committee share jurisdiction over some areas related to nuclear weapons with the armed services committees, for example oversight of the national laboratories and nuclear waste policy.

b Exceptions include the Export–Import Bank and the international monetary institutions, which are generally overseen by the banking committees, and food aid, overseen by the agriculture committees. Anne C. Richard, Superpower on the Cheap? (Paris, France: Institut Français des Relations Internationales (IFRI), December 2002), 31.

Table 9.6 Some committees of jurisdiction for homeland security in the 110th Congress

Department or agency	House	Senate
Operating components of the Department of Homeland Security		
Coast Guard	Homeland Security; Judiciary; Transportation and Infrastructure	Commerce, Science and Transportation
Immigration and Customs Enforcement	Judiciary; Ways and Means	Judiciary; Finance
Customs and Border Patrol	Homeland Security; Judiciary; Ways and Means	Finance; Judiciary
Citizenship and Immigration Services	Judiciary	Judiciary
FEMA	Homeland Security; Transportation and Infrastructure	Homeland Security and Governmental Affairs
Transportation Security Agency	Homeland Security	Commerce, Science, and Transportation
Secret Service	Judiciary	Judiciary
Homeland security activities in other departments		
Department of Defense	Armed Services	Armed Services
Department of Justice	Judiciary	Judiciary
Department of Health and Human Services	Energy and Commerce	Health, Education, Labor, and Pensions
Department of Energy	Energy and Commerce	Energy and Natural Resources

In addition, in the Senate's case, the Homeland Security and Governmental Affairs Committee (HSGAC) holds jurisdiction for general government oversight as well as for some parts of homeland security.

Most of the federal activities and programs for security and international affairs are funded through annual appropriations, as discussed in the next section.[15] House and Senate rules limit the content and reach of annual appropriations bills in two ways, however. First, annual appropriations bills are generally not meant to change substantive laws (though there are exceptions, as discussed below). Second, agencies are generally allowed to spend the money provided through annual appropriations only if that spending is first authorized.[16] Typically the authorization comes through an authorization act.

The frequency of authorization bills and the degree to which they shape policies and budgets have varied over time. Today they vary widely among national defense, homeland security, and international affairs. For defense, Congress passes and the President signs a National Defense Authorization

Act (NDAA) almost every year. The annual NDAA heavily influences both policy and funding for virtually every aspect of defense.

In contrast, a foreign relations authorization act, intended to provide policy and funding guidance for operations of the State Department, is required by law only every two years, and that requirement is often waived. Stand-alone foreign assistance authorization acts, meant to guide the foreign-aid component of international affairs, have been absent in recent decades.[17] Lacking such stand-alone legislation, the requisite authorizing measures for international affairs activities are often folded directly into appropriations bills. Partly as a result, the impact of the authorization step in the foreign affairs area is very weak.

Since its creation in early 2005, the House Homeland Security Committee has attempted to establish an annual authorization process for the Department of Homeland Security. The committee prepared bills in 2005, 2006, and 2007 for the upcoming fiscal years. Late in FY 2008, the Senate HSGAC also introduced an annual authorization bill for FY 2008 and FY 2009. All of those bills died, generally after becoming bogged down in multiple committees of the House or Senate.[18] Nevertheless, Congress has passed several important non-annual authorizing acts for homeland security, including the Homeland Security Act of 2002 that created the Department of Homeland Security.

The next section describes the idealized flow of an annual authorization act through Congress. Thereafter, three subsections offer more details about the frequency and impact of authorizations for national defense, homeland security, and foreign relations.

A Typical Authorization Process

For annual authorizations, the legislative process usually begins in February, shortly after the administration submits the President's budget to Congress.[19] In each chamber, each authorizing committee divides its part of the budget request among its subcommittees. The committee and its subcommittees then hold hearings with executive branch leaders and, in the case of national defense, senior members of the uniformed military. Other witnesses at authorizing committee or subcommittee hearings might include experts from the congressional support agencies and from commercial firms, universities, think tanks, and other non-governmental organizations. In the areas of security and international affairs, such experts might be asked to offer their understandings of broad strategies and budgets or of specific programs and activities under consideration.

The process continues with subcommittee markups, meetings in which the subcommittees consider every aspect of the administration's request and draft the language of the authorizing act. Subcommittee markups are usually the main avenue for changes to the President's request.

In an ideal situation, the Concurrent Budget Resolution is completed before the markups begin in earnest, and the markups can reflect the budgetary realities that the resolution imposes. When the budget resolution is late, however, authorizers may need to rework their markups after the resolution passes.

After a subcommittee has completed its markup, the resulting bill is referred back to the full committee. Subcommittees attract members who have the greatest interest in their areas of jurisdiction, and the full committee generally defers to the subcommittee markup.

The markups result in authorization bills voted on by the authorizing committees. Once a bill is agreed to by the authorizing committee in either chamber, it is sent to the floor of that chamber for votes and amendments by the full House or Senate. Markups proceed separately in the House and the Senate, so the resulting bills often differ substantially. After each chamber passes its bill, a conference committee (with members from the authorizing committee of each chamber) is formed to resolve the differences between the House and Senate versions.

The leadership of the full committee appoints the members who will represent that committee in conference.[20] Usually, but not always, the conference committee is constrained to resolving those issues on which the House and Senate versions differ. Both chambers vote on the version agreed to in conference. If that version passes in both chambers, it goes to the White House for signature by the President, at which point it becomes law.

The authorizers may also tack a "statement of managers" at the end of the bill. Such a statement does not have the force of law, but it often contains interpretations, suggestions, or warnings that agencies should heed as they implement the budget.

Like any other legislation, authorization acts can get hung up at any point in the process for reasons of policy, budgets, politics, or because of disagreements over specific programs. Subcommittee and committee markups can slow down because of disagreements over the total budget to which they should mark, particularly if the budget resolution is late or absent. On the floor, they may be slowed down by amendments that may or may not be related to the authorization at hand (see discussion in the next section of the Defense Authorization Act for FY 2008). They may also be slowed down at any point by the threat of a presidential veto, or by an actual veto.

Authorizations for National Defense

The NDAA authorizes the appropriation of funds for the coming budget year. For example, the NDAA for FY 2009 authorizes funds

> to be appropriated for fiscal year 2009 for procurement for the Army as follows: (1) for aircraft, $4,848,835,000; (2) for missiles, $2,207,460,000;

(3) for weapons and tracked combat vehicles, $3,516,398,000; (4) for ammunition, $2,280,791,000; (5) for other procurement, $11,143,076,000; (6) for the Joint Improvised Explosive Device Defeat Fund, $200,000,000.[21]

An NDAA often calls directly for a department or agency to adopt a specific policy. For example, Section 220 of the NDAA for FY 2009 requires the following:

Except as provided pursuant to subsection (b), effective as of October 1, 2012, each airborne intelligence collection system of the Department of Defense that is connected to the Distributed Common Ground/Surface System shall have the capability to operate with the Network-Centric Collaborative Targeting System.[22]

One policy of special interest to the members of the armed services is the size of the military pay raise that typically goes into effect on January 1 each year. That policy is determined by the annual NDAA. For example, the NDAA for FY 2009 increases the rates of basic pay for military personnel by 3.9 percent, effective January 1, 2009.[23] The inclusion of the pay raise makes it particularly important that lawmakers pass the NDAA by January 1.[24]

Partly because it includes the military pay raise, the defense authorization is generally considered to be "must pass" legislation. This makes the defense bill in either chamber a valuable target for amending hard-to-pass legislation that may have nothing to do with defense. Often the defense authorization carries such riders straight through the legislative process. Sometimes this strategy does not work, however. An example related to the NDAA for FY 2008 shows how complex the politics can become.

In September 2007, the Senate added to the defense authorization bill an amendment to expand the protection of earlier hate-crimes laws to victims based on sexual orientation or gender.[25] The House had already passed a stand-alone version of the same hate-crimes provision, and did not include it in its defense authorization.[26]

Unfortunately for Democrats backing the hate-crimes amendment, a sizeable number of House Democrats were already planning to vote against the defense bill when it emerged from conference, because it lacked the timeline for withdrawing from Iraq the Democrats wanted. Many House Republicans vowed to vote against the bill because of the hate-crimes amendment. With so many votes at risk on both sides of the aisle, House leaders feared that there would be no defense authorization at all. In December, the conference committee agreed to drop the hate-crimes provisions from the bill, and it passed in both chambers. The bill was signed into law on January 28, 2008.[27]

To avoid a situation in which service members did not receive the planned pay raise, President Bush early in January 2008 issued an executive order boosting pay. Congress rescinded that order and established its own pay increase in the final version of the authorization act.[28]

NDAAs can also establish policy by setting limits on the use of any funds that are appropriated for an activity until specific conditions are met. For example, Section 223 of the FY 2009 NDAA prohibits the obligation or expenditure of funds to purchase and field a long-range missile defense system in Europe until the host nation signs and ratifies the basing and status of forces agreements that "allow for the stationing in such nation of the radar and the personnel to carry out the proposed deployment."[29]

The NDAA also typically requires the departments involved in national defense to submit reports, assessments, and certifications aimed at identifying and shaping policy. Sometimes those reports are required before funds can be expended, as in this example from Section 217 of the 2009 NDAA:

> The Secretary of Defense, in consultation with the Director of National Intelligence, shall develop a comprehensive plan to conduct and support research, development, and demonstration of technologies that could evolve into the next generation of overhead nonimaging infrared systems...
> ...Not more than 50 percent of the amounts authorized to be appropriated for fiscal year 2009 ... for research, development, test, and evaluation for the Air Force and available for the Third Generation Infrared Surveillance program may be obligated or expended until the date that is 30 days after the date on which the Secretary submits to Congress the plan required.[30]

Just because an activity is authorized does not mean that money will be provided to pay for it. Sometimes the authorizers provide the authorization to appropriate, but the appropriators do not make the money available. This is rare in defense, but it does sometimes happen. For example, after the NDAA authorized so-called concurrent receipt, allowing military retirees to collect retirement pensions without an offset for any veterans' disability benefits they received, it was several years before the authorization was backed up with appropriated funding.

Like appropriation acts, authorizing legislation is susceptible to unrequested funding, including earmarks. Unrequested funding is money provided by Congress for activities or programs that were not included in the administration's budget request.[31] Earmarks are unrequested funding where Congress names the recipients.[32] One non-profit group identified "447 earmarks worth $7.6 billion" in the NDAA for FY 2008, shortly after the House passed a rule aimed at reducing earmarks through public disclosure.[33]

Defense authorization acts were not always as detailed as they are today. Some observers question whether the lines between defense authorization and appropriation have become too blurred. Such questions are not new. Relationships and jurisdiction between authorizers and appropriators are not cast in stone, and they tend to shift over time.[34] The relative power of authorizers as compared with appropriators has also varied over time.[35]

Since authorization acts establish the policy that underpins federal budgets and are required in advance of spending, one would expect them to be completed before the appropriations acts. In the case of national defense, the annual authorization and appropriation acts are both meant to be completed by September 30 for the fiscal year that begins the next day. In recent years, this has rarely been the case (see Table 9.7).

Some observers argue that the passage of authorization acts after appropriations are already out the door signal a decline in the relevance of authorizing committees and the authorization process. Regardless of timing, however, the NDAA remains an important source of guidance and policy, and the departments involved generally hew to its requirements.

Authorizations for International Affairs

Authorization acts for international affairs traditionally fall into two categories: foreign relations acts, which establish policy and authorize appropriations for the running of the State Department, and foreign assistance acts, which set policy and authorize appropriations for foreign aid.[36] The House Foreign Affairs Committee and the Senate Foreign Relations Committee hold jurisdiction for both of those types of acts.

Table 9.7 Dates of defense authorization and appropriation acts for FY 2000–FY 2009

Act for fiscal year	National defense authorization signed into law	Defense appropriation signed into law
2000	October 5, 1999	October 25, 1999
2001	October 30, 2000	August 9, 2000
2002	December 28, 2001	January 10, 2002
2003	December 2, 2002	October 23, 2002
2004	November 24, 2003	September 30, 2003
2005	October 28, 2004	August 5, 2004
2006	January 6, 2006	December 30, 2005
2007	October 17, 2006	September 29, 2006
2008	January 28, 2008	November 13, 2007
2009	October 14, 2008	September 30, 2008[a]

Source: Table by Miranda Priebe based on information from http://thomas.loc.gov and on Linwood B. Carter and Thomas Coipuram Jr., "Defense Authorization and Appropriations Bills: A Chronology, FY1970–FY2006," CRS Report 98-756 (Washington, DC: Congressional Research Service, May 23, 2005).

Note
[a] Incorporated as Division C of the Continuing Resolution, PL 110-329 (September 30, 2008).

Standing law requires the biannual authorization of appropriations for the State Department and foreign affairs. Since the mid-1990s, that requirement has been honored in the breach.[37] For example, for FY 2008, the annual appropriation for the State Department and foreign operations was included as Division J of the Consolidated Appropriation Act for 2008, which waived the authorization requirement.[38]

Since 1985, there has been no stand-alone foreign assistance authorization act.[39] Instead, authorization language for foreign assistance often gets folded into foreign relations authorization bills and, since 1995, from there into appropriations acts.[40]

The paucity of stand-alone, biannual authorizing legislation reflects a general decline in the power of authorizers relative to appropriators in the area of international affairs. In the case of foreign assistance, it also reflects the lack of domestic political support for money that will be spent in other countries. Within any congressional district, voting for foreign assistance is a net loser: it creates jobs for almost nobody, and to some constituents it looks like waste. From the point of view of a member of Congress running for re-election, it is best not to create any more opportunities to vote on foreign aid than are absolutely necessary.[41]

Even though stand-alone authorization acts for foreign affairs and foreign assistance are rare, Congress still plays an active role in shaping foreign policy through the budget. For example, the FY 2008 Appropriations Act for the Department of State, Foreign Operations, and Related Programs forbids spending to expand the US diplomatic presence in Vietnam without presidential certification, requires the Secretary of State to set up facilities to process visas in Iraq, and bans the funding of abortions using development aid money.[42]

Authorizations for Homeland Security

Despite the creation of homeland security committees in the House and Senate, as of early 2009 Congress has not yet passed a stand-alone annual authorization act either for the Department of Homeland Security or for the overall homeland security function. Outside of the annual process, however, Congress has passed several major authorization acts in the homeland security area since 2001. Moreover, lawmakers have completed important authorizing legislation for various components of the department.

Between 2001 and 2008, two authorization acts were central in reorganizing federal government and setting broad policy for homeland security: the Homeland Security Act of 2002 and the Implementing Recommendations of the 9/11 Commission Act of 2007.[43] The Homeland Security Act of 2002 created DHS and defined the mission, functions, and general structure of the new department. The Implementing Recommendations Act requires the allocation of state and local preparedness grants based on risk, establishes a stand-alone federal grants program for interoperable communications for state and local first responders, and calls for a top-to-bottom quadrennial homeland security review at the beginning of each presidential term.

Other authorization acts since 2001 direct homeland security activities in specific areas. For example, the Secure Fence Act of 2006 requires the Secretary of Homeland Security to beef up surveillance and infrastructure to secure the nation's land and maritime borders.[44]

Much of the authorizing legislation related to homeland security emanates from committees other than the homeland security authorizing committees. For example, the transportation committees developed the Coast Guard and Maritime Transportation Act of 2006, as of February 2009 the last major authorization for appropriations for the Coast Guard.[45] Between 2001 and 2008, Congress passed four major pieces of authorizing legislation related to countering biological threats or dealing with the homeland security aspects of pandemic disease.[46] All of those acts started in the House Energy and Commerce Committee or the Senate Health, Education, Labor, and Pensions Committee. Similarly, the annual defense authorization acts developed by the Armed Services Committees in the House and Senate include policy guidance as well as authorization for appropriation for the homeland security activities of the Department of Defense.

Appropriations Committees and Legislation

The Appropriations Committees of the House and Senate are responsible for the annual funding bills that provide the money that runs the federal government. Each chamber's committee currently has 12 subcommittees, whose jurisdictions are generally aligned the same way in each chamber (see Table 9.8). Jurisdictions of the subcommittees are roughly aligned with specific departments and agencies of the executive branch, and each subcommittee is responsible for one of its chamber's 12 annual appropriation bills.

Four subcommittees in each chamber hold jurisdiction over funding for most aspects of security and international affairs. The Defense Subcommittees of the House and Senate manage appropriations for the Department of Defense (DOD) (with the exception of military construction) and for most of the intelligence community. The Subcommittees on Military Construction, Veterans Affairs, and Related Agencies handle the military construction side of DOD. The State, Foreign Operations, and Related Programs Subcommittees exercise jurisdiction over State Department and foreign assistance budgets.[47] The Homeland Security Subcommittees are generally aligned with DHS.

Nevertheless, every subcommittee in each chamber has jurisdiction over funding for some aspect of national security, in part because federal homeland security funding is dispersed across so many executive branch departments and agencies. In FY 2008, about one-half of the money going to federal

Table 9.8 Subcommittees of the House and Senate Appropriations Committees in the 110th Congress

Subcommittee	Some areas of jurisdiction for statecraft and security
Agriculture, Rural Development, Food and Drug Administration, and Related Agencies	FDA and Agriculture food safety and defense programs; USDA foreign agricultural service
Commerce, Justice, Science, and Related Agencies	FBI national security and intelligence programs; Office of US Trade Representative
Defense	DOD, except for military construction and family housing, base realignment and closure, and civil works of Army Corps of Engineers; CIA; Intelligence Community Staff; Defense Security and Cooperation Agency[a]
Energy and Water Development, and Related Agencies	Nuclear weapons activities of DOE; naval reactors; Defense nuclear facilities safety board; civil works of Army Corps of Engineers; DOE infrastructure protection
Financial Services and General Government	Banking issues related to countering terrorism; appropriation for the Executive Office of the President, including the National Security Council
Homeland Security	All DHS
Interior, Environment, and Related Agencies	Protection of infrastructure at national parks and forests
Labor, HHS, Education, and Related Agencies	HHS grants to states, localities, and health care providers; NIH development of medical countermeasures; HHS biosurveillance; CDC national stockpile of medicines and vaccines to counter biological terrorism
Legislative Branch	Protection of infrastructure in congressional buildings

Subcommittee	Jurisdiction
Military Construction, Veterans Affairs, and Related Agencies	Military family housing construction, operation and maintenance; base realignment and closure accounts; military construction; Department of Veterans Affairs
State, Foreign Operations, and Related Programs	Department of State; USAID; Foreign Military Financing and International Military Education and Training (DOD); Defense Security and Cooperation Agency (DOD);[a] foreign debt restructuring, international affairs technical assistance, International Monetary Fund, multilateral development banks (Treasury); Export–Import Bank; Millennium Challenge Corporation; Overseas Private Investment Corporation; Peace Corps; Trade and Development Agency; Broadcasting Board of Governors; US Institute of Peace
Transportation, Housing and Urban Development, and Other Agencies	Transportation infrastructure protection

Sources: House Committee on Appropriations, "Subcommittee Jurisdiction," 110th Congress, 1st Session (Washington, DC: GPO, January 16, 2007); Senate Committee on Appropriations, "Subcommittee Jurisdiction," 110th Congress (March 2007), Senate Prin. 110–11; Office of Management and Budget, "Crosscutting Programs" *Analytical Perspectives, Budget of the United States for FY 2009* (February 2008), 17–35.

Note
[a] In the Senate, jurisdiction is shared between the Defense subcommittee and the State, Foreign Operations, and Related Programs subcommittee.

homeland security efforts went to DHS and thus fell under the purview of the Homeland Security Subcommittees. Another one-quarter went to DOD and was managed by the Subcommittees on Defense or the Subcommittees on Military Construction, Veterans Affairs, and Related Agencies. Other subcommittees held responsibility for the remaining one-quarter of federal homeland security appropriations.

Types of Appropriations and the Appropriations Process

Congress passes three types of appropriations: regular appropriations, continuing resolutions, and supplemental appropriations. Each has its own processes and its own rules.

Regular Appropriations

The regular appropriations process begins in each chamber with hearings by the subcommittees. Traditionally, appropriation legislation begins in the House. The subcommittees of the two chambers typically work in parallel to ready the bills for action, however. In recent years, the full Senate has often voted on its bill before the House has gotten its own version through the Appropriations Committee.[48]

A critical step in the process is the allocation of money among the appropriations subcommittees. In each chamber, the Chairman of the Appropriations Committee has broad authority for this allocation. Beginning with the 302(a) allocation to the Appropriations Committee that resulted from the Concurrent Budget Resolution, the chairman distributes to the subcommittees their so-called 302(b) allocations.[49] This authority helps to make the chairmen of the House and Senate Appropriations Committees two of the most powerful players in Congress.

Each subcommittee drafts a single appropriations bill and an accompanying report. The subcommittees send their recommendations to the full Appropriations Committee, which considers and ultimately votes on the bill. Traditionally, the Appropriations Committees report each of their 12 bills separately to the floor of the chamber. The full chamber then has an opportunity to amend and vote on the appropriation. After the House and Senate both pass their own versions of the individual appropriation, a conference committee addresses differences. Both chambers vote on the final bill, which is sent to the President for signature—preferably before October 1, the first day of the new fiscal year.

In recent decades, Congress has often broken with tradition by combining multiple appropriations into a single "omnibus" measure. A good example is the consolidated appropriation for FY 2005, which pulled together appropriations for Agriculture; Commerce, Justice, and State; Energy and Water; Foreign Operations; Interior; Labor, HHS, and Education; Legislative Branch;

Transportation and Treasury; and Veterans Affairs and Housing and Urban Development into a single act.[50]

Omnibus or consolidated spending acts are not necessarily a sign of weakness in the appropriation process. The subcommittee hearings and committee markups and reports from each chamber, together with the budget levels granted through a consolidated appropriation, generally provide the budget guidance expected of appropriators. The omnibus tool does allow Congress to avoid the restrictions on funding that might otherwise apply as well as the scrutiny by members and the public to which separate bills would likely be subjected.

More importantly, the omnibus vehicle is a tool that allows lawmakers to deal with contentious policy debates that underlie the federal budget. A consolidated appropriation can combine politically unpopular appropriations, for example for foreign aid, with those that enjoy broad support, such as agriculture and transportation. It also opens greater room for tradeoffs and negotiation of differences between the chambers or between Congress and the administration.[51]

Appropriations of all types are susceptible to earmarks and other unrequested spending, which directs spending to activities and programs that were not included in the administration's budget request. Earmarks give individual members of Congress the opportunity to steer jobs to their own states and districts. Unrequested spending of any type can also be a tool for inserting congressional policy choices into budgets. The chairmen of the Appropriations Committees exercise substantial authority over earmarks and other unrequested spending—another source of their power.

Continuing Resolutions

When appropriations acts are unfinished on September 30, Congress typically passes a continuing resolution to provide funds, often using set formulas based on the previous year's appropriations to determine the amounts that will be provided. Sometimes many executive branch departments and agencies operate under a series of successive continuing resolutions, before Congress and the administration finally agree to a full set of individual appropriation measures or an omnibus appropriation that wraps up all of the outstanding bills. In 2007, the last of four continuing resolutions provided funds for all but defense and homeland security all the way through the end of the fiscal year. Similarly, in 2009, all but two appropriations bills were rolled into an omnibus package after a continuing resolution that funded the government through February.

Congressional strictures against policy provisions and unauthorized appropriations do not apply to continuing resolutions. This and the fact that continuing resolutions must be passed to keep the government running after September 30 suits them to legislation that otherwise would be difficult to pass.[52] Congress often uses continuing resolutions as a vehicle for omnibus appropriations, thus combining the logrolling advantages of the omnibus measure with the extra latitude of the continuing resolution.

Since 2001, Congress has generally viewed defense, military construction, and homeland security as areas too important and visible to leave to a continuing resolution. Those appropriations have generally passed as individual bills before the deadline. Foreign affairs appropriations have typically been rolled into continuing resolutions and ultimately packaged with other appropriations into omnibus measures.

Supplemental Appropriations

The third type of appropriation is the supplemental appropriation, usually considered after the fiscal year begins, to provide funds needed because of unforeseen events such as natural disasters or the start of a war. In 2001 and 2002, emergency supplemental appropriations provided a quick infusion of money to deal with the aftermath of 9/11 and the anthrax attacks of October 2001. Since that time, national leaders have found them expedient for other purposes, including the provision of several hundreds of billions of dollars for military, intelligence, and Department of State operations in Afghanistan and Iraq.

In recent years, Congress has used emergency supplemental appropriations to mandate directly policies that might be hard to move through other legislation. For example, the second emergency supplemental appropriation for pandemic influenza preparedness indemnifies those who provide medical countermeasures against claims that result from the administration of those countermeasures during a public health emergency.[53] That policy was included in the early authorization bills that ultimately resulted in the Pandemic and All-Hazards Preparedness Act (PAHPA) of December 2006, but was pushed into the emergency supplemental act as those bills met roadblocks. In another example, the Post 9/11 Veterans Educational Assistance Act, which authorized a major expansion of the GI Bill, was incorporated as Title V of the Supplemental Appropriations Act of 2008.[54] Though popular in Congress because it expanded benefits for veterans in a time of war, the new benefit was opposed by the administration as too costly and potentially harmful to military retention.

From 1986 until 2000, successive administrations and Congresses crafted broad agreements on taxes and spending, aimed at balancing the federal budget and ultimately creating budgetary surpluses. During that period, supplemental spending for emergencies typically fell outside of the spending limits imposed by those agreements. To avoid a situation in which substantial amounts of appropriated funding would fall outside the spending limits, Congress was chary in what it allowed in supplemental acts, generally limiting them to funds for genuinely unforeseen emergencies. What constituted an emergency was never made entirely clear, however, leading to wide latitude in interpretation on Capitol Hill as well as in the executive branch in recent years.

Since 2000, the administration and Congress have made no serious effort to enforce spending limits of the sort that prevailed during the previous 15 years. Should such limits be restored, emergency supplemental appropriations would likely be excluded from the calculation, as they were in the past.

Concerns Raised by Congressional Organizations and Processes

The terrorist attacks of 2001 led Congress to mandate a broad restructuring of the executive branch to consolidate and strengthen responsibilities in the areas of homeland security and intelligence. They also reinforced a sentiment already prevalent in some circles: that in the modern world, functions of intelligence, defense, international affairs, and homeland security that could formerly be considered as relatively independent are deeply intertwined, and should be planned for and funded in a way that recognizes their interdependence.

Congress also reorganized itself, creating new authorizing committees and appropriations subcommittees to deal with homeland security. Nevertheless, the way Congress is organized and the processes and tools it uses to allocate resources among federal activities appear inconsistent with an integrated approach to national security. This section considers concerns in five areas: authorizing jurisdictions for homeland security, the potential utility of cross-committee hearings, the small size of CBO's national security team, the absence of a budget function for homeland security, and the routine use of emergency supplemental appropriations.

Authorizing Jurisdictions for Homeland Security

The web of jurisdictions for DHS and homeland security among congressional authorizing committees causes three problems for congressional resource allocation. Most important, legacy jurisdictions make it easy for the directors of the various DHS operating components to circumvent decisions made by the Secretary of Homeland Security by going around the Secretary to their legacy committees of jurisdiction. This can make it hard for the Secretary to do the job Congress envisioned: unifying the efforts of a consolidated department and aligning homeland security resources to a national strategy.

A second problem is that intersecting jurisdictions within each chamber make it difficult to pass an annual authorization act. The problem is compounded by the fact that jurisdictional lines for some aspects of homeland security still differ between the House and the Senate. The failure to pass an annual authorization act can in part be blamed on the lack of a central committee of oversight in each chamber. (In contrast, the appropriations committees, where jurisdiction for DHS is consolidated within a single sub-committee, generally complete homeland security appropriations bills before the beginning of the fiscal year.)

Pushing through the authorizing legislation that does pass requires enormous effort. The Implementing Recommendations of the 9/11 Commission Act of 2007 went through ten separate House committees and took until July 2007 to complete, even though lawmakers generally agreed to its broad outlines shortly after the 110th Congress convened in January 2007.[55]

A third problem with oversight by so many committees and subcommittees is the policy disarray that can result as the department receives conflicting guidance from multiple committees or their staffs. The proliferation of oversight committees certainly leads to a proliferation of requests for testimony and reports. Between January and July of 2007, DHS provided some 195 witnesses to 141 hearings and presented more than 1,500 briefings.[56]

The 9/11 Commission recommended that each chamber choose a single point of oversight and review for homeland security.[57] A key issue in establishing a single point of oversight is whether the resulting homeland security committees should have oversight over homeland security as a function (about half of which resides in DHS) or over the department itself (which includes substantial non-homeland security activities). Either alignment is likely preferable to today's structure.

Potential Utility of Cross-Committee Hearings

Even if the authorizing jurisdictions are realigned to put responsibility for homeland security or DHS into a single committee, there will still be overlaps of jurisdiction among committees and subcommittees. For example, DOD now has a substantial stake in developing medical countermeasures against biological threats, yet shifting oversight of that work into the homeland security committees is probably unlikely.

Another way to improve the integration of policy oversight and budgets for homeland security is for Congress to conduct regular joint hearings of homeland security programs and activities that cut across committee jurisdictions.[58] The House and Senate homeland security committees could use such hearings every four years to assess the administration's quadrennial homeland security review, now required at the beginning of each presidential term.

More broadly, Congress could use joint hearings to explore activities that span the jurisdictions of multiple authorizing committees or appropriation subcommittees. Such cross-committee hearings could take up broad questions, such as the links between the national security strategy the administration articulates and the budgets it proposes for defense, intelligence, homeland security, and international affairs. They could also be used to assess and influence policies and budgets in more specific areas, such as national risk-management plans, the relationship between the federal effort and state and local responsibilities in homeland security, the restructuring of security assistance to foreign countries, or the allocation of roles and missions for stabilization and reconstruction efforts in Iraq and Afghanistan.

The Small Size of CBO's National Security Division

CBO, CRS, and GAO provide information and analyses that can help Congress exercise its resource allocation and oversight roles. Since 2001, the three support agencies have provided important reports on a variety of topics related to national security, including past and current spending and projected costs, the structure of the executive branch and Congress, the performance and effectiveness of individual programs, and interagency cooperation. The agencies have done less in the way of broad studies that cut across departments and agencies, particularly across the domestic–national security divide.

The CBO in particular lacks the analysts it would need to examine broad tradeoffs routinely for areas that lie at the intersection of national defense, homeland security, and international affairs. Congress may want to expand the National Security Division and the Budget Analysis Division of CBO with additional analysts who would assess the overall federal effort for security and international affairs as well as particular activities that cut across organizational boundaries in the executive branch or Congress.

Useful studies by CBO could include an examination of the roles and missions of the main operating components of DHS; a look at the possible tradeoffs between Department of State and Energy programs to secure nuclear materials in Russia and DHS programs to identify nuclear materials at US ports of entry; or an assessment of the costs, benefits, and risks of various measures to ameliorate the potential consequences of a biological attack. Such studies could improve congressional understanding of the broad resource allocation choices the executive branch has proposed.

The Absence of a Budget Function for Homeland Security

The absence of a homeland security budget function means that the Budget Committees do not get involved in the annual allocation of total resources to homeland security through the Concurrent Budget Resolution. Yet the Budget Resolution constitutes lawmakers' main chance to fill in the full fiscal picture of the federal government for the coming year. The resolution determines both how well spending will match revenues and the alignment of spending to broad national priorities. With homeland security activities divided among many budget functions, Congress forgoes an opportunity to mark its priorities in the budget.

The lack of a budget function for homeland security also inhibits Congress's ability to audit spending transparently and weakens the links between planned and executed budgets. With only half of total funding for homeland security captured in the homeland security appropriation, Congress must rely for information about overall spending for homeland security on OMB's cross-cutting report. Yet that report provides no consistent historical audit of spending. In the future, Congress might want to work with the White House to create a single homeland security budget function.

The Routine Use of Emergency Supplemental Appropriations

The use of emergency supplemental acts to set policy and provide budgets for recurring activities poses three problems. First, emergency supplemental appropriations generally circumvent the congressional authorization process entirely and typically are subject to less scrutiny in the executive branch and Congress than regular appropriations. The result can be weakened oversight in both branches.

Second, the use of emergency supplementals for recurring activities can muddy projections of the federal government's future fiscal picture. When the government uses such appropriations to pay for routine activities, future spending for those activities does not enter into calculations of future deficits by OMB or the CBO, even though they are likely to recur. Finally, when they are excluded from the spending caps imposed under balanced budget agreements, emergency supplemental appropriations can complicate efforts to reduce the federal deficit. The administration's budget for FY 2010 includes war funding directly in the regular appropriation request and also in the estimates of the annual federal deficit.

Chapter 10

The Politics of National Security Budgeting

Introduction

Without resources, national security policy is largely rhetoric.[1] Policy is shaped and implemented through the budget process. Policy debates frequently occur in the framework of a process that decides on the funding that supports that policy.

If the nation is going to war, it must pay for it, as the lengthy debate over funding the war in Iraq has illustrated.[2] If the United States supports Pakistan's efforts to subdue terrorists in their northwest provinces, funds are needed for foreign assistance and troop training. Arms control agreements are only verifiable if there is funding to support the personnel and equipment used for verification. The enforcement of immigration policies requires funding for technology and people.

Funds for national security policy commitments are planned, allocated, and implemented through the budget processes and institutions described in this book. These institutions and processes are not mechanical, however. They are part of a political process.[3] To understand a budgetary outcome, it is important to understand the political process it goes through. This chapter examines how the formal, sometimes technical processes and institutions we have discussed are linked into that wider political process. The chapter discusses several analytical perspectives that can be used to analyze national security budget decisions, and looks at international affairs, defense, and homeland security budget decisions with those perspectives in mind.

The Mystery of National Security Budget Decisions

Examined in isolation from the political process, national security budgets would seem to be the rational result of defining the fiscal requirements of national security policy. The government decides to pursue a certain course of action with respect to national security. The resources to support that action are estimated, submitted in a budget request, and provided by the Congress.

The Soviet Union acts in an aggressive and hostile way; the United States responds by enlarging its military or developing new strategic systems. Congress provides the funds for that capability. The Warsaw Pact dissolves and the United States and other democracies create and fund programs to provide support to the newly emerging democracies.

At other times, this rational, policy-based logic behind national security budget decisions doesn't seem to explain the budget outcome. The total level of national defense, international affairs, or homeland security budgets, or their relative sizes, may seem unrelated to the needs of national security or careful consideration of the balance among the tools of statecraft.[4] The State Department and the US Agency for International Development (USAID) plan the budget for and implement foreign assistance programs, but the Defense Department creates its own major foreign assistance program. Air power is a necessary ingredient of US military capability, but air capabilities are redundantly provided by several military services, at great cost.

The United States established a new Department of Homeland Security (DHS) to centralize budget decisions in the hands of a single Cabinet Secretary, but the shares of the homeland security budget that go to the component parts of the department are the same as they were before the department was created.[5] The military services are lukewarm about national missile defense, but a $10 billion per year program is created, nonetheless. The Secretary of Defense cancels a bomber program, but it re-emerges in another administration. USAID is the primary foreign assistance provider, but an entirely new foreign assistance agency, the Millennium Challenge Corporation (MCC), is created outside USAID.

Analysts of the national security policymaking process rarely dig into the politics of the budgetary process.[6] Resource decisions, if they are discussed at all, are a secondary derivative of policy.[7] Analysts of the federal budget process, moreover, spend little time examining national security budget decisions, focusing instead on the politics of domestic budgets.[8] The result is that there is little understanding of the politics of national security budgeting. Only by focusing on those politics can one unravel the mystery of decisions that do not appear rational when policy considerations alone are taken into account.

Perspectives on National Security Budget Decisions

National strategy, policies, and international events all clearly have consequences for the national security budget institutions and processes we have discussed in this book. The political arena, however, is the context in which these issues are translated into budgets. National security budget decisions can be examined along three different dimensions: international events and national strategy, bureaucratic interests and processes inside government agencies, and politics in the broadest sense—interests and objectives pursued by players at the top of executive branch agencies, at the presidential level, and in and around the Congress. As national security budget decisions are made, all three of these dimensions can have an impact and they clearly interact with each other. Few national security budget decisions can be explained with only one of these dimensions in mind.

The Impact of National Security Strategy and International Events

Decisions on national security budgets are clearly about policy. The policy problem being addressed in the budget may grow out of an international event, the requirements of the nation's national security strategy, or a specific policy decision. Developments in the international system pose specific challenges and opportunities that can lead to budgetary requirements. A terrorist strike, a coup, a change of policy by a key ally may all require a US response. That response needs to be staffed and funded—or "resourced," in budget language. More proactively, the nation's security strategy outlines goals and objectives aimed at meeting international challenges, seizing opportunities, asserting the United States' national interest, or protecting people and infrastructure. The budgets, programs, and activities of the departments and agencies with roles in foreign policy, national defense, and homeland security support the implementation of those strategies and policies.[9]

From this perspective, international challenges and events and national strategy are clear; both have detailed implications for agency programs and budgets. Agencies and the White House estimate the budgetary costs of responding to events and implementing strategies, and request the funds from the Congress. The Congress holds hearings and drafts legislation and appropriations bills that support or alter the administration's requests.[10] This rational view is the explanation generally offered for national security budget decisions. It is the perspective from which security decisions are generally discussed in the media. In strategy and budget documents, administrations defend their national security budget decisions as rational responses to events or the requirements of strategy and policy.[11]

Since World War II, international events and national strategies have clearly been important factors in shaping the nation's security choices and budgets. From the late 1940s until the end of the Cold War, for example, successive administrations' understanding of Soviet capabilities and intentions provided the framework for evolving US national security strategy: deterrence and containment. Spending for conventional forces was reduced as budgets for nuclear forces grew. Later build-ups reflected estimates of growing Soviet nuclear capability and what was seen as the increasing prowess of Warsaw Pact conventional forces. The strategy also dictated the deployment of substantial numbers of military troops and the provision of significant economic assistance to Western Europe, as well as the creation of foreign and security assistance programs for other US allies around the world.

The end of the Cold War dramatically changed the context for US national security policy. With the disappearance of the Soviet threat, US active-duty military forces shrank from some 2.1 million troops in 1989 to roughly 1.4 million by 1995, leading to a smaller defense budget. The United States made a deliberate policy decision to support democracy and free-market economies in the newly independent states that emerged from the break-up of the former Warsaw Pact and Soviet Union. The United States pressed NATO to open its doors to several of the newly independent states and created its own program to train and prepare the militaries of the new states for the responsibilities of NATO membership—the Partnership for Peace program.[12] Significant new foreign assistance programs were also created: the Support for East European Democracies Act (SEED—1989) and the Freedom Support Act (FSA—1991), discussed in Chapter 4. Diplomatic relations with these new countries also required an expansion of the US diplomatic presence in the region, with additional funding for such budget accounts as Overseas Buildings Operations, and Diplomatic and Consular Programs, discussed in Chapter 2.

The events of September 11, 2001 changed the context yet again. The Bush administration's 2002 and 2006 National Security Strategy documents focused on terrorism, the proliferation of weapons of mass destruction, and support for democracy abroad. The administration also articulated multiple strategies for homeland security and counterterrorism, including the National Homeland Security strategies of 2002 and 2007.

Budget allocations reflected these changes. Spending for homeland security rose faster than that of any other category, more than tripling (in dollars unadjusted for inflation) over a period of eight years (see Table 10.1).[13] Shifts in funding within the defense and international affairs categories also reflected changed priorities, with considerable funding for military operations in counterterrorist situations, training non-US security forces for counterterror operations, biological weapons defense, and democracy promotion. Similarly, when the administration identified the AIDS virus as a threat to political and economic stability in Africa, it created a new program combat HIV/AIDS, much of it targeted to Africa, and invested billions of dollars to achieve that goal, as discussed in Chapter 3.

International events and national security strategies do not explain all national security budget decisions, however. There is rarely one correct response to events, one correct strategy, or one correct budgetary response. For example, knowledgeable experts inside and outside government opposed the decisions to enlarge NATO and use US funds to train and equip former Warsaw Pact militaries. There was considerable opposition to creating a ballistic missile defense program to deal with the Soviet nuclear threat.

Moreover, even if an event or a strategy suggests the need for a program, the form the program takes, its placement within the bureaucracy, its timing

Table 10.1 Budgets for security and foreign affairs (budget authority in billions of current dollars)

	FY 2001	FY 2009
National Defense		
Excluding Iraq and Afghanistan	318	550
Iraq and Afghanistan	0	142
Total National Defense	318	692
Homeland Security		
Total Homeland Security	17	72
Homeland Security in DOD	4	20
Homeland Security Net of DOD	13	52
International Affairs	20	45
Total Security and Foreign Affairs	351	789

Source: Authors' table based on Office of Management and Budget, *Budget of the United States Government Fiscal Year 2010: Historical tables*, Table 5.1; Department of Defense, *Fiscal Year 2010 Budget Request: Summary Justification* (May 2009), Table 4-1; Office of Management and Budget, "Crosscutting Programs," *Analytical Perspectives*, Budget of the United States for FY 2010 (May 2009), 15.

and duration, and the size of its budget may bear only an indirect relationship to the security rationale. Budgets for some programs may seem urgent, yet they get deferred or traded off against other urgent needs. Programs, organizations, and funding may emerge or persist with little apparent connection to the logic of events or strategies. Budgets may vary little from year to year, despite important shifts on the international scene; next year's budget looks like last year's with a boost for inflation.[14]

The Impact of Bureaucracy

The executive branch is the starting point for much of this book's discussion of the budgetary process. Every executive branch agency has its own bureaucracy and its unique formal and informal bureaucratic processes. The bureaucracies have their own cultures, rules, processes, standard operating procedures, and program and budgetary histories.[15] Moreover, within agencies there are bureaucratic subcultures that can have a significant impact on budget decisions. The White House has its own budget bureaucracy at the Office of Management and Budget (OMB), with rules and processes that apply to the entire executive branch. The Congress has an elaborate system of budget procedures, structures, and its own bureaucratic turf wars, discussed in Chapter 9.

Bureaucracies typically seek to preserve the budgetary status quo, starting with last year's budget and making changes at the margin. Genuine "zero-based" reviews of programs and activities are rare. These bureaucratic realities have a major impact on national security budgets. They can help explain why some budget decisions seem illogical if viewed solely from the perspective of national security policy.[16]

Bureaucracy and the Department of Defense

Bureaucratic politics within and among the defense components can be a significant ingredient in Defense Department budget decisions.[17] As the largest and most complex federal agency, DOD is a mini-government. It employs one-third of the civilian workforce of the federal government. Defense civilians and active-duty service members make up some 60 percent of the government's full-time equivalent workers, and members of the Guard and Reserve push the proportion even higher. DOD spends more than half of the discretionary budget and buys roughly 75 percent of all the goods purchased by the federal government. DOD and the services operate logistical and supply institutions, health services, grocery stores, school systems, travel operations, and a system of retirement benefits.

The military services are classic bureaucratic organizations, with historically rooted cultures, doctrines, and processes.[18] In combat, each service performs unique missions for which the others are not trained or equipped—naval warfare, ground combat, air combat and air-to-ground support. The culture of each service supports those core missions. Army culture, for example, gives high priority to retaining as many personnel ("billets") as possible, which can lead to budget tradeoffs against weapons programs in the Army budget. By contrast, Air Force culture places a high value on technology, and the service will accept personnel reductions in favor of funds for aircraft. The Navy's air, surface, and submarine subcultures compete among themselves for funding. No service would voluntarily downsize, abandon its missions, or shrink its budget.[19]

At the same time, there is also overlap and duplication among the service capabilities. In operational terms, some duplication may be helpful. Air Force and Navy air capabilities seem redundant, but can actually deliver air interdiction capabilities under different circumstances. The Air Force needs fixed bases or significant tanker capability to operate; the Navy can operate from carriers offshore when fixed bases are not available. Other duplications, such as Marine and Army ground force or Army and Air Force close air support capabilities, may seem less logical. These may stem from a sense in each service that they cannot fully rely on the others for needed support capability, such as communications.[20]

Distinctions in capabilities, service culture, and the desire to ensure important capabilities are owned within one service can all play a role in how the military services interact in the budget process. For decades, the services have come to believe that each must preserve its share of the defense budget, making the principle of "constant shares" a core element of defense budget planning.[21] As one former Vice Chairman of the Joint Chiefs of Staff (JCS) put it:

[T]he appearance of partnership and cooperation among the four US armed services is the biggest illusion of all.... Duplication and redundancy among the different services became the norm, and once in place, redundant programs became heavily vested. Each service worked hard to ensure that it received the funding and operational priority, while working hard to defeat the other services if they developed a rival capability.[22]

None of the services focuses on the overall needs of forces operating in a combat theater. That is the responsibility of the Combatant Commanders in each regional theater, who actually operate the forces. The COCOMS, as they are known, have become another player in the DOD budget process. The Chairman and the JCS also play a role in the process, providing views on resources, military advice to the President, and overall strategic direction to the military forces.[23] All of these bureaucracies must deal with the Office of the Secretary of Defense, which balances these competing needs and budget requests.[24]

Bureaucracy and International Affairs

Bureaucratic considerations are also an important element in budget decisions for international affairs. Most important, no single agency takes control of planning and budgeting for the entirety of the International Affairs budget. As discussed in Chapters 2 and 3, there is no integrated budget process for all of the international affairs budget, and the most visible foreign affairs agency—the State Department—has not yet done integrated strategic planning or resource allocation for its own programs and operations.

The organizational "diaspora" in international affairs is one reason why defense budgets are so much larger than those for international affairs. While the State Department dominated US national security policymaking at the end of World War II, the balance shifted over the years of the Cold War, leading to a relatively coherent Defense Department, but scattered foreign affairs bureaucracies. The smaller role played by foreign policy institutions in US national security policy and their smaller budgets result, in part, from this bureaucratic difference.

The diaspora itself is a result of the bureaucratic culture of the State Department.[25] Starting in the late 1940s, State repeatedly resisted incorporating programs for foreign assistance, public diplomacy, and trade in its core mission. Instead, these programs were created within other federal agencies (Treasury, Agriculture), or in new agencies designed to carry them out (US Information Agency, USAID, or the MCC).

This resistance to program is linked to the Foreign Service, which sets the tone in the department. The Foreign Service culture values the skills of negotiation, analysis and reporting, foreign languages, overseas representation, and an understanding of foreign cultures. Foreign Service training concentrates on these skills, but does include much attention to strategic planning, program development, or program implementation. Few diplomats are exposed, over their careers, to other institutions in the national security arena (NSC, OMB, DOD, Congress); very few have had responsibility for strategic or budgetary planning or program development and implementation. Within the department, Foreign Service Officers tend to be concentrated in the political and economic areas and the regional bureaus, while functional offices at State that deal with such issues as nonproliferation, security assistance, and democracy promotion tend to be staffed by civil servants, who are not part of the dominant culture. Planning and program development did not fit easily into this dominant culture.

The dispersal of international affairs program activity is exacerbated by the growing involvement of other federal agencies in US global engagement, including Commerce, Health and Human Services, Labor, the Environmental Protection Agency, Justice, and Homeland Security, among others. Budgets for these agencies are planned entirely outside the world of Function 150, as seen in Chapters 3 and 4.

As a consequence, the civilian agencies involved in international affairs agencies have no strategic planning or budgetary process comparable to DOD's Planning, Programming, Budgeting, and Execution (PPBE) system. The reforms to State/USAID foreign assistance budget planning initiated in 2006 (and discussed in Chapter 3) fall well short of the PPBE process. Through 2008, this new process was *ad hoc* in the bureaucracy, disconnected from overall strategy, limited to a one-year horizon, and restricted to only those programs for which State and USAID were responsible.

Over the decades, the dispersal of responsibility for planning, budgeting, and implementing civilian US foreign policy and global engagement has undermined the role and responsibilities of the Department of State and weakened State's ability to create, articulate, and implement a coherent case for foreign affairs budgets to the Congress. One consequence is that the more planning-oriented, coherently organized organization—the Department of Defense—has developed capabilities and activities that overlap with those of the State Department, as discussed in Chapter 4.

The Political Crucible

International events, the requirements of strategy, national security policy choices, bureaucratic norms, and turf struggles come together in the crucible of politics. Budgets are the vehicle for the distribution of financial and human resources, probably the most "political" set of decisions the government makes. As Harold Lasswell said, politics is about "who gets what, when, and how."[26]

The political arena is crowded with players, all of whom are connected to the budget process. There are senior appointed policy officials who oversee policymaking and budgeting. There are the most senior elected officials—the

President and Vice President, and the staff and offices they oversee. There are members of Congress, congressional committees, and staff. And there are powerful associations, interest groups, local institutions, and citizens, bringing their views to bear on the budget. Each of these players has interests; each sees value in some part of the budget; each typically sees its own budget goals as "rational," linked to its own particular interests. This examination of the political arena reviews the role of each of these sets of players in turn.

Senior Policy Officials

Senior executive branch policy officials, appointed to top positions in bureaucratic agencies, play a critical role in the national security budget process. Policy officials shape strategy and interpret events. They push the bureaucracy and respond, in turn, to bureaucratic interests and pressures. They bring their own views and personalities to the decision process.[27] Policy officials are not bureaucrats. Within DOD, the State Department, USAID, DHS, and the other departments and agencies, there is a clear distinction between the responsibilities, interests, actions, and culture of career civilians and military officers, on the one hand, and the Assistant Secretaries and Under Secretaries appointed by the President, on the other.[28] Bureaucrats may play a critical role in generating budget options, and a good part of an agency's budget may support a mission defined by bureaucrats. But policy officials are deeply involved in this process. They will redirect the bureaucracy, negotiate across agencies or even with White House offices, advocate for the agency's budget with the Congress, and oversee the implementation of the results.

Presidential Policies and National Politics

Presidents, Vice Presidents, and their staff bring a different dimension to the national security budget process. Unlike senior policy officials, they have been elected to their positions. Most Presidents come to office with a policy agenda, which they seek to implement through the budget. Elements of this agenda may have played an important role in their electoral victory. While in office, they may develop new policy goals that are seen as crucial to future electoral success.

While it is sometimes argued that presidential elections do not turn on national security issues, this view misses important ways in which national security issues are critically important to US presidential elections. Since World War II, presidential candidates have been judged on the basis of their ability to project an image of strength and their commitment to America's international leadership and, especially, its military strength. National security proposals, with budget implications, have been made during the campaign as a way to demonstrate the capacity for such leadership. John F. Kennedy promised to close what turned out to be a non-existent missile gap.[29] Ronald

Reagan promised to restore US strength, particularly through increased defense spending and a stronger US nuclear deterrent. George W. Bush promised to invest in missile defense as a major priority during his 2000 campaign. Barack Obama promised to restore America's international reputation and leadership, in part by committing to doubling foreign assistance spending.

While these promises were probably not the sole cause of their electoral victories, once in office, presidents are expected to follow through on those proposals; their re-election prospects may depend on the degree to which they fulfill their commitments and successfully project an image of international leadership in doing so. Presidential legacies often turn on their international role, leading many presidents to make foreign and security policy a priority. The budget is the tool presidents use to establish such a legacy.

Congressional Politics

Congress is sometimes described as a secondary player in national security policymaking.[30] A budgetary focus changes this perception. When it comes to the budget, Congress plays an equal, even dominant role in funding national security policies, programs, and institutions. The executive branch prepares budget proposals, but it is the Congress that authorizes and appropriates the funds, giving it significant impact on policy, as discussed in Chapter 9.[31] Congressional appropriations provide the funds for defense forces and equipment, intelligence operations, the operation of security checkpoints in airports, security assistance to Pakistan, contingency operations in Iraq and Afghanistan, nonproliferation negotiations with Iraq and North Korea, and preventing the spread of HIV/AIDS in Africa.

Congress's role in national security budgeting has multiple dimensions. Authorizers and appropriators make essential budget decisions, and frequently differ in their views. The Senate and the House regularly disagree on national security budget levels and details. Democrats and Republicans bring contrasting views to the congressional budget debate, and those differences can be critical, especially when one party controls the Congress while the other controls the White House. Members of Congress and the congressional committees are pressured continuously by interest groups, advocacy organizations, industry lobbies, and the general public, all with their own views on national security issues and programs.

These political relationships can become quite complex. In some policy areas and on some programs, members of Congress and their committees, a closely involved lobbying group or groups, and executive branch agencies will work closely together, seeking to ensure funding for an agency or program. These are sometimes described as "sub-governments" or "iron triangles."[32] They can be particularly influential in budget decisions for weapons programs for DOD.

Events, strategies and policies, bureaucratic politics, and the players in the wider political crucible all have an impact on national security budget decisions. Their importance may vary, however. Relying on one of these dimensions alone can often be inadequate to explain a particular budgetary outcome. The interplay of these dimensions is particularly noticeable when it comes to setting the overall budgets for international affairs and defense.

The International Affairs Topline

The International Affairs budget is roughly one-thirteenth the size of the defense budget. Moreover, for decades, the State Department and other foreign affairs agencies have found it difficult to obtain White House or congressional support for significant budget growth. The persistent difficulty in funding international affairs cannot be explained by international events or a lower priority for diplomacy and foreign assistance in national security strategy. The political and bureaucratic dimensions are critical to understanding this budgetary outcome.

Lacking a central budget planning process and with a bureaucratic culture that does not put a high priority on strategic planning, State Department budgets, especially those for foreign assistance programs, are not "requirements driven," and lack the strong analytical backup DOD's budget requests provide. From a political perspective, the senior international affairs policy officials do not have the same systematic, detailed interaction with OMB and the White House that DOD officials have. As a result, OMB and the White House tend to be more skeptical about diplomacy and foreign assistance resource requirements and planning.

Moreover, the political relationships between senior policy officials in the international affairs world can have an impact on budgets for selective parts of the international affairs budget. A close relationship between the Secretary of the Treasury and the White House can lead to budget increases for multilateral development banks, independent of any State Department view on the banks as a budgetary or strategic priority. The Director of the Peace Corps might have an independent political connection with the White House, with the same result for the Peace Corps budget.[33] Until the early 2000s, the Administrator of USAID could and did make a separate case for development assistance funds, sometimes at odds with the Secretary of State's views.[34]

The overall level of the International Affairs budget request can also depend on the political relationship between the Secretary of State and the President, and the willingness of the Secretary to use his or her direct access. Secretary of State Warren Christopher did not make a strong, personal case to the President for the International Affairs budget, while Secretary Madeleine Albright would regularly seek a meeting with President Clinton to appeal for an increase in the budget above the amount set by the Director of OMB. Secretaries Colin Powell and Condoleezza Rice were very successful in obtaining significant increases in the International Affairs topline, because of Secretary Powell's personal stature and Secretary Rice's direct access to the President.[35] Other Secretaries have shown less interest in the budget process, leading to budget reductions at the White House level.

Once it has been transmitted to the Congress, the overall budget level can be significantly affected by congressional politics. The overall cap on discretionary spending set in the Budget Enforcement Act of 1990 and the continuing politics of deficit reduction until 2002 did not favor International Affairs budget requests. For many of those years, the defense budget was protected by a separate budget ceiling in the annual congressional budget resolution. International Affairs budget was grouped together with domestic budgets in the category of "non-defense discretionary" spending. Given the popularity of domestic spending, this congressional budget rule meant the administration's International Affairs budget requests were generally cut in the budget resolution.

Congress can hold down International Affairs budgets because foreign policy and its budget lack a political constituency. The State Department employs roughly 25,000 Americans, half of whom serve overseas and the other half largely in the Washington, DC region. The State Department does little contracting in the United States and only a small amount of grant-making. Grass-roots lobbying for diplomacy is limited to local foreign policy associations or World Affairs Councils, and at the national level to development organizations and a national coalition—the US Global Leadership Campaign.[36]

The political constituency for foreign assistance is not significantly larger. USAID employs roughly 2,000 foreign and civil servants. The aid agency does have a political constituency through its contractors, who provide development services and agricultural commodities through the food assistance programs. As a result there is a collection of private firms, consultants, and non-profit NGOs who actively support the USAID budget request in the Congress. Many of these are members of Interaction, a national coalition that supports development assistance. Interaction, founded in 1984, has 165 member organizations, from the American Red Cross to Church World Service, to Save the Children. This small but vocal constituency plays a role in maintaining funding for these programs in the Congress.[37]

Overall, however, the State Department, USAID, and the other international affairs agencies have significantly less political support in the US political arena than DOD. International events and national strategy may provide a strong case for increasing these budgets, but bureaucratic dispersal, institutional culture, and this weak political base make it hard to build support for an overall budget level that would be fully responsive to those events and strategies.

The DOD Topline

The politics of defense budgets contrast sharply with those of international affairs. All of the perspectives on budget politics—events and strategy, bureaucracy, and politics—combine to reinforce a tendency for high levels of defense spending in the United States. Defense budgets can decline, though peacetime defense spending since the Korean War has remained quite high, in constant dollars. The declines reflect changes in the politics of defense, as well. The politics of the defense budget in the 1990s reflects the interplay of these dimensions.

Whatever the national security "requirements" for national defense, between 1993 and 2001 decisions about the defense topline were clearly made in the political arena, supported by substantial bureaucratic and political pressures to increase funding. The presidential politics dimension was important at the very start of the Clinton administration, as it prepared its first budget in 1993. The outgoing Bush administration had not sent a federal budget proposal forward to the Congress, but did transmit a document describing what spending levels would be if existing programs were simply continued into the future (known as "current services" budgeting).[38]

The timing for Clinton's first budget was compressed, with a final budget proposal due to Congress in April 1993. The normal budget process, which takes more than a year, could not be carried out and no agency, including DOD, had policy officials in place to prepare a budget. As a result, the White House, led by OMB and the new National Economic Council, played the key role in setting all budget toplines, including that for defense.[39] The defense budget level was set by the White House, in the context of a presidential commitment to deficit reduction and increased domestic spending. It was not set in response to any specific judgment at that moment about national security requirements, international events, or even strong pressure by senior political officials at DOD or from Congress or outside interests.

This did not mean, however, that the White House developed the defense budget independent of any national security planning context. The Chairman of the Joint Chiefs, General Colin Powell had developed a framework for retaining a post-Cold War military force sufficiently large to ensure that the defense budget would not go into "free fall" with the end of the Cold War. This "base force" concept was, with some amendment, accepted by Secretary of Defense Les Aspin. But there was no clear defense budget number that coincided with this force. Because DOD policy officials were not central to early White House budget deliberations, the department did not have a major role in setting the final defense topline.[40] Absent these normal political and bureaucratic pressures, the FY 1993–97 defense toplines were set at a level that was cumulatively roughly $120 billion below the levels projected in the Bush "current services" documents, a level the President thought was adequate for US military requirements.

The 1993 budget decision meant that the defense budget topline would be decided largely in the political arena for the remainder of the decade. The budget debate was less about defense requirements or national strategy per se, than it was about the contest between the political parties, using the language of national security. In the 1994 congressional campaign, Republican candidates criticized the administration for what they argued was a decline in military readiness, caused by excessive deployments and inadequate budgets. The 1994 off-year election was hotly contested and the Republican Party successfully made military readiness an issue. The White House and senior policy officials at DOD decided in the fall of 1994, outside the standard DOD budget review, to increase the previously projected defense topline for FY 2006 by $25 billion explicitly focused on readiness investments, to try to prevent a Republican majority.

The effort failed, leading to continuing political struggle over the defense topline between the majority Republican Congress and the Democratic administration for the remainder of the decade. The Republican majority argued vigorously that the White House was under-funding defense. The Senate Armed Services Committee reached into the DOD bureaucracy for agreement, asking the military service Chiefs for an annual "unfunded requirements" letter listing the programs the Chiefs thought they required which had not been included in the administration's defense budget request. As witnesses, the service chiefs had often been asked whether they felt the administration's budget request was adequate. The letter created a more formal, parallel budget process, making it possible for the services to extend the normal Pentagon bureaucratic struggle over budgets to the Congress, where the majority party could make the defense budget issue part of its political struggle with the White House. The White House chose not to intervene in these communications, though they undercut the President's budget request, for fear of being accused of "censoring" the services.

Electoral politics played an important role in this topline battle. The defense spending issue was seen in the Clinton White House as a potential electoral vulnerability in the 1996 presidential election. Determined to keep the issue out of the election, the White House gradually conceded ground to the military service requests for increased funding. At the same time, the White House took maximum advantage of the politics of deficit reduction in its effort to restrain such increases. The Republican majority in Congress was divided on the overall federal budget, making it possible for the White House to work with the congressional budget committees, chaired by Sen. Pete Domenici (R-NM) and Rep. John Kasich (R-OH), to restrain the defense topline in the budget resolution.[41]

White House willingness to concede some ground on the defense budget, while exploiting the cross-cutting pressure for deficit reduction, kept the defense issue out of the 1996 presidential election, but it did not go away. Republican criticism in the Congress continued, combined with growing bureaucratic pressure from the military services to increase defense budgets above the administration's projections. These political and bureaucratic pressures led to another major increase in the defense topline in the FY 2000 defense budget.[42]

The politics of this increase were complex. In 1998, congressional Republicans were determined to break the budget agreement and provide more defense funds. The administration was determined not to take responsibility for breaking the budget agreement, but did not want to concede the defense issue to the Republicans. At a September 29, 1998 congressional hearing, the service Chiefs again brought their concerns to the Congress, discussing readiness problems and funding shortfalls and saying they would need an additional $17.5 billion a year to make up that shortfall.[43] The administration knew the testimony would be delivered, but hoped the Congress would take responsibility for breaking the budget agreement and provide the additional funding.[44]

Inside the administration, the senior officials played an important role in this budget struggle. The services enlisted the Secretary of Defense, former Republican Senator William Cohen, as an advocate. Cohen and the Joint Chiefs argued internally in the fall of 1998 for a significant long-term increase in the defense topline. The Chiefs sought a $148 billion addition over six years to the existing DOD budget projection, but after difficult negotiations with the White House, settled for $112 billion, $28 billion of which was offset by policy and inflation adjustments in the existing budget projection. The Republican Congress then added another $8.4 billion to the President's request.

The budget argument continued to be carried out in the language of military "readiness," which was clearly a national security policy issue. It was not clear, however, that the readiness argument was a critical problem. Nor was there much discussion about the underlying question of "readiness for what"—an analysis of the threats, events, or capabilities of other countries— the strategic considerations that might have played a central role in defense topline discussions, if policy were the critical dimension for explaining these budgetary outcomes.

The 2000 presidential election continued this debate over readiness. Candidate George W. Bush made the issue a central part of his critique of the Clinton–Gore administration, but was careful not to link that argument to a specific commitment to the defense topline. Once in office, the Bush administration confronted the same budget issue the Clinton administration had faced: how to restrain overall federal spending, including defense, within the budgetary caps. Although Secretary of Defense Donald Rumsfeld argued for a large increase in the topline, the White House resisted this demand, given the presidential priority of restraining overall federal spending.[45]

The terrorist attacks of 9/11 and the invasions of Iraq and Afghanistan put an end to this long-term political and bureaucratic saga. National security considerations became the critical dimension for understanding the budget decisions. At virtually the same time, the constraints imposed by the 1990 Budget Enforcement Act caps expired. National security policy and international events superseded political and bureaucratic factors as the dominant explanation for defense toplines from 2001 until at least 2009.[46]

Defense budgets never declined dramatically over this period, however. Constituency politics are an important element in ensuring a floor under the defense budget, regardless of the vagaries of presidential and party politics. Unlike the world of international affairs, the US defense establishment has, since World War II, become a significant presence in the country's domestic political landscape. While the size of the active-duty armed forces has risen and fallen over time, at 1.4 million (the smallest force since 1950) the active-duty military has, for decades, provided roughly one-third of total federal government employment. Including the 700,000 civil servants working for DOD, over 50 percent of all federal employees work for the Department of Defense.

In addition, there are more than 850,000 citizens in the National Guard and the Reserves, over two million military retirees (plus family members), and 26.5 million veterans. This "constituency" is spread across the United States (only 138,000 military and civilian personnel are in the greater Washington, DC area) in cities and rural areas, and on more than 2,500 military bases, offices, and other installations with local economic impact. While this is less than half the number of installations that existed in 1985, the military remains an important presence in such states as Alabama, Alaska, Arizona, California, Hawaii, Missouri, New Jersey, Texas, and Virginia, creating active local support for DOD, its mission, and its budget.

While there were debatable defense policy issues in the 1990s, policy and strategy were not the primary elements in determining the defense budget topline. Decisions were determined by presidential priorities, party politics, broader budget deficit reduction rules, the complexities of the congressional political process, and the broad base of support for defense budgets in American society.

Homeland Security and Counterterrorism Budgets

Budgets for homeland security and counterterrorism might be expected to be most directly explained by international events. Even in this case, bureaucratic and political dimensions played an important part in budgetary decisions. The impact of international and domestic events is clear. There had been terrorist attacks for a decade before 9/11, including the World Trade Center bombing in 1993, the attack in Saudi Arabia on the US military barracks at Khobar Towers in 1996, the bombing of the US embassies in Kenya and Tanzania in 1998, and the attack in Yemen on the USS Cole in 2000. Even before these events, administrations had begun to focus on the terrorism problem. The State Department created the Anti-Terrorism Assistance (ATA) program in 1983, following the attack on the Marine Corps barracks in Lebanon. In 1989, State's Office for Combating Terrorism became the Office of the Coordinator for Counterterrorism, which was made a statutory office in 1994.

The 1993 World Trade Center bombings, combined with growing concern about domestic terrorists (the bombings in Oklahoma City in 1995 and at the Atlanta Olympics in 1996) led to a 1996 OMB-led review of counterterrorist programs and budgets across the government, and a decision to seek an additional $1 billion in counterterrorism funding from the Congress. The embassy attacks in Africa led directly to a significant budget increase for State Department buildings operations to safeguard embassies overseas, discussed in Chapter 2.

Despite this initial effort, there was growing criticism in the 1990s about the inadequacies of US government counterterrorism programs, criticism that was largely independent of partisan or presidential politics.[47] In 2000, a panel chaired by former Republican Virginia Governor James Gilmore found that the federal government had "no coherent, functional national strategy" for combating terrorism and that governmental organization was "fragmented, uncoordinated and politically unaccountable."[48] The panel proposed creating a National Office for Combating Terrorism in the Executive Office of the President, with authority to certify agency budgets, similar to the authority of the Office of National Drug Control Policy (ONDCP) over counternarcotics budgets. A year later, the bipartisan Hart–Rudman Commission asserted that a mass casualty terrorist attack against the United States was likely, and urged the creation of a National Homeland Security Agency "to consolidate and refine the missions of the nearly two dozen disparate departments and agencies that have a role in US homeland security today."[49]

Terrorism became a core concern of US national security policy and spending after the attacks on the World Trade Center and the Pentagon on September 11, 2001. The Bush administration made counterterrorism policy the central focus of its 2002 national security strategy and crafted a National Strategy for Combating Terrorism.[50]

Political considerations almost immediately entered into play, however, as homeland security structures and processes were debated after the 9/11 attacks. The White House resisted the Hart–Rudman proposal for restructuring executive branch institutions to confront the terrorist threat more coherently. Only when it seemed likely that the Congress would create a new federal department, as proposed by Democratic Sen. Joe Lieberman in October 2001, did the administration take the initiative to propose such a department itself in June 2002, pre-empting the Democratic proposal. Moreover, the administration used the issue of creating a new department against the Democrats as part of its effort to regain control of the Senate in fall 2002. The administration argued that Democratic resistance to its bill, focused on an effort to ensure civil service protections would be extended to the new department, reflected a lack of concern for US national security in the face of the terrorist threat. The argument played a key role in returning the Senate to Republican control. The Bush administration signed the new Department of Homeland Security into law in November 2002, significantly restructuring homeland security institutions and budgets.[51]

In the wake of an investigation of the 9/11 attacks by a bipartisan, congressionally chartered commission, Congress also created an entirely new coordinating office for national intelligence policy and budgets—the Office of the Director of National Intelligence (ODNI) and a National Counterterrorism Center (NCTC), reporting both to ODNI and to the President, with the mission of drafting and providing agency guidance for a national plan to implement a counterterrorism strategy, discussed in Chapter 6.[52] The military's Special Operations forces were given the mission of providing the military element in counterterrorism strategy and the Pentagon created, for the first time, a military command responsible for the territorial defense of the United States Homeland (Northern Command).

These decisions to alter US national security bureaucratic structures led to a significant increase in US counterterrorism and homeland security budgets. By FY 2008, the DHS was spending $32.6 billion on homeland security, much of it to protect US borders, integrate US customs and immigration systems, and protect the US transportation system (notably air traffic and airports). Agencies throughout the rest of the US government spent an additional $32 billion on homeland security that year, over $17.3 billion of it at DOD, largely for force protection.[53] In all, 15 federal departments, 16 other agencies, and the District of Columbia had created programs and were spending significant resources on homeland security, largely to deal with the threat and consequences of a terrorist attack.[54]

Bureaucratic factors also played a role in these decisions. Once the White House had decided to create a new homeland security department, it decided to design that consolidation in a small, closed White House group, in order to end-run likely resistance from the existing federal agencies that would lose offices, staff, and programs. Once created, the new department faced powerful internal bureaucracies which resisted changes to their cultures, insisted on continuing funding levels set in their previous bureaucratic homes (as discussed in Chapter 7), and redefined their existing programs and activities as contributions to the "counterterrorism" mission of the new department.[55]

Bureaucratic obstacles and political disagreements could not have been overcome and counterterrorism budget increases would not have happened had there not been a major international and domestic event—a terrorist attack—requiring a response. International events and national security strategy clearly provide the strongest explanation for these organizational and budget decisions.[56] Once the institutional change had been legislated and the first budget written, however, bureaucratic and political elements played important roles in the implementation of the new policy.[57]

National Missile Defense

The importance of the political and bureaucratic dimensions in national security budgeting become even more clear when it comes to budget decisions about major weapons programs at DOD. The decision to create and continue a well-funded program for national missile defense (NMD) is a classic illustration. Continued funding for NMD and its bureaucratic structure as a separate program and budget reporting to the Secretary of Defense can only be understood if political and bureaucratic dimensions are part of the analysis.

The United States has spent more than $150 billion on missile defense since the program was created as President Reagan's Strategic Defense Initiative in 1983. National security policy and strategic considerations clearly played a role in the program, at the start. Conceived in a Cold War framework, missile defenses were proposed as a way to ensure that US strategic nuclear forces survived a Soviet ballistic missile attack, giving the United States an option to retaliate against such an attack. This capability, it was argued, would ensure that the United States retained a strong deterrent, as missile defense would deny the Soviets the option of a successful first strike.[58]

When the Soviet Union dissolved and the Cold War ended, the likelihood of a Soviet nuclear strike diminished, weakening the policy rationale for the missile defense program. Critics of the program argued that the technology would never mature, and that it was, in any case, not possible to develop a system that could frustrate an overwhelming first strike. Advocates argued that a smaller missile defense program could protect the United States and allied countries against a limited nuclear strike from smaller nuclear forces such as China or North Korea. Missile defense, it was argued, would keep the United States from being deterred from overseas military action or coming to the defense of an ally because one of these countries could threaten a nuclear attack.[59] The Clinton administration de-emphasized national missile defense of the United States and focused the program on tactical missile defenses for US forces deployed overseas. In his presidential campaign of 2000, however, George W. Bush revived the argument, making NMD a centerpiece of his national security agenda, and calling for early deployment of a limited system.

Throughout the evolution of the rationale, NMD programs continued to receive substantial funding. Management responsibility for the program, however, was given not to the military services, but to a new organization in the Office of the Secretary of Defense. This agency changed names over the years from the Strategic Defense Initiative Organization (SDIO), to the Ballistic Missile Defense Organization (BMDO), to the Missile Defense Agency (MDA). The national security policy rationale for the program is inadequate to explain either the persistence of funding for this program or its organizational configuration.

The bureaucratic dimension helps answer the organizational question. The military services were never enthusiastic about the NMD mission or the program because it was not central to the services' core cultures or mission, as discussed above. It was not central to the Air Force, which focuses on air superiority and air interdiction, and fighter aircraft as its core technology. The Navy focused on control of the seas, not missile defense. The Army was interested in acquiring a tactical missile defense capability that would defend deployed land forces, but not a national defense against ballistic missile attack. The services were concerned that once missile defense research and development was complete, funding for production, deployment, and operations would become a growing part of service budgets, where it would compete for funding with core programs and missions. This was a particular concern between 1985 and 2000, when overall defense budgets were declining. For program advocates, the NMD mission and funding could only be protected by providing additional defense funding outside the service budgets and making the Secretary of Defense responsible for the management of the program.[60]

Viewed from the political perspective, the survival of NMD makes sense. Some analysts have argued that a political "iron triangle," driven by contractor interests, has been the key ingredient of its success.[61] Certainly, there are contractors who benefit from the program and who lobby Congress for continued funding. But the primary beneficiaries of missile defense contract funds have been smaller research firms with minimal Washington lobbying presence or influence. For the larger firms in the program (Raytheon, Boeing, Lockheed), missile defense is not a core program or the most significant source of their defense revenue, though they do lobby for the funding. But there is not an "iron triangle" ready to protect the program, as the services remain unenthusiastic about NMD.

Presidential and party politics, however, help complete the explanation: NMD was, and has remained, a presidential priority, especially for the Republic Party. It became an important part of the political dialogue when it was announced as a major, game-changing presidential initiative by President Ronald Reagan on March 23, 1983. Reagan was personally persuaded (largely by scientist Edward Teller, an advocate of the technology) that the technology would work and that ballistic missile defenses would change the United States' relationship with the Soviet Union. The Republican Party enthusiastically embraced Reagan's program and, over the succeeding decades, made support for NMD a "litmus test" of Republican loyalty.

Democrats generally opposed the program, repeatedly seeking to restrict its funding while in the congressional majority. The 1994 Republican congressional victory voided this strategy. The "Contract with America" Republican platform, which was the mandate for that new Congress, stated that it should be "the policy of the United States to deploy at the earliest possible moment an antiballistic missile system that is capable of providing a highly effective defense of the United States against ballistic missile attacks." Throughout the 1990s the Republican Congress and the Clinton White House struggled over the program, with the Congress urging increased funding and early deployment, and the White House resisting such pressures.

In 1997, the Republican Congress created a bipartisan "Commission to Assess the Ballistic Missile Threat to the United States," chaired by Donald Rumsfeld and appointed jointly by the President and the congressional leadership to assess "the nature and magnitude of the existing and emerging ballistic missile threat to the United States."[62] The commission concluded that the threat was more serious than previously thought, bolstering the Republican view that missile defense required a higher funding and faster deployment than the Clinton administration had supported.[63] These partisan political differences made NMD a major policy issue in the 2000 presidential election. The Project for the New American Century (PNAC), including many of the defense policymakers of the future Bush administration, criticized the Clinton–Gore defense policies and called for early deployment of NMD.[64] Republican Congressional candidates and all Republican presidential candidates endorsed the Rumsfeld Commission report and the PNAC recommendation.

Candidate George W. Bush made NMD a signature national security commitment of his campaign, endorsing deployment as part of his first major defense speech in 1999 and again in his first press conference as the likely Republican nominee in May 2000.[65] Once in the White House, with Rumsfeld as Secretary of Defense, the Bush administration increased NMD funding to over $10 billion a year, withdrew from the ABM treaty that restricted testing of such programs, restructured the management office in the Pentagon (but retained its relationship to the Secretary of Defense), and deployed early elements of the system in Alaska in advance of the 2004 presidential election, as promised.

The creation of the NMD program, its survival with significant funding, and its organizational structure are more easily explained by the politics of the program, than by its national security rationale. In this case, the key is partisan and presidential politics.

The B-1 Bomber

The B-1 bomber also illustrates the role of party and presidential politics in budget decisions on military hardware programs.[66] The origins of the B-1 program go back to the effort in the late 1960s to determine a successor to the B-52. President Richard Nixon based his case for the B-1 on the inability of the aging B-52 to penetrate Soviet air defenses.[67] This rational proved questionable, both because the B-1 proved less stealthy than promised and because interim upgrades to the B-52 kept them flying for more than 30 years after the Nixon decision.

Democratic presidential candidate Jimmy Carter put the B-1 squarely in the arena of presidential and party politics in 1976, calling for the cancellation of the program. The Democratic majority in the Congress had opened the door to this decision, passing authorizing legislation in 1976 that delayed a final production decision until after the newly elected president took office. Once in office, President Carter cancelled the B-1, fulfilling his campaign promise. The Air Force, which might have been expected to support the program, did not become part of an "iron triangle" calling for it to continue. Instead, it supported the Carter decision. From the Air Force point of view, funds for the B-1 competed with production funding for two emerging Air Force fighter programs—the F-15 and F-16—which were important to the core Air Force mission. The congressional vote to rescind B-1 funding passed by a narrow majority, reflecting the pressures brought to bear by the industrial and local constituencies with a stake in the program.[68]

B-1 production was revived, however, in 1981. Presidential politics were the key ingredient. The 1980 election was one of the few that turned on national security issues. In the wake of the failure of the Iran hostage rescue mission in April 1980, Reagan campaigned on a platform that emphasized restoring America's military strength and global leadership. Strategic nuclear weapons programs and funding were a significant part of the Reagan commitment, but there were limited options for him to demonstrate that commitment. The Trident missile and submarine program could not easily be accelerated. The MX missile was a Carter program and was already in trouble in Congress and with the Air Force because of problems finding a basing mode. The next generation stealth bomber program, the B-2, was a still-classified Carter program. Rockwell International, the B-1 contractor, briefed the campaign and the new President that production could restart quickly and that the program would be affordable. As a result, the B-1 became the symbol of President Reagan's commitment to modernize the strategic nuclear arsenal.[69] Once in office, President Reagan added funds to the Air Force budget to manufacture the aircraft, eliminating the bureaucratic obstacle to its production.

The national security rationale is only minimally useful in explaining the B-1 decisions. Bureaucratic considerations weakened the case for the program, as the Air Force preferred to focus on fighter programs. Contractor lobbying was critical to keeping the option on the table for the Congress. But it took partisan presidential politics to revive the program and provide adequate funding for it to be built and deployed, despite a relatively weak strategic rationale.

US Arrears to the United Nations

The interplay of politics and bureaucracy in international affairs budget decisions is also revealed by an examination of the problem the United States encountered in funding its dues to the United Nations. From the perspective of national security policy, there should be no question that the United States is treaty-bound to provide its share of funding to the United Nations for its administration and for UN peacekeeping operations. During the 1980s, however, the United States began to fall behind in paying its assessments for both purposes. The "arrears," as they came to be known, reached more than $1 billion by the early 1990s. They caused the United States diplomatic difficulties; other UN member states could not understand why the United States could not fulfill a treaty obligation. Although succeeding administrations would request the required amount of funding, the general understanding was that Sen. Jessie Helms (R-NC), Chair of the Senate Foreign Relations Committee and a vigorous critic of the United Nations, stood in the way of full payment.

The key to the inability of the United States to make these payments lay more, however, in the budgetary structures and processes of the Congress and the bureaucratic politics of the State Department than it did in the policy dispute with Sen. Helms. At the time the arrears were accumulating, the State Department's operations budget, out of which UN dues are paid (see Chapter 2), was appropriated by the Commerce, Justice, State Appropriations subcommittee, whose membership did not include Sen. Helms. That subcommittee, like the others, received every year from the Appropriations Committee chair a 302b allocation which was lower than the overall budget requested by the administration for the departments of Commerce, Justice, and State, all of which were in its jurisdiction. The subcommittee chair would then allocate funds to each agency at a level generally below the administration's request.

Technology (Commerce) and policing (Justice) both have important local constituencies for members of Congress. Diplomacy, as noted above, does not have such a constituency. Facing a smaller allocation than the budget request, the subcommittee chair and the staff would ask State officials whether they would prefer to absorb their budget reduction by cutting back on personnel and department operations, or by reducing payments to the United Nations. Though international policy considerations might suggest that fulfilling UN obligations was a priority, bureaucratic considerations prevailed, leading to reductions in the budget amounts for UN operations and peacekeeping.

The solution to this problem was political, as well as international. Overcoming Sen. Helms' resistance was part of the solution, as he had to be persuaded that the United Nations would reform, in exchange for the United States making up its arrears. At the senior official level, the Clinton White House and the State Department developed a proposal that would link such reforms to a schedule for repayment of the arrears. This solution was not enforceable, however, until the Appropriations committee chairs agreed that the subcommittee's budget allocation would be "held harmless" from these costs. Politics and bureaucracy, not international obligations, were key to solving this budgetary dilemma.

Conclusion

National security policy and budget decisions are made in the context of international events, crises, strategic goals, and specific policy decisions. They are explained and justified in the language of policy. The budgets are prepared by the institutions and through the processes we have discussed in this book. Most of these budget decisions are rooted in some sense of policy, strategy, or requirement. Rational policy considerations can make a compelling case for many of them—the expansion of counterterrorism programs, for example. Rational requirements, alone, however, provide an incomplete or less compelling explanation for many budget decisions, such as the international affairs and defense budgetary toplines. While hardware programs like national missile defense and the B-1 bomber are linked to policy issues, politics provides a more compelling case for decisions on their budgets. Policy problems made finding a solution to the UN arrears necessary, but the problem arose and could only be solved by dealing with bureaucratic dilemmas.

This book deals largely with how institutions and processes plan budgets for US national security policy. It is important to understand how the national security budget process works, and, where it seems not to work, to ensure it can operate as efficiently as possible. It is also critical to recognize that the many programs, institutions, and processes we have discussed in the book operate in a political universe, where policy interacts with bureaucratic needs and cultures, and in the political arena of appointed officials, elected presidents, an active Congress, and an engaged set of interests and advocates.

Politics and bureaucracy are the "battleground" in which budget decisions are made. The perspectives and actions of senior policy officials, the commitments and electoral prospects of the President, and party politics all play crucial roles in setting budget priorities and determining budget outcomes. Moreover, the politics of the budget in the Congress gives that institution a more important role in national security policy and budgeting than is sometimes realized. The presence (or in the case of international affairs, the absence) of local constituencies can play an important role in providing support for budgets in the Congress.

No single perspective on national security budgets can explain all budget decisions and outcomes. Most discussions of national security policy begin and end with the policy issue itself, but do not examine the broader political and bureaucratic sources of decisions. If budgets are policy, then an examination of the politics of the national security budgetary process is key to understanding policy itself and the operations of the institutions and processes we have examined in this book.

Chapter 11

The Road Ahead

How Might Budgeting Change?

This book has reviewed a broad array of agencies, institutions, and processes involved in the national security budgeting process.[1] As it stands, every part of the executive branch's national security planning and budgeting system is in flux, from State and the US Agency for International Development (USAID) to defense, to intelligence, to homeland security, to the interagency and White House process. The Congress has made changes to its budgeting structures and processes, as well.

In this chapter, we look at the future of planning and budgeting for national security, focusing on reforms that are under way or have been proposed. These changes grow out of the experience agencies have had dealing with such international events as the terrorist attacks of 9/11 and the post-invasion experience in Iraq. They represent a growing awareness of the defects of current budget processes.

Overall, the reforms being proposed are designed to improve the effectiveness and efficiency of the national security budget process inside agencies and the Congress, increase institutional capacity for strategic planning and the link to budget planning, and develop processes and capabilities to deal with the challenging security issues of the twenty-first century, which cut across agency programs and missions.

Reforms in International Affairs Budgeting

International affairs agencies face a number of planning and budgeting challenges. One is the dispersal of institutions responsible for US foreign relations and foreign and security assistance. Another is the State Department's weakness in carrying out strategic planning linked to budget allocations. This is linked, in turn, to a lack of appropriately trained personnel at State to carry out planning, program development, and implementation or to deal with the challenging new agenda of the twenty-first century, including the problem of failed states. These weaknesses in the civilian agencies have stimulated the creation of a new set of parallel security and foreign assistance authorities and programs in the Defense Department. There is progress, albeit contested, on all of these fronts, but still more reforms to be considered.

The institutional relationship between State and the other international affairs agencies is slowly evolving toward greater integration, as discussed in Chapter 3. State/USAID budget planning has become more integrated and more systematic. Personnel are being added to both agencies to increase their capacity to manage and implement programs.

Much of this institutional evolution remains untested, however, and a number of the reforms have been criticized. Human resources issues remain at both State and USAID. While the Foreign Service is again expanding, training and career paths have not yet been adjusted to the new, broader missions Foreign Service Officers are being asked to carry out.[2] Recruitment needs to focus on attracting candidates with broader skills, including private sector experience, economic knowledge, and management aptitude, in addition to an aptitude for cultural expertise and language skills. Training programs need to expand to include skills in strategic and resource planning and program development, implementation, and evaluation. Mid-career accessions need to grow to bring in planning and management skills early. Career paths need to be redefined, emphasizing service across the foreign policy and national security institutions, including State, USAID, Defense, Justice, and other departments. Over time, these personnel reforms could dramatically alter the culture of the Foreign Service.

More broadly, the civilian institutions need to resolve the relationship between State and USAID, which implies dealing, as well, with the role of development and foreign economic assistance in US statecraft. The integration of USAID budget planning into the new State foreign assistance office and the appointment of a second Deputy Secretary with authority over foreign assistance raised concern in the development community about the potential loss of USAID's focus on "development." Some organizations proposed the creation of a separate, cabinet-level department of global development, as a way to protect this mission.[3] The merits of such an action are unclear, given USAID's dual role in providing development assistance as well as strategy-driven assistance for the State Department. This disagreement will preoccupy State over the coming years, but closer integration with an appropriate elevation of development as an overall US foreign policy objective may be the appropriate outcome.

A similar institutional question has been raised with respect to public diplomacy, which has had lower priority and resource attention since its absorption into State. In 2008, an advisory commission to the Secretary of State recommended recreating the US Information Agency (USIA) as a semi-autonomous public diplomacy agency inside State.[4] Such an agency might also take over responsibility for the increasing number of public diplomacy programs created at the Department of Defense (DOD) over the past ten years.[5]

A third critical structural and budgetary issue for State/USAID is how to build a civilian capability to deal with failed and fragile states, a problem sometimes described as post-conflict stabilization and reconstruction, as discussed in Chapter 4. In the wake of the Iraq experience, State created the Office of the Coordinator for Reconstruction and Stabilization in 2004, with responsibilities for developing civilian plans for post-conflict activities, coordinating the interagency process for specific interventions, and developing, training, and deploying a civilian capability for such operations. Progress has been slow in this area, but began to accelerate with increased congressional funding in 2008–09. There remains a serious institutional question about the relationship between this capability and the pre-existing capabilities of USAID for early intervention in fragile states and post-conflict situations. Some have suggested revising the S/CRS model and possibly redistributing responsibilities, giving S/CRS planning tasks but making USAID responsible for recruiting, training, and operating a civilian capability.[6]

A fourth critical issue is how to strengthen the internal State Department capacity for planning and budgeting security assistance programs. The expansion of DOD security assistance authorities and programs discussed in Chapter 4 stems, in part, from perceived staffing and planning weaknesses at State, inflexibility in State's authorities and program execution, and State's difficulty raising funds from the Congress for security assistance programs. These weaknesses need to be addressed, as well as developing a strategy for rebalancing responsibilities, authorities, and funding for security assistance between State and DOD.[7]

The State/USAID relationship with other international affairs institutions also continues to be a problem for strategic planning and budgeting. A closer relationship between the Millennium Challenge Corporation, the PEPFAR HIV/AIDS programs, and State/USAID needs to be defined, to ensure synergies in strategic goals, budget planning, and program implementation. More broadly, a mechanism needs to be developed to ensure closer coordination of planning and budgeting between the other international affairs agencies, particularly Treasury and State/USAID, which might involve including such agencies in the strategic planning and budget review processes carried out by the second Deputy Secretary of State.

Greater integration among the international affairs institutions is clearly needed. Equally, there is a growing need for a government-wide planning process for foreign policy strategy, policies, priorities, and resources. A number of other agencies, notably DOD, are significantly engaged overseas. There is no natural institutional setting to carry out integrated strategic planning and budgeting for this broader US engagement. The issue needs to be confronted, in part, by strengthening State's own strategic planning capabilities, but there are now proposals for a cross-agency quadrennial review of diplomacy and development, with a key role being played by State.[8]

There are several other reforms, internal to the international affairs budget, that also need consideration. Improved strategic planning at State/USAID should make it less necessary for these agencies to rely on emergency supplemental appropriations, a reform that has begun with the FY 2010 budget submission. A more strategic State Department vision and stronger planning and management capacities could also help State and USAID obtain greater budget flexibility and fewer congressional earmarks on assistance programs. Both are needed for a more agile State Department to be effective in the future. State will need to engage with the Congress on this issue as Congress considers rewriting State's basic authorities in the Foreign Assistance Act.[9]

State also needs to consider reforms to its internal budget processes that could increase its flexibility in using resources. The proposal in the FY 2010 budget requests to integrate all international narcotics programs and all Eastern Europe and Eurasian assistance both move in this direction. The budget planning capabilities for the latter programs, described in Chapter 4, could be expanded to the other regional bureaus at State, with congressional agreement, enhancing the link between policy and budgeting in State Department planning for other regions of the world.

Reforms in DOD Budgeting

The Defense Department system for resource planning is significantly better structured, more coherent, and more disciplined than the system for international affairs. Planning, Programming, Budgeting, and Execution (PPBE) allows the department to link strategy and budgets, requirements and costs, and to project programs and spending over a long-term trajectory. It also permits both top-level visibility into the planning process and ample scope for the multiple levels of planning to have input into the budget process. It is a highly effective system, giving DOD a substantial advantage in the overall government budget process.

There is room, however, for reform in the existing budget planning system. The link between strategic planning documents—the White House national security strategy, the national defense (OSD) and national military (JSC) strategies, the quadrennial defense review (QDR)—and the actual budget process, which begins with strategic guidance, is imperfect. There needs to be greater attention to the timing of these documents in relationship to the overall process, to ensure strategic priorities are clearly reflected in budget planning, and to ensure that resource requirements are included as an important aspect of strategic thinking.

For example, the QDR has never properly included resource planning, which limits the impact its results can have on budgets. Future QDRs should include resource dimensions, linking strategic guidelines and force planning with budget choices. The timing of the QDR should also be reconsidered, in order to have a planning process in the first year of a new administration that can have an effective impact on early defense budgets.

Within the existing PPBE process, it is increasingly clear that meshing the programming and budgeting phases has made careful scrutiny of budgets based on final program decisions difficult. Decisions on budgets and programs are being made simultaneously, and being shipped back and forth in the process in a way that makes timely, informed decisions difficult. Although moving the programming phase to a point where it precedes budget decisions would squeeze the planning phase, it may make sense, in order to simplify the budgeting phase and discipline budget choices.

The joint review process, which brings OMB into DOD budget planning, also needs attention. Both agencies have had ambiguous feelings about the joint review, but on balance, it seems advantageous to involve the White House budget office in the DOD process. This involvement needs to be systematic and more institutionalized than it has been in recent years, which means both institutions need to negotiate a framework for the joint review that can be repeated over the years and from administration to administration.

Cost control remains a major budget issue at DOD. The Government Accountability Office has regularly warned that major DOD systems are falling behind schedule and running significantly above costs. The DOD portfolio of major weapons programs had risen over 40 percent in cost between FY 2003 and FY 2007, and fallen an average of 22 months behind schedule.[10] Growing concern about rising costs and delays led the Congress to legislate reforms in the DOD acquisition system, through the Weapons System Acquisition Reform Act of 2009.[11] That Act puts particular emphasis on independent cost estimating, creating a position for Cost Assessment and Program Evaluation, which is to set department-wide guidelines for cost estimating and perform independent cost estimates on major acquisition programs.

More broadly, DOD needs to create a more effective performance evaluation process, the last stage of the PPBE system. Until the April 2009 decisions that Secretary Gates made to terminate the vehicle portion of the Future Combat Systems program, relatively few major systems had been terminated for failure to perform up to expectation. The department needs to give attention to a systematic performance evaluation system that can support such decisions in an institutionalized way.

Finally, DOD needs to review its expanding portfolio of security and economic assistance programs, which were developed in response to the exigencies of operations in Iraq and Afghanistan. These programs broaden the DOD mission into areas that are not the core competence of the services. This mission expansion imposes new training requirements and risks further stress on the forces. The programs place additional demands on DOD fiscal resources. The new authorities intrude into competences and authorities of the State Department, which needs to develop its own competences in these areas through additional funding and personnel. And the mission creates a risk of the "militarization of foreign policy," raised by the Chairman of the Joint Chiefs of Staff, Admiral Mike Mullen in 2009.[12]

The Obama administration took office in 2009 emphasizing the need for more effective government management and performance. The White House and the Defense Department leadership disciplined the FY 2010 budget more significantly than had been done in previous years, including a lower overall budget number than internal military planners had projected in 2008, several difficult decisions to terminate weapons programs that were judged no longer needed or non-performing, and a careful scrutiny of the "unfunded requirements" letters the service chiefs were asked to send to the Congress.[13] The Secretary of Defense has also expressed a willingness to review DOD's security and foreign assistance authorities and programs, in conjunction with the State Department. These first steps suggest that reforms in budget planning and discipline at DOD may be forthcoming.

Reforms in Intelligence Budgeting

The Intelligence Reform Act of 2004 was one of the most significant reforms in intelligence community organization and planning processes since the CIA was created in 1947. It put greater authority in the hands of the Director of National Intelligence (DNI) for overseeing, prioritizing, and apportioning intelligence funds than that possessed by the previous Director of Central Intelligence. These authorities have not, however, been fully tested, particularly the relationship between the DNI and the Secretary of Defense, who controls the bulk of intelligence spending. Moreover, the DNI office has not yet fully developed and implemented a budget planning system with the structure and discipline of the PPBE architecture at DOD, though such a system may emerge in the future. If ODNI is to be effective in setting intelligence program and resource priorities, it will be important to begin testing the existing authorities and creating a disciplined planning system to support them.

Reforms in Homeland Security Budgeting

Homeland security budgeting, both government-wide and in the relatively new department, will require significant attention. The new department does not have responsibility for all homeland security programs, but does have responsibility for many programs that are not homeland security. Many of the organizations inside the department remain legacy programs from previous agencies, with cultures and budget shares that have frustrated department-wide planning and priority-setting.[14]

It is not yet clear that the department's use of PPBE-like budgeting and program analysis has been effective in setting priorities or establishing clear budget discipline. The new quadrennial strategic planning system remains untested. The components of DHS have largely continued to plan their own agendas and successfully lobby for, and retain, the budget shares they had prior to the creation of the department. Few redundant activities have been eliminated.

As DHS moves forward, it will be critical to institutionalize an effective QHSR, which should consider strategies, programs, and budgets in relationship to each other. The senior leadership of the department needs to be fully engaged in that review, as well as in the budget process. In the end, with an internally divided portfolio, some of which is not homeland security, and limited authority over other departments implementing homeland security programs, the department will not be fully effective without reforms in both the White House and the Congress, discussed further below.

Reforms in the White House: OMB and NSC

The major security issues that confront the United States are interagency in character. Neither the interagency planning system nor the White House budget system are yet structured, staffed, or capable to carry out cross-agency program and budget planning to confront such major problems as terrorism at home and overseas, proliferation, climate change, development, or fragile and failed states, which are only a few of the cross-agency challenges that confront the national security system. There was a good deal of discussion about this dilemma in the wake of the peacekeeping interventions of the 1990s and the experience of Iraq reconstruction, Afghanistan assistance, and counterterror operations in the first decade of the twenty-first century.[15]

The White House responsibility for strategic and resource planning needs to be more institutionalized than it is today. The White House should oversee a mandatory quadrennial national security review, which would go beyond the current national security strategy to identify key national security priorities. That review should be conducted jointly by OMB and NSC, with agency participation, parallel to the defense and foreign policy reviews conducted in the relevant agencies. A classified National Security Guidance should grow out of that review, and be conducted every two years. The guidance should provide a detailed roadmap to agencies, including budgetary guidance, focusing on key national security priorities.

Using the strategy and guidance as a guidepost, OMB should prepare a single budget document, bringing together international affairs, defense, intelligence, and homeland security budgets and focusing particularly on priority policy areas across agencies. That document should be submitted to Congress as part of an administration's annual budget request.[16]

This tandem relationship between OMB and NSC also needs to be institutionalized with respect to several critical cross-agency planning issues. Failed and fragile states policy is one of these. NSC and OMB need to take a significantly more active role in coordinating planning for overseas contingency operations by civilian and military forces, strengthening the current coordinating system described in Chapter 4. A similar coordinating mechanism needs to be created to deal with security assistance programs, which cut across agencies and lack a strategic orientation, as well as with foreign economic and development assistance, public diplomacy, and climate change and the global environment, among other priority areas.

Homeland security programs and budgets require particular attention. The Obama administration has already moved the Homeland Security Council (HSC) into the National Security Council staff, retaining the HSC as an organizing structure for deliberations on homeland security issues.[17] As of June 2009, there had been no statement about budget coordination for homeland security, however. The White House should request that the Congress move to create a single budget function for homeland security and ensure that the NSC staff for homeland security work closely with OMB in reviewing homeland security programs and funding.

Both OMB and the NSC are highly competent organizations, though only the latter has an institutionalized structure, permanent civil service, and standing authority over the budget process. Both need strengthening to execute this agenda.[18] OMB tends to focus on the short term and the operation of the budget process. It needs to develop a long-term strategic planning cell with additional personnel trained in program analysis and long-term planning. NSC needs to create a similar capability. Together these cells should take the lead in overseeing the quadrennial national security review and the biennial national security guidance processes.

In addition, OMB needs internal reforms. The agency needs to strengthen its process for conducting regular cross-cut reviews of interagency programs and budgets in key policy areas. In the homeland security area, in particular, the OMB process is significantly stovepiped. There needs to be a single point of focus in the agency for homeland security which can work with the NSC homeland security staff, integrated into the national security program area at OMB. OMB also needs to propose a more formal joint review structure for its relationship with DOD, to avoid the uneven application of this review from administration to administration.

Reforms in the Congress

Congress has played a critical role over the past 20 years in legislating new national security programs and reforms to planning and budgeting processes in the executive branch. Jointness at DOD owes much to the Goldwater–Nichols reform bill passed in 1986. Senators Sam Nunn and Dick Lugar sponsored landmark legislation creating a DOD program that reduced the nuclear arsenal of the former Soviet Union; both played a role in creating foreign assistance programs for Eastern Europe and the new nations that were once part of the Soviet Union. Congress created the Department of Homeland Security and the Office of the Director of National Intelligence.

There is, nonetheless, a strong need for reform in the way the Congress deals with national security budgets. Reforming the executive branch so it can do program and budget planning in a more integrated, interagency manner will be minimally effective if Congress remains stovepiped. Under the current congressional budgeting structures and process, once the budget resolution has been passed there is no further attention paid to programs and funding across agencies. Authorizing committees deal with issues inside their areas and appropriating committees further subdivide the national security program and budget universe.

The growing overlap in programs, budgets, and missions among the national security agencies needs careful congressional attention across committees. If congressional restructuring across agency lines is too difficult, the leadership at least should consider expanding the rare practice of holding joint hearings on cross-agency programs and budgets in the key policy areas such as fragile and failed states and security assistance. Appropriations subcommittees should invite other subcommittee members to participate in markup sessions on cross-cutting issues.

In the critical area of homeland security, Congress should consider ways to restructure authorizing and appropriating committee jurisdictions in order to bring more integrated scrutiny to homeland security programs and budgets. In particular, the budget committees need to establish a budget function for homeland security, in order to begin a more integrated review.

With respect to international affairs, the Congress has taken the first important step of integrating virtually all of the appropriations responsibilities in a single subcommittee. Action is needed, however, to strengthen the authorizing committees in both chambers and restore a process of annual authorization bills for the foreign policy institutions. The House Foreign Affairs Committee began to address this weakness in 2009, considering a Foreign Relations Authorization Act and beginning to draft a bill to reauthorize foreign assistance, which has not been done since 1986. The Senate Foreign Relations Committee intends to take similar steps.

Congress should also consider legislating requirements for the executive branch to carry out a quadrennial national security review, provide national security budget and program guidance, and transmit to the Congress a single national security budget document as part of the budget request.

Finally, the Congress needs to strengthen its analytical capabilities in national security by adding staff to the Congressional Budget Office (CBO), particularly in homeland security and international affairs. They should also task CBO to carry out systematic reviews of cross-agency programs and budgets, as well as an examination of the single national security budget document.

Conclusion

Reforms and changes are already under way in the national security budget process. This book has frozen some of these changes in time, but the institutions and processes that plan and budget for national security will continue to evolve. The reforms we have discussed here will not eliminate bureaucratic and political influences on national security budgets and the budget process. They will add rationality to that process, however, and greatly improve the attention paid to the cross-cutting security agenda the nation faces. And they will increase the transparency of the process, which will help diminish some of the distortions that bureaucratic culture and the political process create in national security budgets. Above all, the demanding agenda of national security issues the nation faces makes it important to give urgent attention to the weaknesses we have discussed in this book.

Notes

2 Resource Planning for International Affairs and State Operations

1 The internal State Department culture was, and largely remains, dominated by the traditional diplomatic perspective, a culture that is reinforced through the recruitment, training, and promotion of Foreign Service Officers focused on that set of skills. For more discussion of the cultural issues at State, see Gordon Adams, *The Politics of National Security Budgets*, Policy Analysis Brief (Muscatine, IA: The Stanley Foundation, February 2007). Elmer Plischke notes that if State were to manage all the foreign affairs activities of the United States, it would need to become a "full-fledged Department of Foreign Affairs," with operational duties. This model, he points out, "has been rejected by ... reform studies and the traditional attitude of the State Department and other Departments and independent agencies." *US Department of State: A Reference History* (Westport, CT: Greenwood Press, 1999), 462 and 477.

2 Former Congressional Research Service analyst Larry Nowels notes that:

> Like new aid policy goals that have emerged over the years, these new structures have been added but not necessarily *integrated* into a coherent organizational framework, a situation that only compounds the problems of efficient coordination, duplication of effort and bureaucratic rivalries.
>
> "Foreign Aid Reform Commissions, Task Forces, and Initiatives: From Kennedy to the Present," in *Security by Other Means: Foreign Assistance, Global Poverty, and American Leadership*, ed. Lael Brainard (Washington, DC: The Brookings Institution, 2006), 269–70.

3 Thomas C. Schelling pointed out that "[w]hen Secretary McNamara assumed office [1961], he was at least 15 years ahead of where the Secretary of State is now in having a recognized budget. There is a 'defense budget;' there is not a 'foreign affairs budget.'" (The budget called "foreign affairs" by the Director of the Bureau of the Budget "is a composite figure that makes a lot of sense to the Director of the Budget but has no official status and corresponds to no appropriations procedure.") "PPBS and Foreign Affairs," *The Public Interest*, No. 11 (Spring 1968), 30.

4 Schelling noted that

> by putting some of the specialized professional responsibilities in quasi-independent agencies such as AID, USIA, and Peace Corps, the Executive Branch and the Congress have precluded the State Department's acquiring the professional talents, the internal organization and the executive experience to lord it over these other agencies.
>
> "PPBS and Foreign Affairs," 32.

5 State Department offices are designated by letters of the alphabet. Offices reporting directly to the Secretary generally begin with S/, followed by a specific letter
   for that office.

6 The separation of State operations and foreign assistance funding reflected the
   division of congressional jurisdiction over operations and foreign assistance
   appropriations. For decades, the congressional appropriations subcommittees for
   Commerce, Justice, and State, had jurisdiction over State Operations budgets,
   while the separate Foreign Operations appropriations subcommittee had jurisdiction over foreign economic and security assistance funding. The two subcommittees were merged in the House in 2005, and in the Senate in 2007.

7 In the State Department structure, a Bureau ranks higher than an Office.

8 During the Bush administration, for example, S/P was centrally involved in
   designing a new budget process for foreign assistance (see Chapter 3).

9 All quotes from US Department of State, 1 Foreign Assistance Manual 041 (April
   23, 2002). Hereafter cited as 1 FAM.

10 Functional bureaus and offices at State have responsibilities that cut across
   regions. P also oversees the Bureau of International Narcotics and Law Enforcement Affairs (INL), discussed in Chapter 4.

11 See Title XIII, Section 1313, of the Foreign Affairs Agencies Consolidation Act of
   1998, PL 105-277 (October 21, 1998), 112 Stat. 2681-776 and 112 Stat. 2681-825.

12 The programmatic activities of these bureaus and offices are discussed in Chapter 4.

13 There is often tension in State between the dominant regional bureaus and the
   functional bureaus reporting to the Under Secretary for Global Affairs, as many
   of the programs for which G is responsible are implemented in regions and countries for which the regional bureaus are responsible.

14 State, 1 FAM 044.1.

15 A number of smaller accounts are included in State Operations. Some are
   personnel-related: representation allowances, funding for the protection of foreign missions and officials, emergencies in the diplomatic and consular service,
   repatriation loans, and contributions to the Foreign Service Retirement and Disability Fund. Some fund small non-State institutions, including the American
   Institute in Taiwan (the US presence in lieu of diplomatic relations), the Asia
   Foundation, the East–West Center, and a few small earmarked fellowship and
   exchange programs. Still others fund US participation in cross-border commissions with Canada and Mexico: the International Boundary and Water Commission, the International Fisheries Commission, and the Border Environment
   Cooperation Commission established in the North American Free Trade Agreement (NAFTA).

16 State's local employment overseas is sometimes defined as "locally engaged staff"
   (LES), which includes Americans who are overseas residents and employed by
   the embassy.

17 US Department of State, Bureau of Human Resources, HR Fact Sheet (Washington, DC: June 30, 2008).

18 These include individuals from the Secretary of State down through the level of
   Deputy Assistant Secretaries, Bureau Directors, Chiefs of Mission, and their
   immediate staffs. Calculations are based on the FY 2009 budget request to the
   Congress of $5.3 billion for D&CP in US Department of State, FY 2009 Budget in
   Brief (Washington, DC: February 2008).

19 These officials are responsible for political and economic reporting, representation, and negotiations on such issues as arms control, nonproliferation, trade,
   and human rights.

20 The consular system handles passport and visa operations, border security operations, and assistance to US citizens abroad, and staffs the consular offices.

21 This element has grown significantly since the late 1990s and includes employee protection, security operations, information protection, and counterintelligence, among other activities.

22 This includes administrative support, personnel and financial management services, property management, and building operations.

23 This includes informational and cultural operations administered at State, but not educational and cultural exchanges.

24 The remaining 8 percent pays for participation in international conferences, training services, medical services, rental payments in the United States, and travel.

25 See Harry Crosby, a pseudonym for a younger FSO, for an irreverent treatment of the career expectations for Foreign Service Officers. "Too at Home Abroad," *The Washington Monthly* (September 1991).

26 In 2002, State reported a staffing shortfall of more than 1,300, nearly 550 of which were Foreign Service Officers. US Government Accountability Office, *State Department: Staffing Shortfalls and Ineffective Assignment System Compromise Diplomatic Readiness at Hardship Posts*, GAO-02-626 (Washington, DC: June 2002).

27 Foreign Affairs Council, *Secretary Colin Powell's State Department: An Independent Assessment* (Washington, DC: March 2003).

28 Ibid., 7.

29 US Commission on National Security/21st Century (Hart-Rudman Commission), *Road Map for National Security: Imperative for Change*, Phase III Report (Washington, DC: March 15, 2001), 94–6. A "float" means that enough personnel are employed to allow some to participate in training or change of station or to be on leave, and still fill all of the job slots in the organization.

30 Ibid., 61. This report echoed the 1999 report of the Kaden Commission, which underlined the broad new agenda of issues facing American diplomacy. US Department of State, *America's Overseas Presence in the 21st Century* (Kaden Commission) (Washington, DC: November 1999).

31 See also Henry L. Stimson Center, *Equipped for the Future: Managing US Foreign Affairs in the 21st Century* (Washington, DC: October 1998), esp. 12–13, and Council on Foreign Relations/Center for Strategic and International Studies, *State Department Reform: Report of an Independent Task Force* (Carlucci Commission) (Washington, DC: 2001).

32 Grant Green, Under Secretary of State for Management from 2001 to 2005, noted that most Foreign Service Officers saw no reward from in-service training: "People saw no advantage in it. To them it was a waste of time, with no relationship to better assignments or promotion. They saw senior officers who had risen to the top without training." Nicolas Kralev, "Diplomatic Reorientation," *Washington Times* (April 12, 2004).

33 Foreign Affairs Council, *Secretary Colin Powell's State Department* (2003). Recruitment budgets increased under Secretary Powell, the number of people taking the Foreign Exam rose from 8,000 in FY 2000 to 20,000 in FY 2004, and refusals of offers fell dramatically. Ibid., 3.

34 Crosby, in "Too at Home Abroad," noted his view that the State Department culture did not favor working with other agencies. "Whatever else Defense, Commerce, and Treasury might be, they weren't your friends."

35 Condoleezza Rice, *Transformational Diplomacy: Remarks at Georgetown School of Foreign Service* (Washington, DC: January 18, 2006).

36 Ibid. Secretaries Powell and Rice also moved to address the need for a civilian capability that could deploy rapidly to post-conflict areas for reconstruction tasks. See Chapter 4 for a discussion of the office of the State Coordinator for Stabilization and Reconstruction.

37 There was renewed support for an expansion of funding and personnel in the October 2008 report of the Henry L. Stimson Center and the American Academy of Diplomacy, *A Foreign Affairs Budget for the Future* (Washington, DC: Henry L. Stimson Center, October 2008). The report called for an additional 3,500 State Department personnel to meet necessary staffing levels and cope with "new programmatic and substantive requirements." The first budget of the Obama administration appeared to reflect this concern, providing for significant Foreign Service growth.

38 CA provides services to more than two million Americans overseas, including dealing with arrests, death, emergencies, notary services, and disasters, through its Office of American Citizens Services and Crisis Management. US Department of State, *FY 2008 Budget in Brief* (Washington, DC: 2007), 14.

39 US Department of State, *FY 2009 Foreign Operations Congressional Budget Justification* (Washington, DC: 2008), 34.

40 Crosby, "Too at Home Abroad."

41 US Department of State, *Remarks of Maura Harty, Assistant Secretary of State for Consular Affairs*, Migration Policy Institute (March 25, 2004), http://travel.state. gov/law/legal/testimony/testimony_809.html.

42 Border Security Program investments have also been directed to State's Bureaus of Diplomatic Security, Information Management, and Intelligence and Research. State, *FY 2008 Budget in Brief*, 47–55.

43 In particular, the State program has close links to the US-VISIT (Visitor and Immigrant Status Indicator Technology) program operated by the Customs and Border Protection division of the Department of Homeland Security. US Government Accountability Office, *Border Security: US-VISIT Program Faces Strategic, Operational and Technological Challenges at Land Ports of Entry*. GAO-07-248 (Washington, DC: December 2006).

44 Ralph Blumenthal, "US Planning to Ease Rules on Passports, Official Says," *New York Times* (June 8, 2007).

45 The 1999 Kaden Commission report noted: "We were dismayed to find that our embassies are equipped with antiquated, grossly inefficient, and incompatible information technology systems incapable of even the simplest electronic communications across department lines that are now commonplace in private-sector organizations." State, Kaden Commission, 56.

46 Stimson Center, *Equipped for the Future*, 20. The Stimson Center (21–2) urged a major investment in technology, to create a government-wide system linking all agencies with overseas interests, through a working capital fund into which all agencies would contribute, and provides a detailed list of technology improvements that would be included in such a system.

47 State's Under Secretary for Management initially resisted the fencing off of these fees, arguing that they gave the Secretary flexibility to deal with currency value changes and "change of station" allowances. OMB insisted on transmitting the fencing language to the Congress, however, and the Department agreed, later, that this action was critical to the modernization of the Department's IT system. Author's personal experience.

48 US Department of State, Bureau of Public Affairs, Office of the Historian, *History of the Department of State During the Clinton Presidency (1993–2001)* (Washington, DC: June 2001), www.state.gov/r/pa/ho/pubs/c6059.htm.

49 Foreign Affairs Council, *Secretary Colin Powell's State Department* (2003), 4.

50 Ibid.

51 Ronald Reagan, *Staffing at Diplomatic Missions and Their Overseas Constituent Posts*, National Security Decision Directive 38 (June 2, 1982), http://ftp.fas.org/ irp/offdocs/nsdd38.htm. The State Department Authorization Act of 1980 pro-

vided that "all executive branch agencies with employees in the host country must keep the COM fully informed at all times of their current and planned activities." Foreign Service Act of 1980, PL 96-465 (November 26, 1980).

52 This language was used in the standard Letter of Instruction from President George H.W. Bush, dated July 12, 1990, to new ambassadors. The language changes little from administration to administration.

53 On occasion, the short-term deployment of other agency personnel appeared to violate the authority of the Chief of Mission under NSDD-38. In 2003, US Ambassador to Jordan Edward M. Gnehm learned informally from the defense attaché that a Pentagon intelligence team was being sent to Amman to gather information about the stability of the Jordanian government. The note asked that the defense attaché not notify the ambassador or the CIA station in Jordan about this team. "The message made it clear that these guys were going to be acting under the authority of the secretary of defense," Gnehm said. When he called two other ambassadors in the Middle East he discovered that teams had been sent their way, also without notification. Thom Shanker and Mark Mazzetti, "New Defense Chief Eases Relations Rumsfeld Bruised," *New York Times* (March 12, 2007). The extent of this problem, particularly with respect to counterterror operations, was underlined by a Senate Committee on Foreign Relations staff report in December 2006. *Embassies as Command Posts in the Anti-Terror Campaign: A Report to the Members of the Committee on Foreign Relations*, 109th Congress, 2nd Session, Senate Print 109-52 (Washington, DC: Government Printing Office, December 15, 2006), www.fas.org/irp/congress/2006_rpt/embassies.html.

54 Omnibus Consolidated Appropriations Act of 1997, PL 104-208 (September 30, 1996).

55 US Department of State, *Foreign Affairs Handbook*, 6 FAH-5 H-000, "ICASS Organization," Section H-013-2 (July 21, 2006).

56 US Department of State, *6 Foreign Assistance Manual* 911.4.

57 State, 6 FAH-5, Section H-012-4. The following services are generally covered through ICASS: motor pool and vehicle maintenance, travel services, reproduction services, mail and messenger services, information systems management, reception and telephone system services, purchasing and contracting, personnel management, cashiering, vouchering, accounting, budget preparation, nonresidential security guard services, and building operations. Section H 011-2. In addition, the costs of regional services, such as regional finance centers, and such central services as medical programs and overseas schools may be included.

58 State, 6 FAH-5 H-012.1-3.

59 State, 1 FAM 225.1.

60 State, 6 FAH-5 H-411.2.

61 State, *FY 2008 Budget in Brief*, 58.

62 State, Kaden Commission, 15.

63 Ibid., 19–20.

64 US Government Accountability Office, *Embassy Construction: State Has Made Progress Constructing New Embassies, but Better Planning Is Needed for Operations and Maintenance Requirements*, GAO-06-641 (Washington, DC: June 2006), 4.

65 US Government Accountability Office, *State Department: Management Weaknesses in the Security Construction Program*, GAO/NSIAD/92-2 (Washington, DC: November 1991).

66 GAO, *Embassy Construction*, 4–5.

67 US Department of State, *Report of the Accountability Review Boards: Bombings of the US Embassies in Nairobi, Kenya and Dar Es Salaam, Tanzania on August 7, 1998* (Washington, DC: State, January 1999).

68 The Kaden Commission recommended the creation of a separate, government-run corporation that would be in charge of embassy facility construction and would own, rent, operate, and maintain the buildings. See State, Kaden Commission, 49–51.

69 GAO, *Embassy Construction*, 19. The Kaden Commission was equally critical of the previous arrangement:

> The Department has not put in place a disciplined decision-making process to provide FBO with a firm set of priorities for its capital programs. Instead, FBO has been faced with shifting priorities and protracted negotiations within the Department and with embassies overseas. This contributes to project delays, cost overruns, and inordinately long project-completion timelines.
> State, Kaden Commission, 47.

70 GAO, *Embassy Construction*, 19–20.

71 Office of Management and Budget, *Detailed Information on the Capital Security Construction Program Assessment* (2004), answers to questions 1.4 and 1.5, www.whitehouse.gov/omb/expectmore/detail.10000378.2005.html. GAO also noted the improvements at OBO:

> Strategic and procedural reforms implemented by State—including the creation of OBO, the implementation of performance management and strategic planning principles, and the use of the design-build contract delivery method and a standard embassy design—resulted in reduced project cycle times and costs.
> GAO, Embassy Construction, 10.

72 OMB, Detailed Information.

73 US Department of State, Capital Security Cost-Sharing Program, Briefing (November 2006), slide 3, www.state.gov/obo/c11275.htm. See also State, Kaden Commission, 5.

74 The 2005 language creating the CSCS made it clear that shared funding and "right-sizing" of the embassies were linked: "Implementation of this subsection shall be carried out in a manner that encourages right-sizing of each agency's overseas presence." FY 2005 Consolidated Appropriations Act, Division B, PL 108-447 (December 8, 2004).

75 GAO, *Embassy Construction*, 27. Overseas buildings O&M costs are funded through different parts of the budget, including ICASS, Diplomatic Security, and Diplomatic and Consular Programs, but are not aggregated in one operations and maintenance line item. Ibid., 36.

76 State, 1 FAM 280, "Overseas Buildings Operations," Sec. 280 and 286.

77 US Department of State, Bureau of Diplomatic Security, *A Brief History*, www.state.gov/m/ds/about/history/index.htm. The DS Bureau was created by the Omnibus Diplomatic Security and Antiterrorism Act of 1986, PL 99-399 (August 27, 1986). The Inman panel also recommended that the Marines provide security services at all sensitive posts. Susan B. Epstein, *Embassy Security: Background, Funding, and the Budget*, CRS Report RL30662 (Washington, DC: Congressional Research Service, October 4, 2001), 2.

78 US Department of State, Bureau of Diplomatic Security, *Securing Our Embassies Overseas*, www.state.gov/m/ds/about/overview/c9004.htm.

79 US Department of State, Bureau of Diplomatic Security, *Overview: Keeping American Diplomacy Safe*, www.state.gov/m/ds/about/overview.

80 Epstein, *Embassy Security*, 5. Marine Guards are funded through the Defense Department appropriation, while direct USAID security funding was provided through the foreign operations appropriation.

81 In addition to its formal assessments, the United States makes voluntary contributions to several of these organizations, notably the International Atomic Energy Agency. In addition, some UN-related programs and organizations are not covered in the regular UN budget—UN Development Program (UNDP), the UN Children's Fund (UNICEF), the UN High Commissioner for Refugees (UNHCR), and the World Food Program (WFP). These are funded entirely through voluntary contributions from the UN members. Voluntary US contributions to international organizations are budgeted through the International Organizations and Programs account, covered in Chapter 3.

82 These include such organizations as the Food and Agricultural Organization (FAO), the United Nations Educational, Scientific, and Cultural Organization (UNESCO), the International Labor Organization (ILO), the World Health Organization (WHO), and the International Atomic Energy Agency (IAEA).

83 Other regional organizations include the Organization for Economic Cooperation and Development (OECD), and the Asian Pacific Regional Cooperation Forum (APEC). For a complete listing, see State, *FY 2009 Foreign Operations Congressional Budget Justification*, 619–20.

84 The UN scale of assessments is adjusted to reduce payments for the poorest countries, with a ceiling on the share a low-income country should pay.

85 State, *FY 2009 Foreign Operations Congressional Budget Justification*, 620.

86 US funding for peacekeeping operations that are not voted by the UN Security Council is provided through direct US military spending or as a voluntary (non-assessed) contribution to the operation. See discussion of the Peacekeeping Operations (PKO) account in Chapter 4. In addition, other US military, diplomatic, and foreign assistance activities can support UN peacekeeping indirectly. The Government Accountability Office estimated, for example, that from 1995 to 2001 the United States spent $3.45 billion in direct costs for UN peacekeeping. At the same time, the United States spent an estimated $24.2 billion in indirect support of UN peacekeeping missions, 90 percent of that through military operations in such places as Kuwait, Kosovo, and Bosnia-Herzegovina. US Government Accountability Office, *U.N. Peacekeeping: Estimated US Contributions, Fiscal Years 1996–2001*, GAO-02-294 (Washington, DC: February 2002), 25, Appendix IV, Table 2.

87 For a complete listing of UN peacekeeping operations and projected US assessments, see State, *FY 2009 Foreign Operations Congressional Budget Justification*, 751–70.

88 Marjorie Ann Browne, *United Nations Peacekeeping: Issues for Congress*, Issue Brief IB90103 (Washington, DC: Congressional Research Service, July 5, 2006). For an excellent bibliography on peacekeeping operations, see Virginia C. Shope, *Peacekeeping: A Selected Bibliography*, Carlisle Barracks, PA: US Army War College Library, May 2004, www.carlisle.army.mil/library/bibs/peace04r.htm.

89 This was adjusted to just over 26 percent for 2007–09. United Nations, *Implementation of General Assembly Resolutions 55/235 and 55/236: Report of the Secretary General*, A/61/139 (New York: July 13, 2006), 17.

90 GAO, *U.N. Peacekeeping*, 6. For 2006–07, see United Nations, *Approved Resources for Peacekeeping Operations for the Period from 1 July 2006 to 30 June 2007*, A/C.5/61/18 (New York: January 15, 2007).

91 The FY 2010 State Operations budget request sought $145 million to begin moving these payments to earlier in the United Nations' fiscal year.

92 Browne, *United Nations Peacekeeping*, 9, 11.

93 For details on this process, see Vita Bite, *U.N. System Funding: Congressional Issues*, CRS Report IB86116 (Washington, DC: Congressional Research Service, November 15, 2001).

94 The IO&P account is authorized by Section 301 of the Foreign Assistance Act of 1961, PL 87-195 (September 4, 1961), which states that "when he determines it to be in the national interest, the President is authorized to make voluntary contributions on a grant basis to international organizations and to programs administered by such organizations."

95 State, *FY 2009 Foreign Operations Congressional Budget Justification*, 140.

96 State, 1 FAM 330.

97 The United States also has permanent missions to the United Nations in Geneva, Rome, and Vienna.

98 For a brief history of the emergence of public diplomacy as a function of statecraft, see Walter R. Roberts, "The Evolution of Diplomacy," *Mediterranean Quarterly*, Vol. 17, No. 3 (Summer 2006), 55–64. For a discussion of the meaning of "public diplomacy," as distinguished from "public affairs" and "propaganda," see the Public Diplomacy Alumni Association, "Public Diplomacy Web Site," www.publicdiplomacy.org, a website established by the USIA Alumni Association, particularly Michael McClellan, Counselor for Public Diplomacy, US Embassy, Dublin, *Public Diplomacy in the Context of Traditional Diplomacy*, Remarks to the Vienna Diplomatic Academy (October 11, 2004), www.publicdiplomacy.org/45.htm.

99 USIA could trace its antecedents back to World War I, but was more closely connected to the establishment of libraries and binational centers created during World War II, and the creation of the Office of War Information and the Voice of America in 1942. See USIA homepage, preserved at http://dosfan.lib.uic.edu/usia.

100 Ibid. USIA was the fourth "foreign service," with the State Department, the Foreign Agricultural Service, and the Foreign Commercial Service. Of the latter two, see Chapter 4.

101 Ibid.

102 The reorganization was legislated in the Foreign Affairs Reform and Restructuring Act of 1998, PL 105-277 (October 21, 1998). It created a Bureau of International Information Programs (successor to the USIA Information Activities office), a Bureau of Education and Cultural Affairs (for exchanges and fellows programs), and a Bureau of Public Affairs (overseeing spokesperson activities). State, 1 FAM 046. See also, US Department of State, Bureau of International Information Programs, www.state.gov/r/iip.

103 US Government Accountability Office, *US Public Diplomacy: State Department Efforts Lack Certain Communication Elements and Face Persistent Challenges*, Statement of Jess T. Ford, Director, International Affairs and Trade, to the Subcommittee on Science, the Departments of State, Justice and Commerce, and Related Agencies, House Committee on Appropriations, GAO-06-707T, May 3, 2006, 4.

104 Ibid., 7.

105 US Government Accountability Office, *US Public Diplomacy: State Department Expands Efforts but Faces Significant Challenges*, GAO-03-951 (Washington, DC: September 2003), 6.

106 For a review of polling data on overseas attitudes toward the United States, see Ole R. Holsti, *To See Ourselves As Others See Us: How Publics Abroad View the United States After 9/11* (Ann Arbor: University of Michigan Press, 2008) and Pew Global Attitudes Project, *Global Public Opinion in the Bush Years*, Report (December 18, 2008), Blackboard and http://pewglobal.org/reports/pdf/263.pdf.

107 US international broadcasting also expanded services in the region. For more information on MEPI, see Chapter 4.

108 State, *Congressional Budget Justification, FY 2009*, 13.

109 Ibid., 15, quoting the memorandum creating the office.

110 US Department of State, Office of Policy, Planning and Resources for Public Diplomacy and Public Affairs, www.state.gov/r/ppr.

111 GAO, *US Public Diplomacy* (May 3, 2006), 9. A 2008 independent study recommended staffing increases and program changes for public diplomacy at State. Stimson Center/American Academy of Diplomacy, *A Foreign Affairs Budget*, 24–36.

112 See Secretary of State's Advisory Committee on Transformational Diplomacy, *A Call to Action* (Washington, DC: State, January 2008), 7.

113 See Stimson Center/Academy of American Diplomacy, *A Foreign Affairs Budget*, 67–8.

114 For a discussion of the broader issues of funding and coordination, see Bruce Gregory, "Public Diplomacy as Strategic Communication," in *Countering Terrorism and Insurgency in the 21st Century: International Perspectives*, Part III, ed. James J.F. Forest (Westport, CT: Praeger, 2007), 336–57; US Department of Defense, Defense Science Board, *Strategic Communication*, Report of a Task Force (Washington, DC: Office of the Under Secretary of Defense for Acquisition, Technology, and Logistics, October 2004); the many reports reviewed in Susan B. Epstein and Lisa Mages, *Public Diplomacy: A Review of Past Recommendations*, CRS Report RL33062 (Washington, DC: Congressional Research Service, October 31, 2005); and US Advisory Commission on Public Diplomacy, *Building America's Public Diplomacy Through a Reformed Structure and Additional Resources* (Washington, DC: State, 2002).

115 Foreign Relations Authorization Act, PL 94-350 (July 12, 1976).

116 The two services merged in 1976.

117 This restructuring was enacted through the International Broadcasting Act of 1994, PL 103-236 (April 30, 1994).

118 This reorganization would not take effect until October 1, 1999.

119 Consolidated Appropriations Act for FY 1999, PL 105-277 (October 21, 1998). The BBG also absorbed the transmission services of the IBB.

120 Alhurra also has an Iraqi and a European service. For a critique of the effectiveness of Alhurra, see Craig Whitlock, "US Network Falters in Mideast Mission," *The Washington Post* (June 23, 2008).

121 The BBG notes that Congress located it outside State because

> credibility would be at risk if the various broadcast services were placed inside the Department of State where they would be perceived by foreign audiences as mere adjuncts of the Department, and where they would be subject to the daily pressures of diplomacy.
> Broadcasting Board of Governors, *Marrying the Mission to the Market: Strategic Plan, 2002–2007* (Washington, DC: 2002), 15.

122 Services to East Asia consume 17.5 percent, to Latin America 11.8 percent, and to Africa 3.5 percent. These are all shares of the broadcasting services of BBG, which are 57 percent of the total BBG budget. The IBB technical and support operations consumed the other 42.5 percent of the FY 2008 BBG budget.

123 US Government Accountability Office, *US Public Diplomacy: Interagency Coordination Efforts Hampered by the Lack of National Communications Strategy*, GAO-05-323 (Washington, DC: GAO, April 2005), 18.

124 Broadcasting Board of Governors, *FY 2006 Performance and Accountability Report* (Washington, DC: November 15, 2006).

125 National Endowment for Democracy, *Idea to Reality: A Brief History of the National Endowment for Democracy*, www.ned.org/about/nedhistory.html.

126 NED was authorized in the State Department Authorization Act for fiscal years 1984–85, PL 98-164 (November 22, 1983).

127 National Endowment for Democracy, *Strengthening Democracy Abroad: The Role of the National Endowment for Democracy*, www.ned.org/about/principlesObjectives.html.

128 State, *FY 2009 Budget in Brief*, 141–51.

3 Foreign Economic Assistance Budgeting and Programs

 1 The State Department uses the term "foreign operations" to describe foreign assistance programs, consistent with the pre-2005 structure of the congressional appropriations committees, one for Commerce, Justice, State, which appropriated State Operations funding, and the other for Foreign Operations. In FY 2007, funding for foreign and security assistance constituted 74 percent of the total International Affairs budget, while budgets for State operations and related activities accounted for 26 percent of the total.

 2 These are current dollars. FY 1977 is the first year for which consistent, comparable data on US foreign assistance can be collected. This number covers all economic and security assistance programs and all budgets, including emergency supplemental funding, based on Congressional Research Service calculations using OMB and congressional appropriations committee data. Larry Nowels, *Foreign Policy Budget Trends: A Thirty-Year Review*, CRS Report RL33262 (Washington, DC: Congressional Research Service, January 31, 2006), 10–11.

 3 Budgets peaked in the mid-1980s, because of a large amount of supplemental economic and security assistance funding for Israel, Egypt, and Jordan, a backlog of payments to the World Bank, and famine relief for Africa. They fell in the mid-1990s, because of the end of the Cold War and deficit reduction efforts, then rose, again, in the early 2000s, largely in response to the 9/11 attacks, post-conflict Iraq programs, and presidential initiatives on HIV/AIDS and development such as the Millennium Challenge Corporation.

 4 These are not official budget categories, but a way of grouping programs adapted by the authors from Nowels, *Foreign Policy Budget Trends*.

 5 Ibid., 13.

 6 Ibid.

 7 Curt Tarnoff and Larry Nowels, *Foreign Aid: An Introductory Overview of US Programs and Policy*, CRS Report RL98-916 (Washington, DC: Congressional Research Service, January 19, 2005), 5, Figure 1.

 8 Nowels, *Foreign Policy Budget Trends*, 16.

 9 Tarnoff and Nowels, *Foreign Aid*, 5.

10 For a thorough discussion of early efforts at coordinating internal State Department, USAID, and International Affairs budgets, see William J. Bacchus, *The Price of American Foreign Policy: Congress, The Executive, and International Affairs Funding* (University Park, PA: Pennsylvania State University Press, 1997), especially Chapter 2, "Impediments to Coherent Foreign Affairs Budgeting," 31–62.

11 MPPs and BPPs were considered only semi-effective in linking strategy and policy to budget planning at State. Bacchus quotes a career officer at State: "MPP is strong on program and policy objectives and weak on consolidation, resource allocation, staffing, and funding." Bacchus, *The Price of American Foreign Policy*, 269, footnote 8.

12 Bacchus, *The Price of American Foreign Policy*, 271, based on an internal State Department memo of January 20, 1994, and interviews with senior officials.

13 State describes the Secretary's role in non-State agency budgeting as follows: "The Secretary of State not only determines the resource and program request of the

Department but also, as ombudsman for the Function 150 account, must make tradeoffs and set priorities for the larger foreign affairs community." US Department of State, *Foreign Affairs Handbook*, 4 FAH-3 H114, "Budget Process," Section 114.1 (February 17, 2005). Since USAID, ACDA, and USIA all dual-reported to the Secretary and to the President, State had slightly more leverage over their planning and budgeting. With the absorption of the latter two into State in 1999, arms control and public diplomacy budgeting became part of the internal State operations budget process described in Chapter 2.

14 This Assistant Secretary also became the Chief Financial Officer of the State Department.

15 US Department of State, *1 Foreign Assistance Manual* 221.4 (April 23, 2002). Hereafter cited as 1 FAM.

16 State, 1 FAM 225.

17 State, *Foreign Affairs Handbook*, Sections 114.2–2.

18 Ibid., Section 120.

19 US Department of State and USAID, *Strategic Plan: Fiscal Years 2004–2009: Aligning Diplomacy and Development Assistance* (Washington, DC: State and USAID, August 2003), 37. See also the subsequent plan: US Department of State and USAID, *Strategic Plan: Fiscal Years 2007–2012: Transformational Diplomacy* (Washington, DC: State and USAID, May 2007).

20 US Department of State, *Fact Sheet: New Direction for US Foreign Assistance* (January 19, 2006). The F Director was not named a Deputy Secretary of State because of resistance in the Foreign Service to creating a second Deputy Secretary position.

21 Since the Director was not a confirmation position, dual-hatting the position as the USAID Administrator provided the Congress with some accountability for foreign assistance decisions. Confidential interviews (2006).

22 The Director was given authority

> to provide for continuous supervision and general direction of development and other economic assistance, military assistance, military education and training, and foreign military financing, designing a US foreign assistance strategy and budgetary approach, determining whether there shall be a program for a country and the amount thereof, and approving the programming of foreign assistance.

US Department of State, "Delegation of Authority 293: Organizations, functions, and authority delegations: Director of Foreign Assistance, et al.," Section 1(a), *Federal Register*, Vol. 71, No. 128 (July 5, 2006), 38202-05, www.state.gov/s/l/treaty/authorities/domestic/69286.htm.

23 US Department of State, Office of the Director for US Foreign Assistance, *Fact Sheet: Frequently Asked Questions About US Foreign Assistance Reform* (June 15, 2006). The Congressional Research Service estimates that State/USAID disbursements in calendar year 2005 were 55 percent of all US government foreign assistance, with DOD responsible for 19 percent (mainly assistance in Iraq and Afghanistan) and other departments and agencies responsible for 26.5 percent. Larry Nowels and Connie Veillette, *Restructuring US Foreign Aid: The Role of the Director of Foreign Assistance*, CRS Report RL33491 (Washington, DC: Congressional Research Service, September 8, 2006).

24 Congressional Research Service estimates of calendar year 2005 US foreign assistance disbursements show that DOD was responsible for another 19 percent (mainly assistance in Iraq and Afghanistan), while other departments and agencies were responsible for 26.5 percent. Nowels and Veillette, *Restructuring US Foreign Aid*, 3.

25 State, *Fact Sheet: New Direction.*
26 Israel and Cyprus, for example. Confidential interviews (2006).
27 Iran, North Korea, and Cuba, for example. US Department of State, Office of the Director of US Foreign Assistance, *Foreign Assistance Framework* (January 28, 2007). As a revision, the matrix later added a "global or regional" category to cover funding for "activities that advance the five objectives, transcend a single country's borders, and are addressed outside a country strategy." The F office also created a highly detailed "Standardized Program Structure," defining the program areas that fit under the broader objectives. Programs listed under the "Peace and Security" objective, for example, included "Counter-Terrorism," "Combating Weapons of Mass Destruction," "Stabilization Operations and Security Sector Reform," "Counter-Narcotics," "Transnational Crime," and "Conflict Mitigation and Response."
28 One source described this as "changing the Ambassador's role from planner to implementer." Confidential interviews (2007).
29 The F process also required embassies and missions to analyze and distribute appropriated funds for a given fiscal year through a Mission Operational Plan.
30 See, for example, Gordon Adams, "Don't Reinvent the Foreign Assistance Wheel," *Foreign Service Journal* (March 2008), 46–50, and Gerald Hyman, "Assessing Secretary of State Rice's Reform of US Foreign Assistance," Carnegie Paper No. 90, Democracy and Rule of Law Program (Washington, DC: Carnegie Endowment, February 2008).
31 The F process decisions needed to be cross-walked from the matrix categories to appropriations accounts, which proved complex and confusing to the Congress. Glenn Kessler, "Hill, Aid Groups: One Opaque System Replaced Another," *The Washington Post* (July 22, 2007).
32 There was an extensive debate over foreign assistance institutional reform in 2007–09. Gordon Adams, *Rebalancing and Integrating the National Security Toolkit,* Testimony for the Senate Foreign Relations Committee (April 24, 2008), http://foreign.senate.gov/testimony/2008/AdamsTestimony080424a.pdf; Gordon Adams, "Getting U.S. Foreign Assistance Right," *Bulletin of the Atomic Scientists* (May 2, 2008), www.thebulletin.org/web-edition/columnists/gordon-adams/ getting-us-foreign-assistance-right; Modernizing Foreign Assistance Network, *New Day, New Way: US Foreign Assistance for the 21st Century* (Washington, DC: Center for Global Development, June 2008), ii, www.modernizingforeignas- sistance.net/documents/newdaynewway.pdf; Anne C. Richard and Paul Clayman, *Improving US National Security: Options for Strengthening US Foreign Opera- tions,* Briefing Paper (Muscatine, IA: Stanley Foundation, 2008).
33 The link between US security interests and development had been underlined by Kennedy National Security Council advisor W.W. ("Walt") Rostow, a develop- ment economist, author of *The Stages of Economic Growth: A Non-Communist Manifesto* (Cambridge: Cambridge University Press, 1960).
34 John F. Kennedy, *Special Message to the Congress on Foreign Aid* (March 22, 1961).
35 Ibid.
36 The need for a separate agency had been noted in 1959 by an advisory committee to President Eisenhower. Joseph M. Dodge, *US President's Committee to Study the US Military Assistance Program (Draper Committee): Records, 1958–59* (Abilene, Kansas: Dwight D. Eisenhower Library), www.eisenhower.archives.gov/ Research/Finding_Aids/PDFs/Dodge_Joseph_Papers.pdf.
37 Kennedy, *Special Message.*
38 For a review of the many task forces that have sought to reform US foreign assist- ance, see Larry Nowels, "Foreign Aid Reform Commissions, Task forces, and Ini-

tiatives: From Kennedy to the Present," in *Security By Other Means: Foreign Assistance, Global Poverty, and American Leadership*, ed. Lael Brainard (Washington, DC: The Brookings Institution, 2007), 255–75. For one significant congressional effort to enact restructuring and reform, see House Committee on Foreign Affairs, *Report of the Task Force on Foreign Assistance* (Hamilton–Gilman Report), 101st Cong., 1st sess. (Washington, DC: GPO, 1989), 27. Prefiguring the Bush–Rice reforms of the early 2000s, Hamilton–Gilman urged (42) that DOD, State, and USAID do a better job of formulating "a comprehensive strategy that integrates economic and military assistance."

39 Foreign Affairs Agencies Consolidation Act of 1998, PL 105-277 (March 10, 1998), 112 Stat. 2681-776 and 112 Stat. 2681-825, and USAID, *Automated Directives System*, Chapter 101, "Agency Programs and Functions" (revised February 1, 2006), 3.

40 State, "Delegation of Authority 293" (July 5, 2006), section 5b.

41 Curt Tarnoff and Larry Nowels, *Foreign Aid: An Introductory Overview of US Programs and Policy*, CRS Report RL98-916 (Washington, DC: Congressional Research Service, April 15, 2004), 4.

42 Office of Management and Budget, *Public Budget Database* (Washington, DC: OMB), annual/www.whitehouse.gov/omb/budget/fy2009/db.html.

43 US Department of State and USAID, *US Foreign Assistance: Reference Guide*, Department of State Publication 11202 (Washington, DC: State and USAID, January 2005), 2.

44 Agricultural Trade, Development and Assistance Act of 1954, PL 83-480 (July 10, 1954).

45 Christopher B. Barrett and Daniel G. Maxwell, *Food Aid After Fifty Years: Recasting Its Role* (London: Routledge, 2005) and Thomas Melito, *Multiple Challenges Hinder the Efficiency and Effectiveness of US Food Aid*, GAO-08-83T (Washington, DC: Government Accountability Office, October 2, 2007).

46 These include the three titles of PL 480, Food for Progress, the McGovern–Dole International Food for Education and Child Nutrition program, the Bill Emerson Humanitarian Trust, the Farmer-to-Farmer program, and the Section 416(b) program from that section of the Agricultural Act of 1949. Title I of PL 480 (which has been phased out) and Section 416(b) programs are administered by the Department of Agriculture.

47 No-year contingency funds are rare in the International Affairs budget world. See discussion of IDFA and ERMA below and Chapter 4 on assistance to Europe and Eurasia, and the Nonproliferation and Disarmament Fund.

48 Government credit programs went on budget with the passage of the Federal Credit Reform Act of 1990, PL 101-508 (November 5, 1990), which required agencies to budget for the "subsidy" value of credit. This is a calculation of the likely cost of providing credit, should it not be repaid, rather than the full value of the lending itself. See also Office of Management and Budget, *Circular A-129: Policies for Federal Credit Programs and Non-Tax Receivables* (Washington, DC: revised November 2000).

49 These include the Economic Support Fund, assistance to Eastern Europe and Eurasia, some of the International Narcotics programs, the PEPFAR program, and threshold country programs related to the Millennium Challenge Corporation.

50 US Government Accountability Office, *Foreign Assistance: Strategic Workforce Planning Can Help USAID Address Current and Future Challenges*, GAO-03-946 (Washington, DC: GAO, August 2003), 7.

51 The PPC office "is responsible for the Agency's overall policy formulation, planning, program, and administrative resource allocation, and evaluation systems."

USAID, *Automated Directives System*, Chapter 200, "Introduction to Programming Policy" (revised March 19, 2004), 4.

> [It] leads Agency efforts in managing for results; defines and enforces USAID's program and research priorities; tracks results; ensures that budget allocations and program content reflect Administration priorities, Agency policies, and program performance, and houses the Agency's independent evaluation, performance measurement, and development information functions.
>
> US Agency for International Development, *Automated Directives System*, Chapter 101, "Agency Programs and Functions" (Revised January 1, 2006), 23.

52 USAID, ADS 101, "Agency Programs and Functions," 8, 17.
53 USAID, ADS 200, "Introduction to Programming Policy," 3.
54 Ibid., 41.
55 USAID describes the MSP as the "authoritative interagency country strategy document." USAID, *Automated Directives System*, Chapter 201, "Planning" (revised September 1, 2008), 10.
56 USAID, *Strategic Management—Interim Guidance: A Mandatory Reference for ADS*, Chapter 201 (revised February 21, 2006), 4.
57 Ibid., 6.
58 USAID defines a mortgage as

> a claim on future resources, which has been authorized in the Operating Unit's Management Agreement; the difference between the total authorized level of funding and the cumulative total amount of funds obligated to a particular strategic objective, intermediate result or activity.
>
> USAID, ADS 200, "Introduction to Programming Policy," 41.

59 The "mortgage" can also create an expectation in the recipient country that USAID has committed funds for the lifetime of a project. USAID Strategic Objective Grant Agreements (SOGA) with a recipient government or agency cover this uncertainty by noting that future funding is "subject to the availability of funds to USAID for that purpose." USAID, *Automated Directives System*, Chapter 350, "Grants to Foreign Governments" (revised July 23, 2003), 3.
60 USAID, Bureau for Policy and Program Coordination, *US Foreign Aid: Meeting the Challenges of the Twenty-first Century* (Washington, DC: January 2004); USAID, *At Freedom's Frontiers: A Democracy and Governance Strategic Framework* (Washington, DC: December 2005); USAID, *Policy Framework for Bilateral Foreign Aid: Implementing Transformational Diplomacy Through Development* (Washington, DC: January 2006).
61 The broader strategy noted that the "the events of September 11, 2001 taught us that weak states, like Afghanistan, can pose as great a danger to our national interest as strong states." The White House, *The National Security Strategy of the United States of America* (Washington, DC: September 2002), 3.
62 USAID's strategy points out that USAID had "a tendency to adopt longer-term traditional development planning horizons" and noted that

> fragile states require a response that is simultaneously robust and flexible. This response requires a stable funding source as well as flexibility in deploying funds. It also must include staff, implementation capabilities, and field platforms specific to fragile states. An integrated plan to assure this robust and flexible response is currently lacking.
>
> USAID, *Fragile States Strategy* (Washington, DC: January 2005), notes 7, 10, and 18.

63 USAID noted it was working closely with S/CRS and would likely "play a major operational role for S/CRS once it actively engages in coordinating post-conflict response in a limited number of high-priority countries." Ibid., 10.

64 USAID's 2004 White Paper argued that "insofar as this is a separate and distinct goal, it is important to identify separate and distinct resources—other than development resources—for addressing challenges in fragile states." This could mean using ESF funds in coordination with State, or creating a new fund to avoid drawing on development resources:

> For other fragile states, USAID will work closely with the Administration and Congress to identify resources (separate from development resources) to be dedicated to promoting stability, recovery, and governance reform. Identifying a separate account will help address more transparently the difficult issue of the balance between development efforts and efforts to strengthen fragile states, and will help avoid policy coherence problems that stem from trying to address both challenges from the same account.
>
> USAID, *US Foreign Aid*, 20.

The later fragile state strategy, however, urged greater flexibility, asking that fragile state funding be free of earmarks and usable for a longer period of time and for a broader range of countries than just those in post-conflict situations. The agency wanted to be able "to shift to funds designated for fragile states," should one of its DA recipients become unstable, rather than divert DA or CSH funding to the fragile state goal. Ibid., 10.

65 Ibid., 15, 21.

66 Ibid., 22.

67 Ibid., 25.

68 The agency continued to argue for separate accounts: "Implementation of this policy would be greatly facilitated by a new set of accounts for foreign aid that correspond to the five core goals." USAID, *Policy Framework*.

69 A 1998 World Bank study found that a "good policy environment" and a "good institutional environment" were two major requirements for successful development assistance. World Bank, *Assessing Aid: What Works, What Doesn't, and Why* (New York: Oxford University Press, 1998).

70 US Government Accountability Office, *Millennium Challenge Corporation: Progress Made on Key Challenges in First Year of Operations*, GAO-05-625T, Testimony before the House Committee on International Relations (April 2005).

71 James W. Fox and Lex Rieffel, *The Millennium Challenge Account: Moving Toward Smarter Aid* (Washington, DC: Brookings Institution, July 2005), 6.

72 Tarnoff and Nowels, *Foreign Aid* (April 15, 2004), 30. MCC was created in Title VI of the Foreign Operations, Export Financing, and Related Programs Appropriation Act, PL 108-199 (January 23, 2003), 118 Stat. 3.

73 The indices are drawn from a number of measurable performance goals designed by public, private, and international institutions, such as the World Bank, the IMF, UNESCO, Freedom House, and the World Health Organization. They include measurements of such things as fiscal policy, inflation rates, education expenditure, civil liberties, and the rule of law, among others. See Millennium Challenge Corporation, *Selection Indicators*, www.mcc.gov/selection/indicators/index.php.

74 According to Sec. 611 of the Millennium Challenge Act of 2003, PL 108-199 (January 23, 2004), as amended, the Board may suspend or terminate assistance if the CEO determines that the country is engaged in activities which are contrary to US security interests. However, the Bush administration pledged to remove US

strategic foreign policy objectives from the assistance distribution process. Tarnoff and Nowels, *Foreign Aid* (April 15, 2004), 2.

75 Between FY 2004 and FY 2006, this minimum income level varied from $1,415 to $3,465.

76 US Government Accountability Office, *Millennium Challenge Corporation: Compact Implementation Structures Are Being Established; Framework for Measuring Results Needs Improvement*, GAO-06-805 Report to the Chairman, Senate Committee on Foreign Relations (July 2006), 7–8.

77 Ibid., 2, 10–11, 19, and 21. Compacts had been signed with Armenia, Benin, Burkina Faso, Cape Verde, El Salvador, Georgia, Ghana, Honduras, Lesotho, Madagascar, Mali, Mongolia, Morocco, Mozambique, Namibia, Nicaragua, Tanzania, and Vanuatu.

78 Tarnoff and Nowels, *Foreign Aid* (April 15, 2004), 18.

79 Interview with USAID official (May 29, 2007).

80 Tarnoff and Nowels, *Foreign Aid* (April 15, 2004) and Steve Radelet, *A Note on the MCC Selection Process for 2005* (Washington, DC: Center for Global Development, September 2004), 5. Section 608 of the Millennium Challenge Act requires the MCC's CEO to provide Congressional justification for those countries that are declared eligible for MCA assistance. The statute does not require the MCC to report on its decision-making process for countries that were not selected.

81 Radelet, *A Note on the MCC Selection Process*, 5.

82 These concerns are discussed in GAO, *Millennium Challenge Corporation* (July 2006), which suggests that MCC had yet to develop essential corporate-wide plans, strategies, and time frames and was encountering problems of internal accountability and human resource management. See also Carol Lancaster, *George Bush's Foreign Aid: Transformation or Chaos?* (Washington, DC: Center for Global Development, 2008), 16–22, 48–54, and 96–102.

83 Tarnoff and Nowels, *Foreign Aid* (April 15, 2004), 3, 28.

84 Absorbing MCC was proposed by the Modernizing Foreign Assistance Network in *New Day, New Way*; and by InterAction, a foreign assistance NGO, in *Proposed Major Components and Organization of a Cabinet-Level Department for Global and Human Development*, Policy Paper (June 2008), http://interaction. org/files.cgi/6306_Cabinet-level_org_paper.pdf.

85 United States Leadership Against HIV/AIDS, Tuberculosis, and Malaria Act of 2003, PL 108-25 (May 27, 2003). The Act allocated PEPFAR funding so that 55 percent would be spent on treatment (three-quarters of that for antiretroviral pharmaceuticals), 20 percent for prevention (one-third of that for abstinence programs), 15 percent for palliative care, and 10 percent for orphans and vulnerable children. Congress authorized $48 billion for HIV/AIDS, malaria, and tuberculosis programs between FY 2009 and FY 2013, in the Tom Lantos and Henry J. Hyde United States Global Leadership Against HIV/AIDS, Tuberculosis, and Malaria Reauthorization Act of 2008, PL 110-293, which was signed into law July 30, 2008.

86 US Government Accountability Office, *Global Health: US AIDS Coordinator Addressing Some Key Challenges to Expanding Treatment, but Others Remain*, GAO-04-784 (Washington, DC: GAO, July 2004).

87 The $15 billion was initially divided into $9 billion of new funding for prevention, treatment, and care, $5 billion for ongoing bilateral programs in more than 100 countries, and $1 billion over five years for the Global Fund to Fight AIDS, Tuberculosis, and Malaria. Office of the US Global AIDS Coordinator, *The President's Emergency Plan for AIDS Relief: US Five-Year Global HIV/AIDS Strategy* (Washington, DC: February 2004), 10, 59.

88 Ibid., 12. See also State, 1 FAM 022.7:

> The US Global AIDS Coordinator oversees all US international HIV/AIDS assistance and coordinates the efforts of the various agencies and departments that deliver it ... [and] has primary responsibility for all resources and international activities of the US Government to combat the HIV/AIDS pandemic.

89 United States Leadership Against HIV/AIDS, Tuberculosis, and Malaria Act of 2003, PL 108-25, Sec. 102.f.2.A and B.

90 OGAC, *Five-Year Global HIV/AIDS Strategy*, 8.

91 OGAC has a relatively small staff drawn largely from implementing agencies, principally the Office of HIV/AIDS within the USAID Global Health Bureau, and the Global AIDS Program at the Center for Disease Control (CDC). See also OGAC, *Five-Year Global HIV/AIDS Strategy*, 58.

92 The goals for the 15 focus countries were known as the 2–7–10 goals: provide treatment to two million HIV-infected people; prevent seven million new HIV infections; and provide care to ten million people infected and affected by HIV/AIDS, including orphans and children. The focus countries are: Botswana, Cote d'Ivoire, Ethiopia, Guyana, Haiti, Kenya, Mozambique, Namibia, Nigeria, Rwanda, South Africa, Tanzania, Uganda, Vietnam, and Zambia.

93 Office of the US Global AIDS Coordinator, *Action Today, A Foundation for Tomorrow: The President's Emergency Plan for AIDS Relief*, Second Annual Report to Congress (March 2006), 169, 147. This process proved to be the pilot for the larger F process in 2006, discussed above.

94 The interagency review is partly based on a country's progress in achieving measurable goals. In conjunction with OMB, OGAC developed a series of joint indicators to measure progress toward the 2–7–10 PEPFAR goals. These indicators included areas such as treatment, care, counseling and testing, and prevention of mother-to-child transmissions. They were employed to establish budget allocations for FY 2006 and FY 2007 PEPFAR funding. Office of the US Global AIDS Coordinator, *The Power of Partnerships: The President's Emergency Plan for AIDS Relief*, Third Annual Report (March 2007), 171.

95 Ibid., 147.

96 The five-year strategy used somewhat ambiguous language to deal with the coordinator's authority to allocate funding to agency budgets: "The Coordinator will not predetermine annual funding levels agency by agency but will instead consult with the agencies and Chiefs of Mission to determine the optimal mix of US Government agency support appropriate for local conditions, capabilities, and needs." Ibid., 65. Operationally, the Coordinator's office relies on its "Government and Public Liaison" unit to develop the annual budget, and act as liaison to the budget offices of other agencies, the White House, and the Congress throughout this process.

97 Tiaji Salaam-Blyther, *US International HIV/AIDS, Tuberculosis, and Malaria Spending: FY 2004–FY 2008*, CRS Report RL33485 (Washington, DC: Congressional Research Service, March 2007). In FY 2010, this became the Global Health and Child Survival account.

98 In FY 2008, for example, PEPFAR's overall program was $5.9 billion. Of this, 69 percent was controlled directly by OGAC, 8 percent by the Department of Health and Human Services, 8 percent by USAID, 1 percent by the Department of Defense and 14 percent contributed to the Global Trust Fund by USAID and OGAC. *US President's Emergency Plan for AIDS Relief, Fiscal Year 2008: PEPFAR Operational Plan* (June 2008), www.pepfar.gov/documents/organization/107838.pdf, 10, Table 1.

99 Raymond Copson, *The Global Fund and PEPFAR in US International AIDS*

Policy, CRS Report RL33135 (Washington, DC: Congressional Research Service, November 2005), 10.

100 The deputates are: Asia; Europe, Eurasia, and the Western Hemisphere; Middle East and Africa; International Monetary and Financial Policy; International Development Finance and Debt; and Trade and Investment Policy; Technical Assistance.

101 This method was developed by the President's Commission on Budget Concepts in 1967. Section 4 of the Bretton Woods Agreement Act, PL 79-171 (July 31, 1945), authorized US participation in the IMF and the World Bank's International Bank for Reconstruction and Development. The Act also established the National Advisory Council on International Monetary and Financial Problems (chaired by the Secretary of the Treasury) to ensure that the IMF served US interests. In 1966, Executive Order 11269 established the National Advisory Council on International Monetary and Financial Policies (also chaired by the Secretary of the Treasury) and authorized the Secretary of the Treasury to instruct representatives of the United States to international organizations (e.g., the IMF, World Bank).

102 US Department of the Treasury, Office of International Affairs, *International Monetary Policy (IMF)*, www.ustreas.gov/offices/international-affairs/monetary_ financial_policy/imf_policy.shtml.

103 Jonathan Sanford and Martin Weiss, *International Monetary Fund: Organization, Functions, and Role in the International Economy*, CRS Report RL32364 (Washington, DC: Congressional Research Service, April 2004).

104 International Monetary Fund, *Fact Sheet: IMF at a Glance* (April 2009), www. imf.org/external/np/exr/facts/glance.htm.

105 Each member receives 250 basic votes and one additional vote for each SDR 100,000 of quota. The IMF Board of Governors reviews quotas every five years, but a change requires an 85 percent majority vote by the Board of Governors.

106 Treasury's justification was that a country's IMF quota is essentially a line of credit extended to the IMF. The IMF uses the line of credit when it finances loans (called "purchases") to recipient countries. Sanford and Weiss, *International Monetary Fund*, 5; and Adam Lerrick, "Funding the IMF: How Much Does It Really Cost?" *Quarterly International Economics Reports* (Carnegie Mellon Gailliot Center for Public Policy, November 2003), 2.

107 Lerrick, "Funding the IMF," 6.

108 International Monetary Fund, *IMF Members' Quotas and Voting Power, and IMF Board of Governors* (updated May 21, 2009), www.imf.org/external/np/sec/ memdir/members.htm, and Lerrick, "Funding the IMF," 3.

109 These are also sometimes referred to as "International Financial Institutions" (IFIs).

110 Jonathan Sanford, *International Financial Institutions: Funding US Participation*, CRS Report RS22134 (Washington, DC: Congressional Research Service, May 2005), 3.

111 Callable capital is not used to finance loans or pay for operating costs. The banks would need to liquidate all other resources before asking members to pay in callable capital.

112 In 2006, the IBRD provided $14 billion in loan commitments for 112 projects. US Department of the Treasury, *Treasury International Programs: Justification for Appropriations, FY 2008 Budget Request* (2007), www.treasury.gov/offices/ international-affairs/intl/fy2008/fy2008-budget.pdf, 37.

113 In 2006, IDA committed $9.5 billion to 160 operations in 66 countries in 2006. Ibid., 35.

114 US Department of the Treasury, *Treasury International Programs: Justification*

for Appropriations, FY 2009 Budget Request (2008), www.treas.gov/press/releases/reports/completefy2009cpd.pdf, 1.

115   International Finance Corporation, *2008 Annual Report* (accessed June 5, 2009), www.ifc.org/annualreport.

116   Asian Development Bank, *Statement of the ADB's Operations in 2006* (accessed May 30, 2007), www.adb.org/Documents/reports/operations/2006/default.asp. For more information on the ADB, see www.adb.org.

117   Ibid.

118   The European Bank for Reconstruction and Development, *Basic Facts: Ownership and Funding* (accessed June 5, 2009), www.ebrd.com/about/basics/members.htm.

119   Treasury, *FY 2008 Budget Request.*

120   Since the FY 1982 Foreign Operations appropriations bill, the United States has provided no funding for the "callable capital" of these institutions which has not been drawn on. The foreign assistance appropriators want to avoid creating a contingency appropriation that might not be used, but could be a target for overall budget cutting by the Congress. Sanford, *International Financial Institutions,* 3.

121   For a list of Congressional conditions on the MDB's, see Jonathan Sanford, *Multilateral Development Banks: Procedures for US Participation,* CRS Report RS20791 (Washington, DC: Congressional Research Service, January 2001), 5–6.

122   US Department of State, *FY 2008 Foreign Operations Congressional Budget Justification* (Washington, DC: February 2007), 145.

123   For details on the HIPC initiative, visit the World Bank website, www.worldbank.org.

124   Treasury, *FY 2009 Budget Request,* 23.

125   Organization for Economic Cooperation and Development, *Glossary of Statistical Terms* (accessed June 5 2009), http://stats.oecd.org/glossary.

126   As of 2008, 13 TFCA agreements have been signed in 12 countries, generating more than $163.5 million for rainforest conservation programs in Bangladesh, Belize, Botswana, Columbia, El Salvador, Guatemala, Jamaica, Panama (two agreements), Paraguay, Peru, and the Philippines. Treasury, *FY 2009 Budget Request,* 26.

127   Omnibus Appropriations Act of 1999, PL 105-277 (October 21, 1998). Technical programs in Central Europe and the former Soviet Union continue to be funded through appropriation transfers from USAID.

128   Peace Corps, *Mission,* updated September 26, 2008, www.peacecorps.gov/index.cfm?shell=learn.whatispc.mission.

129   Peace Corps, *2009 Congressional Budget Justification* (Washington, DC: 2008), 21.

130   Peace Corps, *2007 Congressional Budget Justification* (Washington, DC: 2006), 22.

131   Export–Import Bank Act of 1945, PL 79-173 (July 31, 1945), as amended.

132   Export–Import Bank of the United States (Ex–Im Bank), *Annual Report, 2006* (Washington, DC: 2007).

133   US Government Accountability Office, *Export-Import Bank: Key Factors in Considering Exim Bank Reauthorization,* Testimony of JayEtta Hecker, for the Subcommittee on International Finance, Committee of the Senate Committee on Banking, Housing, and Urban Affairs (July 17, 1997).

134   Export–Import Bank of the United States, *Mission,* www.exim.gov/about/mission.cfm.

135   It has, however, strict guidelines with respect to nuclear power plant exports. Export–Import Bank of the United States, *Nuclear Procedures and Guidelines,* www.exim.gov/products/policies/nuclear/envnucp.cfm. The Bank also has a

Transportation Security Exports Program that supports US exports of screening systems, information collection systems, containers, protection equipment, biometric technology, tagging and bar-coding systems, and computer security systems. Export–Import Bank of the United States, *Transportation Security Exports Program (T-SEP)*, www.exim.gov/products/special/tsep.cfm.

136 Exports intended for military use or for a military organization are covered by this prohibition, but not lifesaving, rescue, or medical equipment, even with a military end-user. The Bank can also support the export of small craft for border patrol, drug interdiction, or natural resource monitoring. William Becker and William M. McClenahan Jr., *The Market, the State, and the Export-Import Bank of the United States, 1934–2000* (New York: Cambridge University Press, 2003).

137 For example, Export–Import Bank of the United States, *Annual Report for 1997*, www.exim.gov/about/reports/ar/ar1997/index.cfm.

138 Overseas Private Investment Corporation, *Financing*, www.opic.gov/financing/index.asp.

139 Ibid.

140 Overseas Private Investment Corporation, *Budget Request, Fiscal Year 2009* (February 2008).

141 US Department of State, *FY 2009 International Affairs (Function 150) Budget Request: Summary and Highlights* (Washington, DC: February 2008), 8.

142 US Trade and Development Agency, *Mission Statement* (accessed June 5, 2009), www.ustda.gov/about/mission.asp.

143 US Trade and Development Agency, *About* (accessed June 5, 2009), www.ustda.gov/about/index.asp.

144 Inter-American Foundation, *Home* (accessed June 5, 2009), www.iaf.gov/index/index_en.asp.

145 Inter-American Foundation, *General Information* (accessed June 5, 2009), www.iaf.gov/about_iaf/general_information_en.asp?geninfo=1.

146 State, *FY 2009 International Affairs*, 1.

147 African Development Foundation, *About* (accessed June 5, 2009), www.adf.gov/about.html.

148 For DOD's humanitarian response capabilities, see Chapter 5.

149 OMB made such a proposal in the mid-1990s. For a discussion of the integration of the two offices, see Steven Hansch, "Humanitarian Assistance Expands in Scale and Scope," in *Security By Other Means: Foreign Assistance, Global Poverty, and American Leadership*, ed. Lael Brainard (Washington, DC: The Brookings Institution, 2007), 149–50.

150 Hansch described OFDA's role in broader US response activities as largely "information gathering, and no attendant controls or budget authorities." Ibid., 138.

151 State, *FY 2008 Foreign Operations Congressional Budget Justification*, 105.

152 State, 1 FAM 520.

153 Major recipients include the Office of the United Nations High Commissioner for Refugees (UNHCR), the International Committee of the Red Cross (ICRC), the United Nations Relief and Works Agency for Palestine Refugees in the Near East (UNRWA), the International Organization for Migration, the United Nations Children's Fund (UNICEF), and the World Food Program (WFP). MRA funding also supports initial resettlement services for a fixed number of refugees admitted to the United States. These funds are provided to US-based NGOs that handle overseas refugee process, transportation, domestic reception, and placement services.

154 State, *FY 2008 Foreign Operations Congressional Budget Justification*, 86.

155 The OECD Development Assistance Committee estimates that 26 US federal agencies provide some kind of foreign assistance, though, by the DAC definition, State, USAID, Treasury, Agriculture, and DOD account for more than 90 percent of total funding. Organization for Economic Cooperation and Development, Development Assistance Committee, *United States (2006) DAC Peer Review: Main Findings and Recommendations* (Paris: OECD, December 2006).

156 Most of this activity was DOD operations in Bosnia. GAO acknowledged that this estimate was subject to error, given the difficulty of establishing a clear definition of what constituted international activities and foreign assistance in non-150 agencies. US Government Accountability Office, *International Affairs: Activities of Domestic Agencies*, Statement of Benjamin F. Nelson, Director, International Relations and Trade Issues, National Security and International Affairs Division, to Task Force on International Affairs, Senate Budget Committee, GAO/T-NSIAD-98-174 (June 4, 1998), 1.

157 Ibid., 10.

158 The DOD was responsible for 10 percent of total disbursements, while other government agencies (including Treasury in the 150 account) administered another 26.5 percent. Nowels and Veillette, *Restructuring US Foreign Aid*, 3.

159 US Department of Commerce, *FY 2008 Budget in Brief* (2007), 1.

160 International Trade Administration, *About ITA* (accessed June 5, 2009), www.trade.gov/about.asp.

161 International Trade Administration, *Overview-2006* (accessed June 5, 2009), www.trade.gov/index.asp.

162 Office of Management and Budget, *Budget of the United States Government, Fiscal Year 2008: Appendix* (Washington, DC: GPO, 2007).

163 Commerce, *FY 2008 Budget in Brief* (2007), 63.

164 BIS also oversees US industry compliance with the Chemical Weapons Convention (CWC), which prohibits the development, production, stockpiling, and use of chemical weapons.

165 US Department of Health and Human Services, *Centers for Disease Control and Prevention Justification of Estimates for Appropriation Committees: Fiscal Year 2008* (2007), 177.

166 US Food and Drug Administration, *Office of International Programs* (accessed June 5, 2009) www.fda.gov/ICECI/Inspections/FieldManagementDirectives/ucm056272.htm.

167 John E. Fogarty International Center, FY 2009 Congressional Justification, 2006.

168 For more information, see US Environmental Protection Agency, *Bilateral and Regional Cooperation* (accessed June 5, 2009), www.epa.gov/international/about/04_oia_strategies_01_brc.htm.

169 US Environmental Protection Agency, *2008 Annual Performance Plan and Congressional Justification Appendix* (2007), 2.

170 For more information, see US Environmental Protection Agency, *Environmental Training Modules: International Catalogue* (accessed June 5, 2009), www.epa.gov/ems/resources/guides.htm.

171 For more information, see US Environmental Protection Agency, *Environmental Persistent Organic Pollutants (POPs)* (accessed June 5, 2009), www.epa.gov/oia/toxics/pop.htm.

172 US Environmental Protection Agency, *FY 2010 EPA Budget in Brief* (2009), 59.

173 US Department of Education, *Fiscal Year 2009 Budget Summary and Background Information* (2008), 65.

174 Ibid.

175 Charles Hanrahan, *Agricultural Export and Food Aid Programs*, Issue Brief IB98006 (Washington, DC: Congressional Research Service, January 2006), 1.

176 US Department of Agriculture, *FY 2009 Budget Summary and Annual Perform-ance Plan* (2008), 15.
177 Ibid., 18.
178 US Trade Representative, *History of the United States Trade Representative* (accessed May 8, 2007), www.ustr.gov/Who_We_Are/History_of_the_United_States_Trade_Representative.html.

4 Political and Security Assistance Budgeting and Programs

1 This figure includes Economic Support Funds (ESF), Assistance for Eastern Europe and Central Asia (AEECA), International Narcotics and Law Enforcement (INCLE), and Nonproliferation, Antiterrorism, Demining and Related Activities (NADR). Total funding for these accounts in the FY 2010 budget request was $14.9 billion. US Department of State, *FY 2010 International Affairs (Function 150) Budget Request, Summary and Highlights* (Washington, DC: 2009).
2 This figure includes Foreign Military Financing (FMF), International Military Education and Training (IMET), and Peacekeeping Operations (PKO). Total security assistance funding request in the FY 2010 budget for these accounts was $5.7 billion, while total US foreign assistance in the Function 150 account was $40.3 billion. Ibid.
3 Congress plays an important role in the allocation of ESF funding, frequently ear-marking allocations to specific countries or insisting that State do so. Many at State assert that the Department does not have adequate flexibility to allocate these funds. Interviews with former State Department officials.
4 For a detailed history of economic and security support programs, see Duncan L. Clarke *et al.*, *Send Guns and Money: Security Assistance and US Foreign Policy* (Westport, CT: Praeger, 1997).
5 From FY 1975 to FY 1981, Israel and Egypt received approximately $10 billion in support assistance, or 75 percent of all ESF grants. Ibid., 17.
6 The International Security Assistance Act of 1978, PL 95-384 (September 26, 1978), amended the Foreign Assistance Act of 1961, PL 87-195 (September 4, 1961), in Section 531(a). This amendment renamed the "Security Supporting Assistance" program. Committee on Foreign Relations/Committee on Interna-tional Relations, *Legislation on Foreign Relations through 2005*, Joint Committee Print, Vol. 1-A (Washington, DC: GPO, January 2006), 280, Note 782. The USAID white paper also notes that ESF recipients do not have to meet develop-ment criteria. USAID, *US Foreign Aid: Meeting the Challenges of the Twenty-First Century* (Washington, DC: 2004), www.usaid.gov/policy/pdabz3221.pdf, 30. There is disagreement in the development community about the extent to which ESF funding is linked to economic development goals. See, for example, Samuel Bazzi *et al.*, *Billions for War, Pennies for the Poor: Moving the President's FY 2008 Budget from Hard Power to Smart Power* (Washington, DC: Center for Global Development, 2007).
7 US Government Accountability Office, *Foreign Aid: Improving the Impact and Control of Economic Support Funds*, GAO-NSIAD-88-182 (Washington, DC: GAO, June 1988), 8.
8 US Department of State and USAID, *US Foreign Assistance Reference Guide*, Pub-lication 11202 (Washington, DC: State, January 2005), 6. As part of this shift in focus, an agreement was reached in 1998 to reduce ESF funding for Egypt and Israel. By FY 2008, Egyptian ESF had declined from a peak of $815 billion to $415 billion, and Israel's ESF funding had ended. For Israel, this reduction was com-

pensated, in part, by an increase in security assistance through the Foreign Military Financing Program, discussed below. For a discussion of the Egypt/Israel focus for US economic and security assistance funds through the 1980s and 1990s, see Clarke *et al.*, *Send Guns and Money*, 169–87. See also Patrick Cronin and Tarek Ghani, "The Changing Complexion of Security and Strategic Assistance in the Twenty-First Century," in *Security By Other Means: Foreign Assistance, Global Poverty, and American Leadership*, ed. Lael Brainard (Washington, DC: The Brookings Institution, 2007), 197.

9   The only other countries receiving funds in excess of $100 million were Sudan ($296 million), where a major civil war was ending but significant strife and genocide were taking place, and Colombia ($200 million), to support economic, governance, and counternarcotics/counterinsurgency efforts. US Department of State, *FY 2010 Foreign Operations Congressional Budget Justification* (Washington, DC: May 2009), 39–41.

10   State and USAID, *US Foreign Assistance Reference Guide*, 6.

11   GAO, *Foreign Aid: Improving the Impact*, 10.

12   See also the discussion of the National Endowment for Democracy in Chapter 2.

13   US Department of State, *DRL Programs, Including Human Rights Democracy Fund*, www.state.gov/g/drl/p (accessed May 27, 2009).

14   US Department of State, *Bureau of Democracy, Human Rights and Labor*, http://2001-2009.state.gov/g/drl/rls/57669.htm (accessed May 27, 2009).

15   US Department of State, *Middle East Partnership Initiative: Mission and Goals*, www.mepi.state.gov/mission/index.htm (accessed May 21, 2009). See also, Jeremy M. Sharp, *The Middle East Partnership Initiative: An Overview*, CRS Report RS21457 (Washington, DC: Congressional Research Service, July 20, 2005), 2.

16   US Department of State, *Middle East Partnership Initiative*, www.mepi.state.gov.

17   In addition to State programs, USAID also supports democracy promotion through its Democracy, Conflict, and Humanitarian Assistance (DCHA) pillar. DCHA uses funds for Development Assistance and its Office of Transition Initiatives to "promote effective and democratic governance in fragile democracies and weak states." The FY 2009 USAID resources for these programs came to $76.5 million. US Department of State, *FY 2009 Foreign Operations Congressional Budget Justification* (Washington, DC: February 2008), 157.

18   Over time, the SEED program has provided assistance to Albania, Bosnia-Herzogovina, Bulgaria, the Czech Republic, Hungary, Kosovo, Macedonia, Montenegro, Poland, Romania, Serbia, Slovakia, and Slovenia. FSA has supported Armenia, Azerbaijan, Belarus, Estonia, Georgia, Kazakhstan, Kyrgyzstan, Latvia, Lithuania, Moldova, Russia, Tajikistan, Turkmenistan, Ukraine, and Uzbekistan.

19   SEED accounted for $7.5 billion; FSA for $9.4 billion.

20   State and USAID, *US Foreign Assistance Reference Guide*, 13.

21   State, *FY 2009 Foreign Operations Congressional Budget Justification*.

22   Ibid., 442 and 473.

23   The State Department has argued that this assistance is important for helping these countries "advance along the path toward becoming stable, pluralistic, and prosperous countries that can assist the United States in combating transnational threats." US Department of State, *FY 2008 Foreign Operations Congressional Budget Justification* (Washington, DC: February 2007), 27.

24   State and USAID, *US Foreign Assistance Reference Guide*, 11. The restrictions target Russia. See also State, *FY 2009 Foreign Operations Congressional Budget Justification*, 410–70.

25   State, *FY 2009 Foreign Operations Congressional Budget Justification*, 410–70. Reflecting the complexity of US foreign assistance, SEED and FSA do not account for all US assistance to these regions. For FY 2005, for example, 16 federal

departments and agencies obligated $636.98 million to the 15 SEED countries, only $357.94 million of which was funded through the SEED account. For the FSA region, 22 departments and agencies obligated $1.93 billion in assistance to 12 countries, less than half of which—$641.52 million—was through FSA funding. Cover letters from EUR/ACE Coordinator Thomas C. Adams in US Department of State, *US Government Assistance to Eastern Europe under the Support for Eastern European Democracy Act* (Washington, DC: January 2009), and *US Government Assistance to and Cooperative Activities with Eurasia* (Washington, DC: January 2009).

26 The Coordinator oversees "the bilateral economic, security, democracy, and humanitarian assistance of all US Government agencies providing assistance to the 27 states of the former Soviet Union and Eastern Europe." US Department of State, *US Assistance to Europe and Eurasia*. Other agencies providing such assistance have included USAID, Defense, Treasury, Energy, Commerce, Environmental Protection, Health and Human Services, and Justice.

27 Foreign Assistance Act of 1961, Section 481(a)(1) and (b)(1).

28 Other government agencies are also significantly involved in international and border-related counternarcotic and law enforcement programs, notably the Department of Justice, Federal Bureau of Investigation, Drug Enforcement Administration, Department of Defense and Department of Homeland Security.

29 Foreign Assistance Act of 1961, Section 481(1)(A–G).

30 Ronald Reagan, *Narcotics and National Security*, National Security Decision Directive 221 (April 8, 1986). This directive also expanded the missions and responsibilities of the departments of Defense, Treasury, Justice, and the Central Intelligence Agency for counternarcotics activities.

31 For a discussion of overall counternarcotics strategy, see US Department of State, Bureau of International Narcotics and Law Enforcement (INL), *2009 International Narcotics Control Strategy Report, Vol. 1: Drug and Chemical Control* and *Vol. 2: Money Laundering and Financial Crimes* (Washington, DC: February 27, 2009), www.state.gov/p/inl/rls/nrcrpt/2009/index.htm; and US Department of State, INL, *FY 2007 Budget: Congressional Justification* (Washington, DC: 2006), 3, www.state.gov/documents/organization/71984.pdf.

32 State, *FY 2009 Foreign Operations Congressional Budget Justification*, 53.

33 Through INL, the State Department also operates an air wing of nearly 200 fixed and rotary wing aircraft used for observation, transportation, and crop eradication. The wing has operated both in Latin America and in South Asia. Executive Office of the President, Office of National Drug Control Policy (ONDCP), *National Drug Control Strategy: FY 2008 Budget Summary* (February 2007), 122; State, *FY 2008 International Affairs: Summary and Highlights*, 35–6; and State, INL, *FY 2007 Budget: Congressional Justification*, 12, 16.

34 United Nations, Office on Drugs and Crime, *2006 World Drug Report* (New York: United Nations Publications, 2006).

35 In Iraq, the INCLE account funded police training and advisors for police, justice, and prison programs. Funding came to roughly $500 million from FY 2006–08. State, *FY 2008 International Affairs: Summary and Highlights*, 107.

36 State, *FY 2009 Foreign Operations Congressional Budget Justification*, 53.

37 Nina M. Serafino, *Colombia: Summary and Tables on US Assistance, FY 1989–FY 2004*, CRS Report RS21213 (Washington, DC: Congressional Research Service, May 19, 2003).

38 Since the program's inception, ACI/ACP funds administered by USAID have financed over 1,000 infrastructure projects and helped an estimated 64,000 families receive financial assistance. State, *FY 2008 Foreign Operations Congressional Budget Justification*, 97.

39 Connie Veillette, *Andean Counterdrug Initiative (ACI) and Related Funding Programs: FY2006 Assistance*, CRS Report RL33253 (Washington, DC: Congressional Research Service, January 27, 2006), 2, figures updated for FY 2008–09; the Consolidated Appropriations Act of 2008, PL 110-161 (December 26, 2007); and the Omnibus Appropriations Act, PL 111-8 (March 11, 2009). There are limitations and earmarks on ACI/ACP funding, including a ceiling on administrative expenses, an earmark for alternative development, and limitations with respect to violations of human rights in Colombia and Bolivia. State and USAID, *Foreign Assistance Reference Guide*, 44.

40 State, INL, *FY 2007 Budget: Congressional Justification*, 4, 11.

41 Ibid., 6.

42 Only once has ONDCP actually threatened to withhold certification of an agency budget because it was seen as inadequate, in this case the FY 1997 Defense Department program. Funds were added to that budget as a result of negotiations between the White House and DOD. The authority has not been used since. For ONDCP's responsibilities and budget role, see Executive Office of the President, ONDCP, *National Drug Control Strategy: FY 2008 Budget Summary*.

43 State, INL, *FY 2008 Budget: Congressional Justification*, 6.

44 US Government Accountability Office, *Department of State: Nonproliferation, Anti-terrorism, Demining, and Related Programs (NADR) Follow Legal Authority, but Some Activities Need Reassessment*, GAO-04-521 (Washington, DC: GAO, April 2004), 4.

45 A small amount of funding supports small/light arms destruction programs.

46 US Department of State, *About Us*, www.state.gov/s/ct/about (accessed May 27, 2009).

47 US Department of State, *Our Mission*, www.state.gov/s/ct/about/c16570.htm (accessed May 27, 2009).

48 US Department of State, *1 Foreign Affairs Manual* (October 2, 2008), Section 022.5.

49 Foreign Assistance Act of 1961, Section 571.

50 GAO, NADR Report, above, 36.

51 ATA funds have provided such support in Afghanistan, Iraq, Sudan, Pakistan, Indonesia, the Philippines, and Columbia, among other countries.

52 US Department of State, *Helping Other Nations Fight Terrorism*, http://www.state.gov/m/ds/about/overview/c9007.htm (accessed May 21, 2009), and State, *FY 2008 Foreign Operations Congressional Budget Justification*, 88.

53 Foreign Assistance Act of 1961, Sections 571–2; the restrictions referred to are in Sections 502B and 620A. Section 620 contains a longer list of restrictions that are waived for ATA funds. The Assistant Secretary of State for Democracy, Human Rights, and Labor must be consulted in determining country eligibility.

54 Foreign Assistance Act of 1961, Section 573 (a-c) and GAO, *Department of State: NADR*, 36.

55 Foreign Assistance Act of 1961, Sections 581 and 582.

56 Like ATA funding, nonproliferation funds are free of many Foreign Assistance Act restrictions, except for countries violating human rights or supporting terrorism.

57 Freedom Support Act, PL 102-511 (October 24, 1992), Section 504.

58 GAO, *Department of State: NADR*, 9.

59 The projects are approved by a Review Panel composed of State, DOD, DHS, Energy, OMB, NSC, and CIA representatives, with input from the regional bureaus, Justice and Treasury.

60 US Department of State, *Nonproliferation and Disarmament Fund*, http://www.state.gov/t/isn/ndf (accessed May 27, 2009). For the Kazakhstan case, see William

C. Potter, "The Changing Nuclear Threat: The Sapphire File," *Transition* (November 17, 1995), and John A. Tirpak, "Project Sapphire," *Air Force* (August 1995).

61 US Department of State, *Nonproliferation of WMD Expertise*, www.state.gov/t/isn/c12265.htm, *The US Bio-Chem Redirect Program*, http://biistate.net/chemconference/about.html, and *BioIndustry Initiative*, www.nti.org/e_research/official_docs/dos/dos091603_bioinit.pdf (accessed May 21, 2009). The FY 2008 budget for GTRP was $53.5 million. GAO, *Department of State: NADR*. Voluntary IAEA contributions can be as much as $30 million, over and above the US assessed contribution of roughly $58 million. CCTB contributions are generally $18 million. The United States has not ratified the CCTB treaty.

62 Federation of American Scientists, *Man-Portable Air Defense System (MAN-PADS) Proliferation*, Issue Brief No. 1 (January 2004), www.fas.org/programs/ssp/asmp/MANPADS.html, and "Interview With Assistant Secretary of State John Hillen," *Defense News* (October 9, 2006).

63 US Department of State, *Bureau of Political-Military Affairs*, www.state.gov/t/pm (accessed May 27, 2007).

64 GAO, *Department of State: NADR*, 48.

65 US Department of State, *Post-Conflict Reconstruction: Essential Tasks* (Washington, DC: State, April 2005).

66 Interviews with executive branch officials.

67 Interviews with executive branch officials.

68 For the first three years, the S/CRS staff numbered roughly 50 people, many of them from other agencies. Its operating and personnel budget rose from $12.8 million in fiscal year (FY) 2005 to $20 million in FY 2007.

69 Section 1207 of the National Defense Authorization Act of FY 2006 makes $100 million in DOD funds available for each of two years, for transfer to State for "immediate reconstruction, security, or stabilization assistance to a foreign country." This authority was extended through FY 2011.

70 Defense Institute of Security Assistance Management, *DISAM's Online Green Book* (November 2007), Appendix 2, www.disam.dsca.mil/pubs/DR/greenbook.htm.

71 For a detailed discussion of the history and organization of security assistance programs, see Clarke *et al.*, *Send Guns and Money*, Chapter 1.

72 Cronin and Ghani, "The Changing Complexion of Security," 195–224.

73 Clarke *et al.*, *Send Guns and Money*, Chapter 1. The MAP concept was reauthorized in the Foreign Assistance Act of 1961:

> The President is authorized to furnish military assistance, on such terms and conditions as he may determine, to any friendly country or international organization, the assisting of which the President finds will strengthen the security of the United States and promote world peace and which is otherwise eligible to receive such assistance by ... acquiring from any source and providing (by loan or grant) any defense article or defense service.
>
> Foreign Assistance Act of 1961, Part II, Chapter 2, Section 503.

74 Clarke *et al.*, *Send Guns and Money*, 15–16.

75 Defense Security Cooperation Agency, *Foreign Military Sales, Foreign Military Construction Sales, and Military Assistance Facts as of September 30, 2005* (September 2005), USAID, *Overseas Loans and Grants* (USAID Greenbook); and State, *FY 2009 Foreign Operations Congressional Budget Justification*.

76 State, *FY 2009 Foreign Operations Congressional Budget Justification*, 816–20.

77   Under the direction of the President, the Secretary of State shall be responsible for the continuous supervision and general direction of economic assist-

ance, military assistance, and military education and training programs, including but not limited to determining whether there shall be a military assistance (including civic action) or a military education and training program for a country and the value thereof, to the end that such programs are effectively integrated both at home and abroad and the foreign policy of the US is best served thereby.

> Foreign Assistance Act of 1961, Section 622(c).

The AECA makes this primacy explicit with respect to arms sales and exports. The Secretary of State is responsible for

> the continuous supervision and general direction of sales, leases, financing, cooperative projects, and exports under the AECA, including, but not limited to, determining—1) whether there will be a sale to or financing for a country and the amount thereof; 2) whether there will be a lease to a country; 3) whether there will be a delivery or other performance under the sale, lease, cooperative project, or export, to the end that sales, financing, leases, cooperative projects, and exports will be integrated with other US activities and to the end that the foreign policy of the US would best served thereby.
>
> Arms Export Control Act of 1976 (PL 90-629) (October 22, 1968), Chapter 1, Section 2.

DOD's Defense Security Cooperation Agency (DSCA) reiterates State's primacy: "The Secretary of State provides continuous supervision and general direction for SA [Security Assistance], including determining what programs a given country will have, as well as their scope and content." DSCA, "What Is Security Cooperation?" *Frequently Asked Questions*, www.dsca.osd.mil/PressReleases/faq.htm#What%20is%A0Security%20Cooperation.

78 The American Academy of Diplomacy and Henry L. Stimson Center 2008 study proposed adding significantly to PM personnel to enhance State's capabilities for planning and managing security assistance programs. *A Foreign Affairs Budget for the Future* (Washington, DC: October 2008), 50.

79 Defense Security Cooperation Agency, *Security Assistance Management Manual*, www.dsca.mil/samm.

80 Department of Defense, Defense Security Cooperation Agency, "Defense Security Cooperation Agency Strategic Plan: 2006–2011," February 13, 2006.

81 Foreign Assistance Act, Section 623.

82 That part of the FMF program that involves acquiring the military equipment, providing training, or supplying personnel for the programs is the responsibility of the military services, each of which maintains a security assistance office.

83 Defense Institute of Security Assistance Management, "Security Assistance Organization (SAO) Responsibilities," Briefing at www.disam.dsca.mil/Research/Presentations/dl_presentations.htm. See also, DISAM, *Online Green Book*, Chapter 4.

84 COCOMS operate on a regional basis *and* have extensive relationships with national militaries in the region. See Dana Priest, *The Mission: Waging War and Keeping Peace with America's Military* (New York: W.W. Norton, 2003).

85 See Government Accountability Office, *Security Assistance: State and DOD Need to Assess How the Foreign Military Financing Program for Egypt Achieves US Foreign Policy and Security Goals*, GAO-06-437, April 2006, Appendix III, 28.

86 The FMS program was first authorized under the Foreign Military Sales Act of 1968 (PL 90-629) and again in the Arms Export Control Act of 1976, Sections 21–3. Countries may be obligated to use the US government as the agent or, because they have limited experience of US contracting, prefer to have DOD act as the agent

dealing with the manufacturer. They may also be seeking a close relationship with the US military, so prefer to work through military procurement offices. Department of Defense, Defense Institute of Security Assistance Management, "Appendix 6: A Comparison of Direct Commercial Sales and Foreign Military Sales for the Acquisition of US Defense Articles and Services," *The Management of Security Assistance*, 17th ed. (Wright-Patterson AFB, OH: May 1997).

87 Source: DSCA, "Historical Facts Book," as of September 30, 2007.

88 Congressional notification is required if the sale is more than $14 million for major defense equipment, $50 million for the value of the full case, or $200 million for design and construction services. These ceilings are higher ($25 million, $100 million, and $300 million) if a NATO member, Japan, Australia, or New Zealand is the buyer. DSCA is responsible for drawing up an annual Congressional notification of all arms sales or transfers it anticipates taking place in the next year, the "Javits report." This report forecasts all FMS transfers, direct commercial sales, or excess defense articles (see below) worth more than $7 million for equipment or $25 million for military support or services. Arms Export Control Act of 1976, Section 25.

89 Direct Commercial Sales (DCS) do not have a budgetary impact. However, they do require an export license from the US government. Both State (Office of Defense Trade Controls) and DOD (National Disclosure Process) have a role in granting such licenses. See John J. Hamre *et al.*, *Technology and Security in the Twenty-first Century: US Military Export Control Reform* (Washington, DC: Center for Strategic and International Studies, May 2001).

90 Initially this program was conducted using MAP funding; since 1975 it has been administered through IMET. Clarke *et al.*, *Send Guns and Money*, 20–1.

91 US Department of State, *FY 2007 Foreign Operations Congressional Budget Justification* (Washington, DC: 2006), 211, and Foreign Assistance Act of 1961, Chapter 5, Section 441, for the "Extended IMET Program" (E-IMET).

92 See, for example, Center for International Policy, "IMET: International Military Education and Training" (Washington, DC: May 31, 2007), at www.ciponline.org/facts/imet.htm.

93 On a regional basis, central Europe and Eurasia received over one-quarter of IMET funds in FY 2009, followed by the Near East (18 percent), Africa (15 percent), Western Hemisphere (14 percent), South and Central Asia (11 percent), and East Asia (9 percent). IMET funds are available for one year. State/USAID, *US Foreign Assistance Reference Guide*, 34.

94 US assessments for peacekeeping operations conducted under a UN Security Council resolution are funded through the Contributions to International Peacekeeping Activities (CIPA) account.

95 This authority was contained in the International Security Assistance Act of 1978, Section 12(a), which created Title 6, "Peacekeeping Operations," of the Foreign Assistance Act of 1961.

96 State and USAID, *US Foreign Assistance Reference Guide*, 35.

97 State, *FY 2009 Foreign Operations Congressional Budget Justification*, 103.

98 US Department of State, *FY 2008 International Affairs (Function 150) Budget Request: Summary and Highlights* (Washington, DC: February 2007), 40, and Mark Wong, *Counterterrorism Assistance Issues and Approaches*, working paper for CSIS Task Force on Non-Traditional Security Assistance (May 2005 draft), 5.

99 US Department of State, *Global Peace Operations Initiative Team*, http://www.state.gov/t/pm/ppa/gpoiteam (Accessed May 27, 2009). The following discussion is based on Nina Serafino, *The Global Peacekeeping Operations Initiative*, CRS Report RL32773 (Washington, DC: Congressional Research Service, February 8, 2006), and interviews with former State Department officials.

100 PKO can fund police training through GPOI because Congress agreed to waive Section 660 of the Foreign Assistance Act of 1961, which prohibits US foreign assistance to police, prisons, or laws enforcement forces. Serafino, *Global Peace-keeping Operations*, 6. See also, US Department of State, *GPOI Program Management and History*, http://www.state.gov/t/pm/gpoiteam/gpoi/c20197.htm, and *Objectives and Activities*, www.state.gov/t/pm/ppa/gpoiteam/c20337.htm (accessed May 27, 2009).

101 In addition, under Section 610(a) of the Foreign Assistance Act of 1961, $15 million a year in FMF funds can be transferred to PKO, and under Section 552(c), up to $25 million a year can be drawn down from any agency's commodities and services for PKO programs.

102 Clarke *et al.*, *Send Guns and Money*, 24, and US Department of State, *FY 2001–2008 Foreign Operations Congressional Budget Justifications.*

103 No more than $75 million of this may come from DOD and not more than $75 million may be provided for counternarcotics programs.

104 Interviews with former State Department and Congressional staff, and Defense Security Cooperation Agency, *Security Assistance Management Manual* (October 3, 2003), Chapter 11, "Drawdowns," www.dsca.mil/samm, 479.

105 For a discussion of this problem, see American Academy of Diplomacy and Henry L. Stimson Center, *A Foreign Affairs Budget*. In the area of counterterrorism, a Senate study warned that

> the current budgets of the civilian foreign affairs agencies do not reflect their key role in the conduct of the war against terror. In fact, it can be argued that the disparity in the ratio between investments in military versus civilian approaches threatens US success.

Senate Committee on Foreign Relations, *Embassies As Command Posts in the Anti-Terror Campaign: A Report to Members of the Committee on Foreign Relations*, United States Senate, 109th Congress, 2nd Session, Senate Print 109-52 (Washington, DC: GPO, December 15, 2006), 3.

106 On US overseas basing, see Jon D. Klaus, *US Military Overseas Basing: Background and Oversight Issues for Congress*, CRS Report RS21975 (Washington, DC: Congressional Research Service, November 17, 2004). On the role of the regional combatant commanders, see Dana Priest, *The Mission*.

107 For additional discussion of the new DOD portfolio, see Cindy Williams and Gordon Adams, *Strengthening Statecraft and Security: Reforming US Planning and Resource Allocation* (Cambridge, MA: MIT Security Studies Program Occasional Paper, June 2008), Chapter 4, 57–79; Center for Strategic and International Studies, *Integrating 21st Century Development and Security Assistance*, Final Report of the Task Force on Non-Traditional Security Assistance (Washington, DC: CSIS, January 2008); and American Academy of Diplomacy and Henry L. Stimson Center, *A Foreign Affairs Budget*.

108 Eric Edelman, *Testimony Before the House Armed Services Committee on Train and Equip Authority* (April 7, 2006), www.dod.mil/dodgc/olc/testimony_old/109_second.html. Doug Sample, "Wolfowitz Seeks Flexibility in Security Assistance Spending," *American Forces Press Service* (April 29, 2004), www.defenselink.mil/news/newsarticle.aspx?id=26784; and author interviews with DOD and State Department officials. According to DOD's 2006 Quadrennial Defense Review,

> existing authorities governing planning, financing and use of these instruments for shaping international partnerships do not accommodate the dynamic foreign policy demands of the twenty-first century. Based on recent

operational experience, the Department seeks a continuum of authorities from Congress balancing the need to act quickly in the war on terrorism with the need to integrate military power to meet long-term enduring foreign policy objectives.

US Department of Defense, *Quadrennial Defense Review* (Washington, DC: DOD, February 2006), 87–91.

109 US Department of Defense, *Defense Security Cooperation Agency Strategic Plan: 2006–2011* (February 13, 2006). The full DOD legislative proposal, *Building Partnership Capacity*, can be found at www.dod.mil/dodgc/olc/proposals_old/index. html. See also, US Department of Defense, *Building Partnership Capacity: QDR Execution Roadmap* (May 22, 2006), www.ndu.edu/itea/storage/790/BPC%20 Roadmap.pdf.

110 Office of Management and Budget, *FY 2004 Emergency Supplemental Request* (September 17, 2003), www.whitehouse.gov/omb/budget/amendments/supplemental_9_17_03.pdf.

111 Pat Towell *et al.*, *Defense: FY 2008 Authorization and Appropriations*, CRS Report RL33999 (Washington, DC: Congressional Research Service, July 2007), 29–30; Consolidated Appropriations Act of 2008, PL 110-161, Division L—Defense Supplemental Appropriations; US Government Accountability Office, *Securing, Stabilizing, and Reconstructing Afghanistan: Key Issues for Congressional Oversight*, GAO-07-801SP (Washington, DC: GAO, May 2007), 13.

112 US Department of State, Bureau of Political-Military Affairs, *Report to the Congress: Section 1206(f) of the 2006 National Defense Authorization Act* (July 3, 2007), www.fas.org/asmp/resources/110th/1206report.htm. The 1206 program is further restricted from providing police training or assistance to countries that would otherwise be prohibited by law from receiving US assistance.

113 According to the GAO report, for FY 2006 projects, coordination occurred in only five of 14 instances before proposals were submitted for joint DOD and State review. US Government Accountability Office, *Section 1206 Security Assistance Program—Findings on Criteria, Coordination, and Implementation*, GAO-07-416 (Washington, DC: GAO, February 28, 2007), 3. The Senate Committee on Foreign Relations staff report also found that Section 1206 regional programs initiated by the combatant commands did not receive the same level of embassy input as bilateral programs. Senate Committee on Foreign Relations, *Embassies as Command Posts*, 12.

114 According to DOD data, the Section 1206 program provided $454 million in T&E support for Indonesia, Sri Lanka, Malaysia, and the Philippines in Asia; Macedonia, Albania, Georgia, Ukraine, and Azerbaijan in Europe; Pakistan, Yemen, Lebanon, Bahrain, and Kazakhstan in South and Central Asia; Nigeria, Chad, Djibouti, Mauritania, Tunisia, Kenya, and other unnamed nations in Africa; as well as various Latin American and Caribbean nations, including Mexico. US Department of Defense, *Section 1206 Global Train and Equip Projects Summary, FY06 through FY08*, supplied to the Bipartisan Policy Council, March 2008. In late FY 2008, DOD announced an additional set of projects totaling $98 million, in 19 countries, including Mexico, Pakistan, Belize, Honduras, Guyana, Surinam, Albania, Malaysia, Kyrgyzstan, Benin, Cameroon, Cape Verde, Gabon, Ghana, São Tomé and Príncipe, Togo, Guinea, and Sierra Leone. Sebastian Sprenger, "Final FY-08 'Section 1206' Aid Packages Target Pakistan and Mexico," *Inside the Pentagon* (September 25, 2008).

115 Although DOD has sought a $750 million ceiling for the program, Congress authorized first $200 million, then $300 million and, in the FY 2009 authorization bill, $350 million over two years. The program received a direct appropria-

tion in the Consolidated Appropriations Act of 2008, PL 110-161. The Senate report on the FY 2008 budget request for Section 1206 noted that it had reluctantly agreed to fund the program through DOD, but that "the Department of State normally is tasked to perform this critical function … the Committee believes the responsibility to train and equip foreign military forces should rest with the Department of State." Senate Committee on Appropriations, *Department of Defense Appropriations Act, 2008*, Senate Report 110-155 (Washington, DC: GPO, September 14, 2007).

116 Department of Defense and Emergency Supplemental Appropriations for Recovery from and Response to Terrorist Attacks on the US Act, PL 107-117 (January 10, 2002), 200.

117 2002 Supplemental Appropriations Act for Further Recovery from and Response to Terrorist Attacks on the US, PL 107-206 (August 2002).

118 Recipients have included Georgia, the Kyrgyz Republic, Lithuania, Mongolia, Poland, Romania, Ukraine, and Uzbekistan. US Department of Defense, *FY 2008 Global War on Terror Request* (February 2007), 52.

119 Alan K. Kronstadt, *Pakistan-US Relations*, CRS Report RL33498 (Washington, DC: Congressional Research Service, January 11, 2008, data updated March 5, 2008). This CRS report describes nearly $10.7 billion in total US assistance to Pakistan between FY 2001 and the FY 2009 budget request, virtually all of which qualifies as "security assistance." ESF funding totaled $2.3 billion, while FMF came to over $1.5 billion. See also, Craig Cohen and Derek Chollet, "When $10 Billion Is Not Enough: Rethinking US Strategy Toward Pakistan," *The Washington Quarterly*, Vol. 30, Issue 2 (Spring 2007), 12; Craig Cohen, *A Perilous Course: US Strategy and Assistance to Pakistan* (Washington, DC: Center for Strategic and International Studies, August 2007); and Karen DeYoung, "Congress Moves to Set Terms for Pakistan Aid," *The Washington Post* (April 9, 2009).

120 CTFP follows IMET program development timelines and uses IMET rates for training course costing. US Department of Defense, Defense Security Cooperation Agency, Defense Institute for Security Assistance Management, *Implementation Guidance for Regional Defense Counterterrorism Fellowship Program Interim Guidance Memorandum No. 3* (May 2005), www.defenselink.mil/policy/sections/policy_offices/gsa/ctfp/sections/enclosures/pdf/may_1_06_final_guidance_message_3.pdf.

121 "AFRICOM has responsibility for the military's Combined Joint Task Force Horn of Africa (CJTF-HOA), the Trans-Sahara Counterterrorism Partnership (TSCTP), and the East Africa Counterterrorism Initiative (EACTI)." Theresa Whelan, DASD for African Affairs, DOD, quoted in John Kruzel, "Pentagon Official Describes AFRICOM's Mission, Dispels Misconceptions," *American Forces Press Service* (August 3, 2007) www.defenselink.mil/news/newsarticle.aspx?id=46931&446931=20070803.

122 The AFRICOM model has also been adopted by the military's regional command for Latin America and the Caribbean—SOUTHCOM—which also has a civilian deputy to the Commander. US Southern Command (SOUTHCOM) has expanded its staffing to include State and USAID officials. SOUTHCOM Commander Admiral James Stavrides described the goal of this expansion as follows: "We want to be like a big Velcro cube that these other agencies can hook to so we can collectively do what needs to be done in this region." Remarks to Smart Power Lecture Series, Center for Strategic and International Studies (January 16, 2008).

123 For details, see Stewart Patrick and Kaysie Brown, *The Pentagon and Global Development: Making Sense of the DOD's Expanding Role*, Working Paper 131 (Washington, DC: Center for Global Development, November 12, 2000), and

Lauren Ploch, *Africa Command: US Strategic Interests in Africa and the Role of the US Military in Africa*, CRS Report RL34003 (Washington, DC: Congressional Research Service, December 12, 2007). AFRICOM has not been universally welcomed in Africa. Its search for an African headquarters was rejected or set aside by all African countries the command visited except Liberia. According to one US military officer, "it was seen as a massive intrusion of military might onto a continent that was quite proud of having removed foreign powers from its soil." Karen DeYoung, "US Africa Command Trims Its Aspirations," *The Washington Post* (June 1, 2008).

124   For a detailed discussion of the origins of CERP, see Mark Martins, "No Small Change of Soldiering: The Commander's Emergency Response Program in Iraq and Afghanistan—CERP," *Army Lawyer* (February 2004), 1–20. CERP was expanded to the Philippines in the FY 2008 Supplemental Appropriations Act, PL 110-252 (June 30, 2008).

125   CERP was initially authorized by a June 2003 memo from CPA administrator Ambassador L. Paul Bremer. Fragmentary Order 89 of the Commander of the Combined Joint Task Force 7 implemented the CERP on June 19, 2003.

126   CERP has been significantly more agile and flexible than the formal economic assistance programs created in Iraq as part of the Iraq Relief and Reconstruction Fund (IRRF). Special Inspector General for Iraq Reconstruction (SIGIR), *Iraq Reconstruction: Lessons in Contracting and Procurement* (July 2006), 84, www.sigir.mil/reports/pdf/Lessons_Learned_July21.pdf.

127   Mark Martins, "The Commander's Emergency Response Program," *Joint Force Quarterly*, Issue 37 (2005), 47.

128   House Armed Services Committee, *Agency Stovepipes versus Strategic Agility: Lessons We Need to Learn from Provincial Reconstruction Teams in Iraq and Afghanistan*, Staff Report, Subcommittee on Oversight and Investigations (Washington, DC: GPO, April 2008).

129   The SIGIR expressed concern about the absence of an institutionalized process to coordinate State and USAID projects with the CERP program in Iraq. Special Inspector General for Iraq Reconstruction (SIGIR), *Management of the Commander's Emergency Response Program (CERP) for FY 2005*, SIGIR-05-025 (January 23, 2006).

130   The 2007 State Department report on the Section 1206 program requested that CERP authority be made permanent and global, though it also proposed that State and DOD jointly develop procedures to use the authority. US Department of State, Bureau of Political-Military Affairs, *Report to Congress: Section 1206(f) of the 2006 National Defense Authorization Act* (July 3, 2007).

131   The legal attaché budget was $79 million in FY 2008. Federal Bureau of Investigation, *FY 2008 Authorization and Budget Request to Congress* (Washington, DC, February 2007).

132   Federal Bureau of Investigation, *National Security Branch*, www.fbi.gov/hq/nsb/nsb.htm, and *Counterterrorism*, www.fbi.gov/terrorinfo/counterrorism/waronterrorhome.htm (accessed June 1, 2009). In addition, the National Central Bureau (USNCB), co-managed by DOJ and DHS, coordinates US involvement in the International Criminal Police Organization (INTERPOL). INTERPOL facilitates international police cooperation with respect to international crime. In FY 2008, the USNCB budget was $23.7 million. US Department of Justice, *US National Central Bureau of INTERPOL*, www.usdoj.gov/usncb (accessed June 1, 2009).

133   US Customs and Border Protection, *Container Security Initiative*, Fact Sheet (March 27, 2008).

134   Department of Homeland Security, *Performance and Accountability Report FY 2006: Federal Law Enforcement Training Center*.

135 US Department of Homeland Security, *FY 2008 Budget in Brief*, 51.

136 US Department of Energy, *FY 2008 Congressional Budget Request: Budget Highlights* (February 2007), 65. See also, the National Nuclear Security Administration (NNSA), *Strategic Plan* (Washington, DC: November 2004), http://nnsa.energy.gov/about/documents/NNSA_Strategic_Plan_Nov_2004.pdf.

137 NNSA was created in the National Defense Authorization Act for FY 2000, PL 106-65 (October 5, 1999). See also, US Department of Energy, *National Nuclear Security Administration*, www.energy.gov/organization/nnsa.htm.

138 The ODNN mission is

> to provide policy and technical leadership to limit or prevent the spread of materials, technology, and expertise relating to weapons of mass destruction; advance the technologies to detect the proliferation of weapons of mass destruction worldwide; and eliminate or secure inventories of surplus materials and infrastructure usable for nuclear weapons—in short, to detect, secure, or dispose of dangerous nuclear material.
>
> US Department of Energy, *FY 2009 Congressional Budget Request: National Nuclear Security Administration*, DOE/CF-024, Vol. 1 (February 2008), 453.

The ODNN programs are discussed in this document from 445–544.

5 Planning, Programming, Budgeting, and Execution in the Department of Defense

1 The authors wish to acknowledge substantial contributions made to this chapter by Miranda Priebe.

2 Activities that rely on annual appropriations for their funding are called discretionary; entitlements like Social Security, Medicare, and Medicaid, whose benefits are outlined in existing law, are referred to as mandatory, and make up about two-thirds of the federal budget.

3 For the origins of PPBS, see Alain C. Enthoven and K. Wayne Smith, *How Much Is Enough? Shaping the Defense Program 1961–1969* (1971; repr. Santa Monica, CA: RAND, 2005). The basis of PPBS—systems analysis—was developed at RAND during the 1950s. Charles Hitch and Roland McKean, *The Economics of Defense in the Nuclear Age* (Santa Monica, CA: RAND, 1960).

4 Enthoven and Smith, *How Much Is Enough?*

5 Ibid. Previously, "requirements were derived without reference to costs, and budget ceilings were derived without an analysis of requirements." The result was an annual "confrontation between large, open-ended requirements and much smaller, arbitrary budgets." Amos A. Jordan *et al.*, *American National Security*, 5th ed. (Baltimore, MD: Johns Hopkins University Press, 1998), 201.

6 The changes were formalized in US Department of Defense, *Implementation of a 2-Year Planning, Programming, Budgeting, and Execution Process*, Management Initiative Decision 913 (May 22, 2003).

7 The QDR is meant to tie together the department's view of the long-term national security landscape, its plans for forces and equipment, and its planned budgets. The first QDR was mandated by the National Defense Authorization Act for FY 1997, PL 104-201 (September 23, 1996), Sections 923, 925. Three years later, the National Defense Authorization Act for FY 2000, PL 106-65 (October 5, 1999), Section 901, established a permanent requirement for a QDR to be submitted by September 30 in the first year of every presidential term. The National Defense Authorization Act for FY 2003, PL 107-314 (December 2, 2002), Section 922 changed the timing of submission to February of the second year of each presidential term.

8 US Department of Defense, Directive Number 5141.01, *Director, Program Analysis and Evaluation (PA&E)* (March 16, 2006).

9 Ibid.

10 For more on the CAIG, see Donald Srull, ed., *The Cost Analysis Improvement Group: A History* (McLean, VA: Logistics Management Institute, 1998).

11 Members of the SLRG include the Secretary and Deputy Secretary of Defense; the Secretaries or Under Secretaries of the three military departments; the five Under Secretaries of Defense (or their principal deputies); the Deputy Chief Management Officer; the Defense Chief Information Officer; the Assistant Secretaries for Legislative Affairs and Public Affairs; the DOD general counsel; the Director of Administration and Management; the Director, PA&E; the Chairman and Vice Chairman of the JCS; the Chiefs or Vice Chiefs of the four military services (Commandant or Assistant Commandant in the case of the Marine Corps); the Director of the Joint Staff; and the Chief of the National Guard Bureau. US Department of Defense, Directive number 5105.79, *DOD Senior Governance Councils* (May 19, 2008), Enclosure 3, 7.

12 Membership in the DAWG is the same as in the SLRG, with a few exceptions: the Secretary of Defense is not a member of the DAWG (as the DAWG is chaired by the Deputy Secretary); the Principal Deputy Director of PA&E is included in the DAWG, as are the Commander, US Special Operations Command, and from the Joint Staff, the J5 (Director, Strategic Plans and Policy) and the J8 (Director, Force Structure, Resources, and Assessment). Principal Deputies may, and often do, serve on the DAWG in place of their principals. Ibid., Enclosure 4, 8.

13 Chairman of the Joint Chiefs of Staff Instruction 8501.01A, *Chairman of the JCS, Combatant Commanders, and Joint Staff Participation in the Planning, Programming, Budgeting, and Execution System* (December 3, 2004; directive current as of February 12, 2008), A-1, A-2, and GL-2.

14 Ibid., A-2 to A-4.

15 Ibid.

16 Enthoven and Smith, *How Much Is Enough?*

17 Interviews and discussions with numerous participants in the process (2005–09).

18 The National Defense Authorization Act for FY 1986, PL 99-145 (November 8, 1985), requires that the DOD submit a biennial budget. Appropriators act on an annual basis, however. DOD went through the motions of biennial budgeting for a few years after 1986, but then largely reverted to a process that looked about the same from one year to the next. To make two-year budgeting a reality, Secretary Rumsfeld established and generally enforced rules about the sorts of issues that can be raised during an off-year.

19 The DOD currently labels its part of this phase as "enhanced planning."

20 The Goldwater–Nichols Act called for the President to submit a national security strategy to Congress in February each year, in conjunction with the annual budget request. Goldwater–Nichols Department of Defense Reorganization Act of 1986, PL 99-433 (October 1, 1986), Section 603. In recent decades, administrations have published such strategies, but not annually.

21 Ibid.

22 "The National Defense Strategy … flows from the NSS [national security strategy] and informs the National Military Strategy." US Department of Defense, *National Defense Strategy* (Washington, DC: DOD, June 2008), 1.

23 For example, the first QDR of the George W. Bush administration was completed in September 2001, but the administration did not release its first national security strategy until September 2002. DOD published a *National Defense Strategy* in March 2005; that strategy generally became the basis for the 2006 QDR, which the Secretary of Defense submitted to Congress with the budget in February 2006. The national security strategy was not published until March 2006. Of course, the

department is not generally left wholly without White House guidance. Even in the absence of a recently signed national security strategy, DOD can revert to previously published strategy or may incorporate an understanding of more current White House thinking based on executive directives, meetings, or early drafts of the national security strategy.

24 National Defense Authorization Act for FY 1997, PL 104-201 (September 23, 1996), Sections 923, 925; National Defense Authorization Act for FY 2003, PL 107-314 (December 2, 2002), Section 922.

25 The first QDR report was published in May 1997 by William Cohen; it included an estimate of the resources that would be required. The second QDR, submitted by Donald Rumsfeld just weeks after the 9/11 attacks of 2001, argued that it was not yet possible to estimate the resources needed to deal with the terrorist threat. The third QDR, submitted by Rumsfeld in February 2006, dismissed the notion that a discussion of resources was relevant or necessary.

26 The group of leaders that includes the SLRG and the COCOMs is called the Strategic Planning Council, or SPC. Even in so-called on years, the Secretary may decide that a new SPG is not needed.

27 Presentation by OSD staff member (June 6, 2006).

28 Ibid.

29 Ibid.

30 Gordon England, Memorandum from the Office of the Deputy Secretary of Defense, *Capability Portfolio Management Way Ahead* (February 7, 2008).

31 Christopher J. Castelli, "QDR Shakes Up Planning Process for Future Military Missions," *Inside the Pentagon*, Vol. 25, No. 21 (May 28, 2009), 1.

32 The term is pronounced in various ways, depending on the office. In OSD, it is usually the fiddup. In the services, it is variously fye-dep, fye-dip, or fyedup.

33 Program element examples are drawn from budget item justifications in US Department of Defense, "Research, Development, Testing, and Evaluation (RDT&E) Programs (R-1)," *Department of Defense Budget for Fiscal Year 2008* (February 2007), www.defenselink.mil/comptroller/Docs/fy2008_r1.pdf. The program elements are coded to capture the major force program, the category of research and development in which the activity falls, the type of equipment or activity, and the service or defense agency; for an explanation of the code system, see US Department of Defense, *DOD Program Element Code System* (accessed May 6, 2009), www.dtic.mil/descriptivesum/dod_pe.html.

34 DOD, "RDT&E Programs (R-1)" for FY 2008.

35 Presentation by OSD participant in the process.

36 Secretary McNamara's once top-secret memorandum for the President outlining the changes was downgraded to an unclassified document on May 29, 1975: Memorandum for the President, *Recommended FY 1964—FY 1968 Strategic Retaliatory Forces* (November 1962).

37 Interviews with OSD and service participants (2006–08).

38 US Department of Defense, *Other Secretary of Defense Decisions*, Program Budget Decision 753 (December 23, 2004).

39 Mark P. Keehan, *Planning, Programming, Budgeting, and Execution (PPBE) Process*, Teaching Note (Washington, DC: Defense Acquisition University, April 2006), 11.

40 Ibid. When a program fails to obligate or expend funds on schedule, it is unlikely to be in a position to absorb the following year's money effectively. The failure to spend money on schedule is often also a signal of weakness in technical performance or program management.

41 Ibid. For example, the full funding principle generally applies to procurements: the Air Force is not permitted to purchase half of an airplane one year and the other

half the next year, but must commit to the full aircraft in a single year. This stands in contrast to incremental funding, which has been permitted for some ships in recent years.

42 Ibid.

43 Ibid.

44 Ibid, 12.

45 Presentation by an OSD staff member (June 6, 2006).

46 Interviews with OMB and DOD participants in the process.

47 DOD was not always required to submit its FYDP to Congress, and the requirement to transmit a five-year or six-year program is by no means the norm for other federal departments. Secretary of Defense Robert McNamara introduced the annual FYDP (which at the time stood for five-year defense program) as part of the initial PPBS in the early 1960s. Until the late 1980s, the FYDP was strictly an internal document. The submission of the FYDP to Congress each April was first required by the National Defense Authorization Act for FY 1988 and FY 1989, PL 100-180 (December 4, 1987). Mary T. Tyszkiewicz and Stephen Daggett, *A Defense Budget Primer* (Washington, DC: Congressional Research Service, December 9, 1998), 27.

48 DOD, MID 913, 7.

49 Philip G. Joyce, "Linking Performance and Budgeting: Opportunities in the Federal Budget Process," in *Integrating Performance and Budgets: The Budget Office of Tomorrow*, eds. Jonathan D. Breul and Carl Moravitz (Washington, DC: IBM Center for the Business of Government, 2007), 23.

50 Government Performance and Results Act of 1993, PL 103-62 (August 3, 1993).

51 Joyce, "Linking Performance and Budgeting," 23.

52 Clinton T. Brass, *The Bush Administration's Program Assessment Rating Tool (PART)*, CRS Report RL 32663 (Washington, DC: Congressional Research Service, November 5, 2004), Summary and 5; Joyce, "Linking Performance and Budgeting," 27.

53 Interviews with participants in the process.

54 Paul L. Posner and Denise M. Fantone, "Assessing Federal Program Performance: Observations on the US Office of Management and Budget's Program Assessment Rating Tool and Its Use in the Budget Process," *Public Performance & Management Review*, Vol. 30, No. 3 (March 2007), 353, 365.

55 US Government Accountability Office, *Performance Budgeting: PART Focuses Attention on Program Performance, but More Can Be Done to Engage Congress*, GAO-06-28 (Washington, DC: GAO, October 2005).

56 Smaller programs are more likely to be adjusted based on such information than larger programs; John B. Gilmore and David E. Lewis, "Assessing Performance Budgeting at OMB: The Influence of Politics, Performance, and Program Size," *Journal of Public Administration Research and Theory*, Vol. 16, No. 2 (April 2006), 185; US Government Accountability Office, *Performance Budgeting: Observations on the Use of OMB's Program Assessment Rating Tool for the Fiscal Year 2004 Budget*, Report to Congress by the United States, GAO-04-174 (Washington, DC: GAO, January 2004).

57 Posner and Fantone, "Assessing Federal Program Performance," 356.

58 Albert T. Church and Ted Warner, "DOD Planning, Programming, Budgeting, and Execution System: A Path Toward Improvement," *Joint Force Quarterly*, Issue 52 (2nd Quarter 2009), 84; interviews with OSD participants in the process.

59 Tyszkiewicz and Daggett, *A Defense Budget Primer*, 61.

60 US Department of Defense, Office of the Under Secretary of Defense (Comptroller), *National Defense Budget Estimates for Fiscal Year 2009* (Washington, DC: DOD, March 2008), 1.

61 Tyszkiewicz and Daggett, *A Defense Budget Primer*, 64.
62 Ibid., 5 and 63.
63 US Department of Defense, *National Defense Budget Estimates for Fiscal Year 2009*, Table 5-11.
64 Interviews with OSD staff members.
65 Discussions with staff members from the services and OSD.

6 Intelligence Planning and Budgeting

1 Mark Lowenthal, *Intelligence: From Secrets to Policy*, 4th Ed. (Washington, DC: CQ Press, 2009), 29–54; Ronald Reagan, *United States Intelligence Activities*, Executive Order 12333 (December 4, 1981; as amended through 2008), www.fas. org/irp/offdocs/eo/eo-12333-2008.pdf.
2 For example, the Central Intelligence Agency (CIA) and the Defense Intelligence Agency (DIA) collect, analyze, and disseminate similar intelligence in similar ways, but the former focuses on national intelligence missions and decision-makers, while the DIA supports the Defense Department and the military command structure.
3 Jeffrey T. Richelson, *The US Intelligence Community*, 5th Ed. (Boulder, CO: Westview Press, 2008), 12. Richelson sorts the intelligence organizations into five categories: (1) National, (2) Department of Defense, (3) Military Service, (4) Unified Command intelligence components, and (5) civilian intelligence organizations. Dan Elkins sorts the agencies into three components: (1) Independent, (2) Department of Defense, and (3) Non-DOD. *Managing Intelligence Resources*, 2nd Ed. (Alexandria, VA: DWE Press, 2006).
4 Overall, the IC continues to be governed by Executive Order 12333, *United States Intelligence Activities*, first issued by the administration of President Ronald Reagan. It has been revised several times, most recently in 2008, in response to changing domestic and international circumstances, and the revelation of abuses in the intelligence process. Richelson, *The US Intelligence Community*, 446.
5 Before 2004, these categories were known as NFIP (National Foreign Intelligence Program), JMIP (Joint Military Intelligence Programs), and TIARA (Tactical Intelligence and Related Activities). NFIP was created by Executive Order 11905, *United States Foreign Intelligence Activities* (February 18, 1976), during the presidency of Gerald Ford. NFIP became NIP as a result of the 2004 intelligence reform legislation. The change was intended to signal that it included domestic sources of foreign intelligence, notably FBI intelligence. Elkins, *Managing Intelligence Resources*, 4-3. DOD combined the two into the MIP when it created the position of Under Secretary for Intelligence in 2002.
6 Stephen Daggett, *The US Intelligence Budget: A Basic Overview*, CRS Report RS21945 (Washington, DC: Congressional Research Service, September 24, 2004). For a detailed discussion, see Elkins, *Managing Intelligence Resources*, especially Chapter 4, "What Are Intelligence Resources?"
7 Elkins, *Managing Intelligence Resources*.
8 Ibid., 1-2.
9 Richelson, *The US Intelligence Community*; Lowenthal, *Intelligence*; John Diamond, *The CIA and the Culture of Failure: US Intelligence from the End of the Cold War to the Invasion of Iraq* (Stanford, CA: Stanford Security Studies, 2008).
10 National Commission on Terrorist Attacks, *The 9/11 Commission Report: Final Report of the National Commission on Terrorist Attacks Upon the United States* (New York: W.W. Norton & Co., 2004).
11 Elkins, *Managing Intelligence Resources*, 2-1. Before 1947, the United States' intelligence capabilities were located in the Armed Services (Army, Navy, Marine

Corps, and Coast Guard), the Department of State, the FBI, and the Atomic Energy Commission. There was no centralized organization responsible for coordinating these agencies.

12 House Permanent Select Committee on Intelligence, *Compilation of US Intelligence Laws and Executive Orders* (Washington, DC: GPO, 1983), 7.

13 Richelson, *The US Intelligence Community*, 15–29; 50 USC 403-4d, *Director of the Central Intelligence Agency*, www.law.cornell.edu/uscode/html/uscode50/usc_sec_50_00000403---004a.html (accessed June 18, 2009).

14 Richelson, *The US Intelligence Community*, 17. GlobalSecurity.org estimated the FY 2009 CIA budget at $10 billion. *FY2009 Intelligence Budget*, www.globalsecurity.org/intell/library/budget/index.html (accessed May 2, 2009).

15 Lowenthal, *Intelligence*, 43.

16 Richelson, *The US Intelligence Community*, 17.

17 This responsibility was transferred to the Office of the Director of National Intelligence in 2004 in the Intelligence Reform and Terrorism Prevention Act of 2004, PL 108-458 (December 17, 2004).

18 NSA's charter is set out in the *National Security Council Intelligence Directive* (NSCID) 6 (January 17, 1972). See also Richelson, *The US Intelligence Community*, 31; James Bamford, *The Puzzle Palace: Inside the National Security Agency, America's Most Secret Intelligence Organization* (New York: Penguin, 1983); and Bamford, *The Shadow Factory: The Ultra-Secret NSA from 9/11 to the Eavesdropping on America* (New York: Doubleday, 2008).

19 Elkins, *Managing Intelligence Resources*, 2-4.

20 Richelson, *The US Intelligence Community*, 31-2. NSA's responsibilities are set out in US Department of Defense, Directive S-5100.20, *The National Security Agency and the Central Security Service* (December 23, 1971).

21 Elkins, *Managing Intelligence Resources*, 2-4.

22 Richelson, *The US Intelligence Community*, 31-2. GlobalSecurity.org estimated the FY 2009 NSA budget at $15 billion. *FY2009 Intelligence Budget*, www.globalsecurity.org/intell/library/budget/index.html.

23 Elkins, *Managing Intelligence Resources*, 2-3.

24 Ibid.

25 Richelson, *The US Intelligence Community*, 60–74. GlobalSecurity.org estimated the FY 2009 DIA budget at $2 billion. *FY2009 Intelligence Budget*, www.globalsecurity.org/intell/library/budget/index.html.

26 Richelson, *The US Intelligence Community*, 37–43.

27 Ibid., 38.

28 Ibid., 41.

29 Ibid. GlobalSecurity.org estimated the FY 2009 NRO budget at $15 billion. *FY2009 Intelligence Budget*, www.globalsecurity.org/intell/library/budget/index.html.

30 Richelson, *The US Intelligence Community*.

31 Elkins, *Managing Intelligence Resources*, 2-5. Until then, these functions were carried out separately by the Defense Mapping Agency (DMA), Central Imagery Office (CIO), National Photographic Interpretation Center (NPIC), offices within the Defense Intelligence Agency (DIA), parts of the Defense Airborne Reconnaissance Office (DARO) and the NRO. NIMA became the NGA in 2003.

32 Ibid.

33 National Geo-Spatial Intelligence Agency, *About*, www1.nga.mil/About/Pages/default.aspx (accessed May 11, 2009).

34 Richelson, *The US Intelligence Community*, 45.

35 Ibid., 51. GlobalSecurity.org estimated the FY 2009 NGA budget at $2 billion. *FY2009 Intelligence Budget*, www.globalsecurity.org/intell/library/budget/index.html.

36 Discussion based on Richelson, *The US Intelligence Community*, 158–63. Before World War II, the FBI had a significant presence in Latin America, which was withdrawn after the war.

37 *The 9/11 Commission Report*, 424–6.

38 Richelson, *The US Intelligence Community*, 159.

39 Ibid.

40 Federal Bureau of Investigation, *Legal Attaché Offices*, www.fbi.gov/contact/legat/legat.htm (accessed May 5, 2009).

41 Elkins, *Managing Intelligence Resources*, 2-10.

42 Federal Bureau of Investigation, *FY 2009 Congressional Budget Justification* (Washington, DC: February 2008), 1–4.

43 Reagan, Executive Order 12333, *United States Intelligence Activities*, Section 1.14, provision c, 59949.

44 FBI, *FY 2009 Congressional Budget Justification*, 1–8. GlobalSecurity.org estimated the FY 2009 FBI intelligence budget at $3 billion. *FY2009 Intelligence Budget*, www.globalsecurity.org/intell/library/budget/index.html.

45 Richelson, *The US Intelligence Community*, 155–66. See also Elkins, *Managing Intelligence Resources*, 2-10. ONSI joined the IC in February 2006 by agreement between the Attorney General and the DNI.

46 Richelson, *The US Intelligence Community*.

47 Elkins, *Managing Intelligence Resources*, 2-10.

48 Ibid.

49 Richelson, *The US Intelligence Community*, 142–5.

50 US Department of State, *FY 2009 Congressional Budget Justification* (Washington, DC: 2008), 173.

51 With the absorption of USIA into the State Department in 1999, INR took on responsibility for commissioning and analyzing overseas opinion polling. Ibid., 174–5. Lowenthal argues that INR's impact on intelligence depends greatly on its access to and use by the Secretary of State, which can vary with administrations. Lowenthal, *Intelligence*, 46.

52 Elkins, *Managing Intelligence Resources*, 2-8.

53 Ibid. INR products are often electronically disseminated through the IC's Intelink system, to which members and staff of the Congressional Intelligence Committees have access.

54 Richelson, *The US Intelligence Community*, 143; State, *FY 2009 Congressional Budget Justification*, 173.

55 Richelson, *The US Intelligence Community*.

56 State, *FY 2009 Congressional Budget Justification*, 89. GlobalSecurity.org estimated the FY 2009 INR intelligence budget at $100 million, but the unclassified State Department request for FY 2009 was $59.8 million.

57 Richelson, *The US Intelligence Community*, 149.

58 US Department of Homeland Security, *Office of Intelligence and Analysis*, www.dhs.gov/xabout/structure/gc_1220886590914.shtm (accessed May 11, 2009). OIA has eight bureaus: Alternative Analysis, Homeland Threat Analysis, Current Intelligence, Collection and Requirements, Information Sharing and Knowledge Management, Plans and Integration, Production Management, and the Homeland Infrastructure and Risk Analysis Center. Richelson, *The US Intelligence Community*, 149.

59 Intelligence Authorization Act for FY 2002, PL 107-108 (December 2001), Section 105, 28. This Act included the Coast Guard in the US Intelligence Community by amending the National Security Act of 1947, PL 61-235 (July 26, 1947), 50 USC 401a(4)(h).

60 US Coast Guard, *Coast Guard History: Frequently Asked Questions*, www.uscg.mil/history/faqs/CGI.asp (accessed May 11, 2009).

61 Elkins, *Managing Intelligence Resources*, 2-11.
62 Ibid.
63 Richelson, *The US Intelligence Community*, 154.
64 National Security Council Intelligence Directive No. 1 of December 1947 established the intelligence responsibilities of the AEC. Ibid., 145.
65 Ibid., 147.
66 Ibid.
67 K. Lee Lerner and Brenda Wilmoth Lerner, eds., *Encyclopedia of Espionage, Intelligence, and Security*, Vol. 2. (Detroit, MI: Gale, 2004), 114–15.
68 Richelson, *The US Intelligence Community*, 88-9.
69 Ibid., 88, 93.
70 Lerner and Lerner, *Encyclopedia of Espionage*, 114–15.
71 Elkins, *Managing Intelligence Resources*, 2-6.
72 Ibid., 2-7.
73 Lerner and Lerner, *Encyclopedia of Espionage*, 336–7 and Richelson, *The US Intelligence Community*, 96.
74 Richelson, *The US Intelligence Community*, 108-9.
75 Lerner and Lerner, *Encyclopedia of Espionage*.
76 "Air Intelligence Agency to become Air Force ISR Agency," *Air Force Print News* (May 15, 2007), www.af.mil/news/story_print.asp?id=123053314.
77 Ibid.
78 Lerner and Lerner, *Encyclopedia of Espionage*, 11–13; Richelson, *The US Intelligence Community*, 101, 106; US Air Force, *Air Force Technical Applications Center* (June 2007), www.afisr.af.mil/library/factsheets/factsheet.asp?id=10309.
79 Richelson, *The US Intelligence Community*, 108.
80 The following discussion derives, in significant part, from Elkins, *Managing Intelligence Resources*, Chapter 4.
81 Elkins, *Managing Intelligence Resources*, 4, 19-20.
82 Reagan, Executive Order 12333, *United States Intelligence Activities*, paras. (1)–(4).
83 Elkins, *Managing Intelligence Resources*, 4-5.
84 These organizations also receive funding through the MIP budget.
85 Elkins, *Managing Intelligence Resources*, 4-7.
86 Ibid.
87 Ibid., 4-8.
88 The final two elements in DOD's part of the NIP are a special reconnaissance program, and DOD's Foreign Counterintelligence Program (FCIP). The Program Manager for the FCIP was the DOD Director for Counterintelligence Field Activity. However, this office, which was controversial, was closed in August 2008, and oversight of the program was transferred to the DIA. Elkins, *Managing Intelligence Resources*, 4-10; Reuters, "Unit Created by Rumsfeld Shut Down," *Gulf Times* (August 6, 2008).
89 Some of the NRO activity is funded through the MIP budget.
90 Elkins, *Managing Intelligence Resources*, 4, 11-12.
91 Ibid., 4, 14.
92 Ibid., 4, 15. See also 3, 2-3, for responsibilities of the USD(I).
93 Ibid., 4, 14.
94 Elkins, *Managing Intelligence Resources*, 4, 15-16, 21.
95 *The 9/11 Commission Report*, 357. One intelligence analyst described the DCI's role in intelligence budgeting as "pressing his nose against the glass looking in." Richard A. Best and Alfred Cumming, *Director of National Intelligence Statutory Authorities: Status and Proposals*, CRS Report RL34231 (Washington, DC: Congressional Research Service, April 17, 2008), 7.

96   *The 9/11 Commission Report*, 410.

97   Commission recommendations are found in *The 9/11 Commission Report*, 403–16. The proposed counterterrorism center should work with the OMB Director to prepare the counterterrorism budget, according to the report. Ibid., 405.

98   Intelligence Reform and Terrorism Prevention Act of 2004, PL 108-459 (December 7, 2004), Section 102A(2)(c)(B).

99   Lowenthal, *Intelligence*, 29.

100 This included the National Intelligence Council (NIC), which prepares National Intelligence Estimates (NIE), the new National Counterterrorism Center (NCTC, which replaced the Terrorist Threat Integration Center directed by the DCI), the National Counterproliferation Center (NCPC previously at the CIA), and the National Counterintelligence Executive (NCIX). Richelson, *The US Intelligence Community*, Chapter 17, "Managing National Intelligence," 445–81.

101 If the two cannot agree, the President must resolve the disagreement.

102 Jack Devine, "An Intelligence Reform Reality Check," *Washington Post* (February 18, 2008).

103 Intelligence Reform and Terrorism Prevention Act of 2004, PL 108-458, Section 102A.a.2.c.1.A. and B; Lowenthal, *Intelligence*, 33. The DNI was to obtain the advice of a Joint Intelligence Community Council in preparing this budget. The Council consisted of the heads of the major NIP agencies plus policy advisors. In practice, the DNI created an Executive Committee (EXCOM) from the agencies. The EXCOM includes the DOD Under Secretary for Intelligence, in addition to the other DOD agencies that are part of the NIP. Lowenthal, *Intelligence*, 200.

104 Best and Cumming, *Director of National Intelligence Statutory Authorities* (April 17, 2008), 8; *The 9/11 Commission Report*, 420.

105 Elkins, *Managing Intelligence Resources*, 3-7.

106 As with the DOD budget, OMB participates in a "joint review" with ODNI and DOD with respect to the NIP and the MIP.

107 Intelligence Reform and Terrorism Prevention Act of 2004, PL 108-458, Section 102A.c.5.B.

108 Richelson, *The US Intelligence Community*, 454; Best and Cumming, *Director of National Intelligence Statutory Authorities*, 8; Elkins, *Managing Intelligence Resources*, 9-14.

109 Intelligence Reform and Terrorism Prevention Act of 2004, PL 108-458, Section 102A.c.5.C and c.7.B.

110 Ibid., Section 102A.d.1.B.

111 Ibid. Section 102A.d.5.A.iv.I and II, and d.5.A.v. See also, Richelson, *The US Intelligence Community*, 454.

112 Intelligence Reform and Terrorism Prevention Act of 2004, PL 108-458, Section 102A.d.1.A. Agencies wishing to transfer or reprogram MIP funds must also consult in advance with the DNI. Ibid., Section 102A.d.1.B.

113 Lowenthal, *Intelligence*, 30. There is some evidence that DNI John Negroponte did intervene to ensure that part of a troubled national imagery architecture program was canceled, over the opposition of the NRO. David E. Kaplan and Kevin Whitelaw, "Remaking US Intelligence," *US News and World Report* (November 13, 2006). In 2008, the Senate and House Intelligence Committees sought to strengthen the DNI's authorities authorizing the Director to "conduct accountability reviews of significant failures or deficiencies within the Intelligence Community." In addition, the Conference Report authorized the DNI to "use National Intelligence Program funds to quickly address deficiencies or needs that arise in intelligence information access or sharing capabilities" and "approve interagency financing of national intelligence centers." House Report 110-478, The FY 2008 Intelligence Authorization Act, PL 110-131 (May 7, 2007), Sections 408, 410, 411.

However, President Bush vetoed the legislation because of other provisions that would have limited the CIA's terrorist interrogation programs. Best and Cumming, *Director of National Intelligence Statutory Authorities* (April 17, 2008).

114 Elkins, *Managing Intelligence Resources*, 3-10.
115 Lowenthal, *Intelligence*, 33.
116 Intelligence Reform and Terrorism Prevention Act of 2004, PL 108-458, Section 102A.p.
117 Ibid., Section 102A.c.3.A, says the DNI "shall participate in the development" of the MIP.
118 Ibid., Section 102A.d.1.B.
119 Lowenthal, *Intelligence*, 43.
120 The MIP budgets are also transmitted via classified annexes to department and agency budgets.
121 *Managing Intelligence: Intelligence Strategy, Vision, Plans and Budgets*, Power-Point Briefing presented at American University (November 3, 2008).
122 Ibid.
123 Intelligence Reform and Terrorism Prevention Act of 2004, PL 108-458, Subtitle B.
124 Ibid., Section 119.d.1.
125 Ibid., Section 119.d.2 and d.3.
126 Karen DeYoung, "A Fight Against Terrorism—and Disorganization," *Washington Post* (August 9, 2006).
127 Interviews with executive branch staff (2006–07).
128 Intelligence Reform and Terrorism Prevention Act of 2004, PL 108-458, Section 1022.
129 Ibid.
130 Lowenthal, *Intelligence*, 215.
131 *The 9/11 Commission Report*, 416.
132 Implementing Recommendations of the 9/11 Commission Act of 2007, PL 110-53 (August 3, 2007), Section 601.
133 Lowenthal, *Intelligence*, 215.
134 Office of the Director of National Intelligence, *DNI Releases Budget Figure for 2008 National Intelligence Program* (October 28, 2008).
135 Lowenthal notes that technical collection systems "are a major expenditure within the US intelligence budget." Lowenthal, *Intelligence*, 69.
136 Commission on Roles and Capabilities of the US Intelligence Community, *Preparing for the 21st Century: An Appraisal of US Intelligence*, Chapter 7 (March 1, 1996).
137 Lowenthal, *Intelligence*, 43.
138 *The 9/11 Commission Report*, 420. See also, Frederick M. Kaiser, *Congressional Oversight of Intelligence: Current Structure and Alternatives*, CRS Report RL32525 (Washington, DC: Congressional Research Service, September 16, 2008).
139 Ibid., 3.
140 Lowenthal, *Intelligence*, 206.
141 *The 9/11 Commission Report*, 420.
142 Kaiser, *Congressional Oversight of Intelligence*, 16.
143 Ibid., 17–18.

7 Resource Allocation and Budgeting for Homeland Security

1 The authors wish to acknowledge substantial contributions made to this chapter by Joshua Itzkowitz-Shifrinson and Miranda Priebe.

2 Homeland Security Act of 2002, PL 107-296 (November 25, 2002).
3 See, for example, the report of the 9/11 Commission, "National Commission on Terrorist Attacks Upon the United States," July 22, 2004, http://govinfo.library. unt.edu/911/report/index.htm. The expectation was also endorsed by Tom Ridge, the first Secretary of Homeland Security, in testimony before the Senate Judiciary Committee before the Homeland Security Act of 2002 was passed. See the statement of Governor Tom Ridge, Director of the Transition Planning Office for the Department of Homeland Security, *The Department of Homeland Security: Making Americans Safer*, submitted to the Senate Committee on the Judiciary on June 26, 2002.
4 Ridge, *The Department of Homeland Security*.
5 "The cost of the new elements…, as well as department-wide management and administration units, can be funded from savings achieved by eliminating redundancies inherent in the current structure." Ibid.
6 Cindy Williams, *Strengthening Homeland Security: Reforming Planning and Resource Allocation* (Washington, DC: IBM Center for the Business of Government, 2008).
7 It is easy to argue over the definition of homeland security. As articulated by both the George W. Bush administration and the Obama administration, homeland security consists of activities to prevent terrorist attacks within the United States, reduce the vulnerability of people and infrastructure to terrorism, and minimize the damage and recover from attacks that do occur. Since Hurricane Katrina in 2005, policymakers have widened the definition to include protection from and preparations to mitigate the effects of natural disasters and naturally occurring disease. For the purposes of this chapter, the authors define homeland security at the federal level as the activities that the White House Office of Management and Budget includes in its roll-up of homeland security budgets in the *Analytical Perspectives* volume of the annual federal budget.
8 The first such strategy was: *The National Strategy For Homeland Security* (Washington, DC: Office of Homeland Security, July 2002). The second and most recent is *The National Strategy for Homeland Security* (Washington, DC: Homeland Security Council, October 2007).
9 Alain C. Enthoven and K. Wayne Smith, *How Much is Enough? Shaping the Defense Program 1961–1969* (1971; repr. Santa Monica, CA: Rand, 2005).
10 The system, revised several times in the intervening decades, was modified and renamed PPBE in 2003.
11 *The National Strategy for Homeland Security* (October 2007) is organized not around those six missions, but rather around four goals: "prevent and disrupt terrorist attacks; protect the American people, our critical infrastructure, and key resources; respond to and recover from incidents that do occur; and continue to strengthen the foundation to ensure our long-term success."
12 Budgets by department and agency for each mission category (six categories during the George W. Bush administration, three in the Obama administration's FY 2010 budget submission) are reported in the "Crosscutting Programs" chapter of the *Analytical Perspectives* volume of the federal budget.
13 US Department of Homeland Security, *DHS Resource Allocation Process*, Presentation (November 18, 2008), slide 4.
14 Memorandum from Acting Deputy Secretary of Homeland Security Paul A. Schneider to the Under Secretaries and component heads, *Fiscal Year 2010–2014 Resource Allocation Plan (RAP) Process* (March 7, 2008).
15 The material in this section is adapted from Williams, *Strengthening Homeland Security*.
16 The description of the process is drawn from the US Department of Homeland

Security, *Planning, Programming, Budgeting and Execution,* Management Directive 1330 (February 14, 2005) and from the presentation by DHS, PA&E, *DHS Resource Allocation Process* (November 18, 2008).

17 White House Homeland Security Council, *National Strategy for Homeland Security* (Washington, DC: The White House, October 2007), 41.

18 The Director of Strategic Plans reports to the Assistant Secretary for Policy.

19 Presentation by DHS, PA&E, *DHS Resource Allocation Process* (November 18, 2008).

20 Schneider, *Fiscal Year 2010–2014 Resource Allocation Plan (RAP) Process* (March 7, 2008).

21 Steve Bennett, DHS Risk Assessment Program Manager, *DHS Bioterrorism Risk Assessment: Background, Requirements, and Overview,* Briefing to the Committee on Methodological Improvement to the Department of Homeland Security's 2006 Bioterrorism Risk Assessment (August 28, 2006).

22 National Academy of Sciences, Board on Mathematical Sciences and Their Applications, *Interim Report on Methodological Improvements to the Department of Homeland Security's Biological Agent Risk Analysis* (Washington, DC: National Academies Press, 2007), 2.

23 Implementing Recommendations of the 9/11 Commission Act of 2007, PL 110-053 (August 3, 2007), Section 2401.

24 Discussions with DHS staff.

25 This section draws heavily on Cindy Williams and Gordon Adams, *Strengthening Statecraft and Security: Reforming US Planning and Resource Allocation* (Cambridge, MA: MIT Security Studies Program Occasional Paper, June 2008), 15–43.

26 Homeland security accounts for about 10 percent of the Department of Justice budget, most of it concentrated in the FBI.

27 Pamela W. Smith, *The National Institutes of Health (NIH): Organization, Funding, and Congressional Issues* (Washington, DC: Congressional Research Service, October 29, 2006), 16.

28 Ibid., 14.

29 The organization was then in the Department of Health, Education, and Welfare, and was initially called the Office of the Assistant Secretary for Program Coordination. Gerald Britten, *Office of the Assistant Secretary for Planning and Evaluation: Brief History* (revised January 22, 2009), http://aspe.hhs.gov/info/aspe-history.shtml.

30 Beryl A. Radin, *Managing Decentralized Departments: The Case of the US Department of Health and Human Services* (Washington, DC: The PricewaterhouseCoopers Endowment for the Business of Government, October 1999), 7.

31 US Department of Health and Human Services, *Strategic Plan, Fiscal Years 2007–2012,* 15.

32 *National Institutes of Health Actual Obligations, Percent of Total, by Institute and Center,* on the website of NIH's Office of the Budget, http://officeofbudget.od.nih.gov.

33 Biographical sketch of Elias A. Zerhouni, MD, Director of NIH, included in his written statement before the Subcommittee on Labor–HHS–Education of the House Appropriations Committee (March 5, 2008), 11.

34 Statement by Gerald W. Parker, Principal Deputy Assistant Secretary, Office of the ASPR, Department of Health and Human Services, *HHS Progress in National Preparedness Efforts,* submitted to the Senate Committee on Homeland Security and Governmental Affairs (October 23, 2007), 1, 4.

35 US Department of Health and Human Services, *FY 2009 Budget in Brief* (Washington, DC: 2008), 5.

8 The Role of the Executive Office of the President in National Security Budgeting

1 The President has had this responsibility since the passage of the Budget Act of 1921, PL 67-13 (June 10, 1921). Previously, executive branch department budgets were bound together, without analysis or change, by the Treasury Department and transmitted to the Congress. Allen Schick, *The Federal Budget: Politics, Policy, Process*, 3rd Ed. (Washington, DC: Brookings Institution, 2007), 17.

2 As elsewhere in this book, we use the term national security to encompass all aspects of national defense, intelligence, international affairs, and homeland security.

3 For a detailed discussion of the history of OMB, see Shelly Lynn Tomkin, *Inside OMB: Politics and Process in the President's Budget Office* (Armonk, NY: M.E. Sharpe, 1998), especially Chapter 3.

4 Ibid., 3, describes this function as an "institutional memory." The "memory bank" function is critical for incoming administrations, especially if the new chief executive and his/her staff have little executive branch or Washington, DC experience.

5 OMB's regulatory responsibilities are carried out through its Office of Information and Regulatory Affairs (OIRA). These touch national security programs less than those of other agencies. On OIRA's role, see ibid., 203–16.

6 OMB's statutory and management offices have less impact on agencies than the budget side of the organization. However, the work of these offices in such areas as contracting for financial services, information policy, or travel management can be reinforced by decisions made on the budgetary side and can have some implications for budgets and spending. For example, a mid-1990s proposal from OFPP to open competition for DOD financial systems consolidation to private sector information systems companies was reinforced by OMB's budget division during budget "passback." The OIRA mission of developing programs to cope with the "Y2K" transition for information systems were similarly reinforced during budget passback.

7 Schick, *The Federal Budget*, 14, 16.

8 Tomkin, *Inside OMB*, 36–7 and 191.

9 Budget and Impoundment Act of 1974, PL 93-344 (July 12, 1974).

10 Gramm–Rudman–Hollings Balanced Budget and Emergency Deficit Control Act of 1985, PL 99-177 (December 12, 1985). This Act was named for its leading co-sponsors, Senators Phil Gramm (R-TX), Warren Rudman (R-NH), and Fritz Hollings (D-SC). For a discussion of deficit reduction legislation and its impact on OMB, see Tomkin, *Inside OMB*, 60–71.

11 The caps created serious constraints on defense budgets in the 1990s. They had an even more dramatic effect on International Affairs spending. For a good part of the period from 1990 to 2002, defense was given a separate cap. International Affairs spending was lumped together with domestic spending, which meant politically attractive domestic programs would benefit, while less popular international spending would be cut in the congressional budget resolution.

12 The BEA also required the executive branch to control "mandatory" spending growth (principally Medicare and Medicaid) or revenue losses (through tax cuts) by providing offsets for legislative proposals that would increase such spending or cause such losses. This was called the "paygo" provision of the law. The paygo requirement had an impact on the negotiation of such trade agreements as the NAFTA or Uruguay Round, as the revenue losses from lower tariffs needed to be "paid for" through tax and fee increases elsewhere.

13 Tomkin notes that "some administrations have not appreciated, trusted, and therefore used OMB." Tomkin, *Inside OMB*, 5. President Truman apparently resisted

the OMB role, initially, but then found it useful in dealing with agencies advocating their own institutional agendas. Ibid., 37.

14 The OMB restructuring in 1994 linked its budget and management offices more closely to each other.

15 The "reconciliation" process forced the Congress to align legislative and budgetary provisions with the budgets Stockman had submitted. For an explanation of the reconciliation process, see Schick, *The Federal Budget*, 142–7. See also, Tomkin, *Inside OMB*, 145–7.

16 The Bush administration left behind a "current services" projection for much of the federal budget. "Current services" is a mechanical extrapolation of the most recent appropriation for an agency, measuring how much current programs and activities would cost in the future, if there were no program changes and budgets only grew by the rate of inflation.

17 Paul O'Neill, once Deputy Director of OMB, described OMB's capabilities as "neutral brilliance." Tomkin, *Inside OMB*, 3.

18 Schick, *The Federal Budget*, 98. Tomkin suggests this was a problem in the initial Reagan–Stockman forecasts and in the way a Gramm–Rudman–Hollings sequester was avoided in the late 1980s. Tomkin, *Inside OMB*, 94, 163–4.

19 Homeland security budgets are the responsibility of other divisions in OMB.

20 The federal fiscal year runs from October 1 through the following September 30.

21 Bob Woodward, *Agenda: Inside the Clinton White House* (New York: Simon and Schuster, 1995), for an informed discussion of Clinton's overall budget and fiscal strategy in 1993.

22 Circulars are the OMB mechanism for providing guidance and instructions to executive branch agencies. A-11 is entitled "Preparation, Submission, and Execution of the Budget." Each year's version differs slightly from prior years, conforming to new White House priorities and policies. It is generally available on the OMB website.

23 A-11 also sets out process and expectations for OMB's apportionment of funds, once appropriated, which deal with the actual execution of agency spending plans.

24 DOD is exempt from this deadline.

25 These explanations are often converted in to the agency's Congressional Justification books.

26 The OMB Deputy for Management also frequently attends these reviews, especially as the role of that office has grown with the Government Performance and Results Act of 1993, PL 103-62 (August 3, 1993).

27 Interviews with senior State Department budget officials (2007–08).

28 For example, disagreements over international affairs programs delayed the process into January 2008. Schick notes that "dozens of decisions are made in the home stretch, when all the numbers have been tallied and the deadline nears for sending the budget to the printer." Schick, *The Federal Budget*, 96.

29 Interviews with senior DOD officials.

30 Interviews with senior White House officials.

31 Interviews with former White House officials.

32 See Chapter 6 and Tim Weiner, "Ultra-Secret Office Gets First Budget Scrutiny," *New York Times* (August 10, 1994); Tim Weiner, "Senate Committee Receives Apology from Spy Agency," *New York Times* (August 11, 1994); Reuters, "White House Decries NRO's $1 b. Hoard," *Washington Post* (September 16, 2005); and Dan Morgan, "$1.6 Billion in NRO Kitty Helped Appropriators Fund Pet Projects," *Washington Post* (October 5, 1995).

33 The final homeland security budget decisions are reported in a separate chapter in the Analytical Perspectives volume of the President's annual budget submission. Cindy Williams, *Strengthening Homeland Security: Reforming Planning and*

Resource Allocation (Washington, DC: IBM Center for the Business of Government, 2008).

34 The Anti-Deficiency Act is not a single act of Congress, but rather stems from a variety of laws that built up over time. It bars agencies from spending more funds for the purposes for which they were appropriated than were made available in the appropriation. The Impoundment Act permits OMB to defer providing some funds to agencies temporarily, or to hold them back pending an administration request to Congress to rescind the funds. US Government Accountability Office, *Antideficiency Act Background*, www.gao.gov/ada/antideficiency.htm (accessed June 1, 2009); and Congressional Budget and Impoundment Control Act of 1974, PL 93-344 (July 12, 1974).

35 Office of Management and Budget, *Circular A-11, Preparation, Submission and Execution of the Budget* (Washington, DC: June 2008), Section 120 on apportionment. Apportionments may be done for all funds appropriated to an agency, on a quarterly basis, or by activity, project, or type of spending (called "objects") such as salaries or travel.

36 This report is the SF 133, "Report on Budget Execution and Budgetary Resources."

37 Tomkin, *Inside OMB*, 187.

38 For the early history of OMB's management responsibilities, see Tomkin, *Inside OMB*, 190–216.

39 Paperwork Reduction Act, 44 USC. 3501 *et seq.*

40 Executive Order 12866, "Regulatory Planning and Review," September 30, 1993.

41 Mark L. Goldstein, "The Flickering 'M' in OMB," *Government Executive*, Vol. 22, No. 3 (March 1990), 28, as cited in Tomkin, *Inside OMB*, 199.

42 31 US C. Chapter 11. The responsibilities of the Office of Federal Financial Management include "implementing the financial management improvement priorities of the President, establishing government-wide financial management policies of executive agencies, and carrying out the financial management functions of the CFO Act." Office of Management and Budget, *Office of Federal Financial Management*, www.whitehouse.gov/omb/financial/index.html (accessed June 1, 2009).

43 Tomkin, *Inside OMB*, 201; US Government Accountability Office, *The Chief Financial Officers Act: A Mandate for Federal Financial Management Reform*, GAO/AFMD-12.19.4 (Washington, DC: GAO, September 1991).

44 Tomkin, *Inside OMB*, 253–4.

45 See US Government Accountability Office, *Results-Oriented Government: GPRA Has Established a Solid Foundation for Achieving Greater Results*, GAO-04-38 (Washington, DC: GAO, March 2004).

46 US Government Accountability Office, *OMB 2000: Changes Resulting from the Reorganization of the Office of Management and Budget*, Testimony before the Subcommittee on Government Management, Information, and Technology of the House Committee on Government Reform and Oversight, GAO/T-GGD/AIMD-96-68 (Washington, DC: GAO, February 7, 1996). OMB 2000 reflected a defensive response by OMB: "it was very clear to OMB staff that if OMB did not reform itself, NPR would do it for them and certainly not to their liking." Tomkin, *Inside OMB*, 240.

47 Internal to the RMOs, these additional personnel were not necessarily seen as a helpful addition. Budget staff did not consider these new staff as equally skilled and, because they were not trained as "examiners," they could not easily be assigned to agency accounts.

48 Unfortunately, the implementation of this law [GPRA] has fallen far short of its authors' hopes. Agency plans are plagued by performance measures that are meaningless, vague, too numerous, and often compiled by people who

have no direct connection with budget decisions. Today, agencies produce over 13,000 pages of performance plans every year that are largely ignored in the budget process.

Office of Management and Budget, *Budget of the United States Government, Fiscal Year 2004* (Washington, DC: February 2003), 49.

49 Office of Management and Budget, *PART 101: Introductory Training*, briefing slides (February 2007).

50 OMB, *Budget of the United States Government, Fiscal Year 2004*, 50–1.

51 ExpectMore.gov, www.whitehouse.gov/omb/expectmore, and OMB, *PART 101*.

52 The following data is taken from the ExpectMore.gov, www.whitehouse.gov/omb/expectmore.

53 Office of Management and Budget, *The President's Management Agenda, Fiscal Year 2002* (Washington, DC: 2001), http://georgewbush-whitehouse.archives.gov/omb/budget/fy2002/mgmt.pdf.

54 On the structure, functioning and evolution of the NSC, see Alan G. Whittaker *et al., The National Security Policy Process: The National Security Council and Interagency System* (Washington, DC: National Defense University, ICAF, November 2008); Loch K. Johnson and Karl F. Inderfurth, *Fateful Decisions: Inside the National Security Council* (New York: Oxford University Press, 2004); David Rothkopf, *Running the World: The Inside Story of the National Security Council and the Architects of America's Power* (New York: Public Affairs, 2006); and Amy B. Zegart, *Flawed by Design: The Evolution of the CIA, JSC, and NSC* (Stanford, CA: Stanford University Press, 1999).

55 The missions of the two organizations are distinct. According to the National Security Act of 1947, PL 61-235 (July 26, 1947), NSC

shall advise the President with respect to the integration of domestic, foreign, and military policies related to the national security ... [and execute] other functions the President may direct for the purpose of more effectively coordinating the policies and functions of the departments and agencies of the government relating to the national security.

OMB, according to *Circular A-11*, "evaluates the effectiveness of agency programs, policies, and procedures, assesses competing funding demands among agencies, and sets funding priorities."

56 Agencies tend not to give budget priority to programs that are White House priorities, expecting that the White House will insist that such programs be funded in addition to the agency's budget request. This leaves room in agency budget ceilings for agency priorities.

57 At various times in the Clinton administration, NSC would transmit a single document aggregating the views of the different offices, but generally without setting out clear priorities.

58 The establishment of HSC early in October 2001 was made official in George W. Bush, *Homeland Security Presidential Directive 1 (HSPD-1): Organization and Operation of the Homeland Security Council* (October 29, 2001). HSPD-1 called for the HSC to "ensure coordination of all homeland security-related activities among executive departments and agencies and promote the effective development and implementation of all homeland security policies." HSC's advice and oversight roles were later codified by Congress in the Homeland Security Act of 2002, PL 107-296 (November 25, 2002), Sections 902 and 904.

59 For a detailed discussion of this coordination issue, see Center for Strategic and International Studies, *Beyond Goldwater-Nichols: US Government and Defense Reform for a New Strategic Era*, Phase 2 Report (Washington, DC: July 2005) and

Project on National Security Reform, *Forging a New Shield* (Washington, DC: November 2008).

60 For details on the strategy documents an administration is required by statute to transmit to the Congress, see Catherine Dale, *National Security Strategy: Legislative Mandates, Execution to Date, and Considerations for Congress*, CRS Report RL34505 (Washington, DC: Congressional Research Service, May 28, 2008).

61 Such steps have been proposed by the Center for Strategic and International Studies and Project on National Security Reform studies. For an application of such a process to priority policy areas, see Cindy Williams and Gordon Adams, *Strengthening Statecraft and Security: Reforming US Planning and Resource Allocation* (Cambridge, MA: MIT Security Studies Program Occasional Paper, June 2008), and Gordon Adams, "Establishing the Next President's National Security Agenda: The Role of the White House," *Bulletin of the Atomic Scientists* (June 30, 2008), www.stimson.org/pub.cfm?ID=642.

62 I.M. Destler, *The National Economic Council: A Work in Progress*, Policy Analysis No. 46 (Washington, DC: Institute for International Economics, November 1996), and Woodward, *The Agenda*.

63 Office of National Drug Control Policy, *Enabling Legislation*, www.whitehousedrugpolicy.gov/about/legislation.html.

64 In 1997 the ONDCP Director, General Barry McCaffrey, did not certify the DOD budget for counternarcotics programs, leading to lengthy negotiations, including OMB, to increase DOD funding. This single decertification was sufficiently controversial to deter future Directors from such a step. US Government Accountability Office, *Drug Control: ONDCP Efforts to Manage the National Drug Control Budget*, Letter Report, GAO/GGD-99-80 (May 14, 1999), 2.

65 NCTC also reported to the new Director of National Intelligence, with regard to its responsibilities for fusing agency intelligence on terrorist activities.

66 Interviews with agency and White House officials.

67 Interviews with HSC, OMB, and DHS officials. The Obama administration incorporated the HSC into the NSC architecture. The White House, *Presidential Policy Directive 1: Organization of the National Security Council* (February 13, 2009), and *Presidential Study Directive 1: Organizing for Homeland Security and Counterterrorism* (February 23, 2009).

68 Priscilla Clapp *et al.* richly describe such agency resistance in *Bureaucratic Politics and Foreign Policy* (Washington, DC: Brookings Institution, 2007).

69 For example, the military service's reluctance to embrace national missile defense leading to the creation of a separate agency to administer the program and additional service resources. See Chapter 10.

70 The fear of an "operational" NSC was reinforced by the Iran/Contra experience in the 1980s, when Oliver North conducted operations through the NSC that violated the law. See John Tower (Chair), *The Tower Commission Report (Report of the President's Special Review Board)* (Washington, DC: GPO, February 26, 1987).

71 Gordon Adams, "Establishing the Next President's National Security Agenda," and "Stabilization and Reconstruction in Iraq," in Williams and Adams, *Strengthening Statecraft and Security*.

72 A white paper describing the PCC-56 structure was provided by the White House. William J. Clinton, *The Clinton Administration's Policy on Managing Complex Contingency Operations*, Presidential Decision Directive 56 (May 1997), http://clinton2.nara.gov/WH/EOP/NSC/html/documents/NSCDoc2.html.

73 James Dobbins *et al.*, *America's Role in Nation-Building: From Germany to Iraq* (Santa Monica, CA: RAND, 2003), xxv.

74 Rajiv Chandrasekaran, *Imperial Life in the Emerald City: Inside Iraq's Green Zone* (New York: Vintage, 2007).

75 Joel Brinkley, "Give Rebuilding Lower Priority in Future Wars," *New York Times* (April 8, 2006).

76 See the reports of the Office of the Special Inspector General for Iraq Reconstruction, at www.sigir.mil, for documentation of the difficulties coordinating and implementing the reconstruction funds.

77 US Department of Defense, Military Support for Stability, Security, Transition, and Reconstruction (SSTR) Operations, Directive 3000.05 (November 28, 2005).

78 George W. Bush, *National Security Presidential Directive 44 (NSPD-44)* (December 7, 2005), www.fas.org/irp/offdocs/nspd/nspd-44.html.

79 Ibid.

80 Interviews with executive branch officials.

81 US Department of State, *FY 2009 Budget in Brief* (Washington, DC: February 2008), www.state.gov/documents/organization/100033.pdf, 63–5. In fall 2008, Congress provided $75 million to State and USAID to begin the process of creating the active, stand-by, and reserve corps to begin the process. The FY 2009 appropriation provided another $140 million. S/CRS has had a personnel and administrative budget of roughly $17 million and no contingency funding to start planning operations or conducting early missions.

82 An Army War College paper describes this as follows: "The principle problem of interagency decision-making is lack of *decisive authority*: there is no one in charge." See Gabriel Marcel, "National Security and the Interagency Process," in *US Army War College Guide to National Security Policy and Strategy*, ed. J. Boone Bartholomees (Carlisle Barracks, PA: Army War College, July 2004), 253.

83 Interviews with NSC staff. Such an NSC role would be consistent with the 2005 recommendation of the Center for Strategic and International Studies. Clark Murdock *et al.*, *Beyond Goldwater–Nichols*, esp. Chapters 2, 3 and 4. Marcel called for an "NSC-centric national security system, consolidating the State Policy Planning Staff and DOD's strategic planning, to deal with the need for authoritative decisions." Marcel, "National Security," 253.

84 For further discussion, see the Henry L. Stimson Center and the American Academy of Diplomacy, *A Foreign Affairs Budget for the Future* (Washington, DC: Henry L. Stimson Center, October 2008), 47–59, and Gordon Adams *et al.*, "Providing Authorities and Resources," in *Civilian Surge, Key to Complex Operations: Preliminary Report*, eds. Hans Binnendijk and Patrick M. Cronin (Washington, DC: Center for Technology and National Security Policy, December 2008), 147–60.

85 Confidential interviews with NSC staff and review of the format documents. The NSC questionnaire asked for a description of the specific program and whether it would require additional funding beyond the President's budget. It asked the amount needed, the timing, what budgetary authorities might be used to meet the need, and the funding sources that might be used.

86 This reformed NSC-OMB planning process may reflect proposals made outside the government during the Bush administration. Williams and Adams, *Strengthening Statecraft and Security*; CSIS, *Beyond Goldwater-Nichols*; Project on National Security Reform, *Forging a New Shield*, 323–51.

87 The Budget Enforcement Act of 1990, PL 101-508 (November 5, 1990) required that new spending be offset by reductions elsewhere in the budget, but provided statutory support for emergency supplemental requests. The Act anticipated that emergency spending needs would arise, but they should not trigger the offset requirement, as they would not be recurring expenditures. The Act did not, however, define precisely what constituted an "emergency." OMB did prepare an internal, operational definition of "emergency" spending, however, as "a necessary expenditure that is 'sudden,' 'urgent,' and 'unforeseen,' and is not 'permanent.'"

This definition is reported in Tomkin, *Inside OMB*, 171. It was part of an OMB report fulfilling the requirements of Supplemental Appropriations Act for FY 1991, PL 102-55 (June 13, 1991), covering emergency supplemental funding for humanitarian assistance around Iraq and peacekeeping. This would have likely been written between 1992 and 1993, though Tomkin provides no date. According to Tomkin, the OMB report went on to qualify this definition by asking that the determination of an emergency be made on a "case-by-case" basis, using "common sense judgment," as to whether the "totality of facts and circumstances indicate a true emergency," and "whether the needs can be absorbed within the existing level of resources available."

88 The 1999 requests also sought $850 million to create a DOD contingency fund to support readiness for future peace operations, which was rejected by the Congress.

89 Amy Belasco, *The Cost of Iraq, Afghanistan, and other Global War on Terror Operations Since 9/11*, CRS Report RL33110 (Washington, DC: Congressional Research Service, May 15, 2009), 10.

90 Stephen Daggett, *Military Operations: Precedents for Funding Contingency Operations in Regular or in Supplemental Appropriations Bills*, CRS Report RS22455 (Washington, DC: Congressional Research Service, June 13, 2005).

91 Gordon Adams, *Budgeting for Iraq and the GWOT*, Testimony before the Committee on the Budget, US Senate (February 7, 2007), www.senate.gov/~budget/republican/hearingarchive/testimonies/2007/2007-02-06Adams.pdf.

92 See Gordon Adams, "Post-Combat Stabilization and Reconstruction: The Lessons for US Government Organization and National Security Resource Planning," in *Iraq and America: Choices and Consequences*, eds. Ellen Laipson and Maureen S. Steinbruner (Washington, DC: Henry L. Stimson Center, 2006), 156–61.

93 On the latter program, see Robert T. Deacon and Paul Murphy, "The Structure of an Environmental Transaction: The Debt-for-Nature Swap," *Land Economics*, Vol. 73, No. 1 (1997), 1–24.

94 Interviews with White House staff.

95 Such offsets were required between 1990 and 2002, as part of deficit reduction. The Budget Enforcement Act of 1990 required the government to "pay" for decisions that lowered federal receipts or increased mandatory spending by finding other offsets in revenues or legislative changes (a process known as paygo). Trade agreements could lower projected federal receipts, thus requiring such offsets. Schick, *The Federal Budget*, 162–90.

9 Resource Allocation and Budgeting in Congress

1 The authors wish to acknowledge substantial contributions made to this chapter by Miranda Priebe.

2 As in the rest of this book, we use the term "national security" to include national defense, intelligence, international affairs, and homeland security.

3 The classic reference on the role of committees is Richard F. Fenno, *Congressmen in Committees* (Boston, MA: Little, Brown and Co., 1973).

4 In some years, there is a fourth product: a reconciliation bill that makes the changes in law that will be needed to carry out the fiscal policies established in the Concurrent Budget Resolution. Reconciliation bills typically apply to revenues and to mandatory programs. Mandatory programs are those whose funding is set in existing law, such as Social Security and Medicare. In contrast, most of the funding for security and international affairs falls in the discretionary category, that is, it is appropriated annually. For a discussion of the reconciliation process, see Bill Heniff Jr., *Budget Reconciliation Legislation: Development and Consideration*, CRS Report 98-814 (Washington, DC: Congressional Research Service, August 12, 2008).

5 Bill Heniff Jr., *Overview of the Authorization-Appropriations Process*, CRS Report RS20371 (Washington, DC: Congressional Research Service, June 17, 2008), 2.

6 Susan B. Epstein, *Foreign Relations Authorization, FY2006 and FY2007: An Overview*, CRS Report RL 33000 (Washington, DC: Congressional Research Service, September 15, 2005).

7 Congressional Budget and Impoundment Control Act of 1974, PL 93-344 (July 12, 1974).

8 Allen Schick, *The Federal Budget: Politics, Policy, Process*, 3rd Ed. (Washington, DC: Brookings Institution Press, 2007), 132. Under House rules of the 111th Congress, the committee should include five members from House Appropriations, five from Ways and Means, and one from the Committee on Rules, and one each chosen by the majority and minority leadership. Members other than the chair and ranking minority member may not serve on the committee for more than four of six consecutive Congresses. See "Election and Membership of Standing Committees," in *Rules of the House of Representatives, 111th Congress* (January 28, 2009), Rule X, clause 5 (a)(2)(A), 11.

9 Schick, *The Federal Budget*, 132.

10 The CBO documents in early 2008 were Congressional Budget Office, *The Budget and Economic Outlook: Fiscal Years 2008 to 2018* (Washington, DC: CBO, January 2008), and *An Analysis of the President's Budgetary Proposals for Fiscal Year 2009* (Washington, DC: CBO, March 2008).

11 These allocations do not specify funding for specific programs, but they sometimes state non-binding assumptions about program costs. The text of the resolution also includes a discussion of budget enforcement mechanisms, statements of budget policy, and reconciliation instructions in the event that a reconciliation bill is required to make changes in law to implement the fiscal policy of the resolution. Senate Committee on the Budget, *The Congressional Budget Process: An Explanation* (Washington, DC: GPO, 1998), S. Prt. 105-67.

12 The 302(a) allocation typically distributes all discretionary spending, as well as any mandatory spending funded through appropriations bills, to the Appropriations Committees.

13 Bill Heniff Jr., *Budget Resolution Enforcement*, CRS Report 98-815 (Washington, DC: Congressional Research Service, November 22, 2006).

14 Heniff, *Overview of the Authorization–Appropriations Process*, CRS Report RS20371 (June 17, 2008), 2.

15 There are exceptions. Some appropriations are provided through emergency supplemental appropriations or continuing resolutions, as discussed in the next section. Other activities, such as Department of Defense retail activities like base exchanges and gas stations, do not require an appropriation at all.

16 The Senate rules in this area are more lax than those of the House, and there are exceptions and waivers in both chambers. Schick, *The Federal Budget*, 191–4. Also, exceptions apply for continuing resolutions, omnibus appropriations, and supplemental appropriations. Ibid., 191, 260.

17 Anne C. Richard, *Superpower on the Cheap?* (Paris: Institut Français des Relations Internationales (IFRI), December 2002), 31–2.

18 H.R. 1817, Department of Homeland Security Authorization Act for FY 2006; H.R. 5814, for FY 2007; H.R. 1684, for FY 2008; S. 3623, for FY 2008 to FY 2009. See http://thomas.loc.gov.

19 The process is similar for multi-year authorizations, but is not conducted every year.

20 Committee chairs and ranking minority members can use this power of appointment to influence the outcome in conference.

21 National Defense Authorization Act for FY 2009, PL 110-417 (October 14, 2008), Section 101.

22 Ibid., Section 220.

23 Ibid., Section 601.

24 In some instances, an NDAA has set a permanent or temporary rule for determining future pay raises through a comparison to wage growth in the private sector. When such a rule is in effect, the corresponding raise will prevail if the NDAA is not passed by January 1. On the other hand, if an NDAA is passed and includes a figure for the pay raise, then the new NDAA prevails for the year it covers, even if that figure differs from the one set in the earlier law.

25 Paul Kane, "Hill Negotiators Drop Hate-Crime Provision," *Washington Post* (December 7, 2007).

26 Ibid.

27 National Defense Authorization Act for FY 2008, PL 110-181 (January 28, 2008).

28 Ibid., Section 601.

29 NDAA for FY 2009, PL 110-417, Section 223.

30 Ibid.

31 Office of Management and Budget, *OMB Guidance to Agencies on Definition of Earmarks* (accessed May 19, 2009), http://earmarks.omb.gov/earmarks_definition. html.

32 Technically, earmarks are unrequested funding for activities or programs in which the executive branch does not retain control over the process by which the money is rewarded to recipients; instead, Congress names the recipients explicitly or includes such explicit provisions that only one recipient can qualify. Ibid.

33 Citizens Against Government Waste, "Pork Alert: Defense Authorization," media alert (May 30, 2007).

34 Schick, *The Federal Budget*, 203, 216–22.

35 Ibid, 216–22.

36 Richard, *Superpower on the Cheap?* 31–2. There are some exceptions; authorizations for the Export–Import Bank and the international monetary institutions are generally handled by the banking committees, and food aid by the agriculture committees.

37 For FY 1996 through FY 2001, the authorization of appropriations for foreign relations was included in appropriations acts (in some cases in omnibus or consolidated appropriations). For FY 2003, there was a stand-alone Foreign Relations Authorization Act, PL 107-228 (September 30, 2002). The requirement for authorization of appropriations for FY 2004 and FY 2005 was waived in successive consolidated appropriations acts. Epstein, *Foreign Relations Authorization* (September 15, 2005), 42.

38 Consolidated Appropriations Act for FY 2008, PL 110-161 (December 26, 2007), Division J.

39 For 1985 to 2005, see Epstein, *Foreign Relations Authorization* (September 15, 2005), Summary. A March 2008 review of authorizing legislation using http:// thomas.loc.gov surfaces no Foreign Assistance Act signed into law since 2005.

40 Ibid.

41 Anne C. Richard, *Superpower on the Cheap?* (Paris: Institut Français des Relations Internationales (IFRI), December 2002), 32.

42 Consolidated Appropriations Act for FY 2008, PL 110-161, Division J.

43 Homeland Security Act of 2002, PL 107-296 (November 25, 2002) and Implementing Recommendations of the 9/11 Commission Act of 2007, PL 110-053 (August 3, 2007).

44 Secure Fence Act of 2006, PL 109-367 (October 26, 2006).

45 Coast Guard and Maritime Transportation Act of 2006, PL 109-241 (July 11, 2006).

46 The Acts are the Public Health Security and Bioterrorism Preparedness and

Response Act, PL 107-188 (June 12, 2002); the Smallpox Emergency Personnel Protection Act, PL 108-20 (April 30, 2003); the Project BioShield Act, PL 108-276 (July 21, 2004); and the Pandemic and All-Hazards Preparedness Act (PAHPA), PL 109-417 (December 19, 2006).

47 Until 2005, the subcommittee jurisdictions for foreign assistance and State were distinct and differed by chamber. Foreign Aid had its own appropriation, but State was included in the Commerce and Justice appropriation. That split complicated any attempt to increase spending for international affairs.

48 Sandy Streeter, *The Congressional Appropriations Process: An Introduction*, CRS Report 97-684 (Washington, DC: Congressional Research Service, September 8, 2006), 6.

49 Like the 302(a) allocation, this distribution is named for the section of the Congressional Budget and Impoundment Control Act of 1974 that requires it.

50 FY 2005 Consolidated Appropriations Act, PL 108-447 (December 8, 2004).

51 Streeter, *The Congressional Appropriations Process* (September 8, 2006), 14.

52 Schick, *The Federal Budget*, 260.

53 Public Readiness and Emergency Preparedness Act, PL 109-148 (December 30, 2005), Division C.

54 Supplemental Appropriations Act for 2008, PL 110-252 (June 30, 2008).

55 Committee on Homeland Security, Press Release, *Chairman Thompson on Passage of H.R. 1 and the Future of Homeland Security* (August 2, 2007).

56 Ibid.

57 Other expert commissions and several think tanks have made other recommendations. For a detailed history and analysis of recommendations by commissions and think tanks, see Michael L. Koempel, *Homeland Security: Compendium of Recommendations Relevant to House Committee Organization and Analysis of Considerations for the House, and 109th and 110th Congresses Epilogue*, CRS Report RL32711 (Washington, DC: Congressional Research Service, March 2, 2007), 63.

58 Of course, cross-committee hearings are complicated by issues of jurisdiction. Even decisions about who sits where and in what order committee members will be permitted to question the witnesses can set off a power contest.

10 The Politics of National Security Budgeting

1 As in the rest of this book, we use the term national security to include national defense, intelligence, international affairs, and homeland security.

2 Amy Belasco, *The Cost of Iraq, Afghanistan, and Other Global War on Terror Operations Since 9/11*, CRS Report RL33110 (Washington, DC: Congressional Research Service, October 15, 2008); Joseph E. Stiglitz and Linda J. Bilmes, *The Three Trillion Dollar War: The True Cost of the Iraq Conflict* (New York: Norton, 2008); US Congress, Joint Economic Committee, *War At Any Price?: The Total Economic Costs of the War Beyond the Federal Budget*, Staff Report November 2007.

3 As Aaron Wildavsky and Naomi Caiden put it: "The budgetary process is an arena in which the struggle for power over public policy is worked out." Wildavsky and Caiden, *The New Politics of the Budgetary Process*, 5th Ed. (New York: Pearson/Longman, 2004), 204.

4 In FY 2008, for example, total budgets (Budget Authority) for International Affairs (Function 150) came to $39.5 billion, which was 5.7 percent of the $693 billion investment in National Defense (Function 050). By contrast, in FY 1976, International Affairs funding was 14.1 percent of the amount for National Defense. Office of Management and Budget, *Budget of the United States Government Fiscal Year 2009: Historical Tables* (Washington, DC: OMB, February 2008), 86, Table 5.1.

5 Cindy Williams, *Strengthening Homeland Security: Reforming Planning and Resource Allocation* (Washington, DC: IBM Center for the Business of Government, 2008), 12–13.

6 One recent exception is Harvey M. Sapolsky *et al., US Defense Politics: The Origins of Security Policy* (New York: Routledge, 2009).

7 In their classic discussion of national security decision-making, Graham Allison and Philip Zelikow note only in passing that "[A] number of established processes fix deadlines that demand action at appointed times," and cite the federal budget process as one of several such processes. Allison and Zelikow, *Essence of Decision: Explaining the Cuban Missile Crisis*, 2nd Ed. (New York: Longman, 1999), 299. Budget processes are largely ignored in Priscilla Clapp *et al., Bureaucratic Politics and Foreign Policy*, 2nd Ed. (Washington, DC: Brookings Institution, 2007); William W. Newmann, *Managing National Security Policy: The President and the Process* (Pittsburg, PA: University of Pittsburg Press, 2003); and Amy Ziegart, *Flawed by Design: The Evolution of the CIA, JCS, and NSC* (Stanford, CA: Stanford University Press, 1999).

8 See, for example, Wildavsky and Caiden, *The New Politics*; Allen Schick, *The Federal Budget: Policy, Politics, Process*, 3rd Ed. (Washington, DC: Brookings Institution, 2007); and Stanley E. Collender, *Guide to the Federal Budget: Fiscal Year 1997* (New York: Rowman and Littlefield, 1996).

9 Political scientist Warner R. Schilling captured this perspective:

> In general, the question can be conceived as one susceptible to a rational solution; it is a question of knowing the dimensions of the security problem at hand, the relative importance of the national ends involved, the nature of the means available, and the consequences that would flow for those ends from the alternative ways in which the available means can be employed to secure them.
>
> Schilling, "The Politics of National Defense: Fiscal 1950," in *Strategy, Politics, and Defense Budgets*, eds. Warner R. Schilling, Paul Y. Hammond, and Glenn H. Snyder (New York: Columbia University Press, 1962), 10.

10 This perspective on decision-making is similar to the "Rational Actor Model" in Allison and Zelikow, *Essence of Decision*, 18. Rationality, in their model "refers to consistent, value-maximizing choice within specified constraints." This model views decisions from a perspective that is, in principle, independent of any given nation. It is tied closely to "realist" thinking about international relations, in which states are unitary actors pursuing rational interests with either perfect or imperfect knowledge about the conditions around them. For a critique of Allison and Zelikow's use of this model, see Jonathan Bendor and Thomas H. Hammond, "Rethinking Allison's Models," *American Political Science Review*, Vol. 86, No. 2 (June 1992), 304–9.

11 The Clinton administration produced the lengthy *A National Security Strategy for a New Century* (Washington, DC: White House, October 1998), which covered virtually every security and international economic issue, as well as regional and functional issues. The George W. Bush administration produced several such documents: *The National Security Strategy of the United States of America* (Washington, DC: White House, 2002 and 2006); *The National Strategy to Combat Weapons of Mass Destruction* (Washington, DC: White House, December 2002); *The National Strategy for Combating Terrorism* (Washington, DC: White House, February 2003 and September 2006); and *The National Strategy for Homeland Security* (Washington, DC: White House, July 2002 and October 2007). Departments also produced such documents. See, for example, Secretary of Defense Donald Rumsfeld, *The National Defense Strategy of the United States* (Washington, DC: Office of

the Secretary of Defense, March 2005); Joint Chiefs of Staff, *The National Military Strategy of the United States* (Washington, DC: Department of Defense, 2004); US Department of State and US Agency for International Development, *Strategic Plan, Fiscal Years 2007–2012* (Washington, DC: Department of State, 2006); and Office of the Director for National Intelligence, *The National Intelligence Strategy of the United States of America* (Washington, DC: ODNI, October 2005).

12 James M. Goldgeier, *Not Whether, But When: The US Decision to Enlarge NATO* (Washington, DC: Brookings Institution, 1999).

13 Table 10.1 exaggerates the rise in homeland security spending, because the Bush administration expanded the list of activities that it reported as homeland security-related during the period between FY 2001 and FY 2009. This definitional expansion was particularly pronounced in the Department of Defense.

14 Wildavsky and Caiden argue that bureaucracy (along with congressional politics) provides the most powerful explanations for federal budget decisions:

> The largest determining factor of this year's budget is last year's.... Budgeting is incremental, not comprehensive. The beginning wisdom about an agency budget is that it is almost never actively reviewed as a whole every year, in the sense of reconsidering the value of all existing programs as compared to all possible alternatives. Instead, it is based on last year's budget with special attention given to a narrow range of increases or decreases ... Political reality, budget officials say, restricts attention to items they can do something about—a few new programs and possible cuts in old ones.
>
> Wildavsky and Caiden, *The New Politics*, 46.

15 In his classic study of bureaucracy, James Q. Wilson noted that bureaucratic institutions defend their turf by seeking out tasks others are not performing, fighting off organizations that try to enter their turf, stick to their core competences, and try to avoid joint ventures with other bureaucracies. Wilson, *Bureaucracy: What Government Agencies Do and Why They Do It* (New York: Basic Books, 1989), 181–95.

16 See Allison and Zelikow, *Essence of Decision*, 143–96, for a discussion of their "Organizational Behavior" model of decision-making, which is a classic description of this perspective.

17 The literature on defense decision-making, particularly on weapons programs, is extensive. See, among others, Gordon Adams, *The Iron Triangle: The Politics of Defense Contracting* (New Brunswick, NJ: Transaction Press, 1981); Michael Armacost, *The Politics of Weapons Innovation: The Thor-Jupiter Controversy* (New York: Columbia University Press, 1969); Robert J. Art, *The TFX Decision: McNamara and the Military* (New York: Little Brown, 1968); Theo Farrell, *Weapons Without a Cause: The Politics of Weapons Acquisition* (New York: St. Martin's Press, 1997); Ted Greenwood, *Making the MIRV: A Study of Defense Decision-Making* (Cambridge: Cambridge University Press, 1975); Lauren Holland, *Weapons Under Fire* (New York: Routledge, 1997); James Kurth, "The Political Economy of Weapons Procurement: The Follow-On Imperative," *American Economic Review*, Vol. 62, No. 2 (May 1972), 304–11; Kenneth Mayer, *The Political Economy of Defense Contracting* (New Haven, CT: Yale University Press, 1991); Harvey Sapolsky, *The Polaris System Development: Bureaucratic and Programmatic Success in Government* (Cambridge, MA: Harvard University Press, 1972).

18 For a classic study of culture of the military services, see Carl Builder, *The Masks of War: American Military Styles in Strategy and Analysis* (Baltimore, MD: Johns Hopkins University Press, 1989).

19 Allison and Zelikow, *Essence of Decision*, 169, describe the military services:

[T]he behavior of each of the US military services ... seems to be characterized by effective imperatives to avoid: (1) a decrease in dollars budgeted, (2) a decrease in manpower, (3) a decrease in the number of key specialists (e.g., for the Air Force, pilots), (4) reduction in the percentage of the military budget allocated to that service, (5) encroachment of other services on that service's roles and missions, and (6) inferiority to an enemy weapon of any class.

20 As Admiral William A. Owens puts it:

[I]n the information age, when technological advances have blurred the traditional boundaries in space and time that long physically separated the Air Force from the Navy and the Army from the Marine Corps, the military services' inability to communicate with one another and their indifference to doing so have set the stage for crisis and disaster.

Owens, *Lifting the Fog of War* (New York: Farrar, Straus, Giroux, 2000), 157–8.

21 The reform of DOD and service structures in the 1980s contributed to considerable progress in breaking down the barriers between the services. For the origins of these reforms, commonly known as "Goldwater–Nichols," see James R. Locher, *Victory on the Potomac: the Goldwater–Nichols Act Unifies the Pentagon* (College Station: Texas A&M University Press, 2002). For proposals that would continue this progress, see Clark Murdock *et al.*, *Beyond Goldwater–Nichols Phase 1 Report: Defense Reform for a New Strategic Era* (Washington, DC: Center for Strategic and International Studies, March 2004), and *Beyond Goldwater–Nichols Phase II Report: US Government and Defense Reform for a New Strategic Era* (Washington, DC: Center for Strategic and International Studies, July 2005).

22 Owens, *Lifting the Fog of War*, 157, 159.

23 The Chairman and the Joint Chiefs are not a "general staff"; they do not have operational command of the COCOMs or combat forces in the field, which is the responsibility of the President and the Secretary of Defense.

24 For examples of such budget balancing, see Cindy Williams, ed., *Holding the Line: US Defense Alternatives for the Early 21st Century* (Cambridge, MA: MIT Press, 2001).

25 Gordon Adams, *The Politics of National Security Budgets*, Policy Analysis Brief (Muscatine, IA: The Stanley Foundation, February 2007).

26 Harold D. Lasswell, *Politics: Who Gets What, When, and How* (Rochester, NY: Whittlesey House, 1936). Schilling underlines the importance of a political perspective in understanding the budget process:

An appreciation of these two central aspects of defense budgeting—the inordinate intellectual difficulty of the problems involved, and the fact that they are resolved through the medium of politics as well as that of analysis—is essential for an understanding of the post-1945 budgeting process and the kind of budgets produced by that process.

Schilling, "The Politics of National Defense," 11.

27 This dimension of the political arena is similar to Allison and Zelikow's "Governmental Politics" model III.

The leaders who sit atop organizations are no monolith. Rather, each individual in this group is, in his or her own right, a player in a central, competitive game. The name of the game is politics: bargaining along regular circuits among players positioned hierarchically within the government.

Allison and Zelikow, *Essence of Decision*, 255–324, at 255.

28 Clapp *et al.* conflate the policy official and bureaucratic levels in their classic study, making it difficult to sort out the influence of bureaucrats from that of policy officials. In reality, much of what they discuss reflects the roles, personalities, and interaction of policy officials. Clapp *et al., Bureaucratic Politics.*

29 John Prados, *Soviet Estimate: US Intelligence Analysis and Russian Military Strength* (New York: Dial Press, 1982).

30 This view is disputed, however, in James M. Lindsay, *Congress and the Politics of US Foreign Policy* (Baltimore, MD: Johns Hopkins University Press, 1994); and James M. Lindsay and Randall B. Ripley, *Congress Resurgent: Foreign and Defense Policy on Capitol Hill* (Ann Arbor, MI: University of Michigan Press, 1993).

31 Article 1, Section 8 of the constitution gives Congress the authority "to raise and support Armies…; to provide and maintain a Navy; [and] to make Rules for the Government and regulation of the land and naval Forces." Article 1, Section 9 provides that "no Money shall be drawn from the Treasury, but in Consequence of Appropriations made by law" Allison and Zelikow, *Essence of Decision,* however, refer only in passing to the role of Congress in national security policymaking and make almost no reference to the congressional budget process.

32 There is an extensive literature on such iron triangles or "sub-governments." Adams, *The Iron Triangle*; Gordon Adams, "Disarming the Military Sub-Government," *Harvard Journal on Legislation,* Vol. 14, No. 3 (April 1977); Joel D. Auerbach and Bert Rockman, "Bureaucrats and Clientele Groups: A View From Capitol Hill," *American Journal of Political Science,* Vol. 22, No. 4 (November 1978); Stephen Bailey, *Congress in the Seventies,* 2nd Ed. (New York: St. Martin's Press, 1970); Douglas Cater, *Power in Washington* (New York: Random House, 1964); J. Lieper Freeman, *The Political Process* (Garden City, NY: Doubleday, 1955); Grant McConnell, *Private Power and American Democracy* (New York: Knopf, 1966); and Lester V. Salamon and John J. Siegfried, "Economic Power and Political Influence: The Impact of Industry Structure on Public Policy," *American Political Science Review,* Vol. 71, No. 3 (September 1977).

33 Mark Gearan, Peace Corps Director from 1995 to 1999, had been a senior White House communications official, which gave him unusual access to the White House to lobby for his budget request. The result often led to an increase in the Peace Corps budget over the amount approved by OMB.

34 During the Clinton administration, USAID Director Brian Atwood cultivated a separate relationship with the White House, including the President, through which he made the case for higher funding levels, and institutional autonomy from the State Department.

35 Note, however, that much of the increase for Function 150 funding during the Powell and Rice tenures was for presidential initiatives—the Millennium Challenge and HIV/AIDS programs. Both Secretaries were able to increase funding for personnel and overseas building construction and embassy security, as well.

36 The US Global Leadership Campaign was created in 1995. It is a coalition of more than 400 business and non-profit organizations, from Boeing and Motorola, to CARE and Mercy Corps, to the American Israeli Public Affairs Committee and the African-American Institute whose explicit purpose is to lobby for increases in the overall International Affairs budget, but not any particular program in that budget.

37 Trading and financial businesses and organizations, such as the National Foreign Trade Council, lobby for the budgets of trade and international finance agencies such as OPIC, EXIM Bank, TDA, and USTR.

38 The Budget Enforcement Act of 1990, PL 101-508 (November 5, 1990) had moved the date for formal submission of the President's budget from early January to early February, after a new president came into office.

39 For a detailed discussion of the economic and budgetary planning process at the start of the Clinton Administration, see Bob Woodward, *The Agenda: Inside the Clinton White House* (New York: Simon and Schuster, 1994).

40 For a discussion of base force planning and its relationship to the budget, seen from the Joint Chief's perspective, see Sharon K. Weiner, "The Politics of Resource Allocation in the Post-Cold War Pentagon," *Security Studies*, Vol. 5, No. 4 (summer 1996), esp. 133, 137, 140.

41 The White House also made a strong effort to keep the 1995 round of base closings from adding to the President's weakness on defense. In particular, the closing of two air logistic facilities in San Antonio, Texas, and Sacramento, California, recommended by the base closing commission, was resisted by the White House in part because of the potential impact of those closures on the President's 1996 re-election prospects.

42 The politics of this defense budget increase is described by George Wilson, *This War Really Matters: Inside the Fight for Defense Dollars* (Washington, DC: Congressional Quarterly Press, 2000), esp. Chapters 1, 5, and 6.

43 Wilson, *This War Really Matters*, 96.

44 In the end, an emergency budget supplemental was agreed to, end-running the problem of the caps.

45 The contrast with 1981 is worth noting, since the Reagan administration came into office with a significant economic agenda, including a major tax cut, which it pushed through the Congress very quickly, despite Democratic opposition. The difference is that Reagan also came into office with a commitment to major increases in defense spending, which were implemented early as well, largely without detailed DOD planning. David Stockman, *The Triumph of Politics: Why the Reagan Revolution Failed* (New York: Avon Books, 1987).

46 Congressional constraints created by fiscal conservatism were largely end-run over these years by funding war costs (and other defense programs) through emergency supplementals. Between FY 2001 and FY 2008, those supplementals provided over $860 billion in defense funding, adding roughly 20 percent to overall projected defense resources. Amy Belasco, *The Costs of Iraq, Afghanistan and Other Global War on Terror Operations Since 9/11*, CRS Report RL 33110 (Washington, DC: Congressional Research Service, October 15, 2008).

47 See, for example, Richard A. Clarke's discussion in *Against All Enemies: Inside America's War on Terror* (New York: Free Press, 2004).

48 Advisory Panel to Address Domestic Response Capabilities for Terrorism Involving Weapons of Mass Destruction (Gilmore Panel), *Second Annual Report: Toward A National Strategy for Combating Terrorism* (Washington, DC: RAND Corporation, December 15, 2000).

49 US Commission on National Security/21st Century, *Roadmap for National Security: Imperative for Change*, Phase III Report (February 15, 2001), vi. The report describes a terrorist attack on the US homeland as "the most dangerous and the most novel threat to American national security in the years ahead." Ibid., 8. See also Chapter 1, "Securing the National Homeland," of the report, which argues that

> a direct attack against American citizens on American soil is likely over the next quarter century. The risk is not only death and destruction but also a demoralization that could undermine US global leadership. In the face of this threat, our nation has no coherent or integrated governmental structures.
>
> Ibid., 10.

50 Bush, *National Strategy for Combating Terrorism* (February 2003), www.globalsecurity.org/security/library/policy/national/nsct_sep2006.htm.

51 James B. Steinberg *et al.*, *Protecting the Homeland, 2006/07* (Washington, DC: Brookings Institution, 2006); Donald F. Kettl, *System Under Stress: Homeland Security and American Politics* (Washington, DC: Congressional Quarterly Press, 2007); and interviews conducted by the authors.

52 National Commission on Terrorist Attacks, *The 9/11 Commission Report: Final Report of the National Commission on Terrorist Attacks Upon the United States* (New York: Norton, 2004); Office of the Director of National Intelligence, *The National Intelligence Strategy of the United States of America.*

53 Office of Management and Budget, "Homeland Security Funding Analysis," *Budget of the United States Government, Fiscal Year 2009: Analytical Perspectives, Supplemental Materials* (Washington, DC: GPO, 2008), 33, Table 3.11.

54 The "homeland security strategy" clearly has terrorism as its *raison d'être*. The "Homeland Security Funding Analysis" chapter in *Analytical Perspectives* of the FY 2009 federal budget described this spending as intended "to prevent terrorist attacks within the United States, reduce America's vulnerability to terrorism, and minimize the damage from attacks that may occur." Ibid., 19.

55 Williams, *Strengthening Homeland Security.*

56 For a more skeptical view of the terrorist threat, see John Mueller, *Overblown: How Politicians and the Terrorism Industry Inflate National Security Threats and Why We Believe Them* (New York: Free Press, 2006).

57 Kettl, *System Under Stress.*

58 Frances Fitzgerald, *Way Out There In the Blue: Reagan, Star Wars and the End of the Cold War* (New York: Simon and Schuster, 2000).

59 James M. Lindsay and Michael E. O'Hanlon, *Defending America: The Case for Limited National Missile Defense* (Washington, DC: Brookings Institution, 2001), 13 and 50–82; and Donald Rumsfeld (Chair), *Report of the Commission to Assess the Ballistic Missile Threat to the United States* (Rumsfeld Commission) (Washington, DC: Central Intelligence Agency, July 15, 1998).

60 Robert Holzer and Amy Switak, "Pentagon Mulls Structural Change for Missile Office," *Defense News* (May 14, 2001), 1. On service resistance to missile defense because of the risk of budget pressures, see Builder, *The Masks of War*, 198–202. A similar strategy of isolating a program and its organization from bureaucratic resistance based on traditional service mission and budgetary concerns was used to develop the Polaris missile program in the 1950s. Sapolsky, *The Polaris System Development.*

61 William Hartung and Michelle Ciarrocca, "Star Wars II: Here We Go Again," *The Nation* (June 12, 2000), and "Star Wars Revisited: Still Dangerous, Costly, and Unworkable," *Foreign Policy in Focus*, Vol. 4, No. 4 (April 2000).

62 National Defense Authorization Act for Fiscal Year 1997, PL 104-201 (September 23, 1996), Section 1321(g).

63 Rumsfeld Commission, "Executive Summary," *Report of the Commission to Assess the Ballistic Missile Threat to the United States*, www.fas.org/irp/threat/bm-threat. htm.

64   While reconfiguring its nuclear force, the United States also must counteract the effects of the proliferation of ballistic missiles and weapons of mass destruction that may soon allow lesser states to deter US military action by threatening US allies and the American homeland itself. Of all the new and current missions for US armed forces, this must have priority.
         Project for the New American Century, *Rebuilding the Nation's Defenses* (Washington, DC: PNAC, September 2000), 6.

PNAC members included Donald Rumsfeld, Dick Cheney, Paul Wolfowitz, Richard Perle, Elliot Abrams, William Schneider, Lewis Libby, and John Bolton.

65 Wade Bose, "Bush Outlines Arms Control and Missile Defense Plans," *Arms Control Today* (June 2000). An excellent compendium of major documents and articles on BMD can be found at Arms Control Association, *Subject Resources: Missile Defense*, www.armscontrol.org/subject/md (accessed June 19, 2009).

66 For a discussion of the politics of the B-1 bomber in the 1970s, see Nick Kotz, *Wild Blue Yonder: Money, Politics, and the B-1 Bomber* (New York: Pantheon Books, 1988).

67 For a detailed discussion of the national security arguments over this and later bomber programs, see Michael E. Brown, *Flying Blind: The Politics of the US Strategic Bomber Program* (Ithaca, NY: Cornell University Press, 1992). Brown deals in less detail with the issue of presidential politics. In his view, bureaucratic imperatives—the Air Force desire for the program—were critical. "[T]he strategic rationale for the program was fuzzy at best and organizationally driven, at worst." Ibid., 261.

68 Parts of the B-1 were manufactured in 48 states and all but a handful of Congressional districts. Gordon Adams, *The B-1 Bomber: An Analysis of Its Strategic Utility, Cost, Constituency and Economic Impact* (New York: Council on Economic Priorities, May 1976).

69 Brown, *Flying Blind*, 271–81.

11 The Road Ahead: How Might Budgeting Change?

1 As elsewhere in this book, we use the term national security to encompass all aspects of national defense, intelligence, international affairs, and homeland security.

2 Henry L. Stimson Center and the American Academy of Diplomacy, *A Foreign Affairs Budget for the Future* (Washington, DC: Henry L. Stimson Center, October, October 2008), 11, www.academyofdiplomacy.org/publications/FAB_report_2008.pdf.

3 Modernizing Foreign Assistance Network, *New Day, New Way: US Foreign Assistance for the 21st Century* (Washington, DC: Center for Global Development, June 2008), ii, www.modernizingforeignassistance.net/documents/newdaynewway.pdf.

4 Secretary of State's Advisory Committee on Transformational Diplomacy, 7 (Washington, DC: Department of State, 2007), www.state.gov/documents/organization/99903.pdf.

5 Stimson Center and American Academy of Diplomacy, *A Foreign Affairs Budget for the Future*, 67–8.

6 Gordon Adams *et al.*, "Providing Authorities and Resources," in *Civilian Surge, Key to Complex Operations: Preliminary Report*, eds. Hans Binnendijk and Patrick M. Cronin (Washington, DC: Center for Technology and National Security Policy, 2008), 147–60.

7 Gordon Adams, *Smart Power: Rebalancing the Foreign Policy/National Security Toolkit*, Testimony before the Senate Committee on Homeland Security and Governmental Affairs, Subcommittee on Oversight of Government Management, the Federal Workforce, and the District of Colombia (July 31, 2008), http://hsgac.senate.gov/public/_files/AdamsTestimony073108.pdf. See also, Gordon Adams, *The Role of Civilian and Military Agencies in the Advancement of America's Diplomatic and Development Objectives*, Testimony before the House Committee on Appropriation, Subcommittee on State, Foreign Operations and Related Programs (March 5, 2009), http://appropriations.house.gov/Witness_testimony/SFOPS/Dr_Gordon_Adams_03_05_09.pdf.

8 Foreign Relations Authorization Act, Fiscal Years 2010 and 2011, HR 2410 (June 10, 2009), Section 302, 78–86. An important role will be played here by the National Security Council and OMB, as well.

9 Initiating Foreign Assistance Reform Act of 2009, HR 2139 (April 28, 2009), introduced by the House Committee on Foreign Affairs, http://frwebgate.access.gpo.
   gov/cgi-bin/getdoc.cgi?dbname=111_cong_bills&docid=f:h2139ih.txt.pdf.
10 US Government Accountability Office, *Defense Acquisitions: Assessments of
   Selected Weapon Programs*, GAO-op-326SP (Washington, DC: GAO, March
   2009).
11 The Weapons Systems Acquisition Reform Act, PL 111-23 (May 22, 2009).
12 Mike Mullen, *Remarks at Princeton University Woodrow Wilson School of Public
   and International Affairs* (February 5, 2009), www.jcs.mil/speech.aspx?ID=1128.
13 Sam Legrone, "Gates Demands Review of US Service Chiefs Wish Lists," *Defense
   News* (May 18, 2009), www.defensenews.com/story.php?i=4094483 (accessed May
   31, 2009).
14 Cindy Williams, *Strengthening Homeland Security: Reforming Planning and
   Resource Allocation* (Washington, DC: IBM Center for the Business of Government, 2008), and "Planning and Resource Allocation for Statecraft and Security,"
   Working Paper for the Tobin Project (November 2008), www.tobinproject.org/
   welcome/conference_security/papers/TobinProject_Williams.pdf.
15 See, in particular, Project on National Security Reform, *Forging a New Shield*
   (Washington, DC: PNSR, December 2008); Robert E. Hunter, Edward Gnehm,
   and George Joulwan, *Integrating Instruments of Power and Influence, Lessons
   Learned and Best Practices* (Washington, DC: RAND Corporation, 2008); Cindy
   Williams and Gordon Adams, *Strengthening Statecraft and Security: Reforming US
   Planning and Resource Allocation* (Cambridge, MA: MIT Security Studies Program
   Occasional Paper, June 2008); Center for Strategic and International Studies, Clark
   A. Murdock *et al.*, *Beyond Goldwater–Nichols Pase II Report: US Government and
   Defense Reform for a New Strategic Era* (Washington, DC: CSIS, July 2005).
16 The George W. Bush administration grouped these budget data together as a
   "security budget" in its FY 2009 budget request to the Congress, but did not integrate the description of national security programs.
17 White House, Statement by the President on the White House Organization for
   Homeland Security and Counterterrorism, Press Release (May 26, 2009).
18 Williams and Adams, *Strengthening Statecraft and Security*.

Bibliography

Adams, Gordon. *The B-1 Bomber: An Analysis of Its Strategic Utility, Cost, Constituency and Economic Impact.* New York: Council on Economic Priorities, May 1976.

———. "Disarming the Military Sub-Government." *Harvard Journal on Legislation,* Vol. 14, No. 3 (April 1977).

———. *The Iron Triangle: The Politics of Defense Contracting.* New Brunswick, NJ: Transaction Press, 1981.

———. "Post-Combat Stabilization and Reconstruction: The Lessons for US Government Organization and National Security Resource Planning." In *Iraq and America: Choices and Consequences,* edited by Ellen Laipson and Maureen S. Steinbruner. Washington, DC: Henry L. Stimson Center, 2006.

———. *The Politics of National Security Budgets.* Policy Analysis Brief. Muscatine, IA: The Stanley Foundation, February 2007.

———. *Budgeting for Iraq and the GWOT.* Testimony before the Senate Committee on the Budget. February 7, 2007. www.senate.gov/~budget/republican/hearingarchive/testimonies/2007/2007-02-06Adams.pdf.

———. "Don't Reinvent the Foreign Assistance Wheel." *Foreign Service Journal,* March 2008.

———. *Rebalancing and Integrating the National Security Toolkit.* Testimony before the Senate Foreign Relations Committee. April 24, 2008. http://foreign.senate.gov/testimony/2008/AdamsTestimony080424a.pdf.

———. "Getting U.S. Foreign Assistance Right." *Bulletin of the Atomic Scientists,* May 2, 2008.

———. "Establishing the Next President's National Security Agenda: The Role of the White House." *Bulletin of the Atomic Scientists,* June 30, 2008.

Adams, Gordon, William Bacchus, and David Glaudemans. "Providing Authorities and Resources." In *Civilian Surge, Key to Complex Operations: Preliminary Report,* edited by Hans Binnendijk and Patrick M. Cronin. Washington, DC: Center for Technology and National Security Policy, December 2008.

Advisory Panel to Address Domestic Response Capabilities for Terrorism Involving Weapons of Mass Destruction (Gilmore Panel). *Second Annual Report: Toward A National Strategy for Combating Terrorism.* Washington, DC: RAND, December 15, 2000.

Allison, Graham, and Philip Zelikow. *Essence of Decision: Explaining the Cuban Missile Crisis.* 2nd Ed. New York: Longman, 1999.

Armacost, Michael. *The Politics of Weapons Innovation: The Thor-Jupiter Controversy.* New York: Columbia University Press, 1969.

Art, Robert J. *The TFX Decision: McNamara and the Military.* New York: Little Brown, 1968.

Auerbach, Joel D., and Bert Rockman. "Bureaucrats and Clientele Groups: A View From Capitol Hill." *American Journal of Political Science*, Vol. 22, No. 4 (November 1978).

Bacchus, William J. *The Price of American Foreign Policy: Congress, The Executive, and International Affairs Funding.* University Park, PA: Pennsylvania State University Press, 1997.

Bailey, Stephen. *Congress in the Seventies.* 2nd Ed. New York: St. Martin's Press, 1970.

Bamford, James. *The Puzzle Palace: Inside the National Security Agency, America's Most Secret Intelligence Organization.* New York: Penguin, 1983.

——. *The Shadow Factory: The Ultra-Secret NSA from 9/11 to the Eavesdropping on America.* New York: Doubleday, 2008.

Barrett, Christopher B., and Daniel G. Maxwell. *Food Aid After Fifty Years: Recasting Its Role.* London: Routledge, 2005.

Bazzi, Samuel, Sheila Herrling, and Stewart Patrick. *Billions for War, Pennies for the Poor: Moving the President's FY 2008 Budget from Hard Power to Smart Power.* Washington, DC: Center for Global Development, March 16, 2007.

Becker, William, and William M. McClenahan Jr. *The Market, the State, and the Export-Import Bank of the United States, 1934–2000.* New York: Cambridge University Press, 2003.

Belasco, Amy. *The Cost of Iraq, Afghanistan, and other Global War on Terror Operations Since 9/11.* CRS Report RL33110. Washington, DC: Congressional Research Service, October 15, 2008.

Bendor, Jonathan, and Thomas H. Hammond. "Rethinking Allison's Models." *American Political Science Review*, Vol. 86, No. 2 (June 1992).

Bennett, Steve. *DHS Bioterrorism Risk Assessment: Background, Requirements, and Overview.* Briefing to the Committee on Methodological Improvement to the Department of Homeland Security's 2006 Bioterrorism Risk Assessment. August 28, 2006.

Best, Richard A., and Alfred Cumming. *Director of National Intelligence Statutory Authorities: Status and Proposals.* CRS Report RL34231. Washington, DC: Congressional Research Service, April 17, 2008.

Bite, Vita. *U.N. System Funding: Congressional Issues.* CRS Report IB86116. Washington, DC: Congressional Research Service, November 15, 2001.

Bose, Wade. "Bush Outlines Arms Control and Missile Defense Plans." *Arms Control Today.* June 2000.

Brainard, Lael, ed. *Security by Other Means: Foreign Assistance, Global Poverty, and American Leadership.* Washington, DC: Brookings Institution, 2007.

Brass, Clinton T. *The Bush Administration's Program Assessment Rating Tool (PART).* CRS Report RL32663. Washington, DC: Congressional Research Service, November 5, 2004.

Broadcasting Board of Governors. *Marrying the Mission to the Market: Strategic Plan, 2002–2007.* Washington, DC: 2002.

——. *FY 2006 Performance and Accountability Report.* Washington, DC: November 15, 2006.

Brown, Michael E. *Flying Blind: The Politics of the US Strategic Bomber Program.* Ithaca, NY: Cornell University Press, 1992.

Browne, Marjorie Ann. *United Nations Peacekeeping: Issues for Congress.* Issue Brief IB90103. Washington, DC: Congressional Research Service, July 5, 2006.

Builder, Carl. *The Masks of War: American Military Styles in Strategy and Analysis.* Baltimore, MD: Johns Hopkins University Press, 1989.

Bush, George W. *Homeland Security Presidential Directive 1 (HSPD-1): Organization and Operation of the Homeland Security Council.* October 29, 2001.

——. *National Security Presidential Directive 44* (NSPD-44). December 7, 2005. www.fas.org/irp/offdocs/nspd/nspd-44.html.

——. *The National Security Strategy of the United States of America.* Washington, DC: White House, September 2002 and March 2006.

——. *The National Strategy for Combating Terrorism.* Washington, DC: White House, February 2003 and September 2006.

——. *The National Strategy for Homeland Security.* Washington, DC: Homeland Security Council, July 2002 and October 2007.

——. *The National Strategy to Combat Weapons of Mass Destruction.* Washington, DC: White House, December 2002.

——. *U.S. President's Emergency Plan for AIDS Relief. Fiscal Year 2008: PEPFAR Operational Plan.* June 2008. www.pepfar.gov/documents/organization/107838.pdf.

Carter, Linwood B., and Thomas Coipuram Jr. *Defense Authorization and Appropriations Bills: A Chronology, FY 1970-FY 2006.* CRS Report 98-756C. Washington, DC: Congressional Research Service, May 23, 2005.

Cater, Douglas. *Power in Washington.* New York: Random House, 1964.

Center for Strategic and International Studies. *Integrating 21st Century Development and Security Assistance.* Final Report of the Task Force on Non-Traditional Security Assistance. Washington, DC: January 2008.

Chandrasekaran, Rajiv. *Imperial Life in the Emerald City: Inside Iraq's Green Zone.* New York: Vintage, 2007.

Church, Albert T., and Ted Warner. "DOD Planning, Programming, Budgeting, and Execution System: A Path Toward Improvement." *Joint Forces Quarterly,* Issue 52 (2nd Quarter 2009).

Clapp, Priscilla, Morton Halperin, and Arnold Kanter. *Bureaucratic Politics and Foreign Policy.* Washington, DC: Brookings Institution, 2007.

Clarke, Duncan L., Daniel B. O'Connor, and Jason D. Ellis. *Send Guns and Money: Security Assistance and US Foreign Policy.* Westport, CT: Praeger, 1997.

Clarke, Richard A. *Against All Enemies: Inside America's War on Terror.* New York: Free Press, 2004.

Clinton, William J. *The Clinton Administration's Policy on Managing Complex Contingency Operation.* Presidential Decision Directive 56. May 1997. http://clinton2.nara.gov/WH/EOP/NSC/html/documents/NSCDoc2.html.

——. *A National Security Strategy for a New Century.* Washington, DC: White House, October 1998.

Cohen, Craig. *A Perilous Course: US Strategy and Assistance to Pakistan.* Washington, DC: Center for Strategic and International Studies, August 2007.

Cohen, Craig, and Derek Chollet. "When $10 Billion Is Not Enough: Rethinking US Strategy Toward Pakistan." *The Washington Quarterly,* Vol. 30, No. 2 (spring 2007).

Collender, Stanley E. *Guide to the Federal Budget: Fiscal Year 1997*. New York: Rowman and Littlefield, 1996.

Committee on Foreign Relations/Committee on International Relations. *Legislation on Foreign Relations Through 2005*. Joint Committee Print, Vol. 1-A. Washington, DC: US Congress, January 2006.

Congressional Budget Office. *The Budget and Economic Outlook: Fiscal Years 2008 to 2018*. Washington, DC: CBO, January 2008.

——. *An Analysis of the President's Budgetary Proposals for Fiscal Year 2009*. Washington, DC: CBO, March 2008.

Copson, Raymond. *The Global Fund and PEPFAR in US International AIDS Policy*. CRS Report RL33135. Washington, DC: Congressional Research Service, November 2005.

Council on Foreign Relations/Center for Strategic and International Studies. *State Department Reform: Report of an Independent Task Force* (Carlucci Commission). Washington, DC: 2001.

Crosby, Harry [pseud.]. "Too at Home Abroad." *The Washington Monthly*, September 1991.

Daggett, Stephen. *The US Intelligence Budget: A Basic Overview*. CRS Report RS21945. Washington, DC: Congressional Research Service, September 24, 2004.

——. *Military Operations: Precedents for Funding Contingency Operations in Regular or in Supplemental Appropriations Bills*. CRS Report RS22455. Washington, DC: Congressional Research Service, June 13, 2005.

Dale, Catherine. *National Security Strategy: Legislative Mandates, Execution to Date, and Considerations for Congress*. CRS Report RL34505. Washington, DC: Congressional Research Service, May 28, 2008.

Deacon, Robert T., and Paul Murphy. "The Structure of an Environmental Transaction: The Debt-for-Nature Swap." *Land Economics*, Vol. 73, No. 1 (1997), 1–24.

Defense Institute of Security Assistance Management. *DISAM's Online Greenbook: The Management of Security Assistance*. 27th Ed. Washington, DC: October 2007. www.disam.dsca.mil/pubs/DR/greenbook.htm.

Destler, I.M. *The National Economic Council: A Work in Progress*. Policy Analysis No. 46. Washington, DC: Institute for International Economics, November 1996.

Devine, Jack. "An Intelligence Reform Reality Check." *Washington Post*. February 18, 2008.

Diamond, John. *The CIA and the Culture of Failure: US Intelligence from the End of the Cold War to the Invasion of Iraq*. Stanford, CA: Stanford Security Studies, 2008.

Dobbins, James, John G. McGinn, Keith Crane, Seth G. Jones, Rollie Lal, Andrew Rathmell, Rachel M. Swanger, and Anga Timilsina. *America's Role in Nation-Building: From Germany to Iraq*. Santa Monica, CA: RAND, 2003.

Elkins, Dan. *Managing Intelligence Resources*. 2nd Ed. Alexandria, VA: DWE Press, 2006.

Enthoven, Alain C., and K. Wayne Smith. *How Much Is Enough? Shaping the Defense Program 1961–1969*. Santa Monica, CA: RAND, 2005. First published 1971 by Harper and Row.

Epstein, Susan B. *Embassy Security: Background, Funding, and the Budget*. CRS Report RL30662. Washington, DC: Congressional Research Service, October 4, 2001.

——. *Foreign Relations Authorization, FY2006 and FY2007: An Overview*. CRS Report RL33000. Washington, DC: Congressional Research Service, September 15, 2005.

Epstein, Susan B., and Lisa Mages. *Public Diplomacy: A Review of Past Recommendations.* CRS Report RL33062. Washington, DC: Congressional Research Service, October 31, 2005.

Executive Office of the President. Office of National Drug Control Policy. *National Drug Control Strategy: FY 2008 Budget Summary.* February 2007.

Export–Import Bank of the United States. *Annual Report, 2006.* Washington, DC: 2007.

Farrell, Theo. *Weapons Without a Cause: The Politics of Weapons Acquisition.* New York: St. Martin's Press, 1997.

Federal Bureau of Investigation. *FY 2009 Congressional Budget Justification.* Washington, DC: February 2008.

Federation of American Scientists. *Man-Portable Air Defense System (MANPADS) Proliferation,* Issue Brief No. 1. January 2004. http://fas.org/programs/ssp/asmp/MANPADS.html.

Fenno, Richard F. *Congressmen in Committees.* Boston, MA: Little, Brown and Co., 1973.

Foreign Affairs Council. *Secretary Colin Powell's State Department: An Independent Assessment.* Washington, DC: March 2003.

Fox, James W., and Lex Rieffel. *The Millennium Challenge Account: Moving Toward Smarter Aid.* Washington, DC: Brookings Institution, July 2005.

Freeman, J. Lieper. *The Political Process.* Garden City, NY: Doubleday, 1955.

Gilmore, John B., and David E. Lewis. "Assessing Performance Budgeting at OMB: The Influence of Politics, Performance, and Program Size." *Journal of Public Administration Research and Theory,* Vol. 16, No. 2 (April 2006).

Goldgeier, James M. *Not Whether, But When: The US Decision to Enlarge NATO.* Washington, DC: Brookings Institution, 1999.

Goldstein, Mark L. "The Flickering 'M' in OMB." *Government Executive,* Vol. 22, No. 3 (March 1990).

Greenwood, Ted. *Making the MIRV: A Study of Defense Decision-Making.* Cambridge: Cambridge University Press, 1975.

Gregory, Bruce. "Public Diplomacy as Strategic Communication." In *Countering Terrorism and Insurgency in the 21st Century: International Perspectives,* Part III, edited by James J.F. Forest. Westport, CT: Praeger, 2007.

Hanrahan, Charles. *Agricultural Export and Food Aid Programs.* Issue Brief IB98006. Washington, DC: Congressional Research Service, January 2006.

Hartung, William, and Michelle Ciarrocca. "Star Wars Revisited: Still Dangerous, Costly, and Unworkable." *Foreign Policy in Focus,* Vol. 4, No. 4 (April 2000).

——. "Star Wars II: Here We Go Again." *The Nation,* June 12, 2000.

Heniff Jr., Bill. *Budget Resolution Enforcement.* CRS Report 98-815. Washington, DC: Congressional Research Service, November 22, 2006.

——. *Budget Reconciliation Legislation: Development and Consideration.* CRS Report 98-814. Washington, DC: Congressional Research Service, December 8, 2006.

——. *Overview of the Authorization–Appropriation Process.* CRS Report RS20371. Washington, DC: Congressional Research Service, December 8, 2006.

Henry L. Stimson Center. *Equipped for the Future: Managing US Foreign Affairs in the 21st Century.* Washington, DC: Henry L. Stimson Center, October 1998.

Henry L. Stimson Center and the American Academy of Diplomacy. *A Foreign Affairs Budget for the Future.* Washington, DC: Henry L. Stimson Center, October 2008.

Hitch, Charles, and Roland McKean. *The Economics of Defense in the Nuclear Age.* Santa Monica, CA: RAND, 1960.

Holland, Lauren. *Weapons Under Fire.* New York: Routledge, 1997.

Holsti, Ole R. *To See Ourselves As Others See Us: How Publics Abroad View the United States After 9/11.* Ann Arbor, MI: University of Michigan Press, 2008.

Hyde Smith, Pamela. "The Hard Road Back to Soft Power." *Georgetown Journal of International Affairs,* winter/spring 2007.

Hyman, Gerald. *Assessing Secretary of State Rice's Reform of US Foreign Assistance.* Carnegie Paper No. 90, Democracy and Rule of Law Program. Washington, DC: Carnegie Endowment, February 2008.

InterAction. *Proposed Major Components and Organization of a Cabinet-Level Department for Global and Human Development.* Policy Paper. June 2008. http://interaction.org/files.cgi/6306_Cabinet-level_org_paper.pdf.

International Finance Corporation. *Highlights of IFC's 2006 Annual Report.* www.ifc.org/ifcext/annualreport.nsf/content/Home.

Johnson, Loch K., and Karl F. Inderfurth. *Fateful Decisions: Inside the National Security Council.* New York: Oxford University Press, 2004.

Joint Chiefs of Staff. *Chairman of the JCS, Combatant Commanders, and Joint Staff Participation in the Planning, Programming, Budgeting, and Execution System.* Instruction 8501.01A. December 3, 2004 (directive current as of February 12, 2008).

——. *The National Military Strategy of the United States.* Washington, DC: Joint Chiefs of Staff, 2004.

Jordan, Amos A., William J. Taylor, Jr., and Michael Mazarr. *American National Security.* 5th Ed. Baltimore, MD: Johns Hopkins University Press, 1998.

Joyce, Philip G. "Linking Performance and Budgeting: Opportunities in the Federal Budget Process." In *Integrating Performance and Budgets: The Budget Office of Tomorrow,* edited by Jonathan D. Breul and Carl Moravitz. Washington, DC: IBM Center for the Business of Government, 2007.

Kaiser, Frederick M. *Congressional Oversight of Intelligence: Current Structure and Alternatives.* CRS Report RL32525. Washington, DC: Congressional Research Service, September 16, 2008.

Keehan, Mark P. *Planning, Programming, Budgeting, and Execution (PPBE) Process.* Teaching Note. Washington, DC: Defense Acquisition University, April 2006.

Kettl, Donald F. *System Under Stress: Homeland Security and American Politics.* Washington, DC: Congressional Quarterly Press, 2007.

Klaus, Jon D. *US Military Overseas Basing: Background and Oversight Issues for Congress.* CRS Report RS21975. Washington, DC: Congressional Research Service, November 17, 2004.

Koempel, Michael L. *Homeland Security: Compendium of Recommendations Relevant to House Committee Organization and Analysis of Considerations for the House, and 109th and 110th Congresses Epilogue.* CRS Report RL32711. Washington, DC: Congressional Research Service, March 2, 2007.

Kotz, Nick. *Wild Blue Yonder: Money, Politics, and the B-1 Bomber.* New York: Pantheon Books, 1988.

Kralev, Nicolas. "Diplomatic Reorientation." *Washington Times,* April 12, 2004.

Kronstadt, Alan K. *Pakistan–US Relations.* CRS Report RL33498. Washington, DC: Congressional Research Service, January 11, 2008 (data updated March 5, 2008).

Kurth, James. "The Political Economy of Weapons Procurement: The Follow-On Imperative." *American Economic Review*, Vol. 62, No. 2 (May 1972), 304–11.

Lancaster, Carol. *George Bush's Foreign Aid: Transformation or Chaos?* Washington, DC: Center for Global Development, 2008.

Lasswell, Harold D. *Politics: Who Gets What, When, and How.* Rochester, NY: Whittlesey House, 1936.

Lerner, K. Lee, and Brenda Wilmoth Lerner, eds. *Encyclopedia of Espionage, Intelligence, and Security.* Detroit, MI: Gale, 2004.

Lerrick, Adam. "Funding the IMF: How Much does it Really Cost?" *Quarterly International Economics Reports.* Carnegie Mellon Gailliot Center for Public Policy, November 2003.

Lindsay, James M. *Congress and the Politics of US Foreign Policy.* Baltimore, MD: Johns Hopkins University Press, 1994.

Lindsay, James M., and Michael E. O'Hanlon. *Defending America: The Case for Limited National Missile Defense.* Washington, DC: Brookings Institution, 2001.

Lindsay, James M., and Randall B. Ripley. *Congress Resurgent: Foreign and Defense Policy on Capitol Hill.* Ann Arbor, MI: University of Michigan Press, 1993.

Locher, James R. *Victory on the Potomac: The Goldwater–Nichols Act Unifies the Pentagon.* College Station: Texas A&M University Press, 2002.

Lowenthal, Mark. *Intelligence: From Secrets to Policy.* 4th Ed. Washington, DC: CQ Press, 2009.

McClellan, Michael. *Public Diplomacy in the Context of Traditional Diplomacy.* Remarks to the Vienna Diplomatic Academy. October 11, 2004. www.publicdiplomacy.org/45.htm.

McConnell, Grant. *Private Power and American Democracy.* New York: Knopf, 1966.

Marcel, Gabriel. "National Security and the Interagency Process." In *US Army War College Guide to National Security Policy and Strategy*, edited by J. Boone Bartholomees. Carlisle Barracks, PA: Army War College, July 2004.

Martins, Mark. "No Small Change of Soldiering: The Commander's Emergency Response Program in Iraq and Afghanistan—CERP." *Army Lawyer*, February 2004.

——. "The Commander's Emergency Response Program." *Joint Force Quarterly*, Issue 37 (2005).

Mayer, Kenneth. *The Political Economy of Defense Contracting.* New Haven, CT: Yale University Press, 1991.

Melito, Thomas. *Multiple Challenges Hinder the Efficiency and Effectiveness of US Food Aid.* GAO-08-83T. Washington, DC: Government Accountability Office, October 2, 2007.

Modernizing Foreign Assistance Network. *New Day, New Way: US Foreign Assistance for the 21st Century.* Washington, DC: Center for Global Development, June 2008. www.cgdev.org/content/publications/detail/16210.

Mueller, John. *Overblown: How Politicians and the Terrorism Industry Inflate National Security Threats and Why We Believe Them.* New York: Free Press, 2006.

Murdock, Clark, Michele Flournoy, Kurt M. Campbell, Pierre A. Chao, Julianne Smith, Anne A. Witkowsky, and Christine E. Wormuth. *Beyond Goldwater-Nichols: U.S. Government and Defense Reform for a New Strategic Era, Phase 2 Report.* Washington, DC: Center for Strategic and International Studies, July 2005.

Murdock, Clark, Michele Flournoy, Christopher A. Williams, and Kurt M. Campbell. *Beyond Goldwater-Nichols: Defense Reform for a New Strategic Era, Phase 1 Report.* Washington, DC: Center for Strategic and International Studies, March 2004.

National Academy of Sciences. Board on Mathematical Sciences and Their Applications. *Interim Report on Methodological Improvements to the Department of Homeland Security's Biological Agent Risk Analysis.* Washington, DC: The National Academies Press, 2007.

National Commission on Terrorist Attacks. *The 9/11 Commission Report: Final Report of the National Commission on Terrorist Attacks Upon the United States.* Washington, DC: GPO, July 22, 2004. http://govinfo.library.unt.edu/911/report/index.htm.

National Nuclear Security Administration (NNSA). *Strategic Plan.* Washington, DC: November 2004. http://nnsa.energy.gov/about/documents/NNSA_Strategic_Plan_Nov_2004.pdf.

Newmann, William W. *Managing National Security Policy: The President and the Process.* Pittsburg, PA: University of Pittsburg Press, 2003.

Nowels, Larry. *Foreign Policy Budget Trends: A Thirty-Year Review.* CRS Report RL33262. Washington, DC: Congressional Research Service, January 31, 2006.

Nowels, Larry, and Connie Veillette. *Restructuring US Foreign Aid: The Role of the Director of Foreign Assistance.* CRS Report RL33491. Washington, DC: Congressional Research Service, September 8, 2006.

Office of the Director for National Intelligence. *The National Intelligence Strategy of the United States of America.* Washington, DC: ODNI, October 2005.

Office of Management and Budget. *Circular A-129: Policies for Federal Credit Programs and Non-Tax Receivables.* Washington, DC: GPO, revised November 2000.

——. *The President's Management Agenda, Fiscal Year 2002.* Washington, DC: GPO, 2001. http://georgewbush-whitehouse.archives.gov/omb/budget/fy2002/mgmt.pdf.

——. *Budget of the United States Government, Fiscal Year 2008.* Washington, DC: GPO, 2007.

——. *Budget of the United States Government, Fiscal Year 2009.* Washington, DC: GPO, 2008.

——. *Public Budget Database.* Washington, DC: OMB, http://annual/www.whitehouse.gov/omb/budget/fy2009/db.html.

Office of the US Global AIDS Coordinator. *The President's Emergency Plan for AIDS Relief: US Five-Year Global HIV/AIDS Strategy.* Washington, DC: February 2004.

——. *Action Today, A Foundation for Tomorrow: The President's Emergency Plan for AIDS Relief.* Second Annual Report. Washington, DC: March 2006.

——. *The Power of Partnerships: The President's Emergency Plan for AIDS Relief.* Third Annual Report. Washington, DC: March 2007.

Organization for Economic Cooperation and Development. Development Assistance Committee. *United States (2006) DAC Peer Review: Main Findings and Recommendations.* Paris: OECD, December 2006.

Overseas Private Investment Corporation. *Budget Request, Fiscal Year 2009.* February 2008.

Owens, William A. *Lifting the Fog of War.* New York: Farrar, Straus, Giroux, 2000.

Parker, Gerald W. *HHS Progress in National Preparedness Efforts.* Statement submitted to the Senate Committee on Homeland Security and Governmental Affairs. October 23, 2007.

Patrick, Stewart, and Kaysie Brown. *The Pentagon and Global Development: Making*

Sense of the DOD's Expanding Role. Working Paper 131. Washington, DC: Center for Global Development, November 12, 2000.

Patterson, Anne W. *Afghanistan Interdiction/Eradication of Illegal Narcotics and US Lead Rebuilding Programs*. Testimony before the House Committee on Appropriations, Subcommittee on Foreign Operations, Export Financing and Related Programs. September 12, 2006. www.state.gov/p/inl/rls/rm/72241.htm.

Peace Corps. *2007 Congressional Budget Justification*. Washington, DC: February 2006.

———. *2009 Congressional Budget Justification*. Washington, DC: February 2008.

Pew Global Attitudes Project Report. *Global Public Opinion in the Bush Years*. December 18, 2008. http://pewglobal.org/reports/pdf/263.pdf.

Plischke, Elmer. *US Department of State: A Reference History*. Westport, CT: Greenwood Press, 1999.

Ploch, Lauren. *Africa Command: US Strategic Interests in Africa and the Role of the US Military in Africa*. CRS Report RL34003. Washington, DC: Congressional Research Service, December 12, 2007.

Posner, Paul L., and Denise M. Fantone. "Assessing Federal Program Performance: Observations on the US Office of Management and Budget's Program Assessment Rating Tool and Its Use in the Budget Process." *Public Performance & Management Review*, Vol. 30, No. 3 (March 2007).

Potter, William C. "The Changing Nuclear Threat: The Sapphire File." *Transition*, November 17, 1995.

Prados, John. *Soviet Estimate: US Intelligence Analysis and Russian Military Strength*. New York: Dial Press, 1982.

Priest, Dana. *The Mission: Waging War and Winning the Peace with America's Military*. New York: W.W. Norton & Co., 2003.

Project on National Security Reform. *Forging a New Shield*. Washington, DC: November 2008.

Project for the New American Century. *Rebuilding the Nation's Defenses*. Washington, DC: PNAC, September 2000.

Radelet, Steve. *A Note on the MCC Selection Process for 2005*. Washington, DC: Center for Global Development, September 2004.

Radin, Beryl A. *Managing Decentralized Departments: The Case of the U.S. Department of Health and Human Services*. Washington, DC: The PricewaterhouseCoopers Endowment for the Business of Government, October 1999.

Reagan, Ronald. *United States Intelligence Activities*. Executive Order 12333. December 4, 1981 (as amended through 2008). www.fas.org/irp/offdocs/eo/eo-12333-2008.pdf.

———. *Staffing at Diplomatic Missions and Their Overseas Constituent Posts*. National Security Decision Directive 38. June 2, 1982. http://ftp.fas.org/irp/offdocs/nsdd38.htm.

Rice, Condoleezza. *Transformational Diplomacy: Remarks at Georgetown School of Foreign Service*. Washington, DC: January 18, 2006.

Richard, Anne C. *Superpower on the Cheap?* Paris: Institut Français des Relations Internationales (IFRI), December 2002.

Richard, Anne C., and Paul Clayman. *Improving US National Security: Options for Strengthening US Foreign Operations*. Briefing Paper. Muscatine, IA: Stanley Foundation, 2008.

Richelson, Jeffrey T. *The US Intelligence Community*. 5th Ed. Boulder, CO: Westview Press, 2008.

Ridge, Tom. *The Department of Homeland Security: Making Americans Safer*. Statement Submitted to the Senate Committee on the Judiciary. June 26, 2002.

Roberts, Walter R. "The Evolution of Diplomacy." *Mediterranean Quarterly*, Vol. 17, No. 3 (summer 2006), 55–64.

Rostow, W.W. *The Stages of Economic Growth: A Non-Communist Manifesto*. Cambridge: Cambridge University Press, 1960.

Rothkopf, David. *Running the World: The Inside Story of the National Security Council and the Architects of America's Power*. New York: Public Affairs, 2006.

Rumsfeld, Donald, chair. *Report of the Commission to Assess the Ballistic Missile Threat to the United States* (Rumsfeld Commission). July 15, 1998.

Salaam-Blyther, Tiaji. *US International HIV/AIDS, Tuberculosis, and Malaria Spending: FY 2004–FY 2008*. CRS Report RL33485. Washington, DC: Congressional Research Service, March 2007.

Salamon, Lester V., and John J. Siegfried. "Economic Power and Political Influence: The Impact of Industry Structure on Public Policy." *American Political Science Review*, Vol. 71, No. 3 (September 1977).

Sanford, Jonathan. *Multilateral Development Banks: Procedures for US Participation*. CRS Report RS20791. Washington, DC: Congressional Research Service, January 2001.

——. *International Financial Institutions: Funding US Participation*. CRS Report RS22134. Washington, DC: Congressional Research Service, May 2005.

Sanford, Jonathan, and Martin Weiss. *International Monetary Fund: Organization, Functions, and Role in the International Economy*. CRS Report RL32364. Washington, DC: Congressional Research Service, April 2004.

Sapolsky, Harvey. *The Polaris System Development: Bureaucratic and Programmatic Success in Government*. Cambridge, MA: Harvard University Press, 1972.

Sapolsky, Harvey, Eugene Gholz, and Caitlin Talmadge, *US Defense Politics: The Origins of Security Policy*. New York: Routledge, 2009.

Schelling, Thomas C. "PPBS and Foreign Affairs." *The Public Interest*, No. 11 (spring 1968).

Schick, Allen. *The Federal Budget: Politics, Policy, Process*. 3rd Ed. Washington, DC: Brookings Institution, 2007.

Schilling, Warner R. "The Politics of National Defense: Fiscal 1950." In *Strategy, Politics, and Defense Budgets*, edited by Warner R. Schilling, Paul Y. Hammond, and Glenn H. Snyder. New York: Columbia University Press, 1962.

Serafino, Nina M. *Colombia: Summary and Tables on US Assistance, FY 1989–FY 2004*. CRS Report RS21213. Washington, DC: Congressional Research Service, May 19, 2003.

——. *The Global Peacekeeping Operations Initiative*. CRS Report RL32773. Washington, DC: Congressional Research Service, February 8, 2006.

Sharp, Jeremy M. *The Middle East Partnership Initiative: An Overview*. CRS Report RS21457. Washington, DC: Congressional Research Service, July 20, 2005.

Shope, Virginia C. *Peacekeeping: A Selected Bibliography*. Carlisle Barracks, PA: US Army War College Library, May 2004. www.carlisle.army.mil/library/bibs/peace04r.htm.

Smith, Pamela W. *The National Institutes of Health (NIH): Organization, Funding, and Congressional Issues*. Washington, DC: Congressional Research Service, October 29, 2006.

Special Inspector General for Iraq Reconstruction (SIGIR). *Management of the Commander's Emergency Response Program (CERP) for FY 2005.* SIGIR-05-025. January 23, 2006.

——. *Iraq Reconstruction: Lessons in Contracting and Procurement.* July 2006. www.sigir.mil/reports/pdf/Lessons_Learned_July21.pdf.

Srull, Donald. Ed. *The Cost Analysis Improvement Group: A History.* McLean, VA: Logistics Management Institute, 1998.

Steinberg, James B., Jeremy Shapiro, Michael B. D'Arcy, Michael O'Hanlon, and Peter Orszag. *Protecting the Homeland, 2006/07.* Washington, DC: Brookings Institution, 2006.

Stiglitz, Joseph E., and Linda J. Bilmes. *The Three Trillion Dollar War: The True Cost of the Iraq Conflict.* New York: Norton, 2008.

Stockman, David. *The Triumph of Politics: Why the Reagan Revolution Failed.* New York: Avon Books, 1987.

Streeter, Sandy. *The Congressional Appropriations Process: An Introduction.* CRS Report 97-684. Washington, DC: Congressional Research Service, September 8, 2006.

Tarnoff, Curt. *Millennium Challenge Account.* CRS Report RL32427. Washington, DC: Congressional Research Service, October 8, 2008.

Tarnoff, Curt, and Larry Nowels. *Foreign Aid: An Introductory Overview of US Programs and Policy.* CRS Report RL98-916. Washington, DC: Congressional Research Service, January 19, 2005.

Tomkin, Shelly Lynn. *Inside OMB: Politics and Process in the President's Budget Office.* Armonk, NY: M.E. Sharpe, 1998.

Towell, Pat, Stephen Daggett, and Amy Belasco. *Defense: FY 2008 Authorization and Appropriations.* CRS Report RL33999. Washington, DC: Congressional Research Service, July 2007.

Tower, John, chair. *The Tower Commission Report (Report of the President's Special Review Board).* Washington, DC: GPO, February 26, 1987.

Tyszkiewicz, Mary T., and Stephen Daggett. *A Defense Budget Primer.* Washington, DC: Congressional Research Service, December 9, 1998.

United Nations. Office on Drugs and Crime. *2006 World Drug Report.* New York: United Nations Publications, 2006.

——. *Implementation of General Assembly resolutions 55/235 and 55/236: Report of the Secretary General.* A/61/139. July 13, 2006.

——. *Approved Resources for Peacekeeping Operations for the Period from 1 July 2006 to 30 June 2007.* A/C.5/61/18. January 15, 2007.

US Advisory Commission on Public Diplomacy. *Building America's Public Diplomacy Through a Reformed Structure and Additional Resources*, Washington, DC: State, 2002. www.state.gov/documents/organization/13622.pdf.

US Agency for International Development. *US Foreign Aid: Meeting the Challenges of the Twenty-first Century.* Washington, DC: January 2004.

——. *The Automated Directives System (ADS).* www.usaid.gov/policy/ads.

——. *Fragile States Strategy.* Washington, DC: January 2005.

——. *At Freedom's Frontiers: A Democracy and Governance Strategic Framework.* Washington, DC: December 2005.

——. *Policy Framework for Bilateral Foreign Aid: Implementing Transformational Diplomacy Through Development.* Washington, DC: January 2006.

——. *Strategic Management—Interim Guidance: A Mandatory Reference for ADS, Chapter 201.* Revised February 21, 2006.

US Commission on National Security/21st Century (Hart–Rudman Commission). *Roadmap for National Security: Imperative for Change.* Phase III Report. Washington, DC: February 15, 2001.

US Congress. House. Permanent Select Committee on Intelligence. *Compilation of US Intelligence Laws and Executive Orders.* Washington, DC: GPO, 1983.

——. House. Committee on Foreign Affairs. *Report of the Task Force on Foreign Assistance* (Hamilton–Gilman Report). Washington, DC: GPO, 1989.

——. Joint Economic Committee. *War At Any Price? The Total Economic Costs of the War Beyond the Federal Budget.* Staff Report. Washington, DC: GPO, November 2007.

——. Senate. Committee on the Budget. *The Congressional Budget Process: An Explanation.* Washington, DC: GPO, 1998.

——. Senate. Committee on Foreign Relations/Committee on International Relations. *Legislation on Foreign Relations Through 2005.* Joint Committee Print, Vol. 1-A. Washington, DC: GPO, January 2006.

——. Senate. Committee on Foreign Relations. *Embassies as Command Posts in the Anti-Terror Campaign: A Report to the Members of the Committee on Foreign Relations.* Senate Print 109-52. Washington, DC: GPO, December 15, 2006. www.fas.org/irp/congress/2006_rpt/embassies.html.

——. Senate. Committee on Appropriations. *Department of Defense Appropriations Bill, 2008.* Senate Report 110-155. Washington, DC: GPO, September 14, 2007.

US Department of Agriculture. *FY 2009 Budget Summary and Annual Performance Plan.* 2008.

US Department of Commerce. *FY 2008 Budget in Brief.* 2007.

US Department of Defense. *DOD Program Element Code System.* www.dtic.mil/descriptivesum/dod_pe.html.

——. *The National Security Agency and the Central Security Service.* Directive S-5100.20. December 23, 1971.

——. *Implementation of a 2-Year Planning, Programming, Budgeting, and Execution Process.* Management Initiative Decision 913. May 22, 2003.

——. *Other Secretary of Defense Decisions.* Program Budget Decision 753. December 23, 2004.

——. *The National Defense Strategy of the United States.* Washington, DC: Office of the Secretary of Defense, March 2005.

——. *Military Support for Stability, Security, Transition, and Reconstruction (SSTR) Operations.* Directive 3000.05. November 28, 2005. www.dtic.mil/whs/directives/corres/html/300005.htm.

——. *Quadrennial Defense Review.* Washington, DC: DOD, February 2006.

——. *Director, Program Analysis and Evaluation (PA&E).* Directive Number 5141.01. March 16, 2006.

——. *Building Partnership Capacity: QDR Execution Roadmap.* May 22, 2006. www.ndu.edu/itea/storage/790/BPC%20Roadmap.pdf.

——. "Research, Development, Testing, and Evaluation (RDT&E) Programs (R-1)." In *Department of Defense Budget for Fiscal Year 2008.* February 2007. www.defenselink.mil/comptroller/Docs/fy2008_r1.pdf.

——. *DOD Senior Governance Councils.* Directive Number 5105.79. May 19, 2008.

——. *National Defense Strategy.* Washington, DC: DOD, June 2008.

——. Defense Science Board. *Strategic Communication.* Task Force Report. Washington, DC: Office of the Under Secretary of Defense for Acquisition, Technology, and Logistics, October 2004.

——. Defense Security Cooperation Agency. *Foreign Military Sales, Foreign Military Construction Sales, and Military Assistance Facts as of September 30, 2005.* September 2005.

——. Defense Security Cooperation Agency. *Strategic Plan: 2006–2011.* February 13, 2006.

——. Office of the Undersecretary of Defense (Comptroller). *National Defense Budget Estimates for FY 2008.* Washington, DC: DOD, March 2007.

——. Office of the Undersecretary of Defense (Comptroller). *National Defense Budget Estimates for Fiscal Year 2009.* Washington, DC: DOD, March 2008.

US Department of Education. *Fiscal Year 2009 Budget Summary and Background Information.* Washington, DC: 2008.

US Department of Energy. *FY 2008 Congressional Budget Request: Budget Highlights.* Washington, DC: DOE, February 2007.

——. *FY 2009 Congressional Budget Request: National Nuclear Security Administration.* DOE/CF-024, Vol. 1. Washington, DC: DOE, February 2008.

US Department of Health and Human Services. *Centers for Disease Control and Prevention Justification of Estimates for Appropriation Committees: Fiscal Year 2008.* Washington, DC: HHS, 2007.

——. *Strategic Plan, Fiscal Years 2007–2012.* Washington, DC: HHS, October 2007.

US Department of Homeland Security. *Planning, Programming, Budgeting and Execution.* Management Directive 1330. Washington, DC: DHS, February 14, 2005.

——. Program Analysis and Evaluation. *DHS Resource Allocation Process.* Presentation. Washington, DC: DHS, November 18, 2008.

US Department of State. *Report of the Accountability Review Boards: Bombings of the US Embassies in Nairobi, Kenya and Dar Es Salaam, Tanzania on August 7, 1998.* Washington, DC: State, January 1999.

——. *America's Overseas Presence in the 21st Century* (Kaden Commission). Washington, DC: State, November 1999.

——. *Foreign Affairs Handbook.* www.state.gov/m/a/ips/c22793.htm.

——. *Foreign Affairs Manual.* www.state.gov/m/a/ips/c22793.htm.

——. *FY 2007 Foreign Operations Congressional Budget Justification.* Washington, DC: State, 2006.

——. *FY 2008 Budget in Brief.* Washington, DC: State, 2007.

——. *FY 2008 Foreign Operations Congressional Budget Justification.* Washington, DC: State, February 2007.

——. *FY 2008 International Affairs (Function 150) Budget Request: Summary and Highlights.* Washington, DC: State, February 2007.

——. *FY 2009 Budget in Brief.* Washington, DC: State, February 2008.

——. *FY 2009 Foreign Operations Congressional Budget Justification.* Washington, DC: State, 2008.

——. *FY 2009 International Affairs (Function 150) Budget Request: Summary and Highlights.* Washington, DC: State, February 2008.

——. *FY 2010 Foreign Operations Congressional Budget Justification.* Washington, DC: State, May 2009.

——. *FY 2010 International Affairs (Function 150) Budget Request: Summary and Highlights*. Washington, DC: State, May 7, 2009.

——. Bureau of International Narcotics and Law Enforcement. *FY 2007 Budget: Congressional Justification*. Washington, DC: State, 2006. www.state.gov/documents/organization/71984.pdf.

——. Bureau of International Narcotics and Law Enforcement. *2009 International Narcotics Control Strategy Report, Vol. 1: Drug and Chemical Control* and *Vol. 2: Money Laundering and Financial Crimes*. Washington, DC: State, February 27, 2009. www.state.gov/p/inl/rls/nrcrpt/2009/index.htm.

——. Bureau of Public Affairs, Office of the Historian. *History of the Department of State During the Clinton Presidency (1993–2001)*. Washington, DC: State, June 2001. www.state.gov/r/pa/ho/pubs/c6059.htm.

——. Secretary of State's Advisory Committee on Transformational Diplomacy. *A Call to Action*. Washington, DC: State, January 2008.

US Department of State and US Agency for International Development. *Strategic Plan: Fiscal Years 2004–2009: Aligning Diplomacy and Development Assistance*. Washington, DC: State and USAID, August 2003.

——. *US Foreign Assistance: Reference Guide*. Department of State Publication 11202. Washington, DC: State and USAID, January 2005.

——. *Strategic Plan: Fiscal Years 2007–2012: Transformational Diplomacy*. Washington, DC: State and USAID, May 2007.

US Department of the Treasury. *Treasury International Programs: Justification for Appropriations, FY 2008 Budget Request*. 2007. www.treasury.gov/offices/international-affairs/intl/fy2008/fy2008-budget.pdf.

——. *Treasury International Programs: Justification for Appropriations, FY 2009 Budget Request*. 2008. www.treas.gov/press/releases/reports/completefy2009cpd.pdf.

——. *Treasury International Programs: Justification for Appropriations, FY 2010 Budget Request*. 2009. www.treas.gov/press/releases/reports/completefy2009cpd.pdf.

US Environmental Protection Agency. *2008 Annual Performance Plan and Congressional Justification Appendix*. 2007.

——. *FY 2010 EPA Budget in Brief*. 2009.

US Government Accountability Office. *Foreign Aid: Improving the Impact and Control of Economic Support Funds*. GAO-NSIAD-88-182. Washington, DC: GAO, June 1988.

——. *The Chief Financial Officers Act: A Mandate for Federal Financial Management Reform*. GAO/AFMD-12.19.4. Washington, DC: GAO, September 1991.

——. *State Department: Management Weaknesses in the Security Construction Program*. GAO/NSIAD/92-2. Washington, DC: GAO, November 1991.

——. *OMB 2000: Changes Resulting from the Reorganization of the Office of Management and Budget*. Testimony before the Subcommittee on Government Management, Information, and Technology of the House Committee on Government Reform and Oversight. GAO/T-GGD/AIMD-96-68. Washington, DC: GAO, February 7, 1996.

——. *International Affairs: Activities of Domestic Agencies*. Statement of Benjamin F. Nelson, Director, International Relations and Trade Issues, National Security and International Affairs Division, to the Task Force on International Affairs, Senate Budget Committee. GAO/T-NSIAD-98-174. June 4, 1998.

——. *U.N. Peacekeeping: Estimated US Contributions, Fiscal Years 1996–2001*. GAO-02-294. Washington, DC: GAO, February 2002.

———. *State Department: Staffing Shortfalls and Ineffective Assignment System Compromise Diplomatic Readiness at Hardship Posts.* GAO-02-626. Washington, DC: GAO, June 2002.

———. *Foreign Assistance: Strategic Workforce Planning Can Help USAID Address Current and Future Challenges.* GAO-03-946. Washington, DC: GAO, August 2003.

———. *US Public Diplomacy: State Department Expands Efforts but Faces Significant Challenges.* GAO-03-951. Washington, DC: GAO, September 2003.

———. *Performance Budgeting: Observations on the Use of OMB's Program Assessment Rating Tool for the Fiscal Year 2004 Budget.* GAO-04-174. Washington, DC: GAO, January 2004.

———. *Results-Oriented Government: GPRA Has Established a Solid Foundation for Achieving Greater Results.* GAO-04-38. Washington, DC: GAO, March 2004.

———. *Department of State: Nonproliferation, Anti-terrorism, Demining, and Related Programs Follow Legal Authority, but Some Activities Need Reassessment.* GAO-04-521. Washington, DC: GAO, April 2004.

———. *Global Health: US AIDS Coordinator Addressing Some Key Challenges to Expanding Treatment, but Others Remain.* GAO-04-784. Washington, DC: GAO, July 2004.

———. *Millennium Challenge Corporation: Progress Made on Key Challenges in First Year of Operations.* Testimony before the House Committee on International Relations. GAO-05-625T. April 2005.

———. *US Public Diplomacy: Interagency Coordination Efforts Hampered by the Lack of National Communications Strategy.* GAO-05-323. April 2005.

———. *Performance Budgeting: PART Focuses Attention on Program Performance, but More Can Be Done to Engage Congress.* GAO-06-28. Washington, DC: GAO, October 2005.

———. *US Public Diplomacy: State Department Efforts Lack Certain Communication Elements and Face Persistent Challenges.* Statement of Jess T. Ford, Director, International Affairs and Trade, to the Subcommittee on Science, the Departments of State, Justice and Commerce, and Related Agencies, House Committee on Appropriations. GAO-06-707T. Washington, DC: GAO, May 3, 2006.

———. *Embassy Construction: State Has Made Progress Constructing New Embassies, but Better Planning Is Needed for Operations and Maintenance Requirements.* GAO-06-641. Washington, DC: GAO, June 2006.

———. *Millennium Challenge Corporation: Compact Implementation Structures Are Being Established; Framework for Measuring Results Needs Improvement.* Report to the Chairman, Senate Committee on Foreign Relations. GAO-06-805. Washington, DC: GAO, July 2006.

———. *Border Security: US-VISIT Program Faces Strategic, Operational and Technological Challenges at Land Ports of Entry.* GAO-07-248. Washington, DC: GAO, December 2006.

———. *Section 1206 Security Assistance Program—Findings on Criteria, Coordination, and Implementation.* GAO-07-416. Washington, DC: GAO, February 28, 2007.

———. *Securing, Stabilizing, and Reconstructing Afghanistan: Key Issues for Congressional Oversight.* GAO-07-801SP. Washington, DC: GAO, May 2007.

Veillette, Connie. *Andean Counterdrug Initiative (ACI) and Related Funding Programs: FY2006 Assistance.* CRS Report RL33253. Washington, DC: Congressional Research Service, January 27, 2006.

Weiner, Sharon K. "The Politics of Resource Allocation in the Post-Cold War Pentagon." *Security Studies*, Vol. 5, No. 4 (summer 1996).

Whittaker, Alan G., Frederick C. Smith, and Elizabeth McKune. *The National Security Policy Process: The National Security Council and Interagency System.* Washington, DC: National Defense University, ICAF, November 2008.

Wildavsky, Aaron, and Naomi Caiden. *The New Politics of the Budgetary Process.* 5th Ed. New York: Pearson/Longman, 1988.

Williams, Cindy, ed. *Holding the Line: US Defense Alternatives for the Early 21st Century.* Cambridge, MA: MIT Press, 2001.

——. *Strengthening Homeland Security: Reforming Planning and Resource Allocation.* Washington, DC: IBM Center for the Business of Government, 2008.

Williams, Cindy, and Gordon Adams. *Strengthening Statecraft and Security: Reforming U.S. Planning and Resource Allocation.* Cambridge, MA: MIT Security Studies Program Occasional Paper, June 2008.

Wilson, George. *This War Really Matters: Inside the Fight for Defense Dollars.* Washington, DC: Congressional Quarterly Press, 2000.

Wilson, James Q. *Bureaucracy: What Government Agencies Do and Why They Do It.* New York: Basic Books, 1991.

Wong, Mark. *Counterterrorism Assistance Issues and Approaches.* Working Paper for CSIS Task Force on Non-Traditional Security Assistance. May 2005 Draft.

Woodward, Bob. *The Agenda: Inside the Clinton White House.* New York: Simon and Schuster, 1994.

World Bank. *Assessing Aid: What Works, What Doesn't, and Why.* New York: Oxford University Press, 1998.

Zegart, Amy B. *Flawed by Design: The Evolution of the CIA, JSC, and NSC.* Stanford, CA: Stanford University Press, 1999.

About the Authors

Gordon Adams is a Professor of International Affairs at the School of International Service at American University. He is also a Distinguished Fellow and Director of the Budgeting for Foreign Affairs and Defense Program at the Henry L. Stimson Center in Washington, DC. In 2006–07, he was a Fellow at the Woodrow Wilson International Center for Scholars. From 1993 to 1997, he was Associate Director for National Security and International Affairs at the Office of Management and Budget in the Executive Office of the President.

Dr. Adams holds a Ph.D. in Political Science from Columbia University. He is the author of *The Iron Triangle: The Politics of Defense Contracting* (Transaction Press 1982), co-author, with Guy Ben-Ari, of *Transforming European Militaries: Coalition Operations and the Technology Gap* (Routledge 2006), and co-author of *A Foreign Affairs Budget for the Future* (Stimson 2008). He was founder and Director of the Defense Budget Project in Washington, DC, and served as Deputy Director of the International Institute for Strategic Studies in London. He is a member of the Council on Foreign Relations and the International Institute for Strategic Studies and has been a member of the Strategic Advisory Board to the Raytheon Corporation. He was awarded the Defense Department's Medal for Distinguished Public Service in 1997 and was a member of DOD's Defense Policy Board at the Department of Defense from 1998 to 2001.

Cindy Williams is a principal research scientist of the Security Studies Program at the Massachusetts Institute of Technology. She was formerly the assistant director for national security in the Congressional Budget Office. Dr. Williams has served as a director and in other capacities at the MITRE Corporation, as a member of the Senior Executive Service in the Directorate of Program Analysis and Evaluation of the Office of the Secretary of Defense, and as a mathematician at RAND.

Dr. Williams holds a Ph.D. in Mathematics from the University of California, Irvine. She is the editor of *Holding the Line: U.S. Defense Alternatives for the Early 21st Century* (MIT Press 2001) and *Filling the Ranks:*

Transforming the U.S. Military Personnel System (MIT Press 2004). She is co-editor, with Curtis Gilroy, of *Service to Country: Personnel Policy and the Transformation of Western Militaries* (MIT Press 2006). She is an elected fellow and a member of the board of directors of the National Academy of Public Administration. She is a member of the Council on Foreign Relations and of the International Institute for Strategic Studies and is a former member of the US Naval Studies Board. She serves on the editorial board of *International Security* and the advisory board of the Scowcroft Institute of International Affairs at the Bush School of Government and Public Service of Texas A&M University.

Index

Note: Page numbers in *italics* denote tables, those in **bold** denote figures or illustrations.